Second   Edition

Communication and the Sexes

Barbara Bate

Judy Bowker
Oregon State University

WAVELAND
PRESS, INC.

Prospect Heights, Illinois

Consulting Editor
Robert E. Denton, Jr.

For information about this book, write or call:
Waveland Press, Inc.
P.O. Box 400
Prospect Heights, Illinois 60070
(847) 634-0081

Preface

When women and men communicate, their experiences can range from satisfying and exhilarating to frustrating and annoying. *Communication and the Sexes* was written to provide readers with resources both to better understand the frustrating experiences and to manage them more effectively. This revised edition outlines the changing dynamics between men and women, particularly with regard to language, family, education, organizations, and mediated communication. Many students have given this text to other family members because it has such a practical, readable format. Teachers have found the book applicable to a wide range of courses—such as those on sex and gender, interpersonal communication, and language—including those in sociology, psychology, anthropology, business, and human resource development.

Defining gender and sex as distinct entities, the text offers four ways to examine what we know (and how we know) about human communication and its impact on women and men. Readers encounter the basic concepts, definition, and approaches in the first four chapters. The last six chapters deal with particular contexts and ways to apply these concepts, definitions, and approaches. Chapter 1 sets forth the book's thesis that communication creates and re-creates gender. It also defines key communication terms such as message and situation, describes clusters of concepts that underlie discussions of gender, and discusses some of the basic life situations that demonstrate how gender ideals can be problematic.

Chapter 2 presents the concepts of theory, vantage points, presumptions, and perspectives. The four basic approaches to the study of communication and the sexes—biology, power, culture, and rhetoric—are then outlined and compared.

Chapter 3 addresses theories, research, and recent controversy about language, as it both defines and omits individuals and as it is used by both sexes in conversation.

Chapter 4 describes the framework for studying nonverbal communication codes and offers the results of some recent research on men's and women's nonverbal behavior.

Chapter 5 outlines the stages of relationship development, compares friendship experiences of the sexes, describes strains in dual-career marriages, and examines conflicts that help or hinder intimate relationships.

Chapter 6 centers on the attempts of the child to interpret interpersonal messages among family members and to meet their expectations for appropriate masculine or feminine behavior.

Chapter 7 addresses the public communication of teachers to students and examines children's peer groups as regulators of gender role communication.

Chapter 8 focuses on communication on the job, on ways that organizational symbols affect cooperation between the sexes, and on the kinds of changes presently occurring in the workplace.

Chapter 9 discusses the influence of mass media and mediated communication on views of gender and on struggles to reach gender ideals.

Chapter 10 examines three issues that center on gender: the impact of both the women's and men's movements, the increase in messages of sexual violence, and changes in personal communication styles.

Efforts have been made to include examples from various cultures (age, nationality, ethnicity, class), but much of the research on sex and gender still is largely based on the experiences of white, middle-class Americans. Student vignettes are used throughout to illuminate various perspectives on gender communication.

A NOTE FROM BARBARA

I am grateful to students, friends, and family who have entrusted me with their stories and their concerns about gender issues in their lives. I appreciate the work of Northern Illinois University colleagues in Women's Studies and Communication Studies, particularly Lois Self, for testing my opinions and sharing my commitment to link theories and human experience.

As the second edition goes to press, I give thanks for the life of Claire Bate, who spent her nearly eighty years in loving service to family and several communities, despite major obstacles. I value the work of my current colleagues in The United Methodist Church's General Board of Discipleship, as we try to address all forms of inequality among persons. Finally, I continue to celebrate the presence and challenge of Joanna Bate, once a tree-climbing preschooler and now a soccer-playing high school sophomore who expects to make a difference in her world. I trust that she and other young women and men will influence the planet and the future that we share.

Barbara Bate

A NOTE FROM JUDY

Thanks to the students from Oregon State University who have contributed so much of themselves to this book. I thank them both for their willingness to contribute stories and their thoughtful criticism of drafts. I also greatly appreciate the friendship and excellent work of Loril Chandler whose cheerful contributions to the revisions kept the process going. I owe Carol Rowe several conference appearances for her vivacious style and her jovial manner; her optimism is infectious. In addition, I deeply appreciate Hilary Jones who not only graciously volunteered her time and expertise to review this work but also provided much-needed inspiration.

Thanks also to my family, especially Robert, Parker, and Hilary. Their lighthearted support and patience continues to be a source of energy and confidence.

Judy Bowker

Contents

4 NONVERBAL MESSAGES   129

5 INTIMACY   163

Chapter 1

Defining Sex, Gender, and Communication

Men and women often disagree. Although we do not plan or expect to make life difficult for each other, we often understand differently or interpret differently the ideas and feelings of a person of the other sex. Harvard psychologist Carol Gilligan accounts for the problem by saying that "men and women may speak different languages that they assume are the same . . . creating misunderstandings which impede communication and limit the potential for cooperation and care in relationships."[1] You think of yourself first as an individual, only subsequently categorizing yourself as female or male. Yet you also may think that a particular woman's or man's behavior or meaning can be predicted in many cases merely by knowing the person's sex. According to Gilligan and others, this assumption often is false.

To increase your awareness of the assumptions most people make about the sexes, think of common phrases in conversation: "That's just like a woman" or "just like a man," "they just don't get it," and "the opposite sex." All these phrases portray the two sexes as thinking and talking differently, even in opposite ways. The last phrase also implies that antagonism might be expected because the sexes are the antitheses of one another. In the context of these often taken-for-granted phrases, confusion and complications can frequently be expected when men and women communicate with each other.

In the past two decades our knowledge about the experiences, concerns, and aspirations of each of the sexes has greatly increased. The contemporary feminist movement in the United States has helped explain forces that have muted women's voices and sapped their self-confidence. During the 1980s in this country, attention was paid to the communication problems faced by men also—such as absence of intimacy from fathers, difficulty in expressing feelings to peers, and conflicting messages in the workplace about productivity versus respect for workers as persons.[2] As a result of this expanded focus, problems related to sex and gender are recognized as everyone's concern. The purpose of this book is to show how these problems develop and to prepare you to analyze and address them for yourself.

CHAPTER OVERVIEW

This chapter presents several ideas essential to examining communication between the sexes in your life. In it, we will discuss the definitions of sex and gender; we also will investigate the nature of communication as well as its critical elements. Consideration of sex stereotypes and gender filters will help explain the functions of sex and gender information over a lifetime. Finally, we will explore the various levels of communication. We begin with the important distinction between the terms, "sex" and "gender" because that distinction lies at the heart of our topic: communication and the sexes as a human problem.

SEX AND GENDER

Scholars from different fields of study distinguish what we will call "sex" and "gender" in different ways. Some refer to sex roles or scripts, but everyone who studies this area differentiates between how we identify ourselves biologically and how we identify ourselves psychologically and sociologically. When you read research literature from different disciplines, then, you will need to determine from the context of the reading the definitions used by the authors. You will find some authors—usually those whose area of interest is not sex and gender but some other topic—who use "sex" in one paragraph and "gender" in the next. A scholar whose focus is argumentation, for example, may not realize the importance of distinguishing between reporting results based on sex contrasted to results based on gender. Once again, as you read this literature, you will need to interpret from the context what information is being presented to you.

For our purposes, "sex" refers to biological characteristics that are present to a large degree from the time of your birth. Different pairs of chromosomes—XX for females, XY for males—provide clear genetic directions except in the few instances when there are abnormalities in the number or mix of chromosomes.

In this book the term, "gender," will be used to refer to the expansion or elaboration of biological sex distinctions, an elaboration which occurs through human communication from infancy on. "Gender" will be used as a term for *learned* communication behaviors, most of which appear to have no necessary connection with biological functions. These behaviors become so strongly linked with the biological categories through association and interpersonal reinforcement, however, that many of us believe biological sex and constructed gender are identical. They are not.

Gender is created through communication in a multitude of contexts—in the family, in school, in the workplace, in intimate relationships, and in the mass media. What you have come to believe about "acceptable" behavior for men or women is no accident. You watched, you listened, and you were rewarded or punished for specific behaviors by people who mattered to you. By all these processes of communication, you learned a gender ideal.

The terms, "masculine" and "feminine," in this book refer to the labels people attach to gender-related behaviors. In some cases, people equate male with masculine and female with feminine, but the two pairs of categories are not necessarily linked. Reconceptualizing sex and gender as separate descriptors can be difficult. Distinguishing gender as a learned concept rather than an innate, biological quality may mean restructuring basic presumptions we have relied on all our lives.

Toward that distinction, we must understand the relationship between gender and communication. The thesis of this book is that *communication creates and re-creates gender.*[3] Our approach can be summed up in the following statements.

1. The biological sex categories, male and female, are experienced by most people as unchangeable facts. In the United States,

identifying a person's sex is fundamental to knowing about that person.

2. The gender categories, masculine and feminine, are experienced by most people as separate, contrasted communication ideals to be achieved. Often they are perceived as distinct categories assigned correspondingly to each sex.

3. People often work to attain a gender ideal despite major costs to themselves.

4. At some times during their lives, most individuals feel torn between trying to attain a gender ideal and trying to escape its limitations.

5. Cultural norms regarding gender are not fixed; they vary with time, situation, global location, and even belief systems. People can intentionally alter these norms if they so choose but usually not without resistance.

6. Communication creates and re-creates gender. Gender ideals are communicated verbally and nonverbally, directly and indirectly, intentionally and unintentionally in the situations of everyday life.

Central to these statements is the idea that gender and communication are intertwined. Communication processes create symbols of gender, and those processes also can re-create the meanings of gender. As people communicate with one another interpersonally, in groups, or through the media, they continually re-create the dispositions of the gender categories.

Table 1.1 Distinguishing between Sex and Gender

Sex	Gender
Biologically given	Socially learned
Treated as permanent fact	Treated as behavioral ideal to achieve; relationship between sex and gender often treated as fact
Descriptive	Both descriptive and valuative
"Female" and "male"	"Masculine" and "feminine"
Innate physical features	Selected interpersonal behaviors and attitudes named as appropriate features
Two categories: male or female	Infinite categories of varied combinations of masculinity and femininity

Whether or not you decided early in life to care about the gender ideal for your sex, someone has had a gender ideal in mind for you. You learned about it from a parent, a friend, your schoolmates, magazines, or television commercials you saw. You probably knew both a positive ideal and a negative image that could be attached to your appearance, words, and actions. Slang terms and familiar phrases—"wimp" versus "stud," "fox" versus "dog," "the strong, silent type," "woman's intuition"—tap into the informal consensus of what males or females should and should not be like.

Gender messages teach not only about differences between feminine and masculine; they also teach evaluation. Whereas establishing difference is an act of description, establishing status or hierarchical preference is an act of evaluation. Identifying sex is generally descriptive; identifying gender often carries with it valuative connotations or denotations. Because our everyday distinctions between sex and gender are fuzzy, evaluations inherent in gender messages often are transferred to sex messages. Gender messages incorporate evaluations about whether or not you are acting in ways appropriate to your sex. They also carry messages about which sex best suits a particular behavior or perspective. Throughout this book you will have a chance to consider how you learned the acceptable and unacceptable gender behaviors for your sex—and what messages you now wish to send and receive about gender in your own life.

THE NATURE OF COMMUNICATION

To understand how sex/gender and communication intertwine, we examine human beings from two perspectives: as human *animals* and as *human* animals. From each of these perspectives, we can see how communication functions to create the world in which we live; we also can see how the world we create affects communication.

THE HUMAN *ANIMAL*

From a biological perspective, humans share some kinds of message making with animals. Both humans and animals make and receive messages through sense data such as sounds and physical movement. For example, tone of voice, intensity of sound, or rapidity of movement might signal danger. The sense data has meaning within itself. While dogs may not know the words humans say, they may respond in specific ways to harsh tones of voice or to another dog's growls.

We do not generally think of these kinds of messages as symbolic in nature because they seem to *be* the message they carry. When someone screams, for instance, we do not think the tone and volume and pitch of the sound represents something else; we often respond physically by being startled. The scream *is* the message. While humans may learn to associate screaming with other things—that someone is being mugged or someone is seeing a horrific sight—the scream itself produces the message of screaming without having to be represented in any other way. Like other animals, human *animals* enact many of these kinds of signals every day.

As we study sex/gender and communication, then, we recognize that similarities and differences in male and female communication exist at this animalistic level. We derive some part of meaning from an instinct or a "knowing" innate to being a human *animal* and being male or female.

THE *HUMAN* ANIMAL

Distinguishing between messages instinctual to a human *animal* and those interpreted by the *human* animal, however, is neither clear nor simple. When we emphasize "human," we refer to a different communicative process. *Human* animals have access to a symbolic system not used by other animals. *Human* animals can use means such as icons and words and nonverbal actions to represent their thoughts. In other words, where animals communicate only the thing itself—or referent—humans have many other means by which to represent the thing. While animals have only the sound and tones of the scream, *human* animals have the scream itself as well as the word, "scream," other words (like "shriek" and "yell"), pictures, or nonverbal means by which to indicate screaming.

The communication process used by the *human* animal is not one that came packaged in biology. It is a process developed by humans over centuries; humans developed languages (which continue to evolve slowly) as well as whole sets of nonverbal codes they teach each other generation after generation. People make decisions not only about what representative icon or word should be used for an idea, but whether an icon should even exist for that idea. Sometimes people have new ideas and develop new icons or words. Those new symbols may generate new ideas that, in turn, generate more symbols. Sometimes people create new icons that other people do not adopt. The point is that *human* animals make the decisions about what to represent and how to represent it. Their decisions are not mandated by biology; their decisions derive from their own thoughts and choices.

Further complicating the process used by *human* animals is yet another layer of decision making. Having learned some part of the symbol system (a system comprised of symbols decided upon by humans singly and collectively), individuals then make decisions about how to use it. *Human* animals make choices about words and icons they will learn, words or gestures they will use from the available selection, and meanings they intend to transmit with those symbols. Since each person makes those decisions individually, communicating becomes a complicated process of determining the referent they wish to represent, selecting the corresponding symbols, and making myriad split-second decisions about such things as appropriateness, interpretative possibilities, accuracy of representation, intention, or mutuality.

All these decisions emerge from, reveal, and create value. If humans did not communicate symbolically but used only the referent itself, we would not make choices about how to represent something. For example, if someone wanted to communicate about a man, that person would have to have the man present. The physical presence or absence of the man would be the message: man, no man. Using a symbol system to communicate, decisions are made not only about which aspects of the man to communicate (he is here; he is not here; he is tall; he looks angry) but also about the way to represent the man in symbols, for example "man," "boy," "stud," "player," or "gentleman." In each case, the symbol user makes valuative rulings including such decisions as what characteristics are most important to represent, what images are most salient, or what features need to be omitted. If "stud" is used as the symbol, different features have been represented than those indicated by using "gentleman." The referent remains the same. The selection of the representative symbol includes a valuative process because the symbol user will choose one way of representation over another.

THE HUMAN *ANIMAL* AND THE *HUMAN* ANIMAL

Neither of these communication processes is separate from the other. Both are braided together closely; sometimes we have difficulty realizing that what we perceive as a human *animal* "reality" might actually be a repetitively communicated *human* animal construction. With regard to sex and gender, *human* animal messages about what are human *animal* features may be so pervasive as to persuade us that, indeed, these features are innate and instinctual. Are females innately more intuitive than males? Are females or males innately more cognitive or emotional? Are males instinctually more aggressive? How does the interaction between the "human" and the "animal" perspectives affect the "human" and "animal" delineations? As each of us examines our own decisions about those delineations, we can better understand the creative and generative powers of our *human* animal practices as those practices affect and are affected by our human *animal* existence.

THE ELEMENTS OF COMMUNICATION

To examine communication and the sexes effectively, you should be able to apply some of the essential concepts that make up the study of communication. At some time or other, we all have enjoyed success at communicating as evidenced by friends we have, essays we have written, jobs we have completed, and people who love us. Yet most of us also have experienced significant misunderstandings, conflicts, or uneasiness in our lives having to do with communication and gender-related issues.

As a prelude to our discussions about sex and gender, we will review several concepts essential to the study of communication so our definitions are clearly established before we look at various applications. First, we will examine the meaning of the term, "communication." When we imagine two people communicating, we can define their exchange from many different perspectives. We may say they are communicating simply because they are talking to each other. Some people argue, however, that unless both parties are consciously processing meaning, communication is not occurring. Imagine this scenario: you are concentrating on your computer screen as you rush to complete a paper due for class tomorrow. Your partner enters the room and begins talking to you. Suddenly, you are interrupted from your thoughts by your partner's annoyed voice saying, "Are you listening to me?" Until that question was asked, did communication occur? One perspective holds that mutuality—shared participation in meaning exchange—must exist before communication occurs. Mutuality does not mean both parties agree or even understand each other; it means that both parties consciously attend the communication act. In this book, we promote mutuality as a critical element of effective communication. We recognize, however, that in sex and gender communication, definitions of what constitutes "shared participation" often lie at the crux of communication complications.

Another perspective on the definition of communication considers intention as a critical element. If you are unaware that you glanced sideways at your partner and your partner interprets that glance as a hostile act, did communication occur? If you answered "yes," then does *any* act interpreted by any person constitute communication? Are those acts different from acts where people intentionally direct messages to each other in the process of negotiating meaning? We consider intention to communicate an important element in defining any communication event; we also recognize that unintentional behaviors may be interpreted as communicating and that under those circumstances, a skilled communicator will avoid making assumptions and engage the other in talk about the perceived event. Such communication about communication is called metacommunication. Metacommunication with regard to sex and gender is vital to defining and understanding each dyad's definition of communication.

While you read the discussions about sex, gender, and communication in this book, reconsider these perspectives on the definition of communication. How we conceptualize and define the phenomenon of communication has a direct bearing on critical communication choices such as how and when we talk to people of the same or other sexes or genders, what we talk about, and how we evaluate other communication styles or content.

Having considered some of the complex issues of defining communication, we now will consider important elements of communication events. Every communication event has these elements in some form: (1) message source/receivers, (2) the message, and (3) a situation or context. In the first element, we recognize that sending and receiving messages are not distinguishable. Both happen simultaneously and each process affects the other. When you talk to your partner about your exam for this class, you may think of yourself as the source of a message. However, you will simultaneously act as receiver because you will gauge your communication based on your partner's reactions as you speak. If your partner seems unconcerned about your disclosures, you may raise your voice or change your emphasis or act unconcerned yourself. Based in part on information you receive while you send, you make instant decisions about what to say and what not to say, how to phrase your idea and what tone to use. In addition, your source/receiver behavior will be affected by the context or situation you are experiencing. Situational influences, such as talking about the exam as you wait in line at the post office, may trigger different communication choices than those you would make while talking in the privacy of your living room.

Recognizing that the first element, source/receiver, interacts with the other two elements, let's look more closely now at the other two central concepts: message and situation or context. All the other communication terms and theories in this book derive from combinations of these three basic concepts.

MESSAGE

Message is defined here as any symbol or set of symbols, verbal or nonverbal, to which someone attaches meaning.

SYMBOL. In this definition of message, the first word to look at is symbol. A symbol is a representation of something else. Understanding that symbols are representative—metaphorical—in nature is critical to understanding some of the complexities in gender and communication. Symbols are usually associated with languages; we refer to objects or events by words. The words are not the objects or events themselves; the words only *represent*. Therefore, when we communicate with each other, we attempt to transfer precise meaning to someone else by choosing the best symbols for that purpose.

Our individual perceptions of the world provide the bases for the ideas or concepts we communicate. Because we are *human* animals, we expect the symbols we use to represent to other people our individual perceptions—what an experience is like for us. If a young woman wants to describe to a friend a man she has just met, she can select from a wide array of symbols. She will mentally survey her perception for her ideas or feelings and select the symbols she believes will most accurately represent those perceptions. Each combination of symbols she selects will offer a number of interpretations. She depends on her friend's ability to "accurately" translate her symbols into concepts or ideas.

For example, if she were to say, "What a hunk!" her friend could—but probably will not—imagine a large slab or chunk. The symbol, "hunk," will operate well for two people if both have experience in using it to describe attractive, well-built males. However, since symbols are not the objects or events, they do not always evoke identical meanings for both communicators. Words like "chick," "stud," "buff," and "girl" have all caused controversy because of different potential meanings and evaluations of those words.

VERBAL AND NONVERBAL. The part of the definition of message that said "verbal and nonverbal" means that we use other means besides words to convey meanings. Verbal communication entails your choices of symbols. Nonverbal communication entails several other dimensions, including kinesics (body movements), chronemics (time), haptics (touch and tactile sensations), proxemics and space, paralinguistics (oral and vocal dimensions such as tone, pitch, volume, rate of speech, or inflection), gesture, and appearance. Nonverbal elements account for at least 50 percent and sometimes as much as 90 percent of the meaning receivers interpret in face-to-face situations.[4] However, by its nature nonverbal communication is more ambiguous than verbal communication. When a message combines nonverbal messages with verbal symbols and the meanings compete with or contradict each other, we are more likely to believe our interpretations of nonverbal messages. In other words, how we interpret "Sure, Mark, I really like your tie" will depend on the nonverbal cues we interpret from the speaker. Problems with interpretation become complicated because the two sexes learn somewhat different nonverbal patterns in early life. In addition, a person's gender may influence and complicate those patterns. This problem of interpretation will be discussed at greater length in chapter 4.

ATTACHING MEANING. The third part of the definition of message, "to which someone attaches meaning," highlights our process of making meanings out of events. Meanings don't just happen to us. Human beings create meaning, partly to give order to our lives. However, we often assume that any observer will attach the same meanings that we do to a communication event. This assumption identifies one of the major "hurdles" in the study of gender and communication.

For example, some men in the United States may compare competition in business with experience in sports. Their language reflects that experience: "This project's a winner," "Take the ball and run with it," "Let's hit a home run with this presentation," or "It's third and goal." Heated competition, winning, and the camaraderie of team effort are often familiar and even desired means by which these men frame their experiences. In contrast, some women in the United States may reject sports competition because it promotes aggression in the participants. These women may object to exhortations to "land a knock-out punch" or to "slam-dunk the opposition," claiming that the emotional and physical costs to the players outweigh the benefits of competing. These viewpoints are by no means the only ones on competition, but they are two that have been linked with the two sexes and appear in casual conversation as well as public debates. The two views represent instances in which human actions receive very different meanings depending on who is observing and evaluating them.

SITUATION OR CONTEXT

The third key term for analyzing communication events related to the sexes is "situation" or "context." These terms refer to the set of features in a particular environment at a given time that can reinforce, limit, or define the messages you send. The situation encompasses myriad factors, including the physical setting, time constraints, social customs, past history, public/privacy issues, and present relationships involving you and any members of your audience. How you perceive a situation will influence whether you take initiative as a communicator, wait for someone else to speak, or leave a particular communication setting.[5]

Being silent is one of your options in many communication situations. If you decide that the negative effects of communicating are likely to be greater than the promise of positive results, you may opt not to speak in certain cases. Sometimes choices to remain silent are easy ones. A woman may choose to ignore the implications of "How can I help you, little lady?" She may choose not to take the time and energy to address the issue with a salesperson she never will see again. On the other hand, sometimes the choices to remain silent are difficult. Men or women who work for a manager who uses sexist language may decide to keep silent to protect their jobs; in these cases, the silence can generate frustration and anger on the part of the subordinates. Context and situation can be pivotal when choosing times to speak and times to remain silent with regard to sex and gender.

As you read this book, consider yourself an active designer and creator of your own messages and a careful evaluator of other people's messages. Even though you may feel severely limited at times by situational or contextual forces outside your control, the choices you make—even under those circumstances—determine the reality of gender you contribute to the world. Verbal and nonverbal choices constitute the means by which gender is created and re-created. When you take an active approach to communicating, you design and alter the local situational components; ultimately, those local components inform the global ones. Your active communication can reestablish gender purposefully and intentionally rather than perpetuating rote and perhaps damaging cultural ideals of masculine and feminine.

SITUATION AS RITUAL. Situations limit the information you have about your alternatives and thus influence your message choices. Tradition or custom in particular situations helps define certain behaviors as "normal" or "expected." You can feel strongly guided or pressured by these customs to make a predictable response to another person. Some situations form the basis for social rituals in which participants are expected to know and play their parts.

One such ritual, the "door-opening ceremony," symbolizes the changes in daily life in the United States, changes that have occurred largely because of awareness raised by the women's movement. This small interaction between men and women that had been nearly automatic (done without thinking) turned into an awkward and sometimes uncomfortable decision-making quandary: "Should I open the door for her?" "Is he going to rush ahead of me to open the door?" "Will she call me polite or a chauvinist?" "Should I ignore the whole thing?" A communication situation moved from being a minor ritual to a self-conscious, problematic gender encounter.

The important point is that new meanings have been constructed from a common situation. Behavior that once could commonly be interpreted to mean "Men open doors for women as a sign of respect" has proliferated into various interpretations including "Women do not need men to open doors for them; they are capable of opening their own doors," "Society does not need socially assigned behaviors based on sex," or even "Society cannot function without rituals of civility." Whether we select or reject any of these statements, the salient fact is that meanings are perceived and communicated. Participating in an interaction—however routine—always carries the possibility that participants may interpret the situation differently and, thus, derive different meanings.

As in any process of change, we experience an uncertain moment between what had been the practice before and what will be the practice now. Active, effective communicators educated about gender and communication can help diminish the negative effects of that moment and reestablish the ritual to reflect rather than dictate preferred gender behavior. Awareness of multiple possibilities for meaning can guard against major misunderstandings; however, the impossible task of anticipating every possibility leads to the topics of the next two sections.

ATTRIBUTION, STEREOTYPING, AND THE GENDER FILTER

THE ROLE OF ATTRIBUTION IN STEREOTYPING

Stereotyping arises at least partly because in a complex and changing world we want to be able to predict the behavior of others. We stereotype to hold constant and make sense of the world we know. If we can interpret behaviors in a way that makes sense to us, we believe we then can predict future behaviors and thereby introduce a measure of order to our world. Stereotyping occurs when we make predictions and preclude from those predictions significant individual differences.

Because we tend to attribute behaviors differently to ourselves than we do to others, our attribution process supports the potential for stereotyping. Psychologists have found that we tend to explain our own actions by attributing them to forces outside ourselves—in other words, to situations. However, we tend to explain the actions of other people by attributing those actions to internal factors, that is, the other's basic character traits and intentions.[6] For example, a person might say, "I'm sorry I'm late. Ms. Roberts couldn't see me until four" (a statement attributing the person's lateness to an external situation caused by Ms. Roberts). However, if the event were interpreted by the person who was waiting, that person might say, "Gail will be late today. She apparently didn't make previous arrangements with Ms. Roberts, so she had to wait until Ms. Roberts returned at four" (a statement indicating Gail's internal failing—oversight in not planning ahead).

Attributing your actions to outside forces can be a self-protective measure. It is less damaging to your self-esteem than saying you erred or willfully chose to act in a particular way. As receivers of communication, we often analyze motives as if other people had no external constraints or limitations affecting their decisions. This kind of analysis can lead us to make character judgments about another's basic qualities as a human being, and these judgments can create stereotypes that both give us inaccurate information and form barriers between people. When men and women interact, attribution can imperil cooperation.

STEREOTYPING BETWEEN THE SEXES

Many of us believe we do recognize the situational pressures and forces that affect people, even people of the other sex or of other genders. Since we have been in similar circumstances, we may assume we "know" how another person feels when facing a similar event. However, in the many cases in which a person of the other sex does not behave as we would have, it is tempting to attribute the discrepancy to the other's character. Making character judgments when we lack direct knowledge of the person's situational limitations and individual concerns is easier than exploring differences—which might lead to disturbing questions about our own behavior. Terms like "male chauvinist pig" or "empty-headed bimbo" provide a simple shorthand for dealing with people who offend or disappoint us. If we are unable to identify with a particular person or situation, character labels offer a sense of superiority over the other person. In addition, such behavior on our part can resolve our confusion and restore our sense of control. However, the labels do not provide any information for explaining what is going on or any methods for finding out more about the other person's perspective. Yet, many of us count on these labels rather than seeking clarification.

Forming stereotypes includes uniformly depicting persons in terms of their membership in a specific group rather than in terms of individual characteristics and experiences. When we work from attributions, we assign certain character traits to a group; then we use those traits to explain behaviors of people within that group.

Stereotypes are not always negative. We may hold a positive stereotype of men, for example, as being able to make household repairs. Based on that positive stereotype, you may expect your friend on the football team to be able to fix a leaky faucet. A positive stereotype can coexist with a negative one about the same group. For example, career counselors sometimes encourage females to pursue data entry because of their "natural" manual dexterity, yet discourage surgical medicine because women are not suited to the rigor of the scientific training. You may be thinking, "Well, most women I know *do* dislike math and science classes." The problem is that unless you know that all members of a given group share a given characteristic, you cannot be sure of the degree to which the next person you meet has the same quality or problem or talent. In addition, your conclusions about the relationship of women and science may be based on suppositions about the nature of science and the system of teaching science in the United States. Generalizations or faulty cause-effect relationships about scientific potential and surgeon's work can lead you to mistaken conclusions.

Stereotyping limits the options both of the person who is being stereotyped and the one doing the stereotyping. If the stereotype deals with a positively evaluated trait, it presents pressures to live up to the ideal: "What do you mean, you don't like to play basketball? All tall guys play basketball!" Or, if the stereotype is negative, it may generate a discouraging message: "Play hockey? You? Are you kidding, Samantha? Girls aren't made for contact sports." These messages present the labeled person with a dilemma: Should I distance myself from the stereotyped group in order to be taken as an individual, or should I allow myself to be labeled with the group and try to avoid the negative personal effects of the stereotype? In any case, the stereotyped person must deal with a label that oversimplifies or misdefines the self. In addition, the person who stereotypes eliminates avenues for exchanging meaning with others. As that person limits the world of the other, limitations also are placed on the world that can be shared between them. Stereotyping reduces the scope of possibilities communicators can use to locate shared meaning.

THE GENDER FILTER

For the purposes of this book, we use "gender filter" to refer to assumptions and expectations—often unexamined—about how members of each sex are likely to behave in various communication settings. That these filters usually are unexamined is key to understanding how they work. The filter itself can be problematic. People learn to use all kinds of filters, such as racial, ethnic, educational, socioeconomic, religiosity, or political ideology. When these filters are put in place and left to function without critique or management, they can produce limited worldviews that disallow understanding and choice. Many people use their gender filter in this way. They rely on a mental filter to increase their ease in predicting others' behaviors.

My cousins are two years apart in age and very different. The older, Mike, is tall and skinny, while Kyle is short and stocky. Kyle is very masculine, while Mike is somewhat feminine. I remember one day Kyle was playing ball in the house, and being very rough. As this activity was typical for a young boy, no one thought anything of it. But Michael was off in the other room playing with a female doll, and watching Cinderella. I remember thinking what Kyle was doing was "normal," but what Michael was doing seemed strange. This was a case of a child's sex setting some expectations for the child's gender.

As a result of their filters, people may stereotype and label each other. People label each other for many reasons; one of the reasons is simple convenience. If you can predict how different kinds of conversations will go, you will have less mental preparation to do. If you have to treat each new encounter (same-sex as well as cross-sex) as if its outcome is totally uncertain, you will need to give attention to dozens or even hundreds of features of the event and the people involved. You may decide that the stresses of all that information processing are not worth the trouble, and you may avoid or short-circuit the interaction. An unexamined gender filter gives you a means to process information swiftly in many communication situations. You can take a quick look at a new acquaintance, make an unexamined prediction about that person's qualities and interests, and adapt your own communication to fit the stereotype you have assigned to the acquaintance. This image of interaction is somewhat oversimplified, but it is likely to fit the patterns most of us follow.

A gender filter that is continually examined, managed, and revised can help us identify those external forces we might otherwise overlook. Regular revision of our gender filter may enhance our sensitivity to aspects of others' individual experiences; our communication with those people can be more appropriate and effective.

We often find ourselves fatigued at the prospect of facing another interaction in which sex or gender ideals are expected to play a part. Many people once believed they knew the rules for first meetings, for expressing affection, for avoiding or ending conflicts—even for everyday office behavior. They now find themselves wondering much of the time which set of rules apply, and to whom. Culture, race, class, and ethnicity combine with sex and gender to create a sometimes bewildering web of variables. Women meeting other women at parties, for example, may struggle to figure out whether their conversations will/should be about child care or careers. Men may grapple with decisions about discussing personal matters with other men. You may once have felt confidence in being able to tell which "type" of male or female you were dealing with and thus which set of responses on your part would bring the results you wanted. Then, to your surprise, you may have found that the other person was not behaving like the expected "sensitive man" or "powerful woman" or "liberated person" you thought you recognized.

I was standing on campus one day when one of the males in my rhetoric class approached me. A couple of points first: there were only ten people in the class, fairly evenly balanced, and we had only talked about the civil rights movement. The classmate asked me if I knew who I was going to do my paper on. It was the way he phrased the question that made me remember this instance. He said, "Did you choose which lady you are going to do your paper on?" Then he quickly explained himself, something about the idea that I was a pretty outspoken female, so he assumed I would do it on the feminist movement and someone from it.

I almost went off on him but instead I kept calm and explained that was not the case.

One response to that discovery is to call the other person a fraud, as if their contradicting your expectations were a deliberate strategy to make you stumble. Being aware of expectations and reconciling them with new information is a more useful method of reacting to an unexpected response than blaming the other person. Most people in this time of shifting roles and rules will be trying to cope with the contradictions in their situations and feelings. In this sense, everyone shares the struggle to make sense of the paradoxes and contradictions surrounding sex and gender in everyday communication.

COMMUNICATION AND THE SEXES THROUGHOUT LIFE

Gender issues in communication are part of your life from the moment you are born until the moment you die. The second half of this book will develop this point in detail, examining communication as it occurs at various life stages and in various settings. For now, let's look briefly at some of the ways gender becomes both a goal and a problem for most people growing up in this society.

EARLY YEARS

Gender ideals start to affect your life as a male or as a female even before you draw your first breath. Parents often express a hope for one sex or the other. A positive or negative value may be attached to the possible sex of the new baby. Some parents hope for a boy so he can "carry on the family name." Others wish for a girl because they are

Yippee!
Announcing our new cowboy...
John Brodie Fuller
May 20, 1996   9:10 p.m.
5 pounds, 13 ounces   18 inches
Proud Parents:
Bret and Shawna (McClure) Fuller

"easier to raise." Interestingly, in the United States we often have the circumstance of a girl who learned to play sports because "my dad wanted a boy." We rarely have the circumstance of a boy who learns to sew because "my mom wanted a girl." Implications of parents' desires for one sex or the other reveal important information about cultural evaluation of sex and, consequently, gender in the United States.

Other arrangements before you were born also reflected gender expectations. Colors and designs of clothes and bedding, talk between parents about names and parenting practices, and family talk about what the future will bring all exhibit cultural gender messages. Gifts given to the couple before the baby is born or to the child after it is born often reinforce gender norms.

The process of giving attention to a child's sex continues and often increases after its birth. Exclamations of "It's a boy!" or "It's a girl!" answer one of the first questions asked both by parents and friends. In the United States culture, identifying the sex of the child is primary information. Adults meeting infants for the first time may feel embarrassed if they are unable to distinguish the infant's maleness or femaleness under pastel blankets. Our cultural ritual of dressing girls in pink and boys in blue helps relieve well-wishers of their dilemma.

Interestingly, those colors have not always been assigned to those sexes. You can gauge the power of your gender training by trying to imagine that in the nineteenth century, blue was assigned to girls (billowy skies and softness) and pink to boys (virile, derived from blood red).

As you moved from infant to toddler, you learned that you were a particular sex and that in all likelihood you would remain that sex the rest of your life. Psychologists explain that between the ages of two and three, children learn not only their sex, but the attending gender expectations. For a time, children resist the mandate to claim a gender. Often, children of those ages engage in mixed-gender play and dress; they hold onto their many behavior choices for as long as possible before they finally relinquish the gender behaviors of the other sex.

A Thorough History of Manliness in America

A Book Review by James North

The color blue for boy infants and pink for girls may sound natural and timeless. But, as Michael Kimmel shows in his superb new book [*Manhood in America: A Cultural History*], this color/gender scheme is surprisingly recent. Until the 1880s, little American boys and girls were dressed in identical white christening gowns. Then rising anxiety over the definition of masculinity in a changing society helped prompt a debate; one magazine, *The Infant's Department*, editorialized in 1918 that pink, as "a more decided and stronger color, is more suitable for the boy; while blue, which is more delicate and dainty, is prettier for the girl." The debate continued until the present arrangement won out.

Kimmel's thorough, impressive and fascinating history shows that the definitions of manhood have changed in many ways over the course of American history. The author, a professor of sociology at the State University of New York at Stony Brook, has pored through the historical record, employing everything from popular plays in the 1790s to 1950s television Westerns to create a well-written and revealing narrative, one that helps us see our past in a new light.

He begins by identifying three models for American manhood. The Genteel Patriarch is a property owner, a benevolent authority with an aristocratic code of honor; Thomas Jefferson at Monticello is an example. The Heroic Artisan is an independent, self-reliant craftsman, like Paul Revere, the Boston silversmith and patriot.

As the 19th century opens, these older archetypes are challenged by a newcomer: the Self-Made Man, who must earn his manhood by succeeding in a fiercely competitive, unstable marketplace, proving himself constantly. Kimmel quotes cultural critic Gary Wills: This "self-maker, self-improving, is always a construction in progress. He must ever be tinkering, improving, adjusting, starting over, fearful his product will get out of date, or rot in the storehouse."

Yet Kimmel shows that the rise of the giant corporation increasingly stymied efforts by males to prove their manhood. Four-fifths of American men worked for themselves in the early 19th century, but by 1870 only one-third did. The corporations turned independent artisans into assembly line workers, and would-be self-makers into white-collar bureaucrats.

Kimmel contends that one important way to view American history is to consider the strategies that men have used to protect themselves from "the fear that they are not powerful, strong, rich or successful enough." One strategy, he writes, is to control themselves, through rigorous programs of diet, temperance, exercise and self-improvement. The latest exercise craze, he indicates, is only the recurrence of an old theme: At the end of the 19th century, middle-class American men surged into gymnasiums, joined cycling clubs and sprinted onto athletic fields to prove they had not gone soft with office work.

Kimmel uses the work of historian David Roediger to suggest that white men have used an artificial concept of "whiteness" to elevate their opinion of themselves as compared to blacks, thus avoiding feeling their own increasing powerlessness in a corporate-dominated world.

Finally, American men have escaped, heading for what Kimmel calls a "homosocial" frontier, where they could leave behind feminization and the responsibilities they feared deep down they could not meet. From James Fenimore Cooper through Clint Eastwood, men have headed for this mythical frontier, in fantasies and sometimes in fact. Theodore Roosevelt is a prime example; he was a sickly, upper-class New Yorker who remade himself (with help from the press) into a strenuous outdoorsman and warrior.

Kimmel sees Franklin D. Roosevelt as one of the last of the Genteel Patriarchs, motorcycle club members as Heroic Artisans. His subject is huge, and he is, perhaps understandably, too brief in some areas. We could use, for example, a more considered look at how middle- and working-class definitions of manhood have varied over the years.

But Kimmel's historical synthesis shows that American male attitudes are clearly linked to the society we live in. He suggests implicitly that we could modify those attitudes by changing society, replacing some of the fierce competitiveness with cooperation and genuine teamwork.

Chicago Tribune, Books Section, March 3, 1996

During childhood, the values attached to sex extends to concerns about gender-appropriate behavior. Children who play at cross-sex pastimes—those associated with the other sex—are sometimes encouraged, sometimes not noticed, and sometimes punished by parents or caregivers. Trucks and Power Rangers for boys, Barbies and doll houses for girls are modeled by television commercials. Culturally assigned colors correspond to the expected gender role, pastels for girls and blacks or browns for boys. Clothes also mirror the ideals of little-boy and little-girl behavior expectations: rugged jeans for the aggressiveness of boys, dresses or lace-trimmed coveralls for the delicateness of girls. While unisex fitness fashions and sweatsuits have entered the market as an option for both sexes, often the design, cut, or color of the outfits perpetuate the use of gender signals to mark sex.

My husband is so afraid of our daughter labeling herself in the stereotypical female role. He doesn't want her to be limited in any way. Because of this, he teaches and plays with her in ways that he sees as fun. From this and some of her own nature, she is very much a tomboy. But he excludes the type of play that he considers feminine, such as dolls and dress-up. What he seems to forget is that we are not her only influences. One day when she was two and a half, she got into the refrigerator and found an eggplant. She took the eggplant and put a diaper on it, then wrapped it up in her blanket with her and took a nap. After the eggplant turned mushy she went to pumpkins. She had one pumpkin that she slept with every night for three weeks.

I think it is amazing how much infants and toddlers pick up that which we take for granted. My daughter already categorizes some responsibilities as "mommy jobs" and "daddy jobs."

In the United States, boys and girls hear more negative messages about boys doing girl-style play than about girls doing boy-style play. "Sissy" (a derivative of "sister") and "wimp" are taken as more derogatory labels than "tomboy." Girls in the same culture have somewhat more freedom of action beyond gender-defined boundaries than do boys. The traditional dominance of male figures on television and in stories means that girls will see and identify with male activities more than boys will see and identity with female activities. The sexes do not simply have different communication experiences in their early years; they also differ in the amount and kind of exposure they have to new information about themselves. This characteristic of the United States culture is an example where difference between the sexes is not the critical issue. Evaluation of that difference—an evaluation that feminine behaviors by males are not acceptable—creates a hierarchy elevating one sex over the other and establishes grounds for problems concerning the self-esteem of both males and females who wish to engage in those behaviors.

If a girl receives more information about boys and men than about girls and women, she may develop an ability to think and talk about the interests of a person of the other sex. She may generate a dual perspective that allows her access to the feminine through her own life experiences and limited access to the masculine through observation. However, chasms of misunderstanding may still occur. Attitudes toward goals offer one example. Presumptions about goal setting and even presumptions about what constitutes a goal may vary dramatically between the male and female experiences. Therefore, the feminine agenda may be quite different from the masculine one, or the feminine conceptualization of "goal" might be at variance in kind or definition with that demonstrated by the masculine. Professionals working with adult women who are homemakers report that the women often are unable to state clear personal goals, although they can state precisely the goals of other family members. One explanation might be that cultural preference for the masculine has led these women to focus on the goals of others. However, another explanation may be that the dual perspective allows these women to recognize goals devised by others, while they may or may not be personally interested in goals. The presumption that goals as defined in others' lives must also be significant for these women may be an inaccurate presumption.

Likewise, young boys may be dissuaded from developing an understanding of the feminine experience by the negative messages about femininity. Boys receive more ridicule for "throwing like a girl" than girls receive for "throwing like a boy." Young boys gain little reward for learning the ways of girls. If a boy receives less information about girls and women than about boys and men, he may not readily develop an ability to think and talk about the interests of a person of the other sex. This inability can adversely affect cross-sex relationships. For example, professionals report that adult men often lack skills to develop intimate relationships. Without a dual perspective, masculine intimacy in a culture that assigns intimate expertise to the feminine might be at variance in kind or definition with intimacy demonstrated by the feminine. Without a dual perspective, a male may have less access to that feminine concept of intimacy.

In addition to the challenges presented by these cultural impacts on our early gender development, we all learned these gender expectations during a time when we had little or no analytical ability to appraise information. As children, we cultivated norms and expectations into our daily routines, enacting gender behavior repeatedly to the effect that the behaviors became "natural." While some of the behaviors might have been mediated by adults, such as our parents, many derived from the media or from other children. Just as learning to play the piano or learning a different language is easier and more enduring when done as a child, so are the cultural lessons of gender easier to learn and more enduring in effect. The tenacity of these unexamined gender stereotypes makes redressing those rote behaviors more difficult for adolescents and adults.

ADOLESCENCE AND ADULTHOOD

Many people presume gender to be universal, necessary, and benevolent. The reality is that gender occurs in a variety of combinations, is not a universal construction, can be unnecessary, and can create malice. The effects of gender expectations and ambitions vary widely across individuals. In many situations gender ideals produce complications or directly damage individuals or relationships. Gender ideals based on the idea that a male must "achieve" masculinity and a female must "achieve" femininity create frustrations for most of us during early adulthood and beyond. Ideals of feminine are generated by both males and females, as are ideals of masculine. As a result, pressure to attain those gender ideals can come from many sources. A human model or example that ostensibly achieves the perfect nonverbal and verbal gender behavior can evoke admiration, envy, or both; however, such a model also presents the facade of a reality that does not exist. No one can continually match the images created by Hollywood or the advertising media. Any communication event that focuses on a man's physical strength and "coolness" or on a woman's beauty and physical attractiveness implies that people who do not conform to gender expectations in appearance are inadequate or deficient. The underlying messages convey that people need to compensate for their gender defects ("Act like a man!"), pretend to ignore their differences ("Superwoman"), or accept a lesser status ("Dress for success!").

A girl I went to high school with had been dating another guy in our class and they broke up. She began to get thinner and thinner and all I saw her eat for lunch was an apple and a pint of skim milk. She was a cheerleader as well as valedictorian. She was very intelligent and had a great figure before she stopped eating. I think the reason she did this (probably subconsciously) was to make Mark want her back. She wanted to be perfect for him, and I think she got messages from society that being thin equates with being perfect. I don't understand (because I haven't "been there" myself) how anyone could let something so powerful take hold of his or her life. I guess it comes from society pushing women to be all to all people. They feel powerless, and controlling the food they eat and how their bodies look is the only control they think they have.

Trying to achieve gender ideals can affect our health. Bulimia is an eating disorder that came to prominent attention during the 1980s; that it affects females almost exclusively suggests that this disorder is an extreme response to the gender ideal of slenderness. Bulimics tend to binge on foods, then purge their systems through vomiting. Their bodies become battlegrounds for the opposite goals of overindulgence—to satisfy desire for food—and lean, gender-idealized bodies—signifying being loved and accepted. The results of this battle can be fatal.

In 1951 Miss Sweden was 5' 7" tall and weighed 151 pounds.

In 1983 Miss Sweden was 5' 9" tall and weighed 109 pounds.

On any given day, 50 percent of all adolescent girls are on a diet.

From Jillyn McCullough, "Poisoning Our Girls?" *Statesman Journal*, January 27, 1996, p. D.1.

In terms of the masculine ideal, some men become addicted to body building or athletic competition in the hope of approaching their own gender ideal. Use of steroids to achieve certain muscular forms becomes routine for some body builders. For other males, drinking alcohol represents masculine control and competitive performance. If a male does not drink alcohol or if he drinks beverages that are identified with women, he may label himself or be labelled by others as a "lightweight," a person not to be admired by some other males or some females. While not all men and women support these ideals, cultural traditions continue to be communicated and recognized by many in the United States, and especially by the advertising industry. A third standard for "masculine" males, sexual success with attractive women, influences many men. The ability to "score" with a desirable woman can earn status with peers who wish for similar sexual success; it also generates status for females who subscribe to particular gender ideals. Each of these patterns promotes polarized, ritualistic gender expectations. Unthinking acceptance of such stereotyped behaviors can become a dangerous influence on the decision making of individuals and groups. Recent studies about date rape have made clear connections between male expectations of conquest and consequent behavior choices.

As women and men age, their gender expectations and gender definitions change. Physical changes during the aging process may affect the parameters of expectation for masculine and feminine but leave intact the tension between experience and expectation. Gender pressures felt by sixteen-year-olds may differ from those experienced by sixty-five-year-olds, but people in both age groups can identify the relative ideals. Gender remains a communication component for the entire life cycle.

INTIMACY

Most of us seek intimacy with others, although we may do so for very different reasons. Messages embedded in gender ideals present different messages to males and females about intimacy, including messages about self-disclosure, conflict, interdependency, and ethics. Both homosexual and heterosexual partnerships include negotiations about what intimacy means. A partner who has learned only a masculine ideal may define intimacy as physical and psychological space, declining opportunities to self-disclose and approaching conflict as a win-lose competition. A partner who has learned only a feminine ideal may work toward closeness and cohesion, may self-disclose often, and may avoid or accommodate conflict. Each individual experiences intimacy differently; what has been learned with regard to gender plays a central role in that individual's expectations and behaviors. In addition, the structure by which that individual thinks about intimacy also has been affected by learned gender differences. Therefore, the partners not only have to deal with present behaviors, but with how each partner structures his or her thoughts about that behavior. Since gender is not a polarized "fact" like sex, partners may combine any number of masculine and feminine behaviors. Intimacy between genders, then, becomes complicated. Since gender does not necessarily coincide with sex, both homosexual and heterosexual partners may experience these intimacy tensions.

Another confounding factor about intimacy concerns differences among genders with regard to public and private communication contexts. In intimate relationships, where the private self is foregrounded, an individual's struggle to deal with gender expectations may become exposed. Communication experts explain, for example, that when males are in the company of other males, they are likely to exhibit masculine gender ideals in a pronounced way. In private, however, these behaviors may change. Consequently, intimate partners may contend with different public and private gender expectations. Negotiating these differences does not always occur explicitly. Sometimes we let our partners know nonverbally that we disagree with their gender behavior, adding to the complexity of our intimacy development.

Trying to establish intimacy between sexes and among genders introduces complicated issues about behavior, gender affiliation, argument strategies and forms, developmental patterns, perceptions and uses of self-disclosure, and functions of communication. Our discussions in the chapter about intimacy will explore these issues.

A commitment to an intimate relationship can result in two people establishing a life together; that life may include children. Upon becoming parents, whether by pregnancy or adoption, these parents begin again the cycle of proliferation of gender definitions and expectations.

INFLUENCES ON THINKING ABOUT SEX AND GENDER

Much of our talk about the sexes will require us to make visible fundamental presumptions we often take for granted. Since these presumptions provide the infrastructure to our thinking, we usually use them but do not examine them. In fact, examining them takes effort and concentration. We should learn to take time to analyze our fundamental presumptions about sex and gender in order to understand ourselves and our communication behaviors better. Try to suspend judgments linked to these presumptions while you examine them. Remember that the point of the examination is not necessarily change; the goal is thorough understanding.

We will examine three substructures of presumption: distinguishing and evaluating; polarizing and creating continua; and concentric perspectives.

DISTINGUISHING AND EVALUATING

DISTINGUISHING. When we think about sex and gender—or any topic—we often begin by distinguishing: male from female, feminine from masculine, sex from gender. The intent is to create discrete forms for reference. When we create the discrete symbol—such as "female"—we then can assign in our minds a discrete referent for that symbol.

However, what constitutes "male," "female," "masculine," and "feminine" is not as objective as we often presume. Critical to our assessment of "female," for example, is both our concept of "female" and our consequent symbolic representation—that is, communication—as we attempt to relay that concept to someone else. That same refracting process—life experience shaping concepts and ideas that are then translated into a communication form and transferred to another person—occurs for others as well. As a consequence, perceptions of sex and gender influence our communication on several levels: conceptualization because of the ways our lives are experienced; translation into what we believe are useful and appropriate communication forms; and choice of means by which to offer that translated conceptualization to another person. The process is complex.

Compounding that complexity is our confusion about same/equal and different/unequal. If we determine that a particular characteristic or behavior of males and females is different, do we also assess the difference as inequality? If we seek equality between males and females, are we seeking sameness? While "different but equal" sounds noble, how do we assess either difference or equality? We may create illusions of distinctiveness and act on those illusions.

The point here is that how we think about divisions such as "equal," "unequal," "same," and "different" derives from our presumptions about these concepts. In negotiating gender parameters we will need to articulate and negotiate these presumptions as well. Making the matter more complex, we will need to determine not only how these concepts might appear to ourselves and others, but also whether these concepts apply. Do men and women need to use identical speech patterns to achieve equality? If a woman perceives a message as belittling and a man perceives it as inconsequential, are we dealing with difference or inequality? How are distinctions to be made? And by whom? Under what conditions? Confronting these difficult questions demands well-developed communication skills because these questions require the blending of the multiple perspectives represented by both sexes and all genders.

EVALUATING. Differentiating one thing from another allows us to create order. That order inherently relies on hierarchy. The conceptual complexity of same/different and equal/unequal is compounded in the United States culture by what Kenneth Burke calls the human tendency toward hierarchy. Kenneth Burke was a contemporary, Western, rhetorical theorist who wrote that human beings make order by ranking people, events, and experiences in terms of higher to lower value.[7] In other words, Burke holds that humans not only differentiate but also evaluate simultaneously. When we distinguish one thing, person, or idea from another, we also tend to make judgments about the relative value of that thing, person, or idea. In other words, when we differentiate male from female or feminine from masculine, we simultaneously assess that differentiation in terms of higher or lower, better or worse. Burke contends that we construct mental hierarchies. We even construct hierarchies of hierarchies. The key, then, becomes not whether female/male or masculine/feminine are different, but whether one consistently is evaluated as higher on whatever hierarchy is used. Where the genders fit on that hierarchy will have a direct bearing on our idea of equality or inequality.

These hierarchical evaluations can undercut our wishes to treat each other "equally." Any comparison between men and women as groups—for example, by physical differences—seems to provide a rationale for hierarchical ordering of how people might perform a job, endure hardship, or overcome obstacles. While such a perspective can provide valuable information, it also can provide inaccurate information. In addition, it focuses on areas of possible inequality and evaluated difference rather than on comparisons of common human value. Without examining our hierarchical tendencies through intentional, rhetorical intervention, messages eventually can be aggregated into a sex or gender stereotype that places one sex or gender in a superior position to another.

The building of mental hierarchies is aided and even created in some cases by images in the media: advertisers often urge you to use their products to achieve a body more similar to that of the televised model, promoting one body type as better than others. Commercials depict characters who envy the product or the result of using a product owned by someone else. Subtle messages about whether men or women are better at certain behaviors are threaded through beer commercials, commercials for laundry products, automobile ads, and even advertisements for clothing.

Yet advertisers do not singlehandedly cause viewers to measure themselves against an unattainable image. People have always been inclined to strive to achieve ideals and to suffer over their imperfections as compared to those ideals. One theory about self-concept suggests we have an ideal self and a self we show others. As the discrepancy between those two selves enlarges, we feel more and more uncomfortable and work to allay the discomfort. Advertising just directs that wish to become perfect toward products and toward competition with others. The sexes are rarely shown in direct competition with each other, but they are typically shown competing with members of the same sex for the favors of an appealing person of the other sex. By implication, then, you are a woman who will "win" the man if your hair gleams, your floors shine, and your laundry is whiter; likewise, you are a man who will "win" the woman if your car goes from zero to sixty in less time, you smell like musk, and you wear certain kinds of sport shoes.

SEPARATION AS A CHOICE. People sometimes choose separation from the other sex to aid their personal development. Both formally and informally, females and males sometimes elect to gather with others of the same sex to share life experiences. Groups of women in the 1980s and even into the 1990s have gathered to clarify their experiences as girls and women and to gain support from other women.[8] Cultural messages such as economic indicators and certain generally accepted language practices indicate that hierarchically, that which is constructed as feminine in the United States culture tends to be subordinated to that which is constructed as masculine. To circumvent these powerful cultural messages, some women often prefer to discuss the gender-related issues of daily life in single-sex settings. Participants in research on women often explain that in regard to many topics, they receive more confirmation from other women than from men. They also say they feel their experiences are better understood. In addition, some women in all-female discussion groups cite feelings of freedom to express their opinions without the fear of interruption or criticism by a dominant male.[9]

Men also have begun to form male-only groups for support, although their groups are not as visible nor as widespread as women's. Traditionally in the United States, men have gathered separately from women for certain kinds of activities, such as athletics, hunting, and male-only parties. Some men experienced all-male communities in military academies. The 1996 Supreme Court decision (regarding the Virginia Military Institute and affecting the Citadel in South Carolina) declared such state-supported all-male institutions unconstitutional; nevertheless, some privately owned institutions still operate with male-only populations.

More similar in kind to the women's groups, other male-only groups have emerged to deal with such issues as redefining male roles, rediscovering masculinity, and examining fatherhood. During the 1980s Robert Bly organized seminars for single-sex discussions and exchanges among men about their lives. Bly's focus was on defining masculinity in its own right rather than as it juxtaposed to femininity. By the mid 1990s, small, independent men's groups continued to generate conversations regarding men's changing roles and challenges. In 1995 several men's groups came together for the Million Man March in Washington, D.C. where speakers exhorted males to re-enter community life as leaders and providers of families. Similarly, Promise Keepers' all-male meetings centered on the male's role in the family.

All-female and all-male conversations can provide important means for discovery and reaffirmation for both men and women. Sometimes, however, the single-sex conversations exacerbate the problems of communication between the sexes by promoting myths and stereotypes that supersede distinction, fostering instead evaluation, suspicion, and dysfunctional competition.

Competition and consequent misunderstanding among men and women flourish in a context of partial knowledge and high stakes. Competitive thoughts about the other sex in the workplace occur now with particular force because phrases like "equal opportunity," "affirmative action," "pay equity," and "reverse discrimination" appear to complicate both men's and women's careers. "Do I have my share?" we ask. "Is anyone keeping me from getting all I deserve?" "What can I do to ensure my chances of success?" Likewise, in the home, unspoken questions like, "Am I doing more than my share?" and "Is my partner considering my needs?" undermine personal relationships. All these lines of reasoning promote emotions such as frustration, anxiety, anger, suspicion, and even paranoia. Balance between segregated conversations and those with the other sex can provide more constructive communication overall.

POLARIZING OR CREATING CONTINUA

This second pair of concepts or assumptions is closely linked with the first set of terms just discussed. These two phrases extend the idea of difference to questions of degree and kind of difference. First, consider the idea of polar opposites. If you see women and men as polar opposites, you are likely to believe features or qualities of men should be absent from women, and vice versa. Thus, to some people, a woman should not interrupt men, use obscene gestures, talk loudly, or wear unfeminine clothes. Likewise, men should control emotions, have solutions for problems, and avoid showing vulnerability.

Researchers have found that large numbers of people now want a combination of the skills and strengths they associate with both women and men. But how do you perceive both gentleness and authority if you believe that only a woman can be gentle and only a man can be authoritative? Research into people's self-reported gender ideals has led to the development of scales to measure a concept called *psychological androgyny*.[10] This concept refers to an individual's ability to demonstrate interpersonal skills associated with both sexes. The idea has wide appeal as well as controversial aspects. The appeal is that an androgynous person has a wider choice of behaviors and communication strategies to use to navigate the world. In addition, androgynous people are no less "female" or "male" in their sexuality but are more able to adapt flexibly to varying communication environments. On the other hand, some critics charge that in practice androgyny means females take on masculine behaviors but males do not act in more feminine ways. Other critics maintain that behaviors are not inherently sex-linked and that the notion of androgyny still functions within the practice of inappropriately pairing certain behaviors with a certain sex.

To achieve communicative flexibility, people have begun to perceive genders not from polarities of masculine and feminine but as a series of continua of wide-ranging behaviors. Assessing gender on the basis of a single measure between masculine and feminine implies the two are opposites and unchanging. Under those conditions, understanding gender means deciding whether a person conforms closely or not to the cultural stereotype; that which is not feminine must be masculine and vice versa. Using multiple continua allows for difference in definition of masculine and feminine and also allows for myriad combinations of masculine and feminine behaviors. For example, a person might be high in both, low in both, or relatively high in one under certain circumstances. The continua of wide-ranging behaviors better describe human behavior since most behaviors do not group neatly around one pole or the other. If a woman opens a door for a man, for example, the behavior might be stereotyped as masculine since this practice traditionally has been performed by males in the United States; however, the behavior might also be interpreted as accommodation, consideration, or even subordination, all descriptors that more accurately fall into the United States stereotype of the feminine pole. Other communication cues such as situation, facial expression, and relationship history will often contribute meaning to the behavior. Depending on the different combinations of variables, the behavior will be located in different places along the behavior continuum.

When we consider how gender construction in the United States appears to people in other cultures, we can more easily see how a continuum of behaviors works more effectively than polarization of the sexes. The custom in the United States of women shaving their legs, for example, is met in many other cultures with confusion and surprise. "Do you also shave your arms?" asked a Chinese friend. The behavior is not inherently a feminine one; the culture in the United States assigns the behavior to the feminine gender. Viewed from an intercultural or international perspective, we see that while we do tend to polarize these behaviors as masculine and feminine, such polarization is artificial and arbitrary.

Working from a continuum of behaviors is especially important in talking to children. Among two-year-olds, for example, children may imagine themselves doing a huge variety of activities, and adults who narrow that range to the "correct" options for one sex immediately make the children's world smaller and less stimulating.

CONCENTRIC PERSPECTIVES

As a last consideration about influences on thinking about sex and gender, we use the concept of concentric perspectives. Each of us has a number of different perspectives from which we both examine events we experience and decide about our own behaviors. These various perspectives exist simultaneously; we select from among them based on situational conditions. For example, when we talk about sex and gender issues, one perspective we might consider is one of human universals. From this perspective, we talk about the human condition—people as a group, separate from animals or plants. Rather than viewing differences between men and women, we see their commonalities as human beings. We might discuss communication needs of human beings, needs shared by both females and males, although perhaps expressed differently. We would talk about communication events we believe to be universally true for men and women, and perhaps we would expand our perspective to include humans of all cultures as well.

Take the following husband-and-wife conversation as an example:

Darinda: Why do you have to go on another trip? You only got back from your last one two days ago.

Luis: It's my job, Darinda. That's what I do for a living.

Darinda: Is your job more important than us?

Luis: Let's don't get into that again.

From our universal perspective, we might say these people are struggling with the tension many humans experience, a tension between time for work and time for personal relationships. We might even say another tension emerges in this conversation between autonomy and interdependence. Without assigning certain roles to certain individuals, our perspective might lead us to discuss issues like William Schutz's theory of inclusion, affection, and control.[11] We might discuss the human need to be a part of a larger group (inclusion), gain the esteem and regard of others (affection), and establish order in our lives (control).

However, in another of the concentric perspectives, we might consider sex and gender from a position in a categorical group, that is, a category of people and their positions with regard to sex and gender. Some religious groups, for example, address sex, gender, and communication through the doctrines of their belief systems. For an individual within this group, considering new interpretations of sex, gender, and communication behavior might provoke confrontation between two principal belief systems. Communication events viewed from this perspective can be described differently in kind and intensity than they are when viewed from a universal perspective. In addition, communication events can be interpreted differently within the categorical perspective when they occur between or within other categories.

Looking back at our conversation example, we might interpret the meaning differently from this second perspective. If either Darinda or Luis believes men are the providers to be supported by their wives, either one might interpret Darinda's comments as undermining and selfish. On the other hand, if either Darinda or Luis categorizes women as the protectors of the home, they might interpret Luis's comments as boorish or quarrelsome. Their perspective will influence their assessments of themselves and the other.

In yet a third concentric perspective, we consider the unique, individual circumstance. Details not evident from either of the other two perspectives come into focus as we examine a single case for its unique, particular situation. While the individual may be a member of a category or may be universally included as a human being, perceiving sex, gender, and communication from this singular, distinct perspective may reveal yet another set of significant factors or life experiences.

Considering our sample conversation from this perspective illuminates different details than we examined previously. Luis might know from their history that Darinda likes to spend time together with him; Darinda might consider the three weeks of stress Luis has just experienced. Rather than assess each other as (universal) humans with generalized needs or as (categorized) male or female with socialized behaviors, each may respond to the other with consideration for the particular situation.

How we might think about a sex, gender, and communication event from each of these three concentric perspectives may be very different, yet all three perspectives may exist in the same space. The old saying that a person "can't see the forest for the trees," does not mean that the forest disappears when the focus is on the trees. Likewise, when we use a particular perspective to view sex, gender, and communication, we merely foreground that perspective, keeping the others viable and accessible in the background. We may consider universal truths about sex and gender while also entertaining the complicating features of the communication event from a categorical or individual perspective. Therefore, developing an ability to simultaneously accommodate discrepancy, contradiction and even antitheses may be our greatest challenge. In so doing, we invite revolt against the hierarchical mandates of human nature described by Burke.

For example, some people have said studying communication and the sexes is not a good idea because it keeps people focused on human differences and the resulting conflicts that already divide us too much. From the perspective of human universals, we agree with that point of view. Yet we also agree that from categorical and some individual perspectives, lack of information about sex and gender and communication may limit options, filter visions, and prevent experiences that could be highly exciting and meaningful. The point is to come to an understanding of our "gender filters" and recognize when we are using gender information as a primary predictor—often the *only* predictor—of how the men and women we meet will behave. Our objective is to learn to use gender information from several perspectives without having it become the only way we can see others. In addition, we can learn to move away from secondhand knowledge about men and women and analyze gender-related communication for ourselves.

COMMUNICATION LEVELS

Earlier in the chapter, we reviewed key concepts in the study of communication. The ongoing process of making meaning through symbols occurs in several different communication levels:

- Intrapersonal, communication with oneself
- Interpersonal, communication in a dyad
- Small group, communication among 3 to 18 people
- Public, communication by one person face-to-face with a group of receivers
- Mediated and mass media, communication with audiences by technological means
- Social movements, communication with groups of people intended to change major policies of a society

This list may suggest that events occur on only one level at a time. Actually, most of us receive and send messages on several of these levels simultaneously. Intrapersonal communication constantly informs each of us about strategies used at each of the other levels. Research has shown that sex and gender influences function differently within each level. In the last decade, new work incorporating information about sex and gender has emerged in all six levels, sometimes changing important theories within that level. In interpersonal communication, relationship development theory has evolved to what some label a more feminine form. In small group, information about masculine and feminine leadership qualities has changed some theorists' approaches to discussions of both process and product. In public communication, new theories about public speaking call for significant adjustments in conceptualization and practice of the traditional "speech." As we consider topics in this book, we can find meaningful intersections among sex, gender, and communication at all levels.

INTRAPERSONAL COMMUNICATION

How a person talks with himself or herself while deciding how to act or what to think is of prime importance in the study of communication and the sexes. Our views of ourselves tend to develop from our interpretations of the messages from important others to us. Our self-concepts and levels of self-esteem in turn affect how we form messages to others. Although most communication research focuses on outward acts, a close link exists between external communication in daily life and inner evaluations of the self.

In *Women and Self-Esteem*, Linda Sanford and Mary Ellen Donovan describe various self-messages that people generate when they have received many negative or contradictory messages about themselves during childhood. Two of the major messages they see as affecting everyday communication are (1) chronic comparisons to others, in which one can never measure up to important other people; and (2) expectations of perfection, in which one believes that one should, but cannot, perform flawlessly in key areas. These negative beliefs often correlate with parents' or peers' messages of nonacceptance and scorn.[12]

Although examining intrapersonal communication systematically is difficult, we need to make an effort to understand how intrapersonal messages function. Self-directed messages affect the ways we send and receive messages of all sorts. For example, if you are a man who believes your physical appearance is not masculine enough to attract the women you admire, you may act in a negative way because of this self-directed message, no matter how well other people treat you. On the other hand, if you became convinced early in life that you were attractive, lovable, and interesting and continue to hold that belief about yourself, snubs by people who show little interest in you may not matter much. In other words, we are not all equally vulnerable to outside attacks or rejections in terms of gender. In chapter 6 particular attention will be given to the intrapersonal level of communication as the child develops a view of the self and important others in and around the family.

INTERPERSONAL COMMUNICATION

As it is used in this text, interpersonal communication refers to the informal interactions of two or occasionally three people, often but not always in face-to-face situations. Interpersonal communication within a dyad happens in a variety of situations for both men and women. Families are the first and often most continuous setting for face-to-face communication by one person to another in our lives. The mother-child pair gets much attention in popular culture from song lyrics to films to names of popular artists like Madonna. In addition, interpersonal dyads within the family take on a variety of compositions: father-child, siblings, grandparent relationships, aunts and uncles. The interpersonal communication that occurs in families has direct bearings on the development not only of ideal sex and gender images but also of the person's perceived ability to attain that ideal. In addition, ideas about appropriate family roles, rules, and functions for each sex influence the family member's self-concept with regard to gender. We will discuss these issues in chapters 6 and 10.

A second way we examine dyadic interpersonal communication is in terms of the communication in adult intimate relationships. Chapter 5, on intimacy, deals with the communication between two people who choose to be together. Liking and loving have been studied at length by sociologists, psychologists, novelists, and others, but studies leave us at a loss to explain some of the surprising communication developments that can occur in an intimate relationship. A pair of people may develop an implied interaction rule in which one person is dominant in public and the other in private. In other cases a high frequency of arguing is accepted as natural by one or both members of the pair. In still other instances a woman who considers herself active and competent in many areas of her life participates in an intimate relationship in which she is frequently criticized but describes herself as secure in her partner's love. In chapter 5, we will look at communication factors that help describe the process of developing and maintaining an intimate relationship, and we will also look at some distinctions and parallels between same-sex and two-sex friendships and love relationships.

SMALL GROUP COMMUNICATION. Particular attention will be paid to small group communication in chapter 8 which examines the cooperative tasks that have to be done on the job in terms of their impact on communication and the sexes. Other small groups such as families, play groups, athletic teams, and adult social interest gatherings are also discussed. Each of these cases is, in some sense, a matter of people doing work together. Whenever several people try to complete a task together for some reward (whether money, fame, or interpersonal closeness) an array of issues emerges: leadership, definitions of teamwork, power and authority, conflict, language symbols, and sexual images as enhancements or barriers to task completion, among others. We will look particularly at the features of the workplace that have changed in the past decade, and we will examine recent efforts to define and regulate sexual harassment.

PUBLIC COMMUNICATION

Defined here as messages sent by one person to a large group of others face-to-face, public communication occurs in differing forms in our society. Often we do not recognize as public communication behaviors such as running a department meeting, explaining a change in policy, talking to the school board about busing boundaries, or even coaching a sports team. While we may now depend more on television to see and hear national or regional leaders, we still depend heavily on public communication for information about our community, out-of-the-home work, schools, churches and special interests. Chapter 7 gives particular attention to the teacher as a communicator who affects how boys and girls see themselves, their options, and their limits. Research and anecdotal information about schools note the difficulties of presenting clear, confident messages about gender to children from different kinds of households and value systems. Subtle messages from school materials, teacher talk, peer groups, and school athletics all influence the creation of gender in educational settings.

MASS COMMUNICATION AND
MEDIATED COMMUNICATION

Communication that uses technology to reach widely separated audiences has been called mass communication. Television, radio, newspapers, and magazines all fall into this category. However, changes in technology are occurring so rapidly that even as this book is being written, terminology for these phenomena is evolving. With the advent of selective media delivery systems such as personal computers, VCRs, Internet, and cable television, the concept of mass communication has been partnered with mediated communication. What was once a relatively universally accessible information source—such as commercial television—now has begun to fragment and specialize, becoming selectively available only to people who have the technology, the equipment, or the skill to receive it. As a result, we will consider in this book the effects of both mass communication and mediated communication on our concepts of sex and gender.

The media surround young children as well as adolescents and adults. Thus your views of yourself and your gender ideal began to form under the influence of the media even before you formally entered school. The central question in chapter 9 is how visual symbols as well as verbal symbols in media influence perceptions of sex and gender. This chapter also explores the intended and unintended effects of the structures and traditions of evolving media systems themselves. No single answer about media effects will fit every person. Yet it is important to understand the wide range of influences enacted by the media with regard to sex and gender to better inform choices you make about how you consume products of technology.

United States society is investing heavily both economically and sociologically in the so-called information superhighway (a term already out of date!). As these technological innovations gain salience as essential information sources, we need to be acutely aware of the power of their influence with regard to creating and sustaining sex and gender images. Even more critical, we must be able to analyze what we consume to discover the fundamental sex and gender ideologies promoted by these profit-driven, business-oriented sociological forces. If you are analytically naive in this age of explosive technological expansion, your choices for sex and gender images will be generated for you. Without analytic ability, you will have trouble assessing these images, understanding their implications and persuasive appeals, and discerning which elements to accept and which to reject. In short, your study of sex, gender, and communication can provide a foundation for generating creative and fulfilling personal choice.

One day I was in the computer lab between classes and I wanted to sent an e-mail to my friend. Since her nickname is Holly Hooters, I wanted to send her an anonymous e-mail that said BOOBS really big with all different ways to say boobs—like hooters, knockers, jugs, etc. Beneath the line where you type in the address for the e-mail is another line that says C.C. and another that says subject. I have always thought C.C. meant who the e-mail was from. No one ever told me otherwise. So, trying to be anonymous, I put in a fictitious name. The first name that came to me was Mike Smith, a professor in the College of Business. He was one of my teachers at the time. Well, come to find out that C.C. stands for carbon copy. I ended up sending a copy of this BOOBS e-mail to Dr. Smith. I really did this e-mail up with huge eighty-point font, color, the works! I found out when I got a reply back stating that I had nice artistic talent, good creativity, etc. So later that day before class, I had to talk to Dr. Smith and explain what I did.

Moral of the story—don't play with mediated communication when you're not sure what you're doing.

SOCIAL MOVEMENT COMMUNICATION

In a sense this book as a whole is a study in social movement communication because the study of communication and the sexes was developed by people who chose to analyze rather than to take for granted the interactions of women and men. This social movement, initially called feminism, has been a mediated communication phenomenon as well. Bulletin boards on the Internet attest to the ongoing conversation among people about the roles of the sexes in United States and other cultures. Other media reports have influenced the public image of feminists, and media technology has increasingly been used to promote or oppose the goal of sex equality. National coverage of events like the Anita Hill/Clarence Thomas hearings and the Million Man March create images of active women and men in the current social movement. Social movement communication is important also because many people see themselves as affected by and reacting directly to what they call Women's Liberation, Women's Lib, the Women's Movement, or the Men's Movement. Movement activists have called for changes in education, employment, language, laws, and even the United States Constitution's definition of equality under the law. Behind the public debates about official policies have been countless individual debates over personal language and nonverbal choices, "political correctness," the meaning and value of the word "feminist," roles and responsibilities of males and females as parents, and the impact of violent sexual communication on the interpersonal communication practices of both women and men. At least one of these issues is addressed in every chapter of this book.

CONCLUSION

We will not use sex and gender as interchangeable terms. The difference between them is central to this book and to an understanding of the phenomenon of women and men in a social society. We argue that human communication creates and re-creates gender ideals for each sex. Individuals struggle both to achieve gender ideals and to cope with the restrictions those ideals produce in their lives.

Message, symbol, meaning, and situation or context are words used here to focus attention on the fact that communication exists in contexts and occurs when people actively construct meanings from events. The absence of objectivity in the use of terms like "equality" and "difference" is complicated by the point of perspective used for interpretation, be that perspective universal, categorical, or individual. These complications indicate some of the difficulties in avoiding stereotyping as well as some of the negative effects of stereotyping. The gender filter is a convenient shortcut for reacting to new people and events, but it can limit our capacity to see and hear women and men as individuals. Communication situations throughout life illustrate both the power and the constraints of gender ideals as a guide to human behavior. Finally, the various communication levels indicate that we receive messages related to sex and gender in virtually every setting in which we interact with others or interpret our experiences.

In the next chapter we will move further into the study of communication and the sexes by examining four viewpoints that influence knowledge and values regarding gender and communication. Having seen evidence that the misunderstandings of men and women are everyone's problem, we will now see four ways in which we tend to justify our beliefs about what both sexes are like and why each sex communicates as it does. Taken together, the first two chapters of the book give you a general picture of the ways sex, gender, and communication present complications in communication situations—complications whose management requires communicators with well-developed, effective skills.

QUESTIONS FOR DISCUSSION

1. What communication situations do you find most comfortable? To what extent are these situations typical for your own sex, for the other sex, or for anyone regardless of sex?

2. Most people do not distinguish sex and gender. How does the distinction change the way you think about being a female or male? What complications for public communication or social movement communication might emerge because most audiences do not make that distinction?

3. What would it mean for the sexes to be "equal"? How do others define that term?

4. How different do you think men and women are as human beings, beyond their differences in anatomy? Compare your views with others of both sexes.

5. How do your current beliefs about what it means to be masculine or feminine compare with the expressed beliefs of your parents or other adults you know? On what points do you and they agree the most? On which do you differ the most?

6. What do you like most about being the sex you are? What do you admire or envy most in people of the other sex?

7. Why is the study of sex and gender important to the study of communication?

CASES FOR ANALYSIS

CASE 1.1   SOCCER GAME

For the fourth time in the soccer game, the referee makes a bad call. From the bleachers, Chris calls out, "Call 'em both ways, ref!" "Yeah!" echoes Pat. "Let's see you call *them* for pushing once in a while!" The referee looks up into the stands and then comes to the sideline to talk to the coach, warning, "I'll red card your team if I hear another outburst from the crowd." The coach flashes a reproving look at Chris and Pat.

1. As you read this scenario, what sexes did you assign to Chris, Pat, the coach, and the referee? Why?

2. How does the scene and the meaning of the communication among the characters change when you change their sexes? Assign a different sex to the characters in various combinations and explain how the event might be interpreted differently.

3. Are you most comfortable when gender conforms to sex in traditional ways (for example, a female acts in traditionally feminine ways) or when gender varies with sex? Explore the limits of what you find comfortable for others to do and what you find comfortable for yourself to do.

CASE 1.2   DEWI AND THE CRISIS

Imagine yourself in the situation of Dewi, a professional who is in a crisis. You have not told Gerry, the manager of the office, that you will not be able to meet the deadline on the project you have been working on for weeks. At least five factors in your current situation account for your missing the deadline.

1. Three nights in a row of less than four hours' sleep.

2. A major new financial obligation that you're worried about meeting.

3. A long, sticky argument with your living partner about roles, priorities, and commitments to each other.

4. The absence of a key assistant, whose health status is uncertain.

5. Your forgetting to bring a crucial file on the day you were going to meet with the consultants to make final decisions.

None of these events necessarily shows you to be incapable of doing the project, but the sum of frustrations has led you to say to yourself, "Would I like to cross this week off the calendar!"

Now imagine how the event might look to Gerry, the manager, unaware of the situational factors that are central on your mind but very much aware of productivity needs.

Here are Gerry's reactions:

Boy, I'm surprised that Dewi hasn't come through on this.

The deadline was decided weeks ago!

I wonder if Dewi is just burning out—it's been four years in the same job.

Maybe we should find someone more reliable.

I like Dewi a lot, but we've got to have a go-getter around here.

1. If you were Gerry, how would you bring up the problem now?
2. If you were Dewi, how would you deal with the problem now?
3. What are the advantages and disadvantages for Dewi of bringing up situational factors in the current problem?
4. Did you imagine Dewi and Gerry as male? As female? Or one of each? Would it make any difference in your approach to the crisis?
5. Is it fair to call your character the sum of your actions? Why or why not?

CASE 1.3 DOUBLE DUTY

Two women in a YWCA locker room are discussing the prospect of having children and the ways it might affect their relationships with their husbands. One woman says that she is sure her husband will do well as a father, for two reasons. The first is that he enjoys playing with the children of other couples they know. The second is that he is well organized and able to get a lot of work done efficiently.

"What do you mean?" her friend asks.

"Well, this past Sunday, he finished all the ironing, replaced two buttons, and sewed up a hole in a pocket on a pair of my jeans—all while he watched the Broncos beat the Forty-Niners!"

1. What were your first thoughts about the husband when you read that he was ironing and sewing while watching football? What were your thoughts about the wife? Compare your responses with

others.

2. How might the ability to do two tasks at once be related to the tasks of parenting?

3. To what degree do you believe that both partners in an intimate relationship should be able to do the same household tasks? To what degree should their tasks differ?

4. How does your own current arrangement of household tasks compare with that of your parents? Of other people you know?

NOTES

[1] Carol Gilligan, *In a Different Voice: Psychological Theory and Women's Development* (Cambridge: Harvard University Press, 1982), p. 173.

[2] Betty Friedan, *The Second Stage* (New York: Summit Books, 1981); Robert Brannon, "Dimensions of the Male Sex Role in America," in *Beyond Sex Roles*, 2d ed., ed. Alice Sargent (St. Paul: West, 1985), pp. 296–316.

[3] The idea for this thesis came originally from Linda Putnam. See "In Search of Gender: A Critique of Communication and Sex-Roles Research," *Women's Studies in Communication* 5, 1 (Spring 1982): 1–9.

[4] Albert Mehrabian, *Silent Messages* (Belmont, CA: Wadsworth, 1971).

[5] For a more complete description of the situational aspect of rhetoric, see Lloyd Bitzer, "The Rhetorical Situation," *Philosophy and Rhetoric* 1, 1 (Winter 1968): 1–14; and "Functional Communication: A Situational Perspective," in *Rhetoric in Transition*, ed. Eugene White (University Park, PA: Pennsylvania State University Press, 1980), pp. 21–38.

[6] Chris Kleinke, *Self-Perception* (New York: W. H. Freeman, 1978), pp. 158–71.

[7] Kenneth Burke, "Definition of [the Human]," *Language as Symbolic Action* (Berkeley: University of California Press, 1968), pp. 1–16.

[8] Thirteen original studies of women talking with women in various settings can be found in Barbara Bate and Anita Taylor, eds., *Women Communicating* (Norwood, NJ: Ablex International, 1988).

[9] Repeated anecdotal reports from students in the undergraduate course "Communication and the Sexes," Northern Illinois University, 1984 to 1986; also from students at University of Oregon and Oregon State University, 1985 to 1996.

[10] Sandra L. Bem, "The Measurement of Psychological Androgyny," *Journal of Consulting and Clinical Psychology* 42 (1974): 155–62. For a revision of the Bem Sex-Role Inventory, see Virginia Eman Wheeless and Kathi Dierks-Stewart, "The Psychometric Properties of the Bem Sex-Role Inventory: Questions Concerning Reliability and Validity," *Communication Quarterly* 29 (1981): 173–86.

[11] William Schutz, *FIRO: A Three-Dimensional Theory of Interpersonal Behavior* (New York: Holt, Rinehart and Winston, 1958).

[12] Linda Sanford and Mary Ellen Donovan, *Women and Self-Esteem* (Garden City, NY: Doubleday-Anchor, 1984), pp. 300–14.

Chapter 2

Getting to Theory

For a society to flourish, many different kinds of actions occur simultaneously: farmers generate food, physicians tend illness and injury, nurturers care for children, community workers provide assistance, and so on. People doing these actions not only learn the special skills that constitute their contribution but also are introduced to a unique and particular frame that lends order to their specialized interest. For example, farmers learn a unique frame through which they experience the world. That frame differs from the one used by physicians. When farmers talk to one another, their conversation can proceed to topics within their frames that cannot so quickly or easily be reached in similar conversations with physicians. Frames not only vary *between* groups but can do so *within* groups as well. Farmers' specific skills differ; individual farmers may differ in how and what they know about weather, soil, climate, crops, and fertilizer, for example.

Like any other group, scholars and researchers contribute to their societies; their contributions consist of attempts to discover, generate, or study knowledge. Scholars also work from a unique and particular frame in pursuit of their goals. In this chapter, we will enter that frame, examining specialized vocabulary; inquiry about vantage points, presumptions, and perspectives; and attention to generating, checking, and critiquing theories. This unique frame is continuously critiqued and modified. After completing this course you may decide to continue your communication studies and to join the constantly changing conversation.

CHAPTER OVERVIEW

In addition to presenting some of these specialized conversations, we will also look at four particular perspectives from which to view sex, gender, and communication. While the specialized nature of the scholarly frame provides possibilities for unique conversation, it also (by its elite nature) excludes topics or considerations that may be critical. The clear, ordered descriptions and explanations sought and sometimes attained by the scholarly community can seduce the conversant to forget the ambiguities that lie outside the frame. Therefore, each scholar—including the beginning scholar—assumes the responsibility to resist the inclination to subscribe unquestioningly to a single perspective. As you read, continuously draw on a variety of resources for checking and rechecking your expectations, information, presumptions, and conclusions.

THE SCHOLARLY FRAME

Four terms essential to understanding the rest of this chapter are "theory," "vantage points," "presumptions," and "perspectives." We will begin by discussing theories—the conclusions which are affected by the three other key elements.

THEORY

Theory is the most formal and most consistently defined of the four terms. Theories are sets of belief statements that connect experiences or phenomena in order to explain or to predict natural or human events. Good theories help us understand our worlds better and give us ways to act or think about our experiences.

A good theory is simply a good idea that provides useful insights. It is not *the* way for us to think; rather, it is *a* way for us to think. Thinking of theories as "Truths" can prevent us from creating other new ideas and ignores the ambiguous, complex world in which we communicate. For example, we have long accepted the Copernican theory that the earth is not the center of the universe and that it revolves around the sun. In 1616, Galileo was tried by the Inquisition for suggesting this and other theories that questioned beliefs of the time. Galileo was forced to renounce his support of such theories or be put to death. For the remainder of his life, Galileo remained under house arrest.

This example illustrates two important facts. First, theories have practical uses and can lead to new ways to conceive of and construct our worlds. Second, building new theories can lead to conflict, often because theories can question our values, our morals, and our basic presumptions about how life proceeds. Theories about sex, gender, and communication frequently generate conflicts over what people believe to be central issues in how they live their lives.

VANTAGE POINTS

As used in this book, a vantage point is your angle of vision as you observe and deal with an aspect of an event. For example, if you watched a dance performance, you would notice different elements of the dance based on where you were seated in the theatre. The relationship of your seat to the stage—your vantage point—would determine those portions of the dance you could see and those you could not. A person who has experienced sexual harassment, for example, would have a different vantage point from which to research sex, gender, and communication than would a person who has not had such experiences. A vantage point may affect the perspective from which you observe relationships among events. Unlike a theory, it is usually not constructed and expressed in systematic language. Your vantage point may become evident from your informal word choices, thoughts, or nonverbal behaviors.

Most of us tend to forget that no two people occupy precisely the same vantage point. We often operate as though our own vantage point with regard to events is "right" and "true." We tend to view critically the vantage points of those with whom we disagree. Since men and women have different vantage points on the topics of sex and gender, the need to understand relative perspectives on communication is critical. Our tendencies to ignore or discount different vantage points compound the problem of evaluating other people's thinking and behavior—especially when the issues involve change or confusion related to sex, gender, and communication. Knowing the "right" way to act or the "right" way to explain actions is not the purpose of our study. Instead, our hope is to increase choices of both actions and explanations.

As we try out various vantage points, we see theories differently. Theories that seemed reasonable to us from one location may seem problematic from another. Likewise, understanding various theories can help us find other points from which we begin again to explain the world around us and to predict behaviors and experiences. Consequently, one goal for studying various vantage points for sex and gender is to observe behaviors from positions other than our familiar one. Studying theories that reflect various vantage points broadens our abilities to explain and predict how and why people act and react in certain ways. Given better understanding and more choices, our abilities to engage in a wide range of communication behaviors improve.

Embracing new vantage points or theories sounds simple, but it can create cognitive and emotional dissonance at fundamental levels of awareness. Engaging and sorting through that dissonance has long been the business of scholars and creative thinkers. Undoubtedly, Galileo had reflected on his theoretical positions and knew they would not be easily accepted by his contemporaries. Galileo's decision to embrace publicly an unwelcome theory meant he had to spend his life confined to his house. While you may not confront changes in your thinking that so dramatically affect your life, you may find that engaging different theories of sex and gender can be uncomfortable and stressful. Your first reaction may be to disavow the vantage point or theory and to dispute the explanation or prediction. We all tend to defend our presumptions and most familiar viewpoints, but we can learn to contemplate new theories or vantage points without feeling threatened. If we welcome new ideas as opportunities to gain better understanding or valuable insight, we extend or reshape our theoretical boundaries.

Pursuing such theoretical diversity means recognizing appropriate occasions for accommodating ideas that may be polar opposites. In Western cultures, such dialectic tension often is interpreted as negative and efforts are made to eliminate the tension. Rather than allowing the opposites to reside together, Westerners may seek to resolve the tension by applying some kind of competitive measure to determine the "winning" theory. As you learn more about theories of communication between the sexes, keep in mind the probability that different vantage points will generate different—and sometimes opposing—theories. On some occasions you may believe privileging one theory over the other is necessary or important; on other occasions such privileging may not be deemed necessary. Make the effort to clarify both the reasons you believe privileging is important and the vantage point you occupy when making this decision. Experiment with the possibilities of accommodating opposing theories simultaneously—establishing more options for different circumstances. Consider the reasons someone else might find the other theory more congruent with his or her experience of communication. Reflect on the effect your vantage point has on that person's position. Understanding your motives and reasons for making choices with regard to theories about sex and gender will advance your understanding of your critical perspective.

Vantage points and theories are closely connected to culture. Each of us has learned much of what we know through our cultural filter. In addition we learned how to learn and what constitutes learning through that same screen. When you contemplate theories of sex, gender, and communication, consider the international or global ramifications of the theory. Referring to our discussion in chapter 1, is the theory based on socialized rituals of the *human* animal (a manifestation of the culture in which you live) or is it based on more generally recognized human *animal* conditions (a manifestation of biological sex, common to all members of the species)? Does the theory account for different socio-economic groups, age groups, nationalities, cultures, races, classes, or ethnicities? Try to locate the cultural parameters implicit in these theories; test their more general applicability. Appraising theories and viewpoints on these grounds often reveals the previously invisible presumptions we make about sex and gender.

PRESUMPTIONS

Our presumptions may be more difficult for us to identify than our vantage points. Presumptions are generated from our most closely held beliefs and expectations. Because we automatically accept our presumptions as true, they can be difficult to recognize and reconsider. Presumptions work like heartbeats; they are integral to our daily lives, but we rarely think about them. As a result, whenever we consider issues of sex and gender, we begin with those "truths" about men and women that we always have "known." For example, if we assert that intimacy means openness, self-disclosure, and altruism, we may research intimate communication presuming women will exhibit more patterns of intimate talk than will men. Because we formulate our theory based on that presumption, we change the nature and outcome of the theory. All theorists and readers of theories operate on presumptions that color their perspectives and conclusions. As you read theories in this book, identify what you believe to be the scholars' basic presumptions. Also, identify your own presumptions about sex, gender, and communication as you hear yourself espousing your own personally constructed theories.

PERSPECTIVES

Theories are built not only on vantage points and presumptions but also on perspectives. In this book, perspectives will refer to those interests or special areas of concern that create filters through which we observe the world. Perspective differs from vantage point; while we may observe from similar positions, each of us may choose to focus on very different aspects of the phenomenon we observe. If we are interested in culture and cultural influences on art, we explain a dance performance very differently than if we are interested in choreography. If we take a rhetorical perspective on a dance and see it as communicating a message to society, we explain the dance in still other terms. Our vantage points determine what aspects of the dance we see. Our presumptions and our perspectives determine which of those aspects we choose to highlight.

In addition, theories will vary depending on our purposes for watching the dance in the first place: Do we want to describe the dance? Do we want to critique it? Do we have some other goal? If we wished to describe the dance, we might generate a theory about how culture affects and is affected by dance using our vantage point, our presumptions, and our perspectives as guides and resources. If we wanted to critique the dance, we might assess the effectiveness with which the dance produces messages in nondiscursive ways. Each of these theories would look very different and would be created for very different reasons. Theories about sex and gender will vary in these same ways; some theories intend to critique the phenomenon, some describe, and still others promote new models.

Although theories derived from different perspectives might disagree or even contradict one another, none would be more "right" than the others. Each may be useful for different purposes. We benefit not only from reading and understanding theories that feel comfortable to us but also from studying those that challenge our customary perspectives.

FOUR PERSPECTIVES ABOUT SEX, GENDER, AND COMMUNICATION

In generating theories about sex, gender, and communication, several perspectives have emerged. These perspectives by no means represent clear and discrete categories. These particular filters are certainly not the only ones available. We will discuss these four perspectives, remembering that as many variations will emerge as we find individuals who contemplate them.

1. Biological: Communication with regard to sex and gender may be predominantly driven by predetermined *biology*.
2. Cultural: Communication with regard to sex and gender may be predominantly driven by *cultural forces*. These forces consist of common and repeated communication patterns. Although originally chosen by specific individuals, the patterns have become ingrained in group behavior. The original reasons for the choice of a particular pattern of behavior may be no longer known or evident.
3. Rhetorical: *Rhetoric* is a means by which biology is mitigated and culture is created. Rhetoric is a means by which men and women individually can create and modify gender.
4. Power: *Power* is an outcome of hierarchically ranking rhetorically constructed gender differences within cultures.

Each perspective we present here emphasizes an aspect of the communicative experience somewhat distinctly from the others. Each perspective allows certain elements and issues to filter through and blocks others. We will discuss them separately but remember that they do not exist discretely; they usually are intricately and uniquely braided together.

We are influenced by *how* we think as well as by *what* we think. The perspectives we use significantly affect our interpretive tools and our choices about what action to consider. If we continually adhere to a single perspective, we deprive ourselves of information we might gain from other perspectives. As you step into each perspective, notice how the perspective changes dimensions of the topic.

BIOLOGICAL PERSPECTIVE

Many of us know someone (it may even be ourselves) who says, "That's just the way women are" or "That's natural; all men do that." Presumptions of a biologically based view of communication between men and women usually lie behind such statements. This perspective assumes that males and females are significantly different from birth because of their sex and that the resulting differences in their communication behavior can be explained largely or even entirely by biological factors. Age, sex, ethnicity, or family training might change our vantage points with regard to this perspective. The degree to which we subscribe to biological determinism can influence our communication with others.

Obstetricians and midwives usually state the sex of a baby at the moment of birth, in almost all cases determining this by visible genitalia. However, the sex-differentiated aspects of male and female infants are more complicated than physical characteristics. These biological sex distinctions exist at several levels: the sex chromosomes; the gonads, or internal sex organs; the sex hormones; the external anatomy; and the brain.[1]

The baby's sex is determined within the first two weeks of pregnancy, based on the pairing of two chromosomes, one from each of the parents. An XX pair produces a female; an XY pair produces a male. A small number of babies are born with other combinations, such as an extra chromosome or a missing chromosome. (Gauge your own socialization about gender by reflecting on your reaction to the last sentence. How do you respond to the notion that a baby might be born without a clear chromosomal indicator of XX or XY?) The Y chromosome carries the genes for a number of hereditary problems such as color blindness and hemophilia, which afflict males more often than females. The determining agent for the sex of the child is the chromosome contributed by the male, in contrast to the belief illustrated in history when male rulers divorced or killed their wives for failing to give them sons.

The second biological sex difference in newborns is that males typically have gonads called testicles, which produce sperm; females usually have gonads called ovaries, which produce eggs. These internal organs make possible the creation of a new life through sexual mating. They are vulnerable to incomplete development.

Another important biological sex difference lies in the hormones of both sexes, produced by the gonads and affected by other glands in the body. Though both sexes carry an amount of the hormones associated with the other sex, males produce a much larger amount of testosterone, and females produce much larger amounts of estrogen and progesterone. Female hormone production has long been known to be cyclical, with levels of both estrogen and progesterone varying throughout the menstrual cycle. Male hormone production is widely thought to be noncyclical, but research done in several countries outside the United States indicates that males experience varying levels of intellectual functioning and aggression related to their varying testosterone production.[2] Hormone levels are affected by stress and by changes in an individual's environment; thus, communication can influence hormonal output and be influenced by it.

Males show more physical aggression from early infancy; females show more skill and interest in language from the first year of life. Both tendencies continue through childhood. In some cases the differences in verbal and aggressive behavior become wider as both sexes grow older. These later differences seem to result primarily from instruction by others about gender rather than from genetic requirements.

Biological factors that most noticeably affect communication include differences in the brain, presence and kinds of hormones, physical size, and expectations for behavior. While much of the research about biological differences is inconclusive, tentative, or contradictory, theories about biological influences on human behavior offer insight into communication issues.

BRAIN. Simon LeVay, a neurobiologist at the Salk Institute, recently reported that a cell cluster (the interstitial nucleus of the anterior hypothalamus) in the brain may be "deeply involved in regulating male-typical sex behavior."[3] Other researchers have discovered differences in sizes of other parts of male and female brains. A team from UCLA discovered that one area (INAH3) was twice as large in men as in women and that area also related to "male sex behaviors, such as attraction to females."[4]

Other research on male and female brains suggests females may use more of their brain for certain processes, such as recognizing rhyming words. Sally and Bennett Shaywitz, codirectors of the Yale University Center for the Study of Learning and Attention, conclude that males and females produce comparable results trying to recognize rhymes, but men use only the left hemisphere of their brains in the process whereas most of the women in their study also used a corresponding segment of the right hemisphere.[5]

Ruben C. Gur of the University of Pennsylvania reports the sexes differ in cognitive abilities, particularly memory and judgment.[6] Men excel in judging how an object will look if it is rotated. Women excel in more abstract judgments such as determining the principles by which colors or shapes might be sorted. In addition, research by the group revealed that the parts of the brain involved in action-oriented responses was more active in men than in women.

What these findings tell us and how important they are to everyday communication is not clear. Are these brain differences the result of lifelong patterns? Do they exist at birth? Certainly responsibility for effective or ineffective communication cannot be unequivocally attributed to the functioning of the brain based on sex. However, the findings do indicate that in the future we may discover some ways communication behavior might be influenced based on biological differences as manifested in the brain.

HORMONES. Some women and men have been known to refer, seriously or sarcastically, to a woman's hormones as a reason for mood changes or indecisive behavior. Premenstrual syndrome, or PMS, has been cited in a few court cases as a factor that can lower a defendant's resistance to committing violent actions. Not everyone agrees that the PMS defense is appropriate, however. Certain attorneys and feminist leaders have claimed that using premenstrual syndrome as a legal defense implies that all women may be subject to dangerous mood swings a few days of every month. If employers believed this stereotype, they might try to keep women from holding any positions for which sound judgment is required. The issue is not whether a given woman acted differently because of an individual problem. Rather, it is whether a nearly universal physical phenomenon, menstruation in women between the ages of 12 and 50, will become linked to a much less widespread malady, premenstrual syndrome, encouraging employers to think of and communicate with all women as "disabled" for part of every month.

In its most restrictive form, this perspective has been taken to mean that women should not be in the workplace at all because of their hormonal fluctuations and the possible damage that work stress might cause to their reproductive capacities. This perspective may have influenced a statement by then Speaker of the House of Representatives, Newt Gingrich, when he lectured to a college class about women in the military: "[F]emales have problems staying in a ditch for 30 days because they get infections and they don't have upper body strength."[7]

Dr. Estelle Ramey has offered one counterargument to the idea that women's hormones make their sex significantly more changeable than the other. Her research has revealed periodic cycles in males that affect their emotions, physical strength, and intellectual functioning. Since men do not bleed on certain days of each month, their cycles are harder to identify. Ramey, however, demonstrates that men are subject to major changes in moods and abilities related to the levels of testosterone and other hormones.[8] Thus far no changes in employment or political policy have been made in light of this knowledge.

Conclusions from research about effects of testosterone on human behavior are tenuous.[9] Janowsky claims that testosterone supplements can change the spatial cognition in older men.[10] Other research suggests testosterone does not seem to be related to aggressive behavior in early childhood.[11] However, winners of chess tournaments had higher testosterone levels than losers,[12] higher levels of testosterone were found in adults with higher levels of aggression,[13] and a significant relationship was found between testosterone levels and adult deviant behavior.[14] Men with high levels of testosterone were found to be less likely to marry and more likely to divorce.[15] Some evidence suggests that testosterone may conflict with achievement of higher-status occupations.[16] While men of some races have, in general, higher levels of testosterone than others, research is not clear about whether these differences are biological or environmental.[17]

PHYSICAL SIZE. That adult male bodies on the average are larger and stronger than adult female bodies establishes a certain physical advantage of one sex over the other. That advantage plays a role in communication, especially in situations that include sexual harassment or intense relational conflict. In addition, that biological difference affects vantage points of men and women. Women may interpret very differently than men communication in such contexts as deserted alleyways or dark campus walkways. Likewise, the physical differential may mediate different interpretations by men and women of imperatives or demands.

BIOLOGY AND EXPECTATIONS FOR BEHAVIOR. Two important distinctions between the sexes that relate to human communicating are verbal fluency and physical aggression. That both verbal responsiveness and physical aggression appear within the first few days of life suggests a strong biological basis for each of them. Various research studies have suggested that female infants respond vocally to the presence of other people more than males do, and that girls under the age of two recognize and respond to language on the average better than boys. Interestingly, women are sometimes described as the more talkative sex, even though research reveals that in mixed-sex groups men talk more.[18] What may lead to the perception of women as the talkers is that female children and adults pay more attention to the details of talk, including correcting their own and others' errors as they speak. An impression easily arises that girls and women are the experts at interaction.

As for physical tension and aggression, male infants on the average appear to make active bodily responses to their environments slightly sooner and to a larger degree than do female infants. In early childhood, males are also more likely than females to deal with a problem by using physical aggression. Not every boy is physically active and aggressive, and not every family treats physical aggression as a central part of the masculine gender ideal. However, parents of boys who get into fights or thrive on contact sports often speak about their sons in terms that reveal an assumption that they are acting "naturally." The adage that "boys will be boys" derives from this assumption.

For most people the biological perspective has particular relevance to questions about who should do what kinds of jobs. A 25-year-old female may be greeted with laughter if she applies for a position supervising a fleet of truck drivers. A 25-year-old male may be questioned if he applies for a position as a nurse. When all our experiences and images of truck drivers or nurses have been with members of one sex, we may respond with skepticism about such attempts. No matter how tall, how assertive, or how confident the woman might be, we may cling to the expectation of a male supervisor for truck drivers. In the second case, we might anticipate that requirements for a nurse to be caring and gentle could not be met by a male. When assumptions like these are brought into the open, we can more easily question which biological or physical factors actually matter and which have simply become traditional expectations.

We also can challenge our presumptions that biology is immutable by questioning ourselves about assumptions concerning "appropriate" behavior. Researchers pursue questions about how to vary and increase brain functioning. Drug therapies, physiological and nutrition education affect hormonal conditions. As people in the United States pursue fitness training, bodies change in size and strength. With new theories come changes in biological expectations or limitations historically assigned to male and female. While these changes do not dissolve differences between females and males, they can change the dimensions of the difference. As we discussed in chapter 1, difference is not the problematic feature. When difference is transposed into discrimination or devaluing, unfair or unacceptable conditions for one sex or the other may result.

Focusing on biological factors behind the communication of women and men can be helpful or hurtful in everyday life. On the one hand, you may find it helpful to identify some of the physical realities of both sexes, such as the early verbal fluency of most females and the muscle tension and activity in many males. On the other hand, adopting the biological perspective as the predominant one from which to critique communication with regard to sex and gender can lead to predicting and judging an individual's behavior on the basis of meager facts and questionable generalizations. Susan will "of course experience and express more emotional diversity than Tony" and she will "be likely to major in English or art." On the other hand, 6-foot-4-inch

Tony will "of course want to go out for varsity basketball more than Susan" and will "be likely to major in math or computers." Recall the concept of range of behaviors from chapter 1. Susan may want to study English or computer science; Tony may want to play basketball or tutor non-native students in history. Limiting either one to a biological category can discourage them both from developing new ways to see themselves and from finding new patterns of relating to others.

CULTURAL PERSPECTIVE

The second perspective on communication and the sexes deals with the different ways people learn to understand and respond to their world based on their participation in social groups. It is described as a cultural perspective because it deals with the various learned views of the world that characterize people from differing backgrounds. The phrase "belief systems" is used here in conjunction with the term culture, since groups of people who grow up and live together in the same social group develop similar beliefs, attitudes, and values about their world.

Anthropologist Margaret Mead did several studies of human cultures in which the actions of women and men varied. She later reported that she had seen a wide variety of ways in which cultures organized themselves according to sex or gender, but that no cultural group she had seen treated sex or gender as unimportant.[19] Humans seem inclined to make something of sexual differences beyond simply recognizing anatomical differences at birth. The cultural perspective emphasizes the learning processes within social groups and the resulting belief systems that members of a group often take for granted.

A COMMUNICATION CULTURE. One way to understand the idea of culture is to think of it as a relatively organized set of beliefs and expectations about how people should talk, think, and structure their lives. Often we mistakenly think of "nation" and "culture" as interchangeable words. A nation is a geographically delineated space in which people live; a culture is identified by the cohesion among its members with regard to standards, behaviors, norms, rules, etc. While the United States may be easily defined as a nation with discrete boundaries and territories, it may not be so easily defined as a culture. Nevertheless, in gross terms we can distinguish it from, for example, Chilean culture by identifying differences in beliefs and expectations in the two groups.

THESE DAYS, *Little Girls* DON'T LIVE DOWN THE LANE.

They DRIVE DOWN IT.

Talented, tenacious and tough to beat. In its
continuing support of women's athletics,
State Farm is proud to be a sponsor of the 1995-1996
USA Basketball Women's National Team.

State Farm Insurance Companies

As a culture, many people in the United States operate under certain beliefs and expectations about sex and gender. For example, in the medical profession, men have traditionally dominated the role of physician and women have traditionally dominated the role of nurse. That tradition is changing, if only with regard to women's roles; in 1994 eighteen of the nation's 126 medical schools reported having more women entering their programs than men.[20] Nevertheless, the culture in the United States maintains the expectation that doctors are male.

As a demonstration of this expectation, ask a few friends to solve this riddle:

A young boy and his father were involved in a violent automobile accident. The father was killed; the boy was critically injured. The boy was rushed to the hospital where he was prepped for emergency surgery. The surgeon entered the room, scrubbed and prepared to operate. Suddenly, the surgeon paled and said, "I can't operate on this patient. He's my son." How could this be?

Most people in this culture will struggle with this riddle; some will never figure out the solution (the surgeon is the boy's mother). Because of cultural influences, we all carry presumptions and expectations about the sexes that are as difficult for us to recognize as the answer to this riddle. Presumptions range widely, including things like colors appropriate for each sex, clothing styles, voice ranges, language usage, physical movements, nonverbal affect, professions, lifestyles, and so on.

These presumptions are unique to the culture. Presumptions about national leadership, for example, demonstrate differences among cultures. In the United States, no woman ever has been elected president; other cultures fully accept women as political leaders. Margaret Thatcher in England, Benazir Bhutto of Pakistan, Corazon Aquino in the Philippines, Violeta Chamorro of Nicaragua, and Khaleda Zia in Bangladesh all served as presidents or prime ministers. Sri Lanka's president in 1995, Chandrika Kumaratunga, is the daughter of a woman who served as prime minister in the 1960s.[21]

While we can see differences from culture to culture, presuming that everyone in the United States operates from the same set of cultural norms ignores the cultural diversity within this nation. Ethnicity, race, socio-economic status, age, and physical distinctions can generate cultural norms that function with or in contrast to the predominant ones created by the dominant group in the culture. Each cultural sphere harbors presumptions and expectations with regard to sex, gender, and communication. The process of creating cultural markers for female and male is the same, although the expectations may be very different. A perspective that examines that process reveals behavior that otherwise might be invisible.

Some people might wonder whether culture or biology is more influential in shaping a person's communication behaviors. Most scholars agree that both are influential, although in varying ratios. Education about the process can provide individuals more insight about their own positions in the "nature/nurture" arguments. In addition, education provides individuals more choices about how they think and act in regard to sex, gender, and communication.

TWO SUBCULTURES BASED ON SEX. Some people perceive males and females as separate subcultures within a larger, more general culture. Each of the subcultures is organized—though not always in obvious ways—by sets of beliefs, behavioral expectations, and verbal and nonverbal symbols subscribed to by a significant number of people. Children are typically taught and encouraged to adhere to the expectations for their sex, to be with peers of the same sex, to talk with and to talk like their peers, and to avoid talking and thinking like members of the other group. The umbrella culture affects and is affected by the norms of these two subcultures; likewise, each of the subcultures affects and is affected by each other.

Deborah Tannen, an advocate of this perspective, points to the very different communication rules and patterns children encounter. Girls often play in dyads and spend long hours with a close friend, talking and sharing secrets. Boys often play in groups, usually participating in some group game or sport. As a result, Tannen says, girls develop very different expectations of interpersonal communication than do boys, and each group presumes the other communicates the same way.[22]

This cultural perspective provides one explanation for some of the diversity in the interests and values of males and females. Although boys and girls are almost never totally segregated from each other during childhood, most families, schools, and communities send and receive messages differently depending on the sex of the young person. In many families in the United States, girls are expected to communicate in more subdued and polite ways than are boys. Boys may receive less censure for using profanity; girls may express emotion more openly. Boys may be allowed to stay out later on dates. In

CALVIN AND HOBBES copyright (1985) Watterson. Reprinted with permission of UNIVERSAL PRESS SYNDICATE. All rights reserved.

public schools, boys receive both more criticism and more praise than girls do (this topic will be discussed in chapter 7). Teen magazines encourage adolescent girls to focus their thoughts romantically on adolescent boys, while adolescent boys are encouraged to think about machinery, cars, and physical skills.

The use or nonuse of profanity has been a major definer of gender ideals; education seems to mediate this cultural norm, as it does others. However, only 20 percent of the population in this culture attend college, and less than 5 percent of the population is in college at any time. Realize as you read this book that your vantage point as a person who chose to attend college is one held by only a minority in the culture. Compared to general populations, men and women in college report gender distinctions in communication behaviors to be less pronounced. For example, college-aged females reportedly use more profanity with their peers of either sex than was true even a decade ago. The "profanity gap" between the sexes is smaller now than in the 1960s. Although the profanity norms may have become more similar for men and women both on and off campuses, differences remain. Personal reports suggest that females still use anatomical terms and obscene terms less often than do males.

In terms of nonverbal cues, females and males learn different patterns of eye contact, gestures, touch, and use of the personal space around the body (chapter 4 takes a closer look at these nonverbal cues). One way to make these cultural nonverbal patterns visible is to see them through the eyes of someone of another culture. A friend from China became perplexed when she first arrived here. She said she realized women in this culture removed hair from legs and armpits. She asked why those particular parts had been selected and why men did not do the same. Other nonverbal practices, such as who winks at whom and who crosses their legs and how, weave together a tapestry of presumptions underlying communication, sex, and gender in this culture.

For both language and nonverbal cues, both sexes receive reinforcements for using expected communication patterns and sanctions for venturing into the other sex's territory. A boy may be taunted if he "throws like a girl." A man with a high-pitched voice can be heckled for sounding like a woman. If a woman uses obscene language or chooses not to shave her legs, she may encounter ridicule or teasing.

One way to see the cultural divisions of sex is to observe popular media scenarios. Recently, a television ad for men's cologne featured a young woman sitting alone on a bed; she was wearing only a man's dress shirt. She moved off the bed and posed in front of a full-length mirror, setting the man's hat jauntily on her head. The phone rang.

She picked up the phone and said, "Oh! Hello, honey! I was just thinking about you." Now imagine that same scenario with the sexes reversed. Imagine a man sitting on a bed wearing only a woman's blouse. He moves off the bed and poses in front of a full-length mirror, setting a woman's hat jauntily on his head. The phone rings. He picks up the phone and says, "Oh! Hello, honey! I was just thinking about you." We find the second scenario funny because the reversal of this scene violates our cultural markers for male and female. Once again, issues of difference are less salient than issues of evaluation of difference.

Think for a minute: If you're male, how do you feel about crying at a sad movie or telling someone you are afraid of something? If you're female, how do you feel about not wearing makeup or asking a male for a first date? And how do you feel about a male or female who does the things listed above? If you respond with some hesitation because these acts seem to communicate inappropriate messages, it may be because your own communication culture limited what your sex could do without being ridiculed or rejected. The more you know about this communication history, the more freedom you have to choose which communication behaviors will serve you well as an adult.

BELIEF SYSTEMS WITHIN COMMUNICATION CULTURES. Assumptive systems characterize whole segments of society, directing the attention of virtually all members toward or away from certain approaches to making decisions and construing human relationships.[23] Researchers examine belief systems to discover how they operate and to detect shifts in patterns. For example, Carol Gilligan says women today make moral decisions differently from the ways that had previously been called universal. Women consider the human contexts involved as they ponder questions of vocation, of whether to terminate a pregnancy, or of responding to illness in themselves or family members. Prior to Gilligan's work, Lawrence Kohlberg's studies of moral development in men had treated decision making as most mature when made in the context of abstract principles such as truth or justice. Women had been viewed as less mature because they gave attention to the concrete issue of caring. Gilligan reframes the earlier information to affirm what she calls "an ethic of care," a value system that treats relationships as essential in life and women's concern for them as a strength rather than a limitation.[24] Her theory extends far beyond seeing the sexes as culturally different based on single communication events. Gilligan outlines a belief and values system that differs fundamentally for males and females.

Likewise, Ruthellen Josselson theorizes that individual development is culturally patterned differently for males and females. Josselson argues that Erikson's idea that self and separation as identity
measures may be single-faceted: "Perhaps a central aspect of identity
is the commitment to a self-in-relation rather than to a self that stands
alone facing an abstract world. Reconceptualized this way, the life
stages for women are perhaps different from those for men."[25] From
Josselson's perspective, communication may be dramatically affected
by presumptions each party makes about an individual's developmental pattern, a pattern Josselson believes to be significantly different for
females and males. These patterned differences may be reflected in
other research that suggests men and women use different means to
determine good and poor arguments.[26] How men and women conceptualize argument and what they deem to be effective and ineffective
may derive from belief systems consistent with culturally learned
matrices.

Robert Bly, whose men's movement we will discuss at length in
chapter 10, writes about unique characteristics of the male culture:
"By the time a man is thirty-five he knows that the images of the right
man, the tough man, the true man which he received in high school
do not work in life."[27] Bly perceives a male culture, a female culture,
and a human culture. He believes investigations by males and females
into their respective cultures are "related to each other, but each
moves on a separate timetable."[28] He objects to the division of men
into "sensitive men" and "construction workers."[29] He suggests the
creation of more inclusive definitions of "masculine" and "feminine"
that better address the masculine in women and the feminine in men.
He also asserts that "there are in reality besides these two states, 'feminine' and 'masculine,' all sorts of degrees, intermediate states,
unions, combinations, special cases, genius exceptions, and so on."[30]
Bly writes that the essence of masculinity experienced by males differs
from the masculinity experienced by females; he conjectures that similar differences may exist in the essence of femininity experienced by
females compared to that experienced by males.

Anne Wilson Schaef in her book, *Women's Reality*, forwards
another theory that two distinct belief systems exist within the larger
culture. She names them the white male system (WMS) and the female
system. Schaef does not claim that all white males hold all the beliefs
of the WMS, but she states that this view of the world exists most com-
fortably in a society in which white males dominate and define what
is going on. Schaef describes the WMS as self-contained, disallowing
any other potential beliefs. It treats its own view as objective and rational. The central focus of the WMS is on self and work. Schaef evaluates

the WMS as believing itself invulnerable to criticism[31] and therefore significantly problematic for anyone—female, Hispanic, black, handicapped—who does not share its central beliefs.

Schaef's female system of beliefs involves areas of focus, values, and behavioral expectations different from those identified with the white male system. Its essential claim is that human relationships are central in life—in direct opposition to the white male system's central focus on self and work. Other distinct features of the female system are viewing time as process rather than as clock time, viewing friendship as based on knowing and being known rather than on activities, and viewing other people as peers rather than evaluating them along a hierarchy of power or resources.[32] Interestingly, the notion of a single, female system has been criticized by many[33] who suggest that multiple female systems exist depending on cultural contexts within which women live. These critics argue that theories espousing one female system describe only the dominant female culture in the United States. In contrast, there are multiple vantage points that only now are beginning to be examined in scholarly literature about sex, gender, and communication. All these theories provide illustrations of the way belief systems can generate communication complexities that extend far beyond solutions that call for simple translation.

THE CULTURAL PERSPECTIVE AND THE TWO SPHERES. Gilligan, Bly, Josselson, Schaef and others have made major contributions to our thinking about sex and gender in daily life. Scholarly work intending to study, critique, transform and reconceptualize the female belief system has been far more prevalent than work on the male belief system. As Robert Bly explained in an interview with Keith. Thompson, "[W]hat males need now is an energy that can face this energy in women, and *meet* it. They need to make a similar connection in their psyches. . . ."[34] Bly pursues a transformation of maleness he believes will allow males greater personal knowledge of themselves outside the cultural expectations of their sex. Because of its nontraditional language and approach, Bly's work may be interpreted as unmasculine in nature and ironically may be perceived to feed the stereotype that unmasculinity means femininity. Likewise, the work of Gilligan and Schaef has freed many people to affirm their own patterns of thought, but it also to some extent has fed the stereotypes of women as concerned only with relationships and men as concerned only with self and work.

In addition, little work has been done to identify who works within these systems. For example, women and men both may operate within and support the white male system; the same could be said for the female system. From the cultural perspective, we may find both a simple system that merely describes men and women as different cultures and a more complex system that describes belief systems generated from communication actions of one sex and enacted by some people of that sex and some members of the other sex as well. This more complex system introduces intriguing questions embraced by theorists who take the fourth perspective, the power perspective.

If one adopts the view that anyone of a given sex automatically adheres to the white male system or the female system, a logical next step is to say that the two systems imply the separation of men into the public world of work, politics, sports, and war and women into the private world of home, family, relationships, and feelings. This view borders on the biological perspective already discussed, since it reinforces the idea that childbearing capacity should determine a woman's sphere of activity while physical strength should determine a man's sphere.

However, the view of communication cultures presented here does not presume that early experience or what people learn from peer groups is beyond changing. When people from a geographically distant culture move into a new culture as permanent residents, they develop new beliefs and attitudes to support them in learning new languages and nonverbal behaviors to fit a new way of life. Similarly, the cultural perspective allows both women and men the possibility of developing flexibility in their communication behaviors, even as it recognizes early learning as powerful and difficult to erase. Modifying those familiar cultural patterns can cause uncertainty and discomfort—feelings often present at moments of change. Using the cultural perspective as a mirror, however, we can begin to identify patterns we choose to keep and those we wish to discard. The cultural perspective is helpful in reminding all communicators that there were probably coherent beliefs and practices that influenced our personal histories. Submerged beliefs and assumptions about gender and communication can remain influential for decades after an individual has first been exposed to them. Recognizing this fact can produce more awareness and empathy as we struggle with our own or others' current communication patterns.

RHETORICAL PERSPECTIVE

The two perspectives discussed thus far both treat the sexes as having distinct features, interests, and attitudes. The rhetorical perspective considers not the sexes themselves, but the interactive process in which people engage as they manage their worlds. By "rhetoric," we mean "an action humans perform when they use symbols for the purpose of communicating with one another."[35] Men and women are considered as individuals who decide how they will talk to other people in particular situations. From a rhetorical perspective, the focus is on their relative responsibilities in any given communication situation and their communication actions with regard to those responsibilities. According to the rhetorical perspective, "When we analyze the process of symbolism, we are taking a rhetorical perspective."[36]

Supporters of the biological perspective believe biology in some part determines communication practices. Supporters of the cultural perspective believe cultural requisites in some part determine communication practices. The rhetorical perspective does not ignore biology and culture, but supporters advocate the power of each individual to belie biology and defy culture if that individual so chooses. Rhetoric is a means by which men and women individually can create and modify gender.

The rhetorical perspective begins with the idea that human beings behave strategically when talking with each other in daily life. Note that by "strategic" we do not mean to connote the actions of a manipulative character who schemes to deceive and trick others. Rather, "strategic" means we organize what we will say and watch for and respond to opportunities in particular interactions, all in order to reach personal goals. Those goals may be small (hoping our friend will understand directions to the restaurant), large (wanting to find a considerate way to break up with a partner), significant (hoping to persuade a partner to marry), or insignificant (acknowledging an acquaintance by nodding "hi" as we pass on the street). In any case, the rhetorical strategies help reveal intent of the speaker and mutuality of the pair.

When we take a rhetorical perspective, we accept that human communication has significant bearing on all aspects of our lives and that we intentionally choose its content, character, timing, and tone. Of the four perspectives, the rhetorical one allows for the highest degree of individual choice. Since communication is a situational phenomenon, every situation presents a unique set of features for a given man or woman to evaluate in deciding what to say. Our choices in that situation may change us, the other person, the environment, or our perception of any of these elements. Because of all the variables involved, analyzing a particular communication event from a rhetorical perspective can be complicated as well as fascinating.

The rhetorical perspective assumes that people of both sexes have significant chances to be active in constructing their interactions.

This point is not to be taken lightly. Much of the literature in psychology and sociology is based on the writings of theorists who view humans as the products of outside forces rather than as the initiators of chosen actions. Using the gender filter on human behavior also leads to ignoring the choices faced by a particular woman or man in everyday interactions. If you expect females to be more passive than males in conversations, or if you believe that "real men" are always aggressively pursuing success, you may limit meanings of possible messages you can exchange with others.

THE ELEMENTS OF INTERPERSONAL RHETORIC. To apply a rhetorical perspective to an interpersonal interaction, use the four concepts listed below as a frame. In each interaction, look for the elements of the situation, evidence of the rhetorical strategies, indicators of the rhetorical roles, and cues about the rhetorical goal.[37] Think of an interpersonal encounter you have had recently (between you and one other person) and apply these elements as you read them.

Elements of the situation. What is the particular set of circumstances of this interaction, especially as they regard sex and gender? What are the constraints of time and space? Might they be different for one sex than another? One gender or another? What issues of relationship history might bear on the content or style of either partner? What issues of past experiences in this place or similar ones might affect the process or outcome of this interaction? What within-self factors help or hinder the sending or receiving of messages? How are those within-self factors affected by the sex or gender of either partner? What dimensions of the situation bear on public or private attitudes toward the sex or gender of one partner or the other?

Rhetorical strategies. What are the various ways each partner brings up ideas or opinions? Are the strategies straightforward and direct? Indirect? Unspoken? Do sex or gender seem to play roles in the selection of strategies? Consider the speaker's strategies. Consider the listener's strategies. Does the combination of male-male, female-female, female-male have a bearing on these strategies? How does each partner defend points of view? Does each defend in similar amounts? Are defenses related to sex or gender (both speaker and listener)? Are the defensive attempts equally successful? Are the means for defense similar or different? In what ways? Are feelings expressed? If so, how? Is sex or gender related to expression of feelings or strategies for expression of feelings? Is attention given to the effects of these strategies? If so, how? If not, are strategies devised to elicit attention?

Rhetorical roles. What set of communication behaviors do partners see as expected of them by the other? Is this set related to sex and/or gender in any way? What set of communication behaviors do partners expect of themselves? Who may change the subject? Who may raise the volume? Who may interrupt? Who is expected to listen? Who is expected to give in? Who may use humor? What kind of humor is expected and accepted? Who may express emotions? What emotions? How do sex or gender affect role expectations? What indicators can you find in the interchange that bring you to these conclusions?

Rhetorical goal. Determine what each partner wants to accomplish by talking with one another. Remember that multiple goals can be sought. Also, once the conversation begins, goals will emerge for both the listener and the speaker. Consider how the goals might be connected to sex and/or gender. Some goals concern the topic: I want my partner to listen to me more carefully. Other goals may concern relationship dimensions: I want my partner to express a desire to be with me. Still other goals may deal with self-disclosure, self-esteem, desiring information, and so on. Look at the interpersonal encounter closely; do not be content to merely name the topic of the conversation. A conversation that begins, "You bounced another check" may be about achieving superiority over a partner and not about economics at all. Examine the conversation for clues about sex and/or gender influences.

These four concepts are basic parts of everyday communication. They may not be equally important within a single conversation nor across conversations. You necessarily deal with all of them to some degree as you talk with another person, except in the most ritualistic kind of talk ("Hi, how are ya?" and "Fine, and you?"). Yet even in this last case, you are probably aware of times when you said hello to someone not to obtain information but to achieve a simple goal of being polite or confirming you made eye contact or expressing a wish to be friendly.

A SHIFT IN THE SEXES' RHETORICAL ROLES. A subtle but significant feature of the current rhetorical environment for women and men is that assumptions have shifted somewhat about which sex has the right to speak, in what settings, and in the pursuit of what public and private goals. In the past women were perceived as the receivers of communication in most settings, if they were perceived as present in those settings at all. The expectation in many societies has been that males would be the speakers in government, in the military, in the mass media, and in intellectual debate. When a female entered one of those communication arenas, she was noticed with surprise and often with some amusement, but she did not receive the calm acceptance that was natural for most of her male counterparts. Women today do not have equal acceptance in active rhetorical roles everywhere, but increasing numbers and increased visibility have helped many women to imagine themselves as competent speakers in a widening range of rhetorical situations.

The feminist movement has asserted, directly and indirectly, that women, like men, are and ought to be rhetoricians—individuals with goals, opinions, styles, and capacities to express themselves. Some scholars have developed theories that women have a rhetoric of their own that operates differently and for different purposes than the traditional model, a model that usually includes persuasion.[38] Foss and Griffin claim that women employ an invitational rhetoric, one that engages opinions, goals, and styles in a less confrontational way.[39]

Behind the idea that women are and can be rhetoricians is the presumption that a female may have opinions as strong and as valid as those of her male peers on topics such as nuclear disarmament, computer software, urban design, or marketing research. She may express them in different ways, accomplishing with different strategies the same or different rhetorical goals. Similarly, this perspective on rhetoric and the sexes implies that any male may have valid opinions and knowledge about raising children, renovating houses, and cooking vegetables; he, too, may exercise or learn different rhetorical strategies for his goals. The difference in the two sexes' experience until recently has been, unfortunately, that when a woman has entered domains associated with males she has been treated as an exception, while males entering traditionally feminine domains have often been received as visiting experts. The new rhetorical perspective on the sexes is intended to increase the number of viable rhetorical choices for each and reduce the use of combative, confrontive styles. Its main idea is that anyone, female or male, can have meaningful goals, clear perceptions of situations, and valid strategies for coping with communication in daily life.

POWER PERSPECTIVE

The power perspective considers how sex differences and rhetorically constructed gender differences can be used to advantage one individual or group over another.[40] That advantage may be embedded in cultural beliefs or may arise in a given situation. In either case, rhetorical strategies may be used to amass and engage power and also to repel it. The success of these strategies may depend on resources and energy.

DOMINANCE. Power as an approach to communication and the sexes has to do with the kind and amount of influence individuals have in relation to each other. In this discussion the first kind of power will be referred to as "power over" people or events or organizations. This power may be used benignly or with malice, but it exists as an advantage under the direct control of one party and not the other. It denotes dominance—the ability to control or direct resources and people. This kind of power presumes the presence of hierarchy, a structured system of differences in status between and among people. For example, dominant power was wielded by the Chinese government with regard to the United Nations' 4th International Women's Conference in 1995, a convention attended by participants from all over the world. Since only sanctioned members who officially represent governments can participate in the formal meetings of the conference, approximately 37,000 activists representing NGOs (Non-Governmental Organizations) planned to meet conjointly at the conference to observe and lobby official conference attendees. Because the NGOs are known to raise controversy, openly disagree with conference representatives, and voice dissent, the Chinese government proposed that the NGOs be housed an hour's travel from the official site in a town with fewer than one-tenth the necessary hotel spaces for the group. In addition, transportation to and from the two locales was scarce. This act of dominant power reflected a hierarchical ordering that devalued women who dissented from the elected authority. It was intended to curtail the activities of the NGOs and reduce their abilities to interact with official conference attendees.

With regard to sex and gender, hierarchy means that the resources, status, or value of one sex or one person of a certain sex are greater than the other sex or one person of the other sex. Dominance does not suggest that power is always in evidence nor that power can be exerted at every point; it only suggests that power or the threat of the use of power supports a communication practice.

A few years ago, the Queer Pride tent on the campus was shot at during Queer [Gay] Pride Week. The tent, located in the quad, was not a direct threat to anyone, yet someone (suspected to be a male) felt threatened by it anyway. When I talk to people about this event, women are usually more appalled and men usually respond with "So what?" or "Well, no one got hurt, so what's the problem?" If people from the tent were actively "recruiting" or otherwise being aggressive, I could understand that people would feel threatened. (I would still not shoot at the tent.) Reacting more aggressively and violently, however, is a stereotypical male response to a threat, whether physical or psychological.

Dominance is the central kind of power evidenced in patriarchy. Patriarchy means literally "rule by the fathers." The word is used to label those societies, past and present, in which males control all or most of the major institutions and govern the ways human activities are planned and evaluated. Some writers claim that all human societies are patriarchal and that this is the natural way for humans to organize themselves.[41] Others claim that women were at the center of very early societies for which there are no records, so that we should not assume male dominance is the only system under which human beings have lived.[42] Whatever you believe about the uses of power in past societies, it is useful to examine the ways it is thought of in present discussions about power among women and men. Arguments about which sex is stronger, more in charge of events, or more able to influence the other sex are all debates about power. Whenever arrangements between people shift, as they are doing in light of the feminist movement and other social changes, concerns about power arise because customary power relationships can no longer be assumed.

Given the importance of power in our society, many men view women's actions toward greater self-confidence and more vocational initiative as threats to the standing of men as providers and heads of households. A study comparing views of males and females in the United States and China found that in both countries males expressed needs to hold dominant power and females expressed needs for equal power.[43] Many times the debates or discussions about these concerns do not include the actual word power, and sometimes even the participants themselves don't recognize that they are struggling with power relations. Much of the discomfort women and men sometimes feel about the changes they are making and observing occurs because the customary power relationship—he dominant, she submissive—has been turned upside down, so that she (often without choosing this role) may seem dominant, and he (without knowing how to enact an alternative role) fears he will have no option but to be a subordinate. Ironically, these fears are products of the dominant power perspective; only when power is viewed in hierarchical terms can it be perceived as a scarce commodity available to only one partner at a time. That hierarchical frame demands the superior/subordinate assignments. Other views about power do not cast participants in these kinds of opposing, competitive positions.

This interpersonal uneasiness is further complicated by the fact that females in our society are not encouraged to learn and talk about power. It has been seen as an alien domain, something that is frequently corrupting but never noble and loving. Many women say they don't want power, meaning that they don't want to use the kind of power that controls or crushes others. Many men say that they take power for granted in their work or in social relations; it is something won through competitive effort and necessary to lead others—to show authority and to be a success. Whereas women often find power distasteful because it connotes domination of others, men see power as a necessary control of events and people. Thus the two sexes have trouble talking with each other because they attach profoundly different values to the same word.

EMPOWERMENT. A second way to understand power is the concept of "power to," or empowerment. This view of power is based on the belief that power involves the ability to accomplish goals and to help others to achieve their goals as well. This second way of understanding power has become more visible in recent years. Empowerment means using power to accomplish your own goals and extending the power you possess to others, enabling them to accomplish their goals as well. The term itself is not new, but it has become more widely known through the experiences of women in consciousness-raising groups, in networking and mentoring on the job, and in a variety of self-help activities in which one woman has helped another to gain the confidence and skills to meet a particular challenge.[44]

Because the empowerment definition maintains the notion of power as an entity outside the relationship to be tapped by partners, it can be considered another version of the dominance definition—a version that shows compassion. Implied in the notion of empowerment is the idea that power can be traded from person to person. Therefore, the onus falls on the giver of power to share resources with others. Power is conceptualized as a commodity, a product.

The empowerment perspective has the advantage of making us look at how individuals—children as well as adults, employees as well as friends—become or fail to become confident and able to move toward their goals. To look at the feminist movement as a campaign for women to take over men's leadership positions or to force all men into subservience is to miss the point. Increases in personal and interpersonal affirmation have changed millions of lives of men as well as of women. Current management theories, as discussed in chapter 8, emphasize the individual's self-esteem as a central resource for orga-nizations. Thus both of these versions of the power perspective, dom-inance and empowerment, offer insight into the communication experiences of women and men.

SYNERGISTIC POWER. A third kind of power can be conceptual-ized as a process rather than a commodity. Synergistic power is gen-erated and controlled by both parties. It functions when both parties have access to resources, energy, and status—all of which may occur in similar or dissimilar forms for each partner. Like two skaters who alternately pull each other ahead, two partners using synergistic power generate more energy from their cooperative use of power than either could generate alone. In addition, they deplete less energy from their reserve when they use power to accomplish their goal. Either party may be the lead skater at any given time; likewise, the roles eas-ily reverse. Partners generate power together, contributing unique perceptions, approaches, and content.

Dominant power requires no trust between parties or groups. In fact, it often fosters suspicion of the dominant group by the subordi-nate one. Outranked parties may act freely within the limits allowed by the dominant power but may act otherwise only with permission. The empowerment relationship is also one in which one party has more power than the other. A different kind of trust is experienced by each partner—the power-giver entrusting the other to act and the power-receiver trusting the other to share. Synergistic power, in con-trast, requires resonant trust between parties because it is regulated from within the relationship communication network. Unlike empow-erment, where one party may generally play the role of compassionate provider, synergistic power requires both parties alternately or in syn-chronization to play multiple roles.

The subordinate in a dominant power partnership achieves sat-isfaction only if he or she is willing to remain within prescribed param-eters. Successful empowerment depends on the perceptive and accommodating skills of the partner or group doing the empowering. Synergistic power expands and contracts with the rhythm and shape of the partners' relationship; partners can adjust those dimensions to include or exclude satisfaction goals. Dominant power partnerships require clear, one-way communication from the dominant to the sub-ordinate partner; communication in the other direction may or may not be useful or necessary. Both empowering and synergistic power require keener, transactional communication skills between partners or groups. Synergistic power requires ongoing, continuously generated, and frequently revised communication that can help explicate and calibrate the process of power.

The assumptions behind the concepts of dominance, empowerment, and synergy are significantly different. Table 2.1 shows three sets of assumptions in order to make clear the distinctions.

Table 2.1 Three Forms of the Power Perspective

Dominance (power over)

1. I can control your access to resources or opportunities.
2. Power is a finite quantity.
3. Power is a zero-sum game. If I win, you lose. The more you gain, the less I have.
4. Power can be used by a single person or group to restrict another person or group; the benefits are one-sided.

Empowerment (power to)

1. I can help you find resources or opportunities.
2. Power is expansive and can accommodate a range of users.
3. Power can help and should be shared. When I help you win, we all benefit. It's possible for everyone to be winners.
4. Power can be used by a single person or group to enhance the possibilities for another person or group; this action benefits both, but often benefits the recipient in more concrete ways than the source.

Synergistic (power with)

1. We discover resources and opportunities together; we value the contributions of the other (although we may negotiate the specific content of the contribution). We create a pool of power resources from our separate vantage points and unique perspectives to which we both have access.
2. Power emerges from and resides in mutuality between partners. Power is a process of the relationship rather than an objective entity to be acquired.
3. Power cannot be captured in a game metaphor (winning and losing) that positions two or more individuals against one another; power is generative in nature—promoting choice, energy, and capability without referencing opposing forces.
4. Power is shared interactively; all parties to the interaction benefit in varying degrees and varying amounts throughout the life of the relationship.

Difficulties between men and women can result when different power strategies come into play in a relationship. Consider for example a long-term relationship where one partner consistently uses a synergistic power style and the other consistently uses a dominant power style. Since the synergistic power style depends on trust and shared responsibility, the partner using that style may become frustrated and discouraged about how to meet relational goals. The partner using the dominant style may view the synergistic mode as weak or threatening because it requires a measure of relinquishing individual control. Even if these partners are skilled in metacommunication, they face a significant—and perhaps lifelong—challenge to restructure their means of negotiating power.

The power perspective is a complicated one to assess. Our experiences have mapped the territory we expect to encounter. Whether we are females or males can dramatically affect how we have experienced the world. Education about communication between the sexes from a power perspective may be a way to achieve better understanding for both females and males.

Conclusion

We suggested in chapter 1 that it is helpful to think of gender-related assumptions as a filter on our communication awareness, adding color to what we see and hear but also distracting us from other features and options in our communication. In this respect, gender acts as a form of psychological noise in the communication process—at times a barrier to the adequate sending and receiving of messages and at other times an illuminator of concepts previously unobserved. The goal of this chapter has been to show you four perspectives that can both help and hinder you in communicating accurately with people of your own sex or of the other sex. This knowledge can make you more sensitive to your own frame of reference and to recognize the frames used by people you know.

As a practical application, think about what assumptions you might make in the following situation. A woman and a man in a business meeting are both discussing the pros and cons of closing a plant owned by their company. The woman talks about how employees will feel when the plant closes, and the man talks about how the plant closure will aid the company in regaining its competitive edge in the market. From the biological perspective, you might say that the woman is more tuned physically to her own and others' emotions because of her hormones and childbearing capacity and that the man is taking a competitive approach because men are biologically the more active and aggressive sex. From the cultural perspective, you could decide that the man is operating from a white male system view which necessarily concentrates on individual success, while the woman is showing a female system concern for relationships. A rhetorical view of the situation would lead you to think about the two individuals' goals in talking about competition or feelings, the constraints that led them to adopt those approaches, and the strategies each is using to support his or her own rhetorical roles during the meeting. Finally, from the power perspective you would focus on the differences between the woman's apparent concern for employees as peers and the man's apparent concern to come out on top in a win/lose contest.

As you review the four perspectives and as we apply them throughout the remainder of this text, you may discover some value or application for a perspective that never before seemed to make much sense. You may still not adopt that particular perspective for yourself, but if you recognize its usefulness as an approach, your understanding of another person who endorses that perspective may increase. Knowing the bases for alternative perspectives also reduces possible sources of communication problems and allows more informed discussions about areas of disagreement.

QUESTIONS FOR DISCUSSION

1. Which perspective seems to you most like the perspective that one or both of your parents held as you were growing up? Which one seems most like the view you yourself hold now?

2. What kinds of power are manifest in your household? What kinds do you feel most comfortable using yourself? Which are you unwilling to use?

3. Do you like or dislike the idea of people of either sex being strategic about their personal relationships? Why?

4. How likely is it that you or someone important to you will develop a new perspective about gender and communication in adult life? What would help or hinder that kind of change?

5. Identify cultural sex markers other than women shaving their legs. How does the culture in which you live mark male and female? How do cultures within cultures (such as ethnic, age,

class, physical distinctions, race) mark male and female? Use personal experiences to explain.

6. Consider the scenario depicted in the ad (about men's cologne) mentioned in this chapter. Why does this culture sanction a woman dressing in man's clothing (in this scene) but not a man dressing in a woman's clothing? Why do we laugh when we think about reversing the sexes? Under what conditions may women emulate men or men emulate women? What conclusions can you draw about the evaluative messages in these instances?

7. Select a short interchange you have experienced that either by its nature or its content concerned issues of sex and gender. Using the four concepts (p. 70–71) as a frame for your rhetorical perspective, analyze the interchange.

8. Using an advertisement that reflects relationships between men and women, assess the images and words for indications of the kind of power implied in the communication. To whom is power attributed? What kind of power is evidenced? What are the implications for its use? What details caused you to reach your conclusions?

Cases for Analysis

Case 2.1   Kid Climber

A three-year-old girl, like many children her age, loves to climb. She has tried to scale everything from clothing racks in stores to the highest bars in playgrounds. Her parents both enjoy her energy and at times fear for her safety. They also notice two distinct reactions when other people see their daughter climbing. The first response tends to sound this way:

"Oh, that poor dear is going to break her neck if she doesn't get away from that high stairway. Did you know she was over there?"

The second response tends toward the following:

"That child seems to be wonderfully acrobatic. Have you entered her in gymnastics classes yet? That's a sport that is really perfect for girls, since it allows them to be so graceful."

The parents have the feeling that both statements come from honest interest and concern, but the two comments have highly different implications for dealing with the child's love of climbing on everything in sight.

1. What point(s) of view do you believe are implied by the first response to the child's climbing? By the second response?

2. Do you find one approach to the child's behavior more valid than the other? Which approach, and why?

3. How do you account for strangers' comments to parents about their child's behavior in a public place? What do you assume about the rhetorical goals of the individuals who give either the first or the second response in this narrative?

4. Discuss with others the degree to which you believe that children will "turn out as they are inclined to," no matter how much parents try to intervene to develop skills or restrain behaviors. Consider where your belief(s) on this issue originated.

CASE 2.2 WHAT KIND OF PARTNERS?

Two good friends of yours married last year. They had talked long and hard before the marriage about their shared priority that the two careers they had begun would not get in the way of their closeness. They had both pledged that long hours of overtime would be avoided and that where possible they would take business trips together. Now one of the two has come to you in anger and frustration, complaining that the other has broken their basic promise to each other. The other's overtime now averages 20 hours per week, out-of-town trips are occurring each month, and the rationale given for accepting these assignments is that a promotion is forthcoming within a few months "if I can just pass these tests of my commitment to the firm."

Your friend is skeptical that the pattern will change, and he/she is afraid that the only way to cope with the absences is to become more absent him/herself and more involved in career advancement.

Responding in a parallel fashion to the spouse seems likely to drive a larger wedge between the couple. Yet as you listen you can see that this kind of "revenge" is an understandable reaction.

1. Consider the culture, or belief systems, perspective in relation to this situation. How might the white male system of assumptions be relevant in talking with your friend? How would you react if the unhappy spouse were the husband? If it were the wife?

2. How could knowing about these systems help the partners to understand each other's concerns?

3. What might the pair do to clarify their perspectives before deciding

how to handle the current career question?

4. What evidence do you see in this story of Carol Gilligan's concept of a different voice, one based on an ethic of care?

CASE 2.3 STRATEGIC SKILLS

The following is an actual letter written to a university alumni magazine.[45] It bears directly on the issue of how we evaluate goals and strategies used in an individual's interpersonal rhetoric. The woman who wrote this letter is responding to an earlier letter by a sociological researcher who had stated that the wage gap between men and women is a product of bias as well as of individual career choices.

> No one ever seems to speak of the *simple* reason why there is a wage gap between men and employed women.
>
> The one-half of the women who do not need to work and do not wish to work are the very ones who would, if they worked, fill top executive positions commanding very high salaries and thus bring the average of women's salaries much higher than it is. But it is just those women who use their superior intelligence to find suitable husbands and make satisfactory lives for themselves and their families within their home.
>
> /s/ Robin Smith

The letter divides women on the basis of social class and financial standing. It implies that the author and her peers choose to use their rhetorical skills to find "suitable husbands" rather than entering the workplace.

1. What do you believe to be the writer's primary goal in writing the letter?

2. Based on what you find in the letter, how would you characterize the writer's attitudes toward other women? Toward gender roles as a factor in communication?

3. How does the letter relate to the stereotype of women as strategic in a negative sense?

4. Look at the letter again, with the information that the letter writer spent most of her adult life as an employed single parent, with jobs mainly in department store merchandising. Answer questions 1 through 3 again in light of this knowledge. Does it make a difference in your evaluation?

Notes

[1] Norma McCoy, "Innate Factors in Sex Differences," in *Beyond Sex Roles*, 2d ed., ed. Alice Sargent (St. Paul: West, 1985).

[2] Estelle Ramey, M.D., "Men's Cycles (They Have Them Too, You Know)," in *Beyond Sex-Role Stereotypes*, ed. Alexandra Kaplan and Joan Bean (Boston: Little, Brown, 1976).

[3] David Nimmons, "Sex and the Brain." *Discover: The World of Science* 15, 3 (1994): 64–71.

[4] Ibid.

[5] Sarah Richardson, "S/He-Brains," *Discover: The World of Science* (June 1995): 36.

[6] Ruben C. Gur, "Sex Differences in Regional Cerebral Glucose Metabolism During a Resting State," *Science* 267, 5197 (Jan. 27, 1995): 528–31.

[7] Associated Press, "Gingrich Fires Off on Battle and Sexes," *Statesman Journal*, Salem, OR (Jan. 19, 1995): 2A.

[8] Ramey, M.D., op cit.

[9] Carolyn Tucker Halpern, "Relationship Between Aggression and Pubertal Increases in Testosterone: A Panel Analysis of Adolescent Males," *Social Biology* 40, 2 (Spring 1993): 8–24.

[10] Jeri S. Janowsky, "Testosterone Influences Spatial Cognition in Older Men," *Behavioral Neuroscience* 108, 2 (April 1994): 325–32.

[11] John N. Constantino, "Testosterone and Aggression in Children," *Journal of the American Academy of Child & Adolescent Psychiatry* 32, 6 (Nov. 1993): 1217–1222.

[12] Allan Mazur, "Testosterone and Chess Competition," *Social Psychology Quarterly* 55, 1 (Mar. 1992): 70–77.

[13] John Archer, "The Influence of Testosterone on Human Aggression," *British Journal of Psychology* 82 (Pt. 1) (Feb. 1991): 1–28.

[14] Alan Booth, "The Influence of Testosterone on Deviance in Adulthood: Assessing and Explaining the Relationship," *Criminology* 31, 1 (Feb. 1993): 93–117.

[15] Alan Booth, "Testosterone and Men's Marriages," *Social Forces* 72, 2(Dec. 1993): 463–77.

[16] James M. Dabbs, Jr., "Testosterone and Occupational Achievement," *Social Forces* 70, 3 (Mar. 1992): 813–24.

[17] William H. James, "Causes of Racial Differences in Testosterone Levels of Men," *Journal of the National Cancer Institute* 5, 6 (Mar. 1993): 506–7.

[18] Elizabeth Aries, "Male-Female Interpersonal Styles in All Male, All Female, and Mixed Groups," in *Beyond Sex Roles*, 2d ed., ed. Alice Sargent (St. Paul: West, 1985), pp. 403–10.

[19] Margaret Mead, *Male and Female; A Study of the Sexes in a Changing World* (New York: Morrow, 1949).

[20] Associated Press, "Male Medical Students Decreasing," *Statesman Journal*,

Salem, OR (May 31, 1995): 8A.

21 Wendy Koch, "Power Eludes U.S. Women," *Statesman Journal*, Salem, OR (May 31, 1995): 8A.

22 Tannen, Deborah. *You Just Don't Understand: Women and Men in Conversation* (New York: Ballantine Books, 1990).

23 For development of this idea, see Fern Johnson, "Genders as Cultural Systems," paper presented to the 3d Penn State Conference on Gender, April 1986; Cheris Kramarae and Paula Treichler, "Women's Talk in the Ivory Tower," *Communication Quarterly* 31, 2 (Spring 1983): 118–32; and Paula Treichler, Cheris Kramarae, and Beth Stafford, *For Alma Mater* (Urbana: University of Illinois Press, 1985).

24 Carol Gilligan, *In a Different Voice* (Cambridge: Harvard University Press, 1982).

25 Ruthellen Josselson, *Finding Herself: Pathways to Identity Development in Women* (San Francisco: Jossey-Bass Publishers, 1987), p. 23.

26 Robert Trapp and Judith K. Bowker, "Personal and Ideational Dimensions of Good and Poor Arguments in Human Interaction," in *Argumentation Illuminated*, ed. Franz H. van Eemeren, Rob Grootendorst, J. Anthony Blair, and Charles Arthur Willard (Dordrecht, Holland: International Center for the Study of Argumentation, 1992), pp. 220–30.

27 Robert Bly, *Iron John: A Book About Men* (New York: Vintage Books, 1992). p. ix.

28 Ibid., p. x.

29 Ibid., p. 235.

30 Ibid., p. 236.

31 For discussion about dominant systems closed to subordinate systems, see Judith K. Bowker, "Rhetorical Predicaments in the Reporting of Sexual Harassment," in *Communication and Sexual Harassment in the Workplace*, ed. Gary Kreps (Cresskill, NJ: Hampton Press, 1993), pp. 195–205.

32 Anne Wilson Schaef, *Women's Reality* (St. Paul: Winston Press, 1981).

33 Marsha Houston Stanback, "Feminist Theory and Black Women's Talk," *Howard Journal of Communications* 1 (1989): 187–84; Marsha Houston, "The Politics of Difference: Race, Class, and Women's Communicaton," in *Women Making Meaning: New Feminist Directions in Communication*," ed. Lana S. Rakow (New York: Routledge & Kegan Paul), pp. 45–59.

34 Robert Bly and Keith Thompson, "What Men Really Want," *Challenge of the Heart: Love, Sex, and Intimacy in Changing Times*, ed. John Welwood (Boston: Shambhala Publications, 1985), p. 115.

35 Sonja K. Foss, Karen A. Foss, and Robert Trapp, *Contemporary Perspectives on Rhetoric*, 2d ed. (Prospect Heights, IL: Waveland Press, 1991), p. 14.

36 Ibid., p. 17.

37 Gerald Phillips and Nancy Metzger, *Intimate Communication* (Boston: Allyn and Bacon, 1976).

38 Karen A. Foss and Sonja K. Foss, *Women Speak: The Eloquence of Women's Lives* (Prospect Heights, IL: Waveland Press, 1991).

[39] Sonja K. Foss and Cynthia L. Griffin, "Beyond Persuasion: A Proposal for an Invitational Rhetoric," *Communication Monographs* 62, 1 (March 1995): 2–18.

[40] For more information, see Hilary M. Lips, *Women, Men, and Power* (Mountain View, CA: Mayfield Publishing Company, 1991).

[41] Estelle Ramey M.D., op cit.; George Gilder, "Men Need Liberating from Women's Liberation," and Steven Goldberg, "The Dominant Male Needs No Liberating," both in *Male/Female Roles*, ed. Bruno Leone and Teresa O'Neill (St. Paul: Greenhaven, 1983).

[42] See Adrienne Rich, "Prepatriarchal Female/Goddess Images," from *Of Woman Born* (New York: Norton, 1976); reprinted in *The Politics of Female Spirituality*, ed. Charlene Spretnak (Garden City, NY: Doubleday/Anchor, 1982), pp. 32–38, 39–48.

[43] Rosina C. Chia, Jamie L. Moore, and Ka Nei Lam, "Cultural Differences in Gender Role Attitudes Between Chinese and American Students," *Sex Roles* 31, 1/2 (1994): 23–29.

[44] See Natasha Josefowitz, *Paths to Power* (Reading, MA: Addison-Wesley, 1980).

[45] Alice Johnson Booth, "Letter to the Editor," *Old Oregon* (June 1985), p. 4.

Chapter 3

Language

Nearly 500 B.C., Confucius wrote that "Without knowing the force of words, it is impossible to know men."[1] In nearly twenty-first century English, we rewrite that idea: without knowing the force of words, it is impossible to know women or men. The irony here lies not only in the power of language in the statement to exclude women, but also in the tenuousness with which we can claim that the words Confucius wrote have been accurately interpreted through time and across languages. Throughout the 2,500 years since this statement was written, language continues to wield the power to create our realities. As Confucius wrote, language is how we "know." People expect words to represent reality; many people equate language with reality. Through language we communicate to each other ideas, ways of thinking, and worldviews—in short, words are our ways not only of communicating our realities to one another but also of creating those realities. Choices we make as we use this symbol system can have real and significant effects on the lives and realities of others.

CHAPTER OVERVIEW

This chapter deals specifically with words and the sexes—words used about the sexes and words used by the sexes in everyday life. Since the 1970s, widespread talk about language bias and possible language change has caused us to challenge many popular assumptions about language. Controversy continues concerning how language should deal with the sexes and how both sexes should speak to be effective communicators. To understand these discussions we will examine some of the characteristics of language in general, some particular problems of meaning and evaluation related to gender, and finally some roots of the recent debates about whether language performance should be changed—by women, by men, or by both—in a variety of communication settings.

POPULAR ASSUMPTIONS ABOUT LANGUAGE

Most people hold some unexamined beliefs about what language is and how it works. Now that controversy over language as a reference system has become a topic of female-male conversations, discussing our assumptions can help clear up potential misunderstandings. Four commonly held (and mythical) assumptions start the discussion:

1. Words have concrete, reliable meanings; if you use words carefully, you can be understood by everyone.
2. Language is not biased; only people using language are biased.
3. Language is a solid, unchanging structure to be protected.
4. By themselves, words and language have little or no power and cannot harm us; we should reject the claim that we can be harmed or can harm others with language.

For people who subscribe to the first myth, language appears to be a neutral tool for anyone's use. Language does not seem to be political or subject to competing points of view. These people think about language simply as a system of units (words), each of which has a reliable definition in the dictionary. This definable quality about words is called denotation. Denotation means that language can designate or symbolize without implication. Denotations are the word meanings reported in dictionaries; they are assumed to be direct and unbiased.

Believing that words are only their denotative meaning is naive; the denotation of words is not their only characteristic.

Words carry a secondary meaning, one that implies more than the denotation. Connotations are the word meanings of implied or expressed values; these meanings will vary across individuals due to differing personal experiences. Some words appear to have straightforward meanings and thus to be free from the complications of differing connotations. However, even a simple word such as "dog" has become laden with gender connotations, since the word is sometimes used to refer to a woman the speaker finds unattractive.

One way to understand how denotation and connotation work is to consider the various words used for an eighteen-year-old male: "kid," "boy," "young man," "man," or "player." If you used one of these words to refer to a person on the street, you would with each word signify the same referent—that person on the street. The denotations for each of these words vary, but the arena of denotative meaning will be relatively small. However, the connotation of each of these words dramatically changes the meaning of your statement. That connotation would depend on the sender, receiver, environment, channel, and noise; all the elements of a communication event are involved in determining the connotation. In addition, connotations vary in a considerably larger range than denotations. Whenever you use the word, "feminist," for example, some people will imagine angry, anti-male marchers, while others will take the word to mean someone convinced that sex equality is a positive goal for all human beings. How you and another person might react to any of the words above may be quite different.

Recently, for example, people from other parts of North and South America have wondered why people from the United States refer only to themselves as "Americans." People from other American countries find that usage to have connotations of exclusion. What a person from one nation might believe to be the denotation of "American" and what another person in another nation might believe to be the denotation can be quite different. We cannot expect language to have universal meanings, and we cannot expect interpretations of meanings to be identical to ours. Language used generically by one group can—intentionally or unintentionally—exclude another group.

We may be able to see these language distinctions when we talk about other cultures or people who are different from us. We may have more difficulty seeing that men and women use language differently: a person who believes that words like intimacy, trust, caring, independence, or aggression hold the same denotive meanings for all men and women may have trouble communicating with the other sex.

The second myth states that language is not biased. Is language neutral? First, we have to consider whether our language has a word for every thought, every idea, every feelin´—everything we can see, hear, touch, smell, know, think about or feel. Obviously, no language has words for everything. Then we must ask, who chooses which things to symbolize? Who determines what is important enough to warrant having a symbol placed in the language system to represent it? Do people from every ethnic group, sex, age, race, and class partake in that selection? Do they determine which words become part of the language system? Insofar as the words that constitute the language are words chosen by a specific group, those words will represent the life experience of that group; the language will reflect a bias towards that group. Critics of standardized tests such as the IQ test, the SAT (Scholastic Achievement Test), and the ACT (American College Test) explain that ideas and scenes used on those tests represent largely the experiences of white, middle-class people. The language symbolizes experiences and vantage points familiar to people of one group but unfamiliar to others. As a result, these critics continue, the tests and the language used in the tests are biased in favor of one group over the others.

Teenagers are a group who often compose a language of their own because the formal language system does not offer them words for their experiences. In a way, they create a private system that is biased toward them; if another person does not know the "right" phrase or uses certain phrases incorrectly, teens can recognize that person as not being in their group. Words like "hip," "cool," "awesome," "duh," and "sweet" all have gone through various stages of being "in" or "out." You can probably think of words being used right now, words used only by people of a certain age or having a certain vantage point on life. Those words are examples of the inevitable bias of language.

The third assumption (that language is a solid, unchanging structure to be protected) is paradoxical. If language is the symbolic representation of referents, do we expect those referents to remain unchanged throughout history? The tension between trying to keep things the same and letting things change is reflected in this myth about language.[2] If language were as changeable as the weather, the people within a culture would have a difficult time communicating with one another. People in the northeastern United States might generate a vocabulary and connotation of meaning vastly different from people in the southwestern part of the nation. On the other hand, if language were not allowed to change, we would not be able to symbolize our new ideas and our new discoveries. How could we talk about computers, for example, if we did not allow the language to change? Likewise, if we find new vantage points or perspectives about sex and gender, how could we talk about them or enact them without changing the language? Language is a reasonably stable part of any culture, but it will move and change with the needs of the culture of which it is a part.

One example of such a change is the rule in English grammar to avoid using "they" as a singular pronoun. Sentences such as "Everyone should bring their own lunch on Friday" were considered incorrect. Students of English were trained to use the words "Everyone should bring his own lunch on Friday," producing agreement in number between everyone (singular) and he (also singular). Language history reveals that this rule of grammar was instituted to fit the preferences of a particular group. Linguist Ann Bodine reports that politics influenced language policy concerning use of the pronoun "they" in eighteenth-century England.[3] A change from "they" to "he" was recommended to the Crown by the Royal grammarians, apparently to clear up the inconsistency in pronoun number between "one" and "they" in sentences such as "Everyone may present their proposal." The grammarians probably felt that "he" was the appropriate replacement because of the prominence of men in public life—not considering the potential effects of this change on women. The effect of this pronoun policy has been to make the pronoun system simpler for one sex, more confusing for the other.

But changing that practice of using the "generic 'he'" has been resisted by people who cling to the myth that language should be unchanging. Research has established the negative effects of this usage, revealing that the generic "he" generates male images more often than images of both sexes, and that "s/he" or "he or she" functions for males similarly to the generic "he" usage.[4] In fact, studies frequently show that males are more male-biased than are females[5] and that even using words like "human" and "person" generate more male images than images of both sexes.[6]

Today the use of "they" as a singular, generic pronoun is well established in adult writing in the United States.[7] Both males and females decode "they" with more images of both males and females than do any of the other forms. Language shapes our realities and our ways of thinking, encouraging certain images and thoughts while discouraging others. Changing the language both to reflect and facilitate changes in the culture is inevitable.

The last assumption about language is that words cannot harm us. People who believe this myth believe words only appear to be harmful when we are not strong enough to defy them and they only harm others because of others' deficiencies. People who criticize sex bias in language are often scoffed at for being irrelevant; they are told they are too sensitive, that they are looking for a fight, or that they are ignoring the "real" problems men and women face in society. Children are taught to reinforce this myth when they chant: "Sticks and stones will break my bones, but words will never hurt me."

Contrary to this myth, language does have the capacity to inflict harm. Black actor and writer Ossie Davis wrote an essay entitled "The English Language Is My Enemy," in which he listed numerous ways that white is identified with good and black with evil.[8] Language not only exerts harmful forces in individual cases—such as males being called "wimps" or "sissies" or females being referred to as "broads" or "cows"—but it exerts a more systematic harm. When the structure of the language is such that it identifies inanimate objects by sex (such as the Spanish or French languages do), it produces a systemic effect of valuing male and female in certain ways. Metaphors for males and females evolve in individual language systems, generating limits of behavior patterns for males and females. Ways of naming and referencing the sexes produce repeated messages about appropriate male and female actions; those messages pervade the content and structure of our means to communicate. We hear the messages from the time we are born; we learn to repeat and perpetuate them. Their cumulative impact should not be confused with the more individually manageable episode of a one-time encounter with a term or phrase.

A group of five men, including a friend of mine, were watching a movie about gangs and in the context of the movie, one man called the other man a "bitch," resulting in the two men fighting. The fighting eventually led to more name calling which resulted in death.

I asked my friend why the word "bitch" was used to describe a man, considering it was most commonly used to describe a female. He explained that this word was probably the most offensive word you could call another man. Every man in the room agreed that they would have become involved in a physical attack in the same way as presented in the movie if they had been called a "bitch." I again replied that it's simply a female word used by jerks to describe a female. They stared at me and all replied, "That's why it's so offensive."

This illustrated to me not only the power of sex and gender labeling but also the perception that many men have of female characteristics being negative or completely offensive. By characteristic, I am not saying that "bitch" by any means is a characteristic of females, but demonstrating that males are more offended being labeled with negative female names than with negative male names.

THEORIES ABOUT LANGUAGE AS A REFERENCE SYSTEM

The work of several well-known language scholars reveals the complex connections among words, thoughts, and evaluations of one human being by another. We will examine the theories of three scholars who discuss language or symbol systems in general and two who write about sexist language in particular. All these writers advocate the idea that language is not just a recording device for persons and events but that language or our symbol system significantly influences our thought patterns.

BENJAMIN LEE WHORF

Whorf began his study of cultures and languages as a hobby. After extensive work with the Hopi, he developed the conviction that language structures influence the way people think about the world. Whorf observed that United States English depends on noun forms and on naming people and things, while the Hopi language uses long phrases about events in process and does not name the separate individuals at all. The contrast can be seen in these two phrases:

United States English: Thanksgiving dinner for all the family at Grandmother's house.

Hopi: going—many—together—eating—smiling.

Our culture uses language to separate things (nouns) from action (verbs). Even when our culture describes action, we often turn it into an event. The Hopi language describes action in progress. Time is not delineated as past, present, or future. The Hopi view the world as an accumulation of actions. In contrast to our culture where action is turned into an event linked to a specific time and place, the Hopi focus on the duration of an action—the accumulation of experiences of that action. The Hopi thought affects the structure of the language; the language reflects and shapes Hopi thought. As a result, the Hopi see the world very differently than we do.

Differences in the structure of language—in one case the naming of things and in the other case descriptions of processes—create significant differences for people who use that language. From the time a child learns the language, one child learns to construct thoughts by naming things while the other learns to think by means of descriptions of processes. How the child thinks and what the child thinks about will be changed by the nature of the language learned. While each language might be used to accomplish the other goal, *the structure of the language* establishes the standard thinking form.

Whorf's major contribution to thought about language and the sexes is the idea that a culture and its people are influenced by the way its language is formed and structured, as well as by the content of its messages.[9] As the culture uses its language, that language will affect the evolution and development of the culture. Based on Whorf's ideas, we can see the importance of studying the United States English language as a means of understanding how our culture might be affected by the names we call ourselves and the actions we attribute to males and females. Later in the chapter, we will talk about names used for people of the different sexes as well as common metaphors this culture uses in referring to male and female.

ALFRED KORZYBSKI

While living in the United States away from his native Poland, Count Korzybski took an interest in the ways language does or does not manage to be clear or "scientific." He believed words should come as close as possible to being reliable representations of what is occurring in the world. His theory encounters criticism on this point because it seems to presume a language created by one group could be used effectively by another to represent their experiences. However, Korzybski's theory is useful to promote the ideal of revising and re-creating a language that achieves the goal of removing judgmental or preferential connotations which have been embedded in the language and mistaken for denotative meaning. His writings attempt to make people more aware of the varying levels of abstraction in language. Korzybski pointed out that perceptions are influenced by undetected abstract levels in language. Subtle mixtures of value words and descriptive words in the same sentence blur the line between abstract and concrete levels of description. For example, compare the following sentences. First, a concrete statement:

Kathleen States lives at 1046 Temple Street in Pekin, Illinois, where she cares for her children and manages the household.

Next, a moderately abstract sentence:

One of the States women is a homemaker.

Finally, a statement of a general stereotype:

Women work at home all day.

Most people use a mixture of these types of statements without recognizing how much less reliable and verifiable the second and third statements are than the first one.

Korzybski believed that the natural world does exist and is knowable. It may be represented well or poorly by a particular language.[10] Korzybski pointed out that Western thought—the tendency to reduce "reality" to an either/or polarization—was not an accurate representation. He urged the expansion of language and thought to recognize the multifaceted nature of reality. He also criticized the Western tradition of separating through language what is not separated in nature: space and time or heredity and environment are two examples. Language is somewhat static and lags behind reality which changes constantly.

Korzybski recommended that people consider the factor of time as well as the levels of abstraction in their language habits. Failing to recognize the factor of time when describing a person or situation can produce misleading communication. Are you exactly the same person you were ten years ago? As a "college student" are you exactly like every other college student? Assumptions about a particular category often are transferred to assumptions about an individual. Korzybski might ask the speaker of the second statement, "Do you 'know' every States female in every geographical location and every woman named States who ever lived, and do you know that one always was a homemaker?" Failing to place one's language and thinking within a context of time, space, and level of abstraction makes it impossible for receivers to judge accurately a speaker's descriptions of events, or expressions of opinion. Abstractions can lead to stereotyping; equally problematic, abstractions can lull us into perceiving our world based on outdated interpretations we fail to adjust to evolving realities.

Consider the following statement: "Oh, Charles can't ever stay in a relationship very long. He's irresponsible." The statement does not make clear whether Charles just left a relationship or has abandoned previous relationships. It is also unclear whether the speaker's sense of Charles's irresponsibility is connected to personal experience with the relationship behavior. Korzybski urges that language reflect change over time so that people are not immobilized by the labels applied to them.[11] Broad, abstract statements about people—in our case particularly about the sexes or genders—may be unrelated to a person's current actions and interests. Using language to represent our thoughts or ideas accurately helps avoid misunderstandings and miscommunication caused by abstractions.

KENNETH BURKE

Philosopher, rhetorician, sociologist, and literary critic, Burke spent his life analyzing how people use symbols. Burke's interests were to examine the process of symbolization and the effects on people of using a symbolic system to make meaning. Burke believed humans conduct all their actions from courtship to war according to how they interpret their own and others' symbols. Burke emphasized that symbol creation and use is a unique and essential capacity of humans. The symbols we create can unite us with others, goad us into trying to achieve superiority over others, and make us miserable trying to reach perfection.

Burke defines humans as "symbol-making, symbol-using, symbol-misusing animal[s], inventor[s] of the negative separated from our natural condition by instruments of our own making, goaded by the spirit of hierarchy."[12] He explains that we are separated from our "natural condition" by our symbol-making, symbol-using, and symbol-misusing practices. When we make, use, and misuse symbols, we operate not on the level of natural things but on a symbolic, representative level. Through symbolic action we seek to place things in an order or hierarchy. This order takes a variety of forms ("Being a boy is better than being a girl" or "I could never wear this shirt to school"). In addition, hierarchy is inherent in our symbol system because we choose to symbolize some things and not others.

When Burke writes about the "negative," he describes it as a fundamental principle of language. Only through a symbol system can we represent that which is not present. "Rock" is not the actual rock; it is only a representative of the rock. In the world, only positives exist. A rock is a rock, and a plant is a plant. In nature, we cannot have a "not rock." That which is "not rock" is something else. Language is the means by which we introduce the negative into the natural world. Burke explains that use of this negative supports humans' practice of creating hierarchies.

Burke's negative has special relevance for discussing the notion that males and females are often called "opposite sexes." The negative provides the means to create two distinct forms which then are interpreted as opposite. In the natural world, females simply are female; males simply are males. In the symbolic world, we call them "opposite sexes." We establish these distinctions as a way to describe what is and what is not; for example, Suzie is a girl, not a boy. This gives humans a way to describe what is true and false, what is correct and not correct. These distinctions play a fundamental role in the hierarchies humans create.

Burke describes a second form of the negative as the pair, "thou shalt and thou shalt not," which directs people toward what they should and should not do.[13] Boys and girls start to hear early in their lives a mixture of messages about gender that are based on the negative. A boy may be told that "boys don't wear pink things." At first this may seem to be a statement describing a fact about biological males. But most boys figure out at some point that the statement is really a directive: it tells them what boys should not do. For boys, then, language that appears to be about biological sex differences refers instead to a gender stereotype to be achieved by avoiding or restricting a behavior that is linked with the feminine role.

The negative as related to girls is even more complicated. A girl may be told that "girls don't swear and spit"; they also may be encouraged to wear pants or join a soccer team. Girls get messages that some stereotypically masculine behaviors are acceptable for them but others are not. For the boys, the negative is clear: masculine is a set of characteristics that are distinct from feminine. For the girls, the message is more ambiguous. Feminine may or may not include elements of masculine. This difference in the ways we delineate masculinity and femininity provide bases for questions of inequality we will discuss later.

In addition, females and males may get different messages about femininity from different factions: age, religious affiliation, race, and class are only a few of the influences that may inform receivers that, for example, feminine means shaved legs-makeup-curled hair-politeness or that it means anything-you-want-to-do. While the expectations for feminine may range more widely than those for masculine, both males and females must assess the consequences of violating the hierarchy of masculine and feminine stereotypes.

Burke uses the concept of a terministic screen to explain how the use of symbols leads people to emphasize certain features of the world and to overlook other features that their language does not mention.[14] We learn to think about and experience the world in a certain way. Those experiences, in turn, blind us to other ways of knowing. People of different sexes may have very different terministic screens through which they experience the world and make meaning. When complexities of gender are added to the screen, differences can be amplified. Both Burke and Whorf claim that a given language selects for users certain features of the self and the world while blocking other features. Their theories of language help explain Deborah Tannen's cultural perspective (see chapter 2).

While Whorf, Korzybski, and Burke did not specifically address gender issues in their writings about language, their ideas do reveal two points that are important in our exploration of how men and women communicate. First, language codes and systems are not universal. Cultures have different ways of forming language and may choose to symbolize different experiences. For example, French has no equivalent to the English "teenager." French speakers may use terms equivalent to "adolescent" or "young person"; English speakers can symbolize "teenagers." Second, language has significant influence over human thought. Although you can have a visual or musical experience without putting it into words, you often will try to communicate about it with words—using names and labels that you or other people have available. The range of those names and labels will affect what you recall, what you can describe to others, and what you will treat as sufficiently important to talk about. In other words, you are largely limited to thinking what your language permits you to think.

You may have experienced these limitations when you have talked with someone about your feelings. Remember a time when you felt anxious, angry, ecstatic, or content. You may have experienced frustration as you attempted to describe the emotion. Our language offers far fewer words for emotions than the number we experience. As a result you may have found yourself settling for a word like "anxious" to describe both the feeling you had before an exam and the feeling you had waiting for a concert to begin. The emotional experiences were immensely different; your language limited you to abstract descriptions. Since distinctions are not available in the language, we may become less attentive to distinctions in our experiences with the emotions. This effect demonstrates the interaction these three theorists describe between a culture and its language.

The three language theorists discussed here also shared an interest in the idea that language, like human beings, changes over time. In situations in which no word seems to do justice to a person, event, or relationship, new terms are often invented, but not until enough people have had enough trouble with the available words to adopt a change willingly. The title "Ms." was first used in businesses in the 1950s not out of a commitment to feminist principles but as a means to avoid offending women correspondents whose marital status was unknown to the writer. In an analogous situation of the 1980s, writers have searched for adequate words to describe pairs of people who share a living space without being in a conventional relationship to each other. "Partner" has taken on a contemporary connotation as has "significant other." Other terms like "single mother," "house husband," or "stay-at-home dad" have generated out of changing lifestyles and roles. In addition, the phrases "spousal abuse," "domestic violence," "sex discrimination," and "sexual harassment" have become familiar terms (to be discussed in chapters 8 and 10) because of ongoing problems between the sexes.

Problems of Meaning

Semantics is the study of the meanings humans attach to words. We continually use, invent, and adapt symbols. As part of this process we are also active in decoding and interpreting our own and other people's symbols. The idea of humans actively interpreting language is important to the study of communication and the sexes. If words are subject to different interpretations depending on the goals and biases of the people doing the interpreting, then meanings related to gender are subject to human choices and agreements rather than lying beyond human influence. For example, the word, "lady," used in the phrase "Lady Diana, Princess of Wales" suggests an image of royal wealth. Shouting the same word in "Hey, lady, get a life!" conveys impatience and a low level of respect for the person addressed.

Denotative meanings can carry subtle value connotations even in apparently objective or value-free contexts. The *American Heritage Dictionary of the English Language* received public acclaim in 1973 because it was the first United States dictionary to include the word, "sexism." The definition was "discrimination by members of one sex against the other, especially by males against females, based on the assumption that one sex is superior." While the editorial board won applause for including the new term, the new thinking was not extended to the meanings of "man" and "woman" in that same dictionary. Even the electronic version of the *Deluxe American Heritage Dictionary of the English Language* published in 1992 carries a definition for "man" that remains almost exactly the same.[15] Following the definition is a long explanation in which the editors acknowledge some of the usages as generic. While they do not reveal the number of men and women on their Usage Panel, they explain that the panel on the whole accepted the generic use of the word, "man," although the women members agreed significantly less than did the male members. The explanation goes on to cite different examples of the use of "man" in generic terms and the percentage of disagreement among male and female panel members.

Whereas the definition of "man" occupied 110 lines in the dictionary (33 lines of definition and 77 lines of explanation), the 1992 definition for "woman" occupied 15 lines of definition and no explanation. Of the seven definitions for "woman," the first ("an adult female human being") is the same for 1973 and 1992; however, the second marks a significant change. In 1973, the example used to illustrate the second definition was "Woman is fickle." The newer version cites Elizabeth Cady Stanton, one of the organizers of the first women's rights conventions held in Seneca Falls in 1848. The 1992 version also includes two new definitions that describe women by their roles as workers outside the home.

Changing the definitions of "woman" functions as an example of the Burkeian and Whorfian theories. The definition itself will reflect gender perceptions and interpretations of the dictionary editors (in this case the Usage Panel) and will affect the gender perceptions and interpretations of readers of the dictionary (and users of the language). Because of these effects and the subjective nature of definition, some authors question whether any group can effectively define another. Simone de Beauvoir asserted in her historic book, *The Second Sex*, that women's nature has been largely unknown because women have been seen as the other sex by those recording human knowledge.[16] Furthermore, by defining woman as a modifier (as in "a woman athlete"), the editors of this dictionary demonstrate Whorf's theory; they point out the cultural practice of using male as standard and female as derivative or modifier. Would we say a "man electrician" or "man athlete"? Further, the explanation at the bottom of the entry of the derivation of the word reminds us that in this language, the word for woman began as a subordinate to the word, "man." Studying these definitions can help reveal how language creates images and reference points for people who use it.

METAPHOR

We use metaphors when we link a word or phrase with something to which it could not literally belong; our purpose is to suggest the two things resemble each other. For example, when we say, "My daughter's a ray of sunshine," we do not literally mean she emanates light shafts. We are using the metaphor of a sunshine ray to highlight the bright, happy quality in her. Likewise, when we say, "He streaked away from the explosion," we do not mean he left marks in the road. We use metaphors to make meaning more clear or to give richness to our explanations. Metaphors constitute "a fundamental characteristic of how people categorize and make sense of their experience."[17] Lakoff and Johnson, authors of *Metaphors We Live By*, explain that our language system is fundamentally a metaphor system.[18] Language is not literally that which it represents; our words simply suggest the direction for meaning. Not only is our language a metaphor itself, but we use the language to create other metaphors. Some scholars explain that metaphors reveal the deeper meaning we may interpret about our responses to our life experiences.[19] As Fiona Wilson wrote, "Metaphor is an essential medium through which reality is constructed."[20]

Because metaphors are so common and so descriptive, a good way to understand meaning with regard to sex and gender is to examine metaphors we use for females and males, women and men. Alleen Pace Nilsen identified four kinds of metaphors used to describe men and women: food, plants, animals, and inanimate objects.[21] While her study was completed more than twenty years ago, the metaphors are still familiar. Metaphors in the plants and inanimate objects categories are few; however, the food and animal categories are revealing. In the following examples, we have included a few metaphors from more recent times although most come from Nilsen's work.

Think of the ways women and men are represented with food metaphors. A woman may be referred to as a "dish" or "good enough to eat." Sometimes women are compared to desserts; for example, a woman might be called a "cupcake," "sweet cakes," "sugar plum," or "shortcake." Women also are referred to as fruits and vegetables, such as "tomato," "peach," or "cherry." Women may be said to have "peaches and cream" complexions. Men also may be compared to food items, most notably "meathead," "big cheese," or "hunk." Both sexes may be called "honey" or "sweetie pie," although those terms generally are reserved for intimates who are using the terms within the parameters of their relationship. If you put these metaphors in the context of a meal, the men would represent the main course and the women would represent side dishes and dessert.

A similar division occurs in the animal metaphors. Men often are compared to aggressive or sexually active animals like "stud," "wolf," or "tiger." Men go to "stag" parties. If a man is kind-hearted or gentle, he might be called a "teddy bear." Females—both girls and women—more often are compared to domesticated animals or baby animals like "kitten," "bunny" (as in Playboy bunny), "chick," or "little lamb." If a woman is unattractive either physically or in personality, she might be called a "bitch," "cow," or "dog." (Another interesting twist: if a man is unattractive in personality, he might be called a "son-of-a-bitch." Notice the man's negativity is reflected on his mother!) If a woman is particularly attractive, she takes on more sly and quick characteristics when she is called a "fox." Either sex can be called a "pig," but often the comparison is made for a woman because of her looks and for a man because of his behavior.

These metaphors reveal basic gender stereotypes carried in the language. As we apply shapes, colors, demeanors, and characteristics to women and men in our everyday language, we create and recreate (and often perpetuate) gender.

HOW LANGUAGE AND LANGUAGE USE CREATE INEQUALITIES

Significant numbers of people now look at language differently because they find racial, ethnic, class, age, gender or sex bias operating in everyday speech and writing. If you have made such a shift, you probably now examine carefully your own use of language related to sex or gender, or survey what you read or hear to see whether a given author or speaker chooses words that indicate fairness or bias. Such a change in awareness is a profound one. The battles over language change have led many people to see that words are related to gender more deeply than they had imagined—not as simple descriptions of people or actions, but as influences on human opportunities and human agreements. Language, in other words, has to do with power.

LANGUAGE, POWER, AND BIAS

Language can produce confusion and frustration in receivers who see themselves as excluded from consideration or symbolized in ways they do not perceive for themselves. For example, a heterosexual couple may reconsider the use of the phrase "man and wife" in the wedding ceremony when they realize the unequal power relationship implied in that phrase. While the male is given a persona, the female is given a role, and that role defines her in relation to the man. The pairing of males and females occurs in language in many ways. The pairing can establish a hierarchical relationship between them, as in the "man and wife" example. It can establish other contrasts where men are persona or adults and women are roles or children. For example, we might say "sorority girls," but we are more likely to say "fraternity men" or at least "fraternity guys." Somehow "fraternity boys" implies youngsters and sounds unacceptable, but "sorority girls" (despite naming individuals of approximately the same ages) is accepted. Likewise, we might say "leading man," but we are not likely to say, "leading woman." We would say, "leading lady" (connotating certain refined features and behaviors), but we do not say, "leading gentleman." In each case, the application of the word, "woman," to females of eighteen years and older is not as likely as is the application of the word, "man," to the same aged group of males. In addition, attention brought to the star of the show highlights the "man" persona of the man but the "lady" role of the woman. As we listen to everyday talk, we will hear "woman" used differently than we hear "man" used. The dichotomies within the language include girl/boy, woman/man, gal/guy, and lady/gentlemen. Yet when we use these pairs, we often create combinations like girl/guy or by calling everyone "guys." One reason we change the pairings is to avoid projecting childlike qualities on males (by using "boy"); we also tend to project connotations of "proper" behavior on women by calling them "ladies." In this way, we can exclude the symbolization of women or symbolize them in ways that represent only certain characteristics.

This same unbalanced use of language also occurs as a result of the way some words in United States English were created. In pairs like prince/princess, waiter/waitress, host/hostess, usher/usherette, and actor/actress, the main word is male and a derivative of that word is female. The "ette" ending indicates diminuative qualities and is applied to females doing the same actions as males. In many cases, new language has been introduced to move us from "steward/stewardess" to "flight attendant" or from "waiter/waitress" to "server." The new language is meant to fulfill Korzybski's imperative that we symbolize our realities as accurately as possible. When we symbolize males as more central than females, we impose a hierarchy that excludes females' senses of centrality; in so doing, we symbolize females in ways that screen out parts of their realities.

For some people, the use of gender-biased language depends on whether they believe their attitudes about women are relevant to the language they use.[22] A recent study revealed that college-aged people are not as concerned about gender-inclusive language as was the cohort group before them.[23] Investigation into effects of instruction in high school about gender equity language reveals it has had little effect on changing students' sexist language practices.[24] Medical students were shown to be least interested in changing their language and had made few attempts to do so.[25] People of the same age who were not in college reported more ease in reforming their language to be gender-inclusive than did college students.[26] While no clear explanation has been made for this difference, the regression in sex/gender equity

CALVIN AND HOBBES copyright (1986) Watterson. Reprinted with permission of UNIVERSAL PRESS SYNDICATE. All rights reserved.

in language over the last decade has been attributed by some to the problem that change has stayed at the level of "PC," political correctness. Important values about equity have not yet been braided into the cultural fabric. Robin Lakoff[27] asserted that directly confronting gender-related speech patterns alone will not change language and social behavior; she believes that only long-term social and political change to more equitable conditions will bring about reform. Jean Kantambu Latting agrees, explaining that we cannot change another person's behavior; we only can "provide the opportunity and space for people to change themselves. . . ."[28]

When we use language that is not equitable, we may do so because we are rotely following the same symbolization process used when we first learned to talk. We blindly comply with its conventions. We do not think about why we are more likely to ask a woman than a man if she will be changing her name when she marries. Some women retain their birth names when they marry; some couples change to hyphenated names or combined names like Douglas-Seymour; and some couples choose to adopt a shared last name, often the man's name in heterosexual couples. Controversy exists about whether the first two patterns indicate less commitment to marriage—with the emphasis on the woman's commitment. Because our symbolization process is nearly invisible to us, we do not recognize the power of the convention. How do we feel if in a heterosexual couple, the husband says he is changing his name to his wife's because she preferred it that way? How do we feel if the sexes were reversed, and the wife says she is changing hers to accommodate him? Even this act of naming ourselves—a central, rhetorical act—carries implications of hierarchy and power. If you are male, try to imagine growing up believing that one day you would change your surname to someone else's. Imagine being Mr. Sue Adams. If you are female, try to imagine growing up never questioning that you would continue for your life to have your birth name. Imagine presuming that someone else would simply change their name to yours. The differences in these two assumptions are significant.

Also significant are formal titles in our language for adult people. In the scenario mentioned before, what would we call Mr. Sue Adams's wife? We could not call her "Mrs. Sue Adams" because in the present English language system, "Mrs." identifies the woman as married. To create for females a system similar to the one now used by males, Sue Adams would need to invent a title that, like "Mr.," carried no message about her marital status and no connotations about her political agendas with regard to sex and gender. In addition to her own title, Sue would need to invent a title for Mr. Sue Adams, one that signified he was married.

In current practice, the formal titles for females include "Mrs.," "Ms.," and "Miss." "Mrs." and "Miss" are used to indicate whether or not the woman is married. "Ms.," a term sometimes received with suspicion or disdain, is currently used for women whose marital status is unknown or by women who do not wish to be identified by their marital status. The formal title for males, "Mr.," does not give information about the man's marital status. Thus, if a person is introduced as "Mrs." or "Miss," the language itself immediately reveals to others a female's eligibility as a potential partner. Unlike men, whose titles only indicate their sex, women must choose a particular title. "Ms." is the only choice that does not announce marital status as the first known characteristic. Research suggests that a woman who uses the "Ms." title is perceived as more oriented toward achievement and less expressive than women who use other titles; if she explicitly asks to be addressed with "Ms.," others will attribute those traits to her more strongly than if she makes her preference known implicitly.[29]

Because of the language, women today must decide how to symbolize themselves for the world. If they concur with convention and tradition, they may decide to be known as "Mrs. Carson States," "Miss Kathleen States," or "Mrs. Kathleen States." If women wish to be known by a symbol that is unique to them, they must decide whether or not they also want to deal with the connotations of the title, "Ms." Women must consider whether the title they choose will interfere with or hinder their careers. They also may consider the effect of their choice on family members or partners. Males may consider implications of titles they use to address females, but males do not have to make such decisions for their own names. Males also make fewer decisions about how to symbolize themselves in terms of their life activities. When men identify themselves, they are more likely than women to say, "I'm a plumber" or "I'm a pharmacist." Most women now expect to spend a large part of their adult lives in paid employment outside the home, but most also expect to be competent in some homemaking activities. Which should be treated as a central identity? In common usage, does "Mrs.," "Miss," or "Ms." connote one identity or the other? Using other kinds of symbols, women make symbolic choices as well. If a woman refers to herself as "one part homemaker and one part top executive," an older relative may discount the executive label, while an employment interviewer may not believe that a woman who mentions her interest in her home can be serious about long-term career ambitions. While men may explain they are fathers or they have families, the connotations for labels for men and women are different. For women, one kind of label may qualify or even cancel out the other.

CAREERS

Language can influence human action directly as well as indirectly. Research by scholars in a variety of fields supports the power of language to help or hinder individuals' career advancement. One effect of language on career development occurs through the labeling and evaluation of jobs typically done by men and those typically done by women. Occupations with masculine labels were perceived as roles for men and not as roles for men and women. People based their judgments about whether an occupation was appropriate for men or for women on the sex composition of that occupation. If mostly females filled a certain occupation—such as nursing—that occupation was considered a female job not to be pursued by males.[30]

One subtle element in this process fits Whorf's idea that language highlighting persons rather than processes tends to influence people to think about identities rather than the actions various people are taking. A frequent practice in social conversation illustrates this tendency to move toward name labels. One person begins a conversation by asking, "What do you do?" The second person answers, "I'm a plumber." Notice that the question was asked in terms of action, but the answer is given in terms of a personal identity. We are so used to this switch from verbs to nouns that we rarely notice it. In fact, if the second person answered the question with "I plumb," you would probably laugh and then ask: "What do you plumb?" Even in that case, the language eventually directs attention toward a noun, a thing, rather than toward a verb or action word.

Nouns for positions also represent the identities of the people who do them. "He's president of WTZ, Inc." implies that his central identity lies in his work and his high status with that firm. Notice the contrast when a woman currently at home with small children is asked in social conversation, "What do you do?" Many women answer the question with some embarrassment, saying, "Oh, I'm just a housewife." Other options include mentioning a hobby that has the potential to earn money, or listing 15 tasks that she has completed that day in managing the household, caring for the children, and preparing meals for her husband and children. Some women answer, "I couldn't begin to tell you all I do," while others say, "Nothing," rather than tell all the routine tasks they do each day.

"Executive" language contrasts with "housewife" language not only in terms of money being paid for the work, but also in the sense that the housewife's job sounds like many small items with no definite skill, status, or product. The executive's job implies an identity as a wise, well-organized person worthy of elevated status and income. The housewife's work, in other words, does not count as work (a point that will be pursued in chapter 8). Her nature, as implied by the language of her job, is scattered and vague. The executive's nature, according to the language of that job, is focused, strong, and impressive.

Men generally gain more status from the language labels that are given to their jobs and thus to them as individuals than do women. For many employed women, the work identity is not the primary identity they report to others. They usually have other major work to do in the home, and many of the sorts of paid work that women currently do—as typists, checkout clerks, waitresses, and receptionists—gain little status for them but offer convenience and support to their bosses and supervisors. In terms of the traditional power viewpoint reported in chapter 2, men's power to control their environments is enhanced by having a support person—female or male. A woman often has her real power to accomplish tasks and develop others' skills elsewhere—through her work as a parent, household manager, volunteer, or friend.

Self-esteem for both women and men is developed through a long and individually varied set of experiences, some of which are directly related to career issues. Language is one way to learn about careers; both sexes receive messages about careers and family responsibilities and are affected by their early histories. Boys learn in their first five years that they will become, and must work to become, men. They gain access to language in a way their sisters do not. The language reinforces the presence, the future prospects, and the necessity for leadership of men. "Someday you will have a family, and you must provide well for them." The reality is that 30 percent of families with children in the United States are single-parent families headed by women, and the large majority of these women are employed for pay while being fully responsible for their children's care. The word "provider" has a male connotation even though it is inaccurate on two counts: Most married couples consist of two employed partners, and many more women than men are employed single parents.

INVISIBILITY

Have you ever wanted to explain a sensation to someone but just couldn't find the right words? The experience can be very frustrating; you want to communicate the feeling but can't find any way to do so. Sometimes you give up, saying, "Never mind. I just can't explain it to you." At that moment, the feeling you had is invisible to the receiver because you cannot symbolize it. When people in a culture have an experience or an idea or a way of thinking that has no representative symbol in the language, those realities are invisible.[31] Language privileges certain experiences by providing the means to make them visible. Users must change the language if they want to share previously invisible experiences. One way to change the language is to create new words, phrases, and constructions. Have you ever played Fictionary? Each player invents plausible dictionary definitions of words selected at random from the dictionary. Players listen to these new definitions and decide which they believe actually came from the dictionary.

Cheris Kramarae designed a similar process, one in which she constructed words that would make visible experiences not represented in present United States English.[32] Asking for contributions from students, friends, acquaintances, and colleagues, Kramarae compiled words people created to symbolize aspects of their own realities—words or definitions not presently in the language. People contributed derivatives and definitions of words to create a new lexicon

For Better or For Worse®
by Lynn Johnston

FOR BETTER OR WORSE copyright (1996) Lynn Johnston Prod., Inc. Dist. by
UNIVERSAL PRESS SYNDICATE. All rights reserved.

to expand their choices as they communicated with one another. Kramarae attempted to make the experiences of a minority group as well represented in language as are the experiences of the majority group. One such entry contributed by Catharine Mackinnon defined sexual harassment as "the unwanted imposition of sexual requirements in the context of a relationship of unequal power."[33]

Sex bias in language emerges from and feeds back into sex bias in the perceptions of individuals and the policies of institutions. To the person who expresses it, the bias may seem to be the truth about one sex; the link often is ignored between making that statement and affecting future behavior toward stereotyped people. One source of bias and stereotyping in our language arises from the phenomenon of two communication cultures, mentioned in chapter 2. When women and men spend a great deal of their time in different locations and activities, both sexes have a limited chance of knowing what the other is thinking, planning, and evaluating in many aspects of daily life. In theory this problem would affect both sexes equally. However, women may hear significantly more about the worlds of business, sports, the military, and criminal activity through the news media and from individual men than men are likely to hear about the actions, relationships, and values of importance to women. One major reason for that difference is the early communication to males to avoid what is female—identified in the effort to achieve a masculine communicator ideal.

THINKING AND LEARNING

Interest in language issues related to gender has led to research about the ways people process information. Scholars have begun to investigate differences in thinking and learning patterns, values, reasoning, and moral decision making. Authors of *Women's Ways of Knowing* theorize that women learn and know in different ways than men.[34] Conceptualizing a different way of knowing is difficult for most of us because we use our familiar "knowing patterns" to attempt to analyze the different way! The authors assert that women's knowing emanates from a concern for understanding (rather than proof) and an interest in connection (rather than an interest in mastering the subject). Since women's process and intent for knowing may differ from men's, many women and men may doubt women's capabilities as intellectuals. Both may see the feminine process as different from the masculine process; because of their social conditioning, both may devalue the feminine process because it does not conform to the masculine one. As a result, women second guess themselves and may feel tentative in forwarding their ideas. Understanding the underlying problem in the contrasts between knowing styles means understanding how language—and the denotations and connotations for words like "intellectual," "logical," and "establishing proof"—affects thinking and learning. The form of the language reveals the Burkean hierarchy of values so that proof has more prestige than understanding and mastery of a subject has more prestige than learning how that subject is contextually connected. This hierarchy privileges one way of thinking over another and privileges life experiences that produce that way of thinking over others. Someone once said, "It takes a smart fish to know it is swimming in water." As we are immersed in our pool of social conditioning and language, conceptualizing and legitimizing any other way of knowing requires constant attention and great effort.

LANGUAGE PERFORMANCE

Most of us have never examined our expectations of how women and men ought to talk. When those expectations are violated, however, we recognize the violation immediately and can find the results humorous. When Robin Williams masqueraded as the housekeeper in *Mrs. Doubtfire*, we found his antics hilarious partly because we recognized the absurdity of a large man wearing stockings and speaking in such prim ways. While the point of the movie was to entertain the audience (and make money!), *Mrs. Doubtfire* was an interesting study in our communication stereotypes for men and for women. These stereotypes have survived despite a great range of individual variation and intentional social change.

This section deals with the expected patterns of language use by men and women. It describes some of the most prominent research findings concerning women's and men's language choices. The main purpose of this discussion is to influence you to be skeptical about any statements that appear to "prove" that someone of one sex or the other will talk certain ways across settings and situations. Any such statements made on the basis of our limited knowledge are merely stereotypes. The knowledge we now have about language performance is based on isolated settings and short periods of time, so much more knowledge is needed about situation differences, about the change process itself, and about the ways people make change as well as respond to change. The chapter ends with an account of the efforts at planned language change that have begun because of feminist analyses and other research on sex bias in language.

PERCEIVING LANGUAGE USE

The first two chapters of this book portrayed human perception as an active process. We do not simply absorb information from the environment; we select it for memory, for close attention, and for active interpretation—although we may not be consciously aware of how or why we have made our choices. This point is relevant to the ways we hear and react to people's talk as well. You may profit from asking yourself what you expect or predict either sex to sound like and to consider how you react to deviations from those expectations. Your image of male and female talk may come from your first family experiences, where both parents might have been soft-spoken and conversational with you. Or you may have had one parent who spoke more abruptly and gave you more orders, while the other parent asked you about your feelings and listened to you more attentively. Your models for how to talk might have been an older child, a teacher, or a valued neighbor or relative. You probably considered the sex of that model as at least a part of his or her appeal to you.

When I was young and my dad told me that I did a good job or a bad job on something (like homework), I would listen and value his opinion. I remember one particular instance when I was in junior high and high school, when I'd get all As and a B on my report card. I'd consider this a good job. My father would ask, "How come these aren't all As?" In an instant I'd go from feeling proud of myself to feeling like a failure.

Under constant parental pressure to perform academically, I did quite well in the formative years. People thought I was smart or gifted. But I didn't feel that way—I was just getting the job done so my dad wouldn't complain that I wasn't trying hard enough. In retrospect, my dad warped my whole view of the education process from getting an education to getting a grade. Basically, my dad doesn't think I'm a good student or that I try hard enough and somehow I ended up feeling the same way. Weird, huh?

Your perception of other people's uses of language is informative. It gives you practical information about how you are likely to be received in various communication settings like schools, workplaces, and social events. Most people adopt different communication rules for different situations. At a party you would be violating a communication rule if you pulled out your briefcase and began demonstrating a new type of calculator to all the guests. Sitting on your supervisor's desk at your workplace would be a violation of a communication rule if you had just been called in to the supervisor's office to correct a serious mistake you had made. A communication rule, then, is a widely shared expectation about the topics, styles, language, and nonverbal elements of messages that will be treated as fitting a given place and time. Being an effective communicator requires that a person know enough of the rules to avoid committing major errors in dealing with other people.

When children and young adults learn how to speak acceptably in various situations, they are learning the pragmatics of human communication. Linguists, psychologists, and sociologists all take an interest in the ways people learn these communicative expectations and modify or break them when necessary. Imagine the words used by a man holding his newborn infant during a midnight feeding; imagine him two days later making a sales pitch to a business client. If you were to describe the man only by the words and movements that separate what is "masculine" (drive, ambition, task orientation) in his behavior from what is called "feminine" (nurturing, calm, and affectionate), you would be missing essential aspects of his two experiences as a communicator.

We have alternatives to saying that women and men each talk a certain way. An alternative approach does not avoid stereotyping altogether, but it moves in the direction of looking at gender-related sets of language features that can be learned or evaluated by anyone, rather than expecting people automatically to have a certain kind of language personality derived from their sex. Table 3.1 shows three sets of language features.[35] A given individual's language pattern will not follow any one language style absolutely. Most of us respond to situations with some degree of flexibility. Yet when looking at these sets of features, people often report they see themselves reflected in one of the patterns more than in the other two. You may want to see whether this is true for you. The description of the nonsexist language style is shorter than the others because it is adaptable to different communication situations depending on the audience and the constraints in each situation.

Table 3.1 Three Gender-Related Language Styles

Indicators of feminine language

1. Content emphasizes feelings and relationships: one's own emotions, the listener's reactions, the feelings of other people. Focus is on identity and relating more than on the physical or technical features of task achievement.

2. Indirectness rather than direct assertions: using questions rather than statements, or "tag" questions that combine elements of both. Indirect verb forms such as might or would are used more than forms like can or will.

3. Respect for or deference to the listener; allowing options to the other, by questions or by references to the other's goals or preferences.

4. Adjectives and adverb qualifiers are used within statements: very, kind of, possibly, really. Effect is to produce few bold assertions.

5. Use of standard speech; rare use of nonstandard or taboo words.

Indicators of masculine language

1. Content deals primarily with tasks, especially jobs done outside the home and with competitive achievements. Time and space elements of action are stressed, and objects are treated as parts of systems.

2. Direct assertions far more often than questions; direct use of present and future verbs such as can or will rather than modal (indirect) forms.

3. Refers to self more than to the listener. May focus on goals, plans, or accomplishments; rarely mentions anxiety, doubts, or personal limitations, except as followed by a "we should do this" statement.

4. Uses unqualified nouns and verbs; rarely uses qualifiers.

5. Uses the language of sports and the military and expects partners in conversation to do the same.

6. Uses nonstandard speech for emphasis, to produce identification in the listener, or to show a bond between self and others.

7. Shows willingness to confront the listener or other persons if necessary.

Indicators of nonsexist or inclusive language

1. Emphasizes both task and interpersonal content of talk.

2. Uses I rather than you at beginning of statements, to convey individual opinion or feeling directly instead of through labeling or attacking the listener.

3. Refers to the listener as a peer, not as a superior or subordinate.

4. Gives evidence in support of own claims, whether about task or interpersonal issues.

These features are summaries of characteristics often expected from members of one sex or the other. They are not meant as actual descriptions of any particular person's talk. Even if all three styles appear to you as stereotypes, the three descriptions can still help illuminate the fact that language is a matter of choice, and more choices are available to speakers than they think.

Descriptions of feminine and masculine language styles have their origins in gender communication ideals as well as in communication acts. Each of the four viewpoints discussed in chapter 2 helps explain why humans believe the sexes speak differently, as well as why some differences are perceived as more important than others.

From the biological perspective, girls and women are often seen as more fluent or skillful with words than are boys and men. This apparent biological advantage is countered with the claim that women's ease with language is "gossip," endless talk about topics of little or no interest to men. Another way the biological advantage of women's language skill is discounted is by devaluing words in general. Language facility and task accomplishment are posed as opposites: "all talk, no action," or "he's just a bag of rhetoric." Underlying these phrases is a defense of the masculine gender ideal that men communicate through physical strength and movement while women communicate with the weaker tool of language.

The three contrasting power perspectives emerge clearly in the gender-based language styles. Feminine language implies shared power (manifested as synergistic or empowerment depending on the distribution of resource) or, if necessary, a speaker's giving up power in favor of a constructive relationship with the other (empowerment). Masculine language, in contrast, implies that the speaker has and will use power to control task accomplishment and the responses of the other, using confrontive tactics if necessary (dominant). This style also fits the individual who wants to show personal superiority in an interpersonal setting, whether by giving solutions, making threats, or telling jokes. Inclusive language balances listener and speaker, task and process (synergistic). Both leadership and cooperation are elicited and necessary.

The cultural perspective emerges through the emphases of the feminine and masculine styles. Feeling-oriented talk is welcomed in intimate settings or in jobs that involve taking care of other people's physical and social needs. Achievement-oriented talk may succeed when there are no perceived barriers to reaching a goal. Barriers tend to appear unexpectedly, however. One woman who worked for an impatient male executive happened to be just outside his office when the executive learned of a major conflict between two workers who were both responsible to him. He came out of the office, waved his arms in disgust, and said to the woman, "Will you fix that up so we can get our work done?" That executive's cultural perspective suggested that a woman should deal with feelings and relationships, even in an employment setting where she has no authority over the people involved in the conflict.

The rhetorical perspective provides the best explanation for why almost no one is likely to use a single gender-related language style all the time. People look at situations in light of the goals they hope to achieve and the limitations placed on them by time, space, and other communicators. A recent study of powerful and less powerful talk suggests the rhetorical perspective may be more important than either sex or gender.[36] The salesman-father feeding his infant in the earlier example might wish that he could find someone to sympathize with his late-night feeding schedule. He might tell himself, however, that men get passed over for promotions if they talk too much about family and not enough about their jobs. A woman who is new to a job setting might feel a similar constraint on talking about a first child who is delighted about learning to read. The sexes may differ widely in what they take into account in choosing their language strategies, but they are similar in thinking about the reactions of others when they deviate significantly from the language style expected of them. So their actions, without being fully determined by the views of others, may be more guarded, and even more sex-stereotyped, in certain situations than would be characteristic in another, freer setting.

LANGUAGE IN CONVERSATION

We do not know the full range of language practices that either women or men can potentially show in different communication situations. Studying conversational patterns is even more complex than studying isolated language features, for our ability to predict individual cases decreases significantly as the number of factors increases. As scholars have begun to study systematically the elements of conversation, their results have increased our understanding of both the stereotypes and the realities of men's and women's talk.

During the 1970s scholars in linguistics and anthropology organized their knowledge about conversations around four basic concepts. Those concepts continue to guide research today:

1. The turn, a segment of talk uttered by one person at a time.
2. The floor, the implied right to be the speaker at a given moment, particularly in groups larger than two persons.
3. The interruption, an act of starting—and continuing—to speak while another person is in the middle of a turn.
4. The overlap, speaking while another person is talking, often briefly and allowing the other to continue the turn.

These concepts have received some research attention in relation to the talk of men and women. The research done thus far has revealed some apparently significant differences between the two sexes in certain features of conversation, the most widely reported finding resulting from a study by Don Zimmerman and Candace West in 1973. Their first study showed that men interrupted women far more often than women interrupted either men or women (96 percent, compared with 4 percent), and much more often than men interrupted other men. This pattern has been confirmed by other researchers, but since the 1973 study the difference in behavior has not seemed as clear-cut as it originally appeared to be. In later work West and Zimmerman found that women who were interrupted by men began to continue speaking instead of becoming silent, sometimes commenting on the event itself with words such as "I'd like to finish."[37] Individual reports reveal women giving support to other women who have been interrupted, often by saying something like "I'd like to hear the rest of her idea." Interruption behavior by both sexes is likely affected by the communicators' attitudes toward each other and themselves, as well as by their knowledge of the specific language to use in responding to an interruption.

Research into overlap behavior and treatment of the conversational floor shows some apparent differences in women's and men's behaviors that may be related to the perspective of power as dominance. When women overlap each other's conversation, often they do so with supportive information or expressions of interest, so that the impact of the overlap is to show involvement in the other's words rather than competition with them. Men have not been observed to use overlaps in that cooperative sense; instead they make sounds that show the receiver's readiness to take a turn himself. The "floor" in traditional parliamentary practice can be held by only one person; yet women have been observed in various settings sharing the floor with other women and treating communication as a jointly built product of individual contributions rather than as an individual act of asserting control. Again, we don't know how often any of these specific behaviors occur in which settings, but they seem to develop less from differing amounts of skill in either sex than from differing values given to the competitive versus cooperative approaches to conversation.

Whatever skills and values are demonstrated by both sexes in conversation, clear patterns of inequality continue to appear in the everyday communication of many women and men. Some analysts of language in conversation attribute the imbalance to women's excessive use of polite language forms and structures, which undercut women's credibility as adult speakers and thinkers. Linguist Robin Lakoff was one of the earliest to claim that women's language is powerless; beginning in 1973 she tried to explain that certain language forms used primarily by women kept them from being perceived as credible speakers. Her major concerns were the tag question, hedges and qualifiers, and adverbs and adjectives used as intensifiers. The literature on these three elements only partly supports Lakoff's assertion that they are part of a woman's language style. More important is the idea that these elements indicate a powerless style, whether or not it is used by women.[38] The three elements do not always appear together, so they need to be examined individually.

The tag question is a combination of a sentence and a question, treated as a unit, for example: "You'll be coming home soon, won't you?" The question has the effect of turning the original statement into a question as well. Whether women or men use this form more in all settings is not clearly shown in the literature; but one significant difference is that women use tag questions with young children much more than men do. One of the authors' children, on reading this section of the book, remarked, "I always hated it when you would say, 'It's time for bed, isn't it?' I didn't want to agree with you but I knew it was time for bed. I would have preferred you just said, 'It's time for bed.'" Lakoff also disliked this structure because it could be interpreted as indicating the woman was uncertain about assertions she had every right to make ("It's a nice day, isn't it?") and to make her appear to wait for agreement or approval when neither is necessary; however, other scholars suggest the tag question may function in another way, as an opening for a conversation. Instead of simply making a demand—"Come home soon" or "Go to bed"—the tag question invites the receiver into a negotiation about the act. Rather than being read as a weak statement of uncertainty, the tag question can be read as a conversation tool that promotes connection.

A second feature presumed by Lakoff to characterize women's language is the use of hedges and qualifiers, such as: "It seems possible that we will be able to take that trip to Arizona." Lakoff and others interpret a phrase such as "it seems possible" as a speaker's way of limiting her own responsibility and thus lowering her own credibility. While hedges studied in a courtroom have been evaluated as showing lack of power and expertise,[39] another study showed that in college discussion groups, males could be credible when they used qualifiers and hedges in their speech, whereas females in the same discussion groups were rated as less credible.[40] Perhaps the factor of expecting males and not females to act as leaders affected the participants' judgments of their language behavior.

The third element of women's language that concerned Lakoff and others is the intensifier "That's really fine," or "I'm tremendously glad for you." In this case a general sex-linked difference seems to hold up over time, in that women have been repeatedly found to use more interpretive, evaluative, and emotive terms in speech. Recently, a picante sauce manufacturer took advantage of this speech quality to add humor to their advertisement. Four weather-beaten men dressed as cowboys are shown out on the range, gathering around a campsite in what appears to be desolate, desertlike surroundings. They describe the sauce with words like "exquisite bouquet" and "delicate balance." The advertisement ends when one cowboy says if he were to serve that sauce, he would have used a "prettier bowl." The juxtaposition of the leather-skinned, worn, rugged appearance of the men and the intensifiers in their talk played on our gender expectations for male and female talk.

It is important not to generalize too soon or too widely about the presence of these elements in women's speech. While interviewing women in managerial positions with a large national retailing firm, one author noticed that only one out of six women used any of the three elements from Lakoff's model more than a single time. Their actions could confirm the rhetorical perspective in that they adapted their words to show a researcher they were comfortable in their jobs. Their omission of three elements of "women's language" also gives support to the claim that women's speech is not always powerless. All six had higher-status positions than do most working women, and they were thus relatively powerful women.

On the other hand, research does indicate that people (both men and women) who exhibit a feminine speech style are perceived as less competent than those using the masculine style. The stereotype of women's speech appeared stronger than a preconceived expectation of the men's style.[41] One reason women may continue to use this style even though it is perceived as less competent may be because some conclude that women who speak in a more tentative style are more influential with men. If the gender inequity is functioning as research indicates, women may use this style as a means to attain power. The style does not seem to function in the same way with other combinations. For example, men who use the feminine style are not persuasive to other men, and the feminine style is not more persuasive for women listeners. These complexities in communication styles create contradictions between the behaviors that seem to bring success in one communication situation and those that are effective in another setting. If you are female, those contradictions can pose major problems, especially if you are trying to balance employment and managing a household. Many white women experience themselves as bilingual, speaking two distinct languages in the two gender-based cultures. Men of color may know a similar experience; women of color sometimes have to juggle three or four "languages" in the course of their day. People who live this sort of split existence have to be continually alert to adapt appropriately to their diverse communication settings. They may feel compelled to limit their talk to on-the-job matters while in their places of employment, and they may try not to talk about the politics of the job when they are with family members at home. To a degree both sexes share this kind of split communicative existence. However, stereotyped expectations for females create a wider discrepancy between the two behaviors.

LANGUAGE CHANGE

The process of language change has been scattered and erratic, but there is evidence of consensus on some issues that was not the case in the early 1970s. That consensus is partly a product of the visibility of women in settings where they were not seen in 1970—as astronaut, vice-presidential candidate, Cabinet members, and Supreme Court justices. The growing agreement about including women in everyday language is also a product of hearing and reading examples of inclusive language from news commentators, teachers, textbooks, and magazines. After the publishing companies of Scott, Foresman (in 1972) and McGraw-Hill (in 1974) put forth guidelines for equal treatment of the sexes in textbooks, professional associations in psychology, sociology, literature, and speech communication developed their own guidelines for publications. These guidelines have served as positive models for writers and speakers to use in portraying sex equality rather than sex bias.

Over the years of persuasion, debate, and often ridicule, certain themes have reappeared. In the ongoing controversy over planned language change to promote sex equity, the following questions represent the most troubling issues in terms of how often they come up in print and in conversation.

Q. How can people use pronouns clearly and fairly without stumbling over themselves with too many he/she's?

A. Use plurals where possible, or use the noun in a later reference to promote clarity. Try to use s/he or him/her as infrequently as possible for ease in speaking. You can sometimes change to you and avoid the third person pronoun altogether. Notice that although this book is about sex and gender, s/he or him and her has appeared infrequently. Most ideas can be expressed in sentences without resorting to either singular or plural generic pronouns.

Q. How can I refer to people by position or occupation without being biased or sounding silly?

A. Choose words that describe functions rather than depending on -man words. For example, use "firefighter" and "letter carrier." "Chair" is a centuries-old term for the person who chairs a committee or a meeting.

Q. How can I refer to a woman I do not know, whether or not she is currently with an intimate partner?

A. If you're not sure of her name, ask her. If she is with a spouse, inquire about her name so you will not label her as "Mrs. X," with no first name to use in conversation. If writing to a female, use Ms. if you do not know her marital status or title. But if she has a professional title such as Dr., use it.

Q. How can I deal with name differences within families—such as in a second marriage, children with different last names, and a wife's name not being the same as her husband's?

A. Again, ask people their names or ask what they prefer to be called. This is the simplest way to avoid your being confused and their being offended.

The common element in each of these questions is how to make language better reflect individuals' views of the world and of themselves, while allowing people to carry on their communication with a minimum amount of disruption. Speakers and writers are most successful with language change when they assess a current situation carefully, as suggested by the rhetorical approach.

People tend to hold existing beliefs as long as possible, even in the face of contradicting information. Psychologists call this tendency the drive toward cognitive consistency or balance. While trying to keep our mental houses in order, we may fight or deny ideas that go against long-standing personal constructs. This tendency explains why many people have chosen not to adopt nonsexist, or inclusive, language forms; some have seen language as a passive instrument that cannot change or a monument that should not be tampered with. In contrast, some individuals have made a definite effort to alter their language practices regarding the sexes. Bates's research on individual language changes made by university professors revealed that the two items that most influenced them to alter their language toward a more inclusive style were the presence of a trusted female who encouraged them to make the change to avoid bias, and information from a person or a written source giving them options for adding terms smoothly to their everyday language. You may find that changing your language habits is harder than you think. You may find that even after a year you fall back into old patterns.

Those who take nonsexist or inclusive language to an extreme often do so out of discomfort with change, leading them to make the entire issue seem ridiculous. Long after the first public controversy about sex bias in language, many people tend to recall the trivial aspects of the controversy. A student newspaper editor at the University of Oregon suggested in 1975 that people give up not only the word, "chairman" but also the word "chairperson," because the latter word contained the syllable "son." The alternative? "Chairperoff-spring"—the only noun free of man-terms. Even a less ridiculous response to language can have the effect of stereotyping the options for change. A department chair announced that one of the secretaries would "man" the phones during a faculty meeting. He received immediate jeers from many of the people at the meeting, both male and female. Following the jeers came suggestions for alternate phrasing, and "person the phones" seemed to be the most popular. This problem-solving attempt was amusing; surprisingly, no one suggested the old-fashioned and nonsexist, "answer the phones."

CONCLUSION

Because many people remember only the humorous or extreme versions of the gender-in-language debate, a central point about language is often missed. Language has a major influence over human thought—as theorists Whorf, Korzybski, and Burke have asserted. Korzybski believed that reality is separate from language but knowable by humans if we take meticulous care to match our representative symbol system to that changing reality. Whorf proposed that symbol systems affect how we perceive reality, and Burke believed that language creates reality. Language symbols select the elements of "man" and "woman" that will be noticed and reinforced. These symbols present females with uncertainties about meaning that can affect learning, career choice, and self-esteem; they present males with demands for uncompromising success that can affect relational development, intimacy, and choice.

What we know about the sexes' language performance in a variety of settings is limited by people's adaptations to situations, by social changes over time, and to some degree by the bias of our expectations for the language behavior of women compared to that of men. Tag questions and other elements of what has been labeled "women's language" seem to be related to power or value differences more than to biological sex.

The current movement for language change has been in process for nearly three decades. Some consensus about acceptable changes have been reached, but there has been no full agreement among people outside the academic world about the effects of "he/man" language on women's self-esteem and on men's perceptions of women. This chapter has demonstrated through research and evidence that gender-related language can affect learning, career development, and personal well-being. It remains to be seen what actions both sexes will take in order to alter the effects of sex bias in language. Words influence particular views; changing language changes understanding. Taking a rhetorical perspective on language means becoming aware of how communication patterns affect our interactions and acting on those insights to effect change.

QUESTIONS FOR DISCUSSION

1. Think of the names you called others or the names others called you when you were a child. What do you remember of your reactions? To what degree do any of these childhood labels still affect your view of yourself and other men and women?

2. Think of something regarding sex and gender that is not represented by a word in the United States English language. Devise a word, a derivation, and a definition. Discuss the word with a group. What are the major advantages and disadvantages of making new words?

3. Listen for metaphors in your speech. Try to identify the kinds of metaphors you are most likely to use with regard to women and men. What conclusions can you draw from the categories you generate?

4. In what ways does contemporary language portray either men or women as predominantly sexual beings? What visual images contribute to this impression?

5. This chapter mentions many ways in which language influences your views of sex and gender. Name several language

practices that influence your thinking about ethnicity, race, class, age, and sexual preference.

6. Can language changes influence attitudes?

Cases for Analysis

Case 3.1   The Parent Group

During an evening meeting at the high school, the male principal asked parents to air any concerns or problems they might have experienced. One parent said she was disturbed by the amount of sexist language she heard both from students and from teachers. She asked if the school might invest in a seminar that could educate the school community about the problems with sexist language. The discussion that ensued was short and included remarks about racist language also.

In the written minutes for the meeting, the discussion was described as one about "the sexes language." The minutes were signed by the principal.

1. What implications might the concerned parent have seen when she saw the phrase changed from "sexist language" to "sexes language?"

2. How might the effects of sexist language used in a high school be significant because of the age of the students? Do you think sexist language has more or less of an effect on college students? People who did not attend college? Older people?

3. Do you recall sexist language being used in your high school? Do you recall any classes or workshops directed at ways to change such language? How would you describe the attitudes of most high school students with regard to sexist language? High school teachers?

4. As a student, what do you do when you hear a college professor use sexist language? How are the reactions of males and females different? Similar?

Case 3.2   Hillary Clinton

Hillary Clinton has generated a significant amount of attention during her years in the White House. Bumper stickers say, "Vote for Hillary's husband" or "Impeach Clinton—and his wife." Her style of speaking has caused some critics to call her cold and unfeeling or "too smart for her own good." Her talk also has prompted people to say, "Finally, a woman in the White House who talks like a partner and an equal instead of an accessory."

1. What phrases and bumper-sticker sayings have you heard about Hillary Clinton? Write down as many as you can recall and explain how language functions to connote certain attitudes about sex and gender.

2. Why do you think her style has generated so much attention? What are the characteristics of speech or presentation that seem to attract the most comments? Imagine a man who conducted himself similarly. How are the two treated differently? What do the two have in common?

3. Think about the phrase, "First Lady." Now that you have read about language equity, do you think that term is an appropriate one? What other terms come to mind?

4. How does the title, "First Lady" fit Hillary Clinton? Barbara Bush? Nancy Reagan? Rosalynn Carter? Pat Nixon? Jacqueline Kennedy? What speech characteristics do you find similar in these women's styles? Which characteristics do you think were most well liked by the public? Which characteristics do you think were most expected?

5. Outline what you think would be a good speaking style for the president of the United States. Examine the feminine and masculine stereotypes. What matches do you find between your first list and the two different styles? What are the implications for males or females who might run for the presidency?

NOTES

[1] Confucian Analects, bk. 20:3, iii from *The Chinese Classics* (1861–1886), vol. I, trans. James Legge.

[2] For an interesting commentary on changing "man" words to "person" words or other neutral indicators, see Alan R. Slotkin, "Media Watch: The TV Verdict on Genderless-Person," *American Speech* 64, 3 (1989): 286.

[3] Ann Bodine, "Androcentrism in Prescriptive Grammar: Singular 'they,' Sex-Indefinite 'he,' and 'he or she,'" *Language in Society* 4 (August 1975): 129–46.

4 Mykol C. Hamilton, "Using Masculine Generics: Does Generic _He_ Increase Male Bias in the User's Imagery?" _Sex Roles_ 19, 11/12 (1988): 785–99.

5 Mykol C. Hamilton, "Masculine Bias in the Attribution of Personhood," _Psychology of Women Quarterly_ 15 (1991): 393–402.

6 Mirian Watkins Meyers, "Current Generic Pronoun Usage: An Empirical Study" _American Speech_ 65 (Fall 1990): 228–37.

7 John Gastil, "Generic Pronouns and Sexist Language: The Oxymoronic Character of Masculine Generics," _Sex Roles_ 23, 11/12 (1990): 629–42.

8 Ossie Davis, "The English Language Is My Enemy," _American Teacher_ (April 1967), reprinted in _Language, Communication, and Rhetoric in Black America_, ed. Arthur Smith (New York: Harper & Row, 1972), pp. 49–57.

9 Benjamin Lee Whorf, _Language, Thought, and Reality_, ed. John B. Carroll (Cambridge, MA: MIT Press, 1956).

10 Ann M. Gill, _Rhetoric and Human Understanding_ (Prospect Heights, IL: Waveland Press, 1994), p. 240.

11 Alfred Korzybski, _Science and Sanity_ (New York: Science Press, 1933).

12 Sonja K. Foss, Karen A. Foss, and Robert Trapp, _Contemporary Perspectives on Rhetoric_, 2d ed. (Prospect Heights, IL: Waveland Press, 1991), p. 198.

13 Kenneth Burke, _A Grammar of Motives_ (Berkeley: University of California Press, 1950).

14 Kenneth Burke, "Terministic Screens," in _Language As Symbolic Action_ (Berkeley: University of California Press, 1968), pp. 44–66.

15 _The Deluxe American Heritage Dictionary of the English Language_, 3rd ed. (electronic version) (Houghton Mifflin Company, 1992).

16 Simone de Beauvoir, _The Second Sex_, trans. H. M. Parshley (New York: Alfred A. Knopf, 1952).

17 R. W. Gibbs, Jr., "Categorization and metaphor understanding," _Psychological Review_, 99, 3 (1992): 572.

18 G. Lakoff and M. Johnson, _Metaphors We Live By_ (Chicago: The University of Chicago Press, 1980).

19 J. Ross, as cited in R. Norton, J. Schwartzbaum, and J. Wheat, "Language Discrimination of General Physicians: AIDS Metaphors Used in the AIDS Crisis," _Communication Research_ 17, 6 (1990): 809–26.

20 Fiona Wilson, "Language, Technology, Gender, and Power," _Human Relations_ 45, 9 (1992): 883–904.

21 Alleen Pace Nilsen, "Sexism in English: A Feminist View," _Female Studies_ VI, ed. Nancy Hoffman, Cynthia Secor, and Adrian Tinsley (Old Westbury, NY: The Feminist Press, 1972), pp. 102–109 as cited in Barbara Westbrook Eakins and R. Gene Eakins, _Sex Differences in Human Communication_ (Boston: Houghton Mifflin Company, 1978), p. 122–23.

22 Kimberly Matheson and Connie M. Dristiansen, "The Effect of Sexist Attitudes and Social Structure on the Use of Sex-Biased Pronouns," _The Journal of Social Psychology_ 127, 4 (1987): 395–98.

23 Donald L. Rubin and Kathryn L. Greene, "Effects of Biological and Psychological Gender, Age Cohort, and Interviewer Gender on Attitudes Toward Gender-

Inclusive/Exclusive Language," *Sex Roles* 24, 7/8 (1991): 391–412.

[24] Diana K. Ivy, Phil Backlund, and Manoocher "Mitch" Javidi, "The Lawyer, the Babysitter, and the Student: Nonsexist Language Usage and Instruction," paper presented at the Communication and Instruction Interest Group of the Western States Communication Association convention (Albuquerque, NM: February 1993).

[25] Jinni A. Harrigan and Karen S. Lucic, "Attitudes About Gender Bias in Language: A Reevaluation," *Sex Roles* 19, 3/4 (1988): 129–40.

[26] N. Henley and D. Dragun, "Survey of Attitudes Toward Changing Sex-Biased Language," paper presented at the Annual Convention of the American Psychological Association (Anaheim, CA: August 1983), as cited in Rubin and Greene, 1991.

[27] Robin Lakoff, *Language and Women's Place* (New York: Harper & Row, 1975).

[28] Jean Kantambu Latting, "Soliciting Individual Change in an Interpersonal Setting: The Case of Racially or Sexually Offensive Language," *Journal of Applied Behavioral Science* 29, 4 (December 1993): 464–84.

[29] Kenneth L. Dion and Albert A. Cota, "The Ms. Stereotype: Its Domain and the Role of Explicitness in Title Preference," *Psychology of Women Quarterly* 15 (1991), pp. 403–10.

[30] Norma J. Shepelak, Darlene Ogden, and Diane Tobin-Bennett, "The Influence of Gender Labels on the Sex Typing of Imaginary Occupations," *Sex Roles* 11, 11/12 (1984): 983–97.

[31] For a discussion about invisibility during the Clarence Thomas/Anita Hill hearings, see Judith K. Bowker, "Voice and Visibility in the Hill/Thomas Hearings," in *Outsiders Looking In*, ed. Paul Siegel (Hampton Press, in press).

[32] Cheris Kramarae and Paula A. Treichler, with assistance from Ann Russo, *A Feminist Dictionary* (London, Boston: Pandora Press, 1985).

[33] Ibid.

[34] Mary Field Belenky, Blythe McVicker Clinchy, Nancy Rule Goldberger, and Jill Mattuck Tarule, *Women's Ways of Knowing: The Development of Self, Voice, and Mind* (New York: Basic Books, Inc., Publishers, 1986).

[35] See Cheris Kramarae, *Women and Men Speaking* (Rowley, MA: Newbury House, 1981); Robin Lakoff, op cit., "Women's Language," *Language and Style* 10, 4 (1977): 222–47; Barbara and Gene Eakins, *Sex Differences in Human Communication* (Boston: Houghton Mifflin, 1978); Betty Lou DuBois and Isabel Crouch, eds., *The Sociology of the Languages of American Women* (San Antonio, TX: Trinity University, 1976); and Cynthia Berryman[-Fink], "Attitudes Toward Male and Female Sex-Appropriate and Sex- Inappropriate Language," in *Communication, Language, and Sex: Proceedings of the First Annual Conference*, ed. Cynthia L. Berryman and Virginia Eman (Rowley, MA: Newbury House, 1978), pp. 195–216.

[36] Jennifer A. Simkins-Bullock and Beth G. Wildman, "An Investigation into the Relationships Between Gender and Language," *Sex Roles*, 24, 3/4 (1991).

[37] Don Zimmerman and Candace West, "Sex Roles, Interruptions, and Silences in Conversations," in *Language and Sex: Difference and Dominance*, ed. Barrie Thorne and Nancy Henley (Rowley, MA: Newbury House, 1975), pp.

105–29; Candace West and Don Zimmerman, "Small Insults: A Study of Interruptions in Cross-Sex Conversations between Unacquainted Persons," in *Language, Gender, and Society*, ed. Barrie Thorne, Cheris Kramarae, and Nancy Henley (Rowley, MA: Newbury House, 1983), pp. 102–17.

[38] See William M. O'Barr and Bowman K. Atkins, "Women's Language or Powerless Language?" in *Women and Language in Literature and Society*, ed. Sally McConnell-Ginet et al. (New York: Praeger, 1980), pp. 93–110.

[39] Jennifer Simkins-Bullock and Beth G. Wildman, "An Investigation into the Relationships between Gender and Language," *Sex Roles* 24, 3/4 (1991): 149–60.

[40] Linda L. Carli, "Gender, Language, and Influence," *Journal of Personality and Social Psychology*, 59, 5 (1990): 941–51.

[41] Kathryn Quina, Joseph A. Wingard, and Henry G. Bates, "Language Style and Gender Stereotypes in Person Perception," *Psychology of Women Quarterly* 11 (1987): 111–22.

Chapter 4

Nonverbal Messages

"It was not *what* he said; it was *how* he said it. I'm convinced he doesn't believe me!" You may have repeated these phrases or have heard someone else say them. If you are like most people in our society, you use more than words to create or interpret meaning. We derive much of our meaning in an interpersonal interaction by interpreting nonverbal elements of the message. These unstated behaviors cover a very broad spectrum from the way you clear your throat to the way you walk across a room to how you embrace a family member. The details of your own nonverbal behavior may be largely invisible to you, while people who know you well may be able to describe or imitate the actions that are your nonverbal signature.

CHAPTER OVERVIEW

Gender roles are built largely on the nonverbal symbols that are encouraged or suppressed by the people important to you in your early years. Throughout life your responses to others' nonverbal cues act as rewards or punishments to those people in daily life. Women who behave in ways outside the nonverbal expectations for their sex—such as talking loudly or showing physical aggression—may be the object of gossip or subject to ridicule. Men who are less than 5 feet 10 inches tall or who have high-pitched, nonresonant voices may face negative reactions from people with whom they work or socialize.

Paul has some nonstandard nonverbal mannerisms. If you overlook or ignore them, he is a wonderful person—creative, cooperative, non-petty. . . . Well, how do you write a recommendation for a secondary elementary education major whose nonverbal presentation is exaggeratedly feminine? Specifically,

- *a high-pitched voice*
- *often with very breathy delivery*
- *mincing steps (when asking a favor), folding hands in a prayer-like pose, midchest, and strong head cant???*

I tried to figure out if I should metacommunicate with him about some of these things and decided to do so. We went to breakfast, chatted while I screwed up my courage. Finally, I said, "Paul, I've noticed some things that might help you be a more effective communicator . . ." Then I described what he did and explained that generally these were not normative for men in public settings. This is an example of men not being "privileged" to adopt "feminine" (in this culture) mannerisms. He was perceived as nerdy, a wimp, and gay (although he was married and has fathered two children).

You may notice some shifting and overlap in the range of nonverbal symbols that are portrayed in popular culture as acceptable for each sex. Yet most of us still find ourselves uneasy when people speak or act in ways that are hard to predict or are outside our own gender training. This chapter may help you recognize and interpret elements of the nonverbal communication patterns that occur around you. It also may help you decide which nonverbal symbols associated with your own sex are worth retaining and which may not fit you as an individual.

EXAMINING YOUR NONVERBAL BEHAVIOR

The following questions are intended to aid you in becoming more aware of your current nonverbal communication patterns. Consider not only which behaviors are characteristic of you but also those which you associate with negative or positive qualities in either men or women.

- Do you usually smile when meeting a stranger?
- Do you initiate a handshake at the start and end of a professional conference, or do you wait for the other person to do so?
- Do you carry a briefcase, a purse, or a fannypack?
- If you wear glasses, are the frames wire or plastic, and do they have initials on the lens or a designer emblem on the temple?
- Do you usually sit with your arms over the backs of the neighboring seats or with your hands held together in your lap?
- When you walk down a street, do you watch an approaching person until the two of you have passed each other, or do you lower your eyes before the other person does?
- Do people describe your voice as pleasing, powerful, sharp, sweet, authoritative, calm, intense, or uncertain?
- How much time did you spend deciding what clothes to wear today?
- How many items of clothing have you bought in the past month?
- Do you know anyone who is a foot taller or a foot shorter than you are? How do you feel about your height?
- When you guess friends' feelings based on their actions rather than their words, how often are you correct?
- Have you ever been told that you have good qualifications for a job but that you need to show more confidence?

Each of the above items involves one or more nonverbal symbols related to gender. The last two messages may seem more like psychology than communication. Of course, communication includes a focus on the ways humans receive and interpret the many nonverbal messages we send.

The major importance of nonverbal messages in daily life is often overlooked in the United States. We are intent on conveying verbal messages and finding, even inventing, the right words to fit almost every human experience. However, evidence suggests we believe what we observe through nonverbal cues more than we believe the words we hear. Often words are completely inadequate when confronting profound experiences of love, grief, gratitude, and empathy. Such dramatic occasions highlight our dependence on nonverbal communication.

The fact that this chapter follows the chapter about language is significant. Nonverbal is not verbal—not words; it is the "other part" of the communication message. Children learn about gender first by touch and sound and by observing what other human beings do in their presence. The foundation of what humans communicate to each other about being masculine and feminine is an enormous set of word-less events and examples, many of which could not be translated into words.

You probably learned your own nonverbal communication patterns through observation and imitation rather than from being "taught." You are not likely to know how you developed a particular gesture or vocal pattern. In fact, you may not even be aware of some of them. Adults often find that changing nonverbal patterns is difficult because these habits have been established for so long that they feel like "us" rather than like separate, alterable communication behaviors.

NONVERBAL IMAGES FROM EARLY LIFE

One way to become more in touch with your own early development of nonverbal patterns related to gender is to imagine communication events that can affect your views about the ways females or males look and sound. Here are some possibilities; some may fit your own experience and others may not. Think of any events that may have taught you something about the subtle, sensory aspects of being female or male in this society. Imagine

- a father leaving for work wearing a dark suit and a tie, a uniform, or work pants and shirt
- a little girl in a ruffled dress, hair bows, and patent leather shoes
- her brother in pants and knit shirt, with short hair that needs no combing
- girls holding dolls when they go to school or to stores
- boys fighting on the grass or walkway, while others watch, smile, and gently shake their heads
- females fixing small items like clothing; males fixing large machines such as automobiles
- couples in which the woman is taller than the man

- tall males smiling down at shorter partners; tall females slouching next to shorter partners
- advertisements with a woman gazing toward a man who is looking away from her
- clothes that hurt or bind: ties for him, shoes for her (or girdles or underwire bras)
- a female family member getting ready to go out for an evening, spending 45 minutes on hair and makeup
- a male family member taking 20 minutes to get ready for a date, 5 minutes of it on his hair
- girls giggling and glancing at boys; boys making efforts to ignore girls
- a pregnant woman being hugged, patted on the belly, and her condition openly addressed by strangers
- mothers hugging and kissing daughters and sons at important moments; fathers hugging daughters and shaking hands with sons

In reading the above series of examples, you may notice that some of the strongest unexamined beliefs you hold are connected with early communication experiences, largely nonverbal, that taught you rather clearly what went with your own or the other biological sex. Recognizing some of this early, unexamined nonverbal experience allows you to be more open to looking at the influences of nonverbal messages in your life.

Physically my sex is female. My parents identify my sex by choosing girl stuff for me. My room is pink; my toys are pink. On the contrary, my brother's stuff is all dark colors such as blue. My parents shaped my view that a girl has to be sensitive, vulnerable, whereas a boy has to be strong. When I fell down, I could cry and my parents would come to hold me immediately, whereas when my brother fell down, they wouldn't come to get him. They always said, "Big boys don't cry. You can get up by yourself." When my brother could get up and didn't cry, my parents would say, "Good boy."

Your own communication style arises from choices you make among the patterns you observe, the people you accept as models, the goals you have for communicating, and—quite importantly—your beliefs about which behaviors are appropriate for members of your sex.

CATEGORIES OF NONVERBAL BEHAVIOR

Nonverbal communication can be studied from a number of different vantage points; we have selected three that cover a wide range of sex and gender messages. Each vantage point offers a different angle of vision for analyzing the nonverbal elements of your daily interactions. We will examine (1) the locations from which nonverbal messages originate, (2) the functions of nonverbal communication in relation to language, and (3) the kinds of meaning that can be attached to nonverbal symbols in interpersonal encounters. In each case we will present basic information presently available on the nonverbal behaviors believed to be characteristic of women and of men.

LOCATIONS

The first way to categorize nonverbal cues is by the locations from which they originate. Nonverbal messages come from four primary locations: voice, face, body, and environment. Vocal cues include pitch, intonation, volume, pace, and vocal quality. Facial nonverbals include smiling, eye contact, head tilt, and other means of expression such as eyebrow or jaw movements. Nonverbals originating from the body in general include posture, gestures, whole-body movements, and touching. Also possible to include in this category are clothing and personal accessories. The environment is a source of nonverbal cues, including the amount of space between communicators, room colors and furnishings, light and noise, and customary uses of certain types of spaces, among other things.

FUNCTIONS

Another way to categorize nonverbal cues is according to the functions they serve in relation to verbal or language cues in communication. The eight major functions are (1) to reinforce the verbal, (2) to qualify the verbal (modify or change), (3) to replace verbal (substitute), (4) to demonstrate control or status, (5) to regulate interaction, (6) to convey cultural messages, (7) to convey relational messages, and (8) to contradict the verbal part of a message. Any nonverbal element may function in more than one of these ways simultaneously.

When someone waves to you, an energetic gesture accompanying the words "Bye for now!" may serve to *reinforce* the words and also to *regulate* the interaction between you. As a reinforcer, the wave gives a second channel through which you can gain information. As a regulator, it indicates your communication is over for now. If the other person says the same words while waving slowly and crying, you interpret the message differently; in this case the wave *qualifies* the verbal message (goodbye) by adding an emotional element of sadness. That emotional element also may function as a *relational message* that reflects on the closeness between you. If the person simply waves without a word, the action *replaces* the language cue; the fact that the person waves while leaving has *cultural implications* because not every culture makes that same gesture at that time. If, as the other person waves, they say, "I'm so sorry you have to go," but their wave is animated and energetic, the wave might function to *contradict the verbal*; you might believe the other person is glad to see you leave! Last, the other's wave may not give you a "goodbye" message at all. The wave may be agitated and forceful, sending you a *controlling* message to "get out of here." While these simple examples seem clear enough, most nonverbal messages are ambiguous and subject to misinterpretation. When they are combined with issues of sex and gender, the ambiguity and room for misinterpretation increases.

MEANING

If you are interested in how your own or others' nonverbal messages will be interpreted by receivers, you can examine the meanings people construct from nonverbal cues.

The meaning will derive from both the content (sometimes called "report") and the relationship (sometimes called "command") dimensions of the message.[1] The content is the information conveyed, whether that information is true or false, valid or invalid. If Jerome says to Louise, "I want to go to a movie tonight," the content consists of Jerome's expressed desires. The relationship dimension identifies the connection between the communicators. Whether Jerome speaks in a loud, directive voice or a soft, whining one establishes his perception of how he sees himself at this moment, how he sees Louise, and how he interprets the connection between them.

The relationship dimension regulates the ways we choose to interpret the message. As a result, Louise will interpret the meaning of Jerome's message based on her reading of his relationship message. If Jerome uses a stern tone and a loud voice, Louise may interpret the message to be a demand and may growl back, "Fine. We always do what you want to anyway." Notice that—as is true with every message we send—Louise is generating a relationship message of her own. If Jerome uses a soft, whiny approach, Louise may interpret his message as a request or a plea and may respond differently.

The meaning that is exchanged between Jerome and Louise includes far more than their relative desires to attend the movie. The relationship dimension—often carried nonverbally—functions in more subtle and more ambiguous ways than the content dimension. We have relatively stable reference systems to understand what Jerome means by "want" and "movie" and "tonight." Extracting meaning from tone of voice or facial expression or situational context is more complicated. The ambiguity of nonverbal communication can cause partners to misunderstand and misinterpret each other.

My boyfriend often comments about how my good friend and I can talk to each other without saying anything. We are able to look at each other and read each other. We are able to determine, without words, what the other is thinking. This is an awesome thing to be able to do. My boyfriend never knows what we are communicating and we rarely let him in on the secret.

Most women I know are able to do this, but I believe that you must have a relationship with someone that is very close. In my lifetime (so far), I have had four friends with whom I can communicate in this way. I like my ability to be able to accurately determine what my friends are communicating to me nonverbally. It is something I learned, and as long as I have close friends my nonverbal skills will continue to blossom.

Traditionally in the United States, women are socialized to be more aware of the subtle relational messages and men are socialized to "get to the bottom line." The common gender stereotype holds that she cares about relationships and feelings while he cares about content, report, and task. As with other stereotypes, some truth may be found in this distinction, as the cultural perspective implies. Yet do not assume that men are only interested in content and task while women are only interested in relationship and connection. When parents deal with their children's issues, both males and females find benefit in combining content and relationship skills; they find that critical to good parenting is understanding both the issue the child names and the relational messages the child may not be able to name. Likewise, in the workplace, using both dimensions to discuss an account with a client works to the advantage of both males and females.

Another way to categorize the kinds of meaning people can attach to their nonverbal encounters is according to levels of dominance (power or status); connection/distance, interest/disinterest, liking/disliking (immediacy), and general responsiveness.[2] Receivers may perceive a person's nonverbal messages as conveying low, moderate, or high levels of any one of these three qualities. Dominance indicators suggest a desire to lead or control an encounter. A person who shows high dominance will convey vocal, facial, and postural cues of being or expecting to be in charge of the situation. If nonverbals don't reflect dominance concerns, the person may not care about control but instead may be looking for means to effectively accomplish a cooperative task. A similar pattern can occur with respect to immediacy. If I act toward you as if it matters greatly to me that we have a friendly interaction, you may decide that the liking or connection dimension of nonverbal communication is most relevant at the moment. But if I act as if our dealings with each other should be on a straightforward, no-nonsense level, immediacy would appear to be irrelevant to me or an unwelcome distraction. The third dimension of meaning, responsiveness, involves how much energy or involvement an individual contributes to a communication encounter. Vocal variety, facial animation, and energetic gestures can all be indicators of high personal involvement and interest. In contrast, such cues as eyes rolled toward the ceiling, arms stretched wide, and long yawns show low involvement or boredom—as many teachers and preachers can confirm! The dimensions of dominance, liking, and responsiveness are useful in revealing aspects of a communication event that you might miss if you looked for meanings only in verbal statements.

Sex-Linked Differences in Nonverbal Behavior

Table 4.1 examines some of the recent findings from research into women's and men's nonverbal communication patterns. Before we summarize any research results, however, a reminder is necessary. Because most people think that learned behaviors based on gender ideals are natural outcomes of one's sex, it can be hard to distinguish which nonverbal patterns are taught to children and adults through modeling and imitation. This table is titled expectations rather than behaviors because we know more about which gender-based message cues people are expected to use than about how often a given individual actually uses any of these cues in a given setting.

Table 4.1 Nonverbal Behavior Expectations Related to Gender Ideals

Nonverbal location	Gender stereotype	
	Feminine	Masculine
Voice	Higher pitch, varied intonation, softer on average	Lower pitch, sometimes monotone, louder on average
Body	Arms and legs crossed, enclosed appearance, head tilted, clothing decorative, may initiate hugs with either sex	Arms and legs stretched, open appearance, head erect, clothing more uniform, may initiate touch of female in work or social settings
Face	Frequent smiles, watch while listening	Reduced facial animation, look away often as speaker or listener
Environment	Claim limited space, use color and objects to convey mood	Claim large personal space, use color and objects to show power

Research results to date concerning nonverbal cues and the sexes reveal several tentative patterns. In one study, for example, the author discovered participants' perceptions about females and males mirrored sex stereotypes: women were perceived by participants to be "fluent, skilled, and involved communicators. Men were perceived as more dysfluent, less skilled, restless, and loud."[3] In general, men tend to expand and women to contract nonverbally when it comes to vocal features and body movements. Women seem to be more expansive in the use of facial nonverbal cues, while men are more restricted in facial expression. As for nonverbals related to the physical environment, the results suggest men occupy and use more space and larger spaces than women; in addition, males and females use objects and colors for different purposes.

These summary statements require two important qualifications. The research on women's communication with other women suggests that women talking with one another may show different nonverbal patterns because they focus less on dominance issues than do their male counterparts, take more pleasure in communicative creativity, and possibly make stronger efforts nonverbally to resolve conflict through identifying with the other.[4] The nonverbal research to date is severely limited as it relates to people of varying races, ages, classes, ethnicities, geographical backgrounds, and sexual orientations. The primary research subject has been the white, middle-class college student under the age of 25, so the conclusions cited here are by no means adequate to describe the behavior of all communicators. You should recall these limitations as you review table 4.1, for it provides only modest predictability about the current nonverbal behaviors of men or women.

VOCAL CUES

What do you expect to be distinctive about women's voices as compared to men's? The most obvious answer is pitch. Pitch can affect both the function of nonverbal communication and the meaning we attribute to it. On the average, the pitch of men's voices after puberty is lower than that of women's voices. That in itself is not surprising, since the vocal folds in the female larynx are generally shorter than the vocal folds in the male larynx. The degree of difference between the sexes widens as boys and girls develop, not only in pitch but also in volume, rate, and quality or timbre.

Jacqueline Sachs found that listeners to audiotapes judged accurately the sexes of 10-year-old male and female children, except when they were hearing girls who considered themselves tomboys. Listeners mislabeled these girls as boys. No physical difference was found in the vocal apparatus of these girls as compared to other girls; the difference was one of vocal quality, a subtle characteristic that was apparently learned along with other skills when the girls engaged in activities that were identified with masculine interests.[5] At the other extreme, certain young girls and women with soft, breathy, high-pitched voices are noticed by voice professionals because they speak at the upper end of their natural pitch range rather than in the middle of their range. Girls may learn to use softer, higher voices because they are seen as conveying a positive gender message of innocence and need for relationship, despite the possible risk of being labeled "flaky" or "bimbo." Since the gender stereotype for a sex is more comfortable for most people than deviation from that stereotype, girls may learn to use higher pitches to enhance the immediacy (liking) component of meaning in nonverbal interactions.

If a breathy, high-pitched, hesitant voice characterizes the gender role stereotype for women, the portrait of the "masculine voice" is quite different. Men's voices are pitched lower than are women's, and young men often work to lower their pitch and increase their volume in order to sound more authoritative. Because lower pitch is equated with credibility, some women undergo similar vocal retraining to improve their prospects for business and political success, especially work in television or radio. In terms of vocal variety and pacing, men generally lower both their pitch and their volume at the end of a sentence, while women often end sentences with an upward intonation, implying either continuation or questioning. These uses of pitch constitute regulatory functions because they guide the interaction through conversation turns. Within a given message, more women than men vary their intonation, or "speech melodies." Men's louder speaking volume often adds to their perceived authority by filling the space in which they are speaking, but that authority is sometimes undercut by monotonous speech patterns and long utterances without a break or a question. The volume also can create the sensation of dominance. A man may speak to a small group in a voice that is louder than necessary for the size of the group. A woman in the same group may direct her message to a single individual, speaking with a voice too low to be heard throughout the group; in this way, she also makes meaning with regard to dominance.

Because we count on vocal differences between the sexes as cues to an individual's sex, we can be unnerved by encountering someone whose voice does not fit a name or appearance. While Barbara was drafting this section of the book, she received a business phone call meant for her husband, and it reminded her forcefully of this problem. The person sounded female, so when she heard the name, "David," at the other end of the line, she asked again for the name, presuming she had heard it wrong. Finally she decided that it was simply a higher-pitched voice in the body of a male. (She later learned to her surprise that David is over 6 feet tall and husky, quite different from her mental picture of him!) The pitch of David's voice gave Barbara a cultural message; in the United States culture, high pitch is equated with femininity. Barbara's responsiveness was mediated in some part by her expectation based on the voice pitch. This small communication episode suggests that people whose voices do not seem to agree with their biological sex category may face more questioning or more distrust from others, since receivers feel more comfortable when the verbal and nonverbal messages fit together.

Each of the vocal patterns described here has a biological element, but each is also largely explainable by the notion that gender-related patterns are created, perpetuated, and evaluated in everyday communication. Voices can even establish or end careers, depending on the perceptions and stereotypes of decision makers. Cheris Kramarae discovered, for example, that the British Broadcasting Corporation had claimed that women newscasters' voices were clear and effective for use on the BBC during World War II, a time when many potential male newscasters were not available. At the end of the war, when these males returned to England, the same women's voices were reevaluated as being unpleasant and inappropriate for reporting serious or "hard" news.[6] Recall our discussion about difference and evaluation. Nonverbal meaning and function is interpretative in nature; the differences between voice pitches becomes problematic only when they are evaluated in such a way as to disadvantage one group and not another.

BODY CUES: POSITION, MOVEMENT, AND TOUCH

As in the case of voices, you will not be surprised by some of the findings about how people use their bodies—in posture as well as in gestures, touch, and general body movements. When people believe their personal space is being invaded, both men and women allow women to come closest to them and both men and women keep men at a distance.[7] Men tend to expand to fill their social space while they are receiving messages, either in work settings or informal social settings. Imagine a male leaning back, his legs stretched out 2 to 3 feet apart or crossed, ankle on knee. His arms are likely to be crossed behind his head or extended across the backs of the chairs beside his own. A clear biological component of these nonverbal behaviors is the size of the person in question. Men with long legs, long trunks, and long arms often describe themselves as cramped in office, theater, plane, or institutional seating. However, biology cannot be the total explanation for these actions, since short men also tend to spread themselves out in similar ways. Status and control can result as a function of this nonverbal use of space; dominance can result as meaning.

As a male, I am aware of the fact that socially, in order to keep my masculinity, I should not cross my legs. This disturbs me because sometimes it is comfortable to cross them. However, every time I do, I become so self-conscious of what I am doing that I am unable to relax. Am I too worried about my image and about how people are viewing me? I have heard women say that they don't find it attractive when men cross their legs. It is not common for them to do so, even though it is a comfortable way to sit.

I think this is an American phenomenon because in Europe the males are not as restricted about crossing their legs. This is very strange but really should be the least of my worries. Why am I self-conscious, and why don't I just sit like I want? I don't know. I'll blame society.

The posture and movement cues of women suggest a different pattern. Women in many settings tend to hold their limbs nearer to their trunks than men do. In small groups or working pairs containing both sexes, women have more often been seen folding their arms or clasping their hands in front of them rather than extending their arms above or away from their bodies. Women's legs are more often crossed ankle to ankle or knee to knee, rather than the knee-to-ankle pattern associated with men. A tilt of the head is seen frequently in photographs of women. It gives the appearance that the woman is shorter than the person she is with, and it is a movement almost never linked with highly "masculine" men. In terms of posture and movement, women in male-female interactions often appear to use as small a space as they can, contracting the body as much as possible. One explanation for this different "feminine" pattern comes from the training to "act like a lady" that many young girls receive. In this training, crossing the legs and keeping the limbs close to the body connotes a propriety that contrasts with the "loose woman" stereotype, in which the woman who fails to protect her body in social settings fails to protect her virginity as well. Despite significant changes since the 1950s when admonitions about "being a lady" were prevalent, how women use their bodies remains similar to patterns at that time.

When my mom is mad she stares at the TV with her legs and arms crossed. She always chews gum at a rather speedy pace. My brothers and I always laugh because she will say nothing is wrong, but she says it in a way so that we know something is wrong.

My baseball coach, however, is much different. When he gets mad, he puts his hands either in his back pocket or hunches his back and puts his hands to his knees. The biggest thing he does is get really close to you. He violates that space or comfort zone. He doesn't have to say one word and you know by his actions that you're in trouble. He can use his eyes to make you wilt.

Research on touch investigates frequency and kinds of touch as well as meaning derived from touch. Men touch other men with the least frequency, perhaps due to homophobic attitudes.[8] Other findings indicate that men touch women more than women touch men,[9] both in work settings and in general social interaction; however, some scholars suggest that males and females touch each other with equal frequency.[10] Because men have more power in the society, women may be more alert to a man's touch, trying to discern meaning. As a result, they may recall those touches more vividly than others or than men recall women's touches.[11] These kinds of considerations in research are important for us to think about.

Research also varies in recording the kinds of touching that occurs. Touch can range from an arm across the other's shoulders, a hand on the other's back, a pat on the head or on the behind, to other gestures that are explicitly erotic. During courtship, males interpret some of these more intimate touches as playful or fun while females often interpret them as unpleasant.[12] The ambiguity of meaning can present difficult communication problems between partners.

Meaning of touch seems to be linked to perceived dominance. In a public context, researchers discovered men responded negatively to women who touched them if the men thought the women were of equal status; men did not respond negatively if they thought the women were of higher status. Men may perceive equals as potential competitors and therefore respond negatively. Women did not respond negatively to men who touched them regardless of the men's status.[13] Perhaps women find touching and being touched more consistent with their gender stereotype, while males seem to find touch warranted only by the higher status of the other person. Touch may be interpreted as assertiveness or aggression; men may perceive the touch from a competitive perspective. These reactions to touch may contribute to the disturbing findings that submissive women are rated as more attractive than dominant ones.[14] The male patterns of response to touch may be traced to research on boys and girls that shows boys engage in defensive self-touching behaviors (like crossing the arms or gesturing with their hands as if to deflect a blow) much more frequently than girls.[15]

When I was growing up, it was not uncommon to show affection to the members of my family and friends. I was brought up to hug people, hold hands and kiss friends on the cheek to show respect and affection. Eye contact and numerous other nonverbals are prevalent in the Filipino culture. It is normal for brothers and sisters in their young adult age to hold hands in public. In the Western culture, that is almost unheard of. Even friendships have more affectionate physical activity than in the Western culture. Growing up with this cultural difference, I have picked up the idea that it is OK to show unconditional affection toward people. I hold more eye contact, display more nonverbals, and physically express my emotions toward other people more often than most males. This is because of my culture and the gender roles it has created for me.

Different kinds of touches can be used by each sex to achieve different goals. Men are more likely to initiate touch when they are dating, perhaps to attract a partner or fulfill a courting ritual. Females interpret more intimate touch as higher relational commitment[16] and are more likely to initiate it after marriage, perhaps to express communion.[17] Another kind of touch has been studied less often but is of equal importance. Observation and personal reports confirm that women initiate hugs and embraces with other women, men, and children far more often than do men. Unlike the patterns of movement already mentioned, the activity of hugging is clearly an expansive movement and a symbol of close relationship. As the cultural viewpoint from chapter 2 suggests, intimacy is part of the sphere in which women are expected to be at ease. In contrast, touches by male to female that reinforce status differences or presume some form of sexual relationship do not necessarily connote affection or interpersonal commitment.

Receivers of touch communication often must analyze whether the touch is intended to convey immediacy or dominance, or—even more difficult—whether the touch is being masked as immediacy while conveying dominance. At the relational level, women and men often differ about where the line exists between a man's expression of friendly affection and his effort to assert sexual dominance. One way to gauge whether a nonverbal gesture connotes immediacy or dominance would be to imagine doing the same gesture to someone who is an equal, a superior, or someone of the same sex. Avoiding messages of sexual dominance and recognizing differences in the meanings construed by males and females with regard to touch can reduce relational tension in a communication environment.

Relational tension may exist because of feelings of attraction. Research about attractiveness consistently finds that men are found attractive based on their faces and women are evaluated based on their faces and their bodies.[18] In Western cultures, such as the United States, visual cues seem more important than, for example, audio ones like voice. How attractive a man's face is seems to be highly correlated with how attractive we find the man to be. When we evaluate a woman, we consider both her face and her body.

In my experience in college, I have only had one boyfriend and dated a couple of others, but no huge significant relationships. At the beginning of this year, my dad decided that I need "girl clothes." He thought this would help me get dates. You see, in high school, I dressed very feminine, yet I was athletic. When I came to college, dressing up for class went away altogether. I only wore jeans, and sometimes ones with holes, baggy shirts, and rarely showered before class. Even though I don't think I was the only college coed who did this, my dad felt as though I should clean up my act because I had become "just one of the guys."

My dad was putting me into stereotypical roles of a female. He felt I needed to dress nice, not sexy but nice and feminine. He was forcing a gender on me that I now recognize did not fit. Although I like to dress nice, I am not stereotypical.

A major form of body communication is clothing. For the sexes, the primary distinction is between the more subdued, basically unchanging business uniform of men and boys and the more vibrant, constantly changing styles for women and girls. Shifts toward greater variety of color and pattern in males' clothing have decreased the ranges of differences, but women's clothing is still more decorative than functional especially in formal or "dress-up" occasions. "No back" dresses, strapless attire, and outfits with plunging necklines all are designed to display women's bodies; jewelry often is used to accentuate the neck or hands. Men's bodies are not exhibited through clothing in a similar way.

Women's clothes are also geared toward demonstrating that a woman is both attractive and linked with someone of high enough status to support her wardrobe preferences. Jewelry may perform the status function, for diamonds and gold are marketed as financial investments as well as symbols of love and social rank.

FACIAL CUES

A basic element of the gender stereotype for either sex is that one's eye movements and facial expression should convey femininity or masculinity appropriately. Most people believe women should look pleasant and receptive, while men should look strong and in control. Deviation from either of these ideal patterns tends to be noticed by observers and can often become a matter of concern. How well do the sexes adhere to these ideals? The research to date confirms that girls smile more often than boys,[19] women smile more often than men,[20] women show anger less often than men,[21] and females sometimes smile when the situation appears to be at odds with their facial expression, such as in the midst of an argument. Recent research explores the possibility that charismatic women (but not men), who are highly expressive and skilled at nonverbal facial expression, may learn to use those skills to mask dominant or aggressive personalities, personalities not acceptable in females in this culture. Perceived by others as friendly, these women may be behaving in culturally acceptable ways that concur with the expectation that women are warm and unthreatening.[22] Males, on the other hand, often show almost no facial expression during a conversation or in conflict, thus giving no cues to others about how to interpret their words or their silences.

These facial cues can be sources of confusion when the sexes interpret them differently. When men interact with women, they may perceive the women as displaying more sexuality than the women perceive of themselves. In addition, the men may interpret the women as having more desire to see them again than the women report having. The differences in interpretation may confuse both men and women, the man calling the woman a tease and the woman calling the man arrogant.[23]

Regarding eye contact, men usually look away from each other in a dialogue or in a small group, both when speaking and when listening to someone else speak. One exception is that a male may return his gaze to the other person's face just at the end of his message, as a signal to the other that he is ready for a response. Women, in contrast, tend to look for extended periods at a speaker when they are listening to an oral message, but some look away from individual listeners much of the time when they are speaking to a group. Further, in passing each other in a hallway, it appears that men continue to gaze toward the person they are passing longer than women continue to look at the person they are passing.

Some analysts of these nonverbal patterns have asserted that women's smiles and gazes show a constant need for approval by the other person. Most interpersonal interactions require far more complex analyses. If you consider male and female behaviors as interdependent during a conversation, you can see that an absence or small amount of verbal or nonverbal cues on the part of the male may allow him to alter the conversation to his advantage.

In my personal relationship, my boyfriend and I have very different notions of communication. He thinks I think too much about little details. This is especially evident when I reflect on a fight or something he said. He can't stand it!

I can't stand it when he never cares about the details of what I have said. What I mean by this is that I often give clues in my communication as to what I need or want. He hardly ever picks up on them. This communication habit gets us both in trouble. I am trying to teach him my communication style but it is rarely effective.

From the power dominant perspective, the person who withholds information from another establishes the more powerful position. If she wishes to gain access to the information, the female must try to learn whatever she can by analyzing the male's nonverbal cues. From a rhetorical position, she may look for nonverbal or verbal cues to discern what little she can about the current level of trust in the relationship. She may engage in an empowerment move by sending cues to demonstrate the intention to promote a positive relationship. If the male partner adheres to a dominant power position, these cues can be interpreted as indicators that she is in a "one-down" position, a subordinate or submissive position. From that dominant perspective, messages requesting connection or cooperation may be interpreted as messages from the less powerful; they may be used to establish her as more in need of the current relationship than he is. The ambiguities and power of nonverbal messages require a great deal of attention in order to perceive the nuances.

ENVIRONMENT

The fourth area of nonverbal distinctions between the sexes involves messages related to one's environment: amounts and types of physical space, uses of color and furnishings, behavior related to objects, amounts and types of light, and noise.

In terms of amounts and types of physical space, men often have larger work spaces available to them than their female co-workers. The nonverbal differences of space are linked with differences of power. People with high status and high incomes tend to occupy large, high-ceilinged, expensively furnished, and private spaces—spaces that those of lower status and income must ask permission to enter.

In face-to-face interactions, women appear to allow other people to stand closer to them than men do, and women seem to command less space when they are moving through social environments. I have sometimes asked students to test these statements by walking down a crowded hallway and watching to see which sex tends to move aside more often. The results have been consistent: women move aside more for both men and women, and they tend to carry their books in front of them so that the overall width of body plus objects is less than it is when a male walks down the hall. How much this particular pattern of female restriction and male expansion is based on direct training or on observation of same-sex models is not clear, but it is clear that many young women do not demand much personal space when in the presence of males.

Culture greatly influences how the sexes use personal space. In countries like Nigeria where males and females are segregated for most of their school years, both sexes use greater space when they meet together.[24] In India, a woman's use and preference for space appears to be related to her class.[25] In other cultures, women's preferences for space—especially with men who are strangers—seem to be related to the culture's norms with regard to violence against women.[26] Understanding how space is used differently in different cultures illuminates the particular functions and meanings of space in the United States.

Regarding color and its uses, women in many cultures seem to use and notice a wider range of color in their home or work environments and in their choices of clothing. Yet this difference is also confounded by other factors. Sex differences in use of color can be attributed partly to a biological difference, for many more males than females are color-blind. Many men report that their wives, professional "shoppers," or other females they know pick out their clothing for them and "match" shirts and pants.

In terms of use of objects, differences between the sexes occur in odd ways. Many old divisions have fallen away. Some employed women have given up purses in favor of briefcases, but "purse" is still the word to refer to the bag carried by a female. Some men who work elsewhere than in business settings now carry backpacks or leather shoulder cases, but they are not referred to as "purses" without some connotation attached. Clothing pieces, like underwear, identify interesting differences. Men perusing the women's lingerie department are more suspect than women in the men's underwear section. If men handle women's underwear, the act often is connected to sexuality, perhaps as an indication of a sexual relationship or imaginary liaison. If women handle men's underwear, the act often is connected to doing laundry!

On the other hand, many objects that once were sex-typed have become more accessible to both sexes: for example, car and car repair parts, construction site objects, athletic accoutrements like shot puts or javelins or soccer balls, kitchen utensils, aprons, and earrings. While progress has been made toward sharing these objects, we still

GUYS SAY WE'RE MOODY AND EMOTIONAL. LET'S SEE HOW THEY FEEL AFTER 8 HOURS IN AN UNDERWIRE.

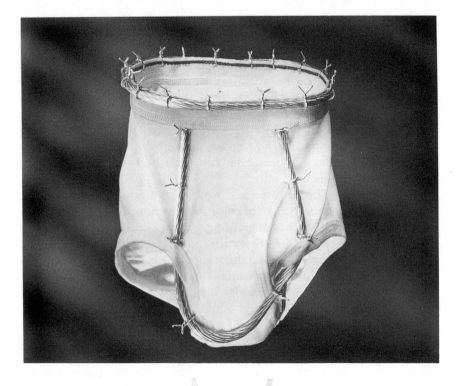

Chances are, few men would choose to wear a device that pokes, pinches and rides up into their delicate parts. So why should we? Introducing Magic Ring, the first true wireless support bra by Lovable. With unique

Magic Ring™
Wearing is believing™

Comfort Panels™ stitched into the garment running from cup to shoulder, it cradles you in soft fabric. Instead of hard steel. Giving you the same shape and support as a wire. Without radically altering your state of mind.

by LOVABLE.♡

The Lovable Company

have masculine and feminine connotations that change the nonverbal message we send and receive by using these objects.

This discussion of sex-linked differences in nonverbal behaviors include qualifiers such as "customary," "tendency," and "in male-female interactions." Research into the nonverbal communication patterns of men and women has focused almost entirely on Caucasian people in the United States, and sometimes on men as the representative adults. Because cultural groups are major agents of instruction in body movement, touch, and other forms of expression, our knowledge is severely limited. As more and more people live and work in circumstances where they can act as partners or colleagues, the literal freedom of movement for both women and men of many ethnicities, ages, races, and classes may increase.

Interpreting Mixed Nonverbal Cues

As mentioned earlier, when the words we hear contradict what we see or believe to be true, most of us believe the nonverbal rather than the verbal information. We may have noticed that many people, including ourselves, can manage to lie to other people with words. Nonverbal cues, however, are harder to control; most of us cannot deceive as well nonverbally as we can verbally. As a result, we have learned to look to the nonverbal cues as carriers of the "real" message even if the words tell us something else.

From the cultural perspective, this reliance on nonverbal meanings makes interpretation of meaning more complex. Consider the example of eye contact. Deborah Tannen explains that during an important conversation between close friends, males may sit side by side, looking down or around the room as they talk. Females may sit face to face, making nearly continuous eye contact, often touching.[27] Now imagine what each of the sexes might interpret from these nonverbal cues if they were to talk with each other. The male may interpret the female's touch or eye contact as invasive and suffocating; the female may interpret the male's lack of eye contact and deflected body position as indifferent and disconfirming. The verbal message between the two may be modified by these relationship messages carried nonverbally.

From a power perspective, the complexity increases. If Charles contradicts his, "Yes, I'm listening!" by burying his face in a newspaper, Carlene is left interpreting cultural differences ("I can listen without making eye contact") and power dimensions as well ("My newspaper reading—or my way of communicating—is more important than you or your way of communicating"). Likewise, a male may experience contradiction when a female says she likes gentleness and emotional expression in males but then is more attracted to males who do not exhibit those behaviors. He may feel he is in a "one down" position because he believes he risked his social status to incorporate these stereotypically feminine behaviors.[28]

Mixed nonverbal cues often are used in music videos where some females may appear in low-cut outfits or suggestive body suits (complying with the feminine stereotype) but may also be screaming into the microphone or engaging in aggressive behaviors (rejecting the feminine stereotype). Likewise, males may be presented with contradictory gender stereotypes. Some of these images may reflect the cultures of certain street communities where mixed cues create paradoxes involving drugs and sexuality.[29]

We use nonverbal cues to determine if we believe the mixed message is strategic and intentional. Nonverbal cues also may inform us that the mixed message is a result of confusion, misinformation, or lack of information. Sometimes metacommunicating about the implicit messages in nonverbal behaviors can clarify meaning. Since nonverbal behavior so often carries relational messages, however, the metacommunication can be tentative, intricate, and difficult to navigate.

NONVERBALS, GENDER, AND POWER

Nancy Henley's book, *Body Politics: Power, Sex, and Nonverbal Communication*, develops the thesis that nonverbal messages particularly reflect and reinforce power. Higher or lower status in a relationship can be conveyed through the nonverbal aspects of an encounter. We can recognize power differences in nonverbal communication not only in male-female encounters but also in those of people of differing ethnic backgrounds, age groups, or educational levels. Henley uses the term, "micropolitical cues," to refer to the small details of nonverbal behavior that indicate the power or status of participants in a given conversation, project, or intimate relationship.[30]

Height and physical attractiveness are strong micropolitical cues in our society. We expect tall, good-looking people to be trustworthy and wise. The political element here is particularly subtle, since people don't control their height and can affect their attractiveness only within limits. What may happen is that a tall, attractive person, customarily a male but now increasingly a female as well, receives general positive reinforcement from others during adolescence and young adulthood, based on the individual's physical appearance and stimulus value to others. The positive verbal and nonverbal messages build confidence, leading the tall, attractive person to act more and more like a leader. The self-fulfilling prophecy is operating here. What we expect to happen is more likely to happen simply because we act as if it will happen. The impact of this phenomenon goes beyond the individual to advertising firms and large corporations. Tall, attractive males are expected by others to be leaders or executives, and they often expect the same of themselves.

Another micropolitical cue concerns the use of silence. Silence often is construed negatively, although this attitude is not universal. Apache couples expect to remain silent for hours at a time, especially during the initial stages of courting. Silence is interpreted as a means to get to know the other.[31] Many of us react less favorably to conversations that contain silences; in fact, research shows we experience more anxiety-producing thoughts if the silences are not accompanied by some kind of activity that warrants them.[32]

As a result of our attitude about silence, silence by one individual in the company of another can reinforce the first person's status and prerogative. Pausing or leaving silent lapses in the conversation are means by which silence is used. Men exhibit more silence in mixed-sex conversations than women. A man's silence in conversation often is interpreted as an agent of power. When men either do not answer a request or do not respond to a woman's talk, their silence is perceived as a means to control both floor and turn in the talk.

Another set of micropolitical cues that have gained attention are visual displays of dominance. When researchers say, "visual dominance," they are referring to the comparative percentage of how much a person looks at another while talking compared to how much the person looks at another while listening. High-power people look at the other person both while speaking and listening; low-power people tend to look at the other person more while listening than while talking. When the task of a mixed-sex group is traditionally feminine in nature (such as quilting or book clubs), women show more high-power visual dominance; however, when the task is either masculine (such as changing a tire or chopping down a tree) or neutral (such as applying the Heimlich maneuver or growing a vegetable garden), men show more high-power visual dominance. One team of researchers found that when both sexes were given special training before the task, the task became more familiar and the sex differences in visual display of dominance and power disappeared.[33] They suggested that the difference in visual dominance display had more to do with preparation than sex differences, but that it also depended on interest, confidence, interpersonal influence, and how familiar the task was to the men and women. These findings indicate that the socialization of the sexes contributes to the power bias in mixed-sex groups more than innate abilities of each sex.

These micropolitical cues can affect the shape and configuration of the conversation. How women conduct conversations with other women differs from the way they conduct conversations with men. In mixed-sex conversations, women converge to men's conversation behaviors.[34] In other words, conversations in mixed-sexed groups and all male groups look very much alike; conversations in all female groups look different than the other two. Some scholars suggest that much of the work about nonverbals, gender, and power has tended to mold women's talk to imitate men's talk rather than integrating the styles to create new patterns.

Managing One's Own Interpersonal Cues

One of the most puzzling communication issues for adult women and adult men today is how to respond to a mixture of pressures to exhibit feminine, masculine, and gender-neutral nonverbal behavior. While men may receive negative responses for enacting feminine behaviors, their pressure to do so generally does not emanate from their source of economic livelihood. The problem is acute for women who interact in both professional and intimate situations. Audrey Nelson has written about an apparent contradiction between women's supposed superiority in interpreting nonverbal messages from others and their frequent inability to show confidence and competence in sending nonverbal messages to others.[35] Nelson does not offer a complete solution to the problem, but she cites the nonverbal rules and examples learned in early life as part of its cause.

Many young girls hear from different sources that they should be restrained and should avoid calling attention to themselves. Boys, in contrast, are told early in life to "stand tall," to "act like a man," and to show confidence and assertiveness even if that means contradicting their inner feelings. These two gender communication stereotypes have traditionally been interdependent. Young girls figure out that others will reward them for being quiet, clean, passive, and polite. Young boys learn that being active in the outdoors and forceful in defending themselves will win praise. Attempts to change the climate for young boys are less visible than those to change the climate for young girls. Demonstrating that change is an advertisement for Nike that reiterates over and over again, "If you let me play sports. . . ." The ensuing message—that playing sports will make girls stronger and healthier and will increase self-esteem—challenges the stereotype of protecting females. The depictions of females diving for soccer balls and stretching up to basketball hoops diverge from the stereotypical feminine picture. This change in climate signals movement toward incorporating masculine activities or values into a female's life; it does not signal incorporation of feminine activities or values into males' lives.

Some women struggle to accommodate both genders. According to researcher-consultant Janet Lee Mills, many women in the workplace have trouble displaying a combination of femininity and power.[36] As we will discuss in chapter 8, our expectations of power and of femininity sometimes are antithetical; women find themselves caught between wanting to assert authority and wanting to maintain their femininity. For example, lower pitched voices are more authoritative; feminine voices are higher pitched. Higher volume indicates power; feminine speakers are taught to lower their volumes. In *Speechless*, Michael Keaton suggests to Gena Davis that if she wants to command the attention of her boss, she should raise the volume of her voice when she speaks to him. She tries it; it works. When she raises her voice to her boss, however, everyone in the office stops and stares. Later, the boss tells her she need not be angry. That scene demonstrates the effects women anticipate when they make choices between femininity and power.

One of the barriers women and men face in learning new and different nonverbal behaviors is the lack of role models who affirm themselves as members of a particular sex but also incorporate images of power and strength for women and images of gentleness and care for men. Misunderstanding the issues of difference and evaluation can cause people to resist the emergence of these role models. For them, seeing an assertive leader who is a woman or a caring manager who is a man violates old stereotypes and threatens their clear divisions between the sexes.

Sensitivity to others and awareness of one's own bodily experience are qualities of potential usefulness to men as well as women. Researchers claim that more "masculine" females and more "feminine" males are better at decoding nonverbal messages.[37] In addition, when both people in a dyad are good at decoding nonverbal messages, they seem to eliminate the effects of traditional sex-role expectations.[38] When both men in an interaction decoded nonverbal messages well, the men rated their interactions as higher in emotional sharing. When both women in an interaction decoded nonverbal messages well, both women rated their interactions as higher in being able to influence each other. This sex-role reversal may suggest that each sex can benefit by learning the behaviors traditionally assigned to the other.

In professional and college sports, males historically were rewarded for ignoring pain and pushing their bodies to extremes. Female athletes are increasing in numbers, and they are being trained in the same mode. Males still dominate the public workplace where people are often rewarded for long hours, frequent travel, long commuting distances—all stresses to the body and mind that go unnoticed when they are considered unchangeable. The fact that men still far outnumber women in stress-related illnesses such as ulcers, heart attacks, and strokes confirms the seriousness of inattention to nonverbal messages from one's own body. As more women have entered the public workplace in the United States, alcoholism and physical illness in females have increased. Unfortunately the development of effective role models who can balance the demands placed upon them with their physical well-being lags behind the changes of the last twenty-five years.

Conclusion

Although we do not have complete knowledge about sex-linked distinctions in nonverbal behavior, differences have been observed between the sexes in eye contact, smiles, amount of personal space, and touching. Power is clearly a factor in nonverbal interactions, and belief systems regarding the centrality of relationships may influence behaviors such as eye contact, hugging, and regulating space between communicators.

Within the limits of gender role training, each person to some degree learns and changes throughout a lifetime, developing new nonverbal as well as verbal responses to circumstances. Knowing a wide array of nonverbal cues and their effects, including those cues that are associated positively with both sexes, can give you more opportunity to develop a set of nonverbal patterns that will meet your individual and interpersonal goals effectively.

QUESTIONS FOR DISCUSSION

1. Think of two or three early nonverbal images you can recall receiving that showed you what men or women were like and how each was expected to behave. Have you seen evidence that any of those early images still has influence in your life?

2. Think of the voices you particularly like or dislike, either in people you communicate with frequently or in media personalities that you see and hear on a regular basis. Have you ever chosen or rejected a television program based on the voice(s) involved? Have you ever reacted to a voice that seemed to you inappropriate for that person's sex?

3. Body ideals are highly visible in the mass media, and body-building or fitness programs are on the increase. How pleased, guilty, ambitious, ashamed, resigned, or otherwise are you about your body, and with whom have you shared those perceptions?

4. How uneasy are you with a woman in the workplace who shows "masculine-identified" nonverbal behavior? With a man who shows "feminine-identified" nonverbal behavior? How similar or different are your evaluations of the two people?

5. Discuss with others your beliefs about (a) how feasible and (b) how ethical it is to change one's nonverbal message sending to better meet personal goals.

CASES FOR ANALYSIS

CASE 4.1   THE UNKNOWN PRESCHOOLER (A STUDENT CONTRIBUTION)

I worked with the local Family Network this summer as the child coordinator. The first day, thirty other people and I were checking in the kids as the parents dropped them off. After the parents had left there was this one kid for whom we did not have a name. The child was approximately three years old but didn't talk very clearly. None of us could decide what sex the child was. The child had long hair but a receding hairline look. The child was built larger than the other children, stocky, and spoke in a very harsh, loud tone. We found later that it was a very boyish-looking girl.

What I found interesting is how important it was that we had to know what sex the child was to really feel comfortable talking to her and directing her to "appropriate activities." Though we had mostly games that both sexes enjoyed, I would not ask a boy if he wanted to play with dolls. After thinking about how big of a dilemma the situation was, I realized how often people do question the sex. When judging a person's actions, we have to ask ourselves, "Is it a boy or a girl?"

1. Think of any experience you have had in which the sex of the other person was ambiguous to you, even for a short time. What did you do? What did you think about? Did you extend an interaction in order to gain a clear answer?

2. Consider the places in your environment where the dress of men and of women is expected to be the most different. Where is it allowed to be the most similar? How important are these variations?

3. What are your own preferences in clothing? In hairstyle?

4. Talk with others about the positive and negative aspects of unisex appearance in women and men.

CASE 4.2   SMILE

Penny sat down on the one soft chair in her apartment, ignoring its softness because she was so angry at herself. She just realized that she had once again let her nonverbal behavior contradict her true feelings about something important to her. Joe, a male friend of hers, had offered ten days earlier to help paint her living room walls. It was a task that required a lot of moving of heavy furniture that she could not move alone. Joe had volunteered to share the job with her, and she had gratefully accepted.

Just a few minutes ago, at the agreed-upon time for the job, Joe had appeared at her front door, clearly not dressed for painting. He said, his head leaning against the door frame and his eyes looking directly at hers, "Something's come up. I hope you are not mad, Pen, but I won't be able to help you after all." Penny winced as she recalled that she had nodded, smiled, and let his change of plans go with a shrug. She was shocked and angry at this last-minute breaking of his promise to her, but she just couldn't find a way to say even a part of what she felt. The memory of her smile and shrug made her feel weak and stupid and powerless. Why couldn't she permit herself to say what really needed saying?

1. Is there anything about Penny's smile and shrug that suggests they may be a part of her gender role training rather than a physiological characteristic from birth?

2. Who have you observed smiling in communication situations that involve argument or difficulty? Have you ever reacted in that way?

3. In what ways can both Penny's and Joe's actions in this situation appropriately be called "micropolitical"? Who has what kind of power here?

4. What suggestions would you make to Penny to help her bring her nonverbal messages closer to expressing her real feelings?

CASE 4.3 THE PLAY

The director for the high school play was rummaging around the costume room, with Peter at his elbow.

"What are you looking for?" I asked as I stuck my head in the door.

"Something filmy and wispy," replied the director.

"What's it for?" I asked.

"Peter is playing the part of Sir Gayhead in the spoof we're putting on. He's going to show up in the middle of the battle scene, dressed in pink, wearing a boa, and carrying a wand. We don't want the audience to miss the message. We're looking for a sash for his tights." Peter and the director laughed and went back to rummaging.

1. Why would Peter and the director think the costume and scene they were planning would be funny to the audience?

2. This event actually occurred in 1993. Imagine yourself as a parent, the "I" in the story, Peter as one of the most popular boys in the school, and the director a well respected teacher. What do you think you *should* have done? What do you think you *would* have done? Discuss the differences.

3. On the night of the performance, the audience laughed uproariously at the scene; in fact, the scene was the one many recalled after the play. If you were in the audience, how do you think you would react? What action would you take? What action could you take?

4. How do you account for such dramatically different reactions in this culture to homosexuality? In this case, the response was noisy laughter. In other cases, gay people have been beaten, abused, or humiliated. What nonverbal codes have been developed in the

United States culture surrounding homosexuality and why do they exist?

NOTES

[1] Paula Watzlawick, Janet Beavin Bavelas, and Don D. Jackson, "Some Tentative Axioms of Communication," in *Pragmatics of Human Communication: A Study of Interactions, Patterns, Pathologies, and Paradoxes* (New York: W. W. Norton & Company, 1967), pp. 48–71.

[2] Albert Mehrabian, *Silent Messages* (Belmont, CA: Wadsworth, 1971).

[3] Nancy J. Briton and Judith A. Hall, "Beliefs about Female and Male Nonverbal Communication," *Sex Roles* 32, 1/2 (1995): 87.

[4] Barbara Bate and Anita Taylor, *Women Communicating* (Norwood, NJ: Ablex International, 1988); Briton and Hall, op cit., pp. 79–90.

[5] Jacqueline Sachs, "Cues to the Identification of Sex in Children's Speech," in *Language and Sex: Difference and Dominance*, ed. Barrie Thorne and Nancy Henley (Rowley, MA: Newbury House, 1975), pp. 152–71; Sally McConnell-Ginet, "Intonation in a Man's World," in *Language, Gender, and Society*, ed. Barrie Thorne et al. (Rowley, MA: Newbury House, 1983), pp. 69–88.

[6] Cheris Kramarae, "The Evaluation of Women's Speech by the British Broadcasting Corporation: A Historical Analysis," lecture at Northern Illinois University (October 1980).

[7] Jay Hewitt and Rebecca Henley, "Sex Differences in Reaction to Spatial Invasion," *Perceptual and Motor Skills* 64 (1987): 809–10.

[8] Neal J. Roese, James M. Olson, Marianne N. Borenstein, Angela Martin, and Allison L. Shores, "Same-Sex Touching Behavior: The Moderating Role of Homophobic Attitudes," *Journal of Nonverbal Behavior* 16, 4 (Winter 1992): 249–59.

[9] See, for example, Brenda Major, Anne Marie Schmidlin, and Lynne Williams, "Gender Patterns in Social Touch: The Impact of Setting and Age," *Journal of Personality and Social Psychology* 58, 4 (1990): 634–43.

[10] Judith A. Hall and Ellen M. Veccia, "More 'Touching' Observations: New Insights on Men, Women, and Interpersonal Touch," *Journal of Personality and Social Psychology* 59, 6 (1990): 1155–1162; Phyllis W. Berman and Vicki L. Smith, "Gender and Situational Differences in Children's Smiles, Touch, and Proxemics," *Sex Roles* 10 5/6 (1984): 347–56.

[11] Deborah S. Stier and Judith A. Hall, "Gender Differences in Touch: An Empirical and Theoretical Review," *Journal of Personality and Social Psychology* 47, 2 (1984): 440–59.

[12] Kevin Lee Johnson and Renee Edwards, "The Effects of Gender and Type of Romantic Touch on Perceptions of Relational Commitment," *Journal of Nonverbal Behavior* 15, 1 (Spring 1991): 43–54.

[13] Debbie Storrs and Chris L. Kleinke, "Evaluation of High and Equal Status Male and Female Touchers," *Journal of Nonverbal Behavior* 14, 2 (Summer 1990): 87–95.

[14] Robert S. Raines, Sarah B. Hechtman, and Robert Rosenthal, "Nonverbal Behavior and Gender as Determinants of Physical Attractiveness," *Journal of Nonverbal Behavior* 14, 4 (Winter 1990): 253–67.

[15] M. D'Alessio and A. Zazzetta, "Development of Self-Touching Behavior in Childhood," *Perceptual and Motor Skills* 63 (1986): 243–53.

[16] Johnson and Edwards, op cit.

[17] Frank N. Willis, Jr. and Leon F. Briggs, "Relationship and Touch in Public Settings," *Journal of Nonverbal Behavior* 16, 1 (Spring 1992): 55–62.

[18] Raines, Hechtman, and Rosenthal, op cit.

[19] Berman and Smith, op cit.

[20] J. A. Hall and A. G. Halberstadt, "Smiling and Gazing" in *The Psychology of Gender: Advances through Meta-Analysis*, ed. A. W. Siegman and S. Feldstein (Baltimore MD: The Johns Hopkins University Press, 1986), pp. 136–58.

[21] Rotter and Rotter, 1988, as cited in Tucker and Friedman, "Sex Differences in Nonverbal Expressiveness: Emotional Expression, Personality, and Impressions," *Journal of Nonverbal Behavior* 17, 2 (Summer 1993): 103–18.

[22] Joan S. Tucker and Howard S. Friedman, "Sex Differences in Nonverbal Expressiveness: Emotional Expression, Personality, and Impressions," *Journal of Nonverbal Behavior* 17, 2 (Summer 1993): 103–18.

[23] Christine Bowman, "The Impact of Mode of Presentation on Gender Differences in Social Perception," *Sex Roles* 32, 3/4 (1995): 169–83.

[24] Bamidele Adepeju Folarin, "Comparison of Personal Space as a Function of Grade and Sex of Interacting Pairs of Children," *Perceptual and Motor Skills* 68 (1989): 873–74.

[25] S. P. Sinha and Neelima Nukerjee, "Marital Adjustment and Personal Space Orientation," *The Journal of Social Psychology* 130, 5 (October 1990): 633–39.

[26] John S. Watson, "Taking a Taxi in Sweden: Front or Back Seat? A Study of Sex Differences among Passengers," *Psychological Reports* 68 (1991): 961–62.

[27] Deborah Tannen, *You Just Don't Understand: Women and Men in Conversation* (New York: Ballentine Books, 1990).

[28] Donald R. McCreary, "The Male Role and Avoiding Femininity" *Sex Roles* 31, 9/10 (1994): 517–531.

[29] Jody Miller, "Gender and Power on the Streets: Street Prostitution in the Era of Crack Cocaine," *Journal of Contemporary Ethnography* 23, 4 (January 1995): 427–52.

[30] Nancy Henley, *Body Politics: Power, Sex, and Nonverbal Communication* (Englewood Cliffs, NJ: Prentice Hall/Spectrum, 1977).

[31] Joseph A. DeVito, "Silence and Paralanguage as Communication," *Et Cetera* 46, 2 (Summer 1989): 153–57.

[32] Helen M. Newman, "The Sounds of Silence in Communicative Encounters," *Communication Quarterly* 30, 2 (Spring 1982): 142–49.

[33] Clifford E. Brown, John F. Dovidio, and Steve L. Ellyson, "Reducing Sex Differences in Visual Displays of Dominance: Knowledge Is Power," *Personality and Social Psychology Bulletin* 16, 2 (June 1990): 358–68.

[34] Anthony Mulac, Lisa B. Studley, John M. Wiemann, and James J. Bradac, "Male/Female Gaze in Same-Sex and Mixed-Sex Dyads: Gender-Linked Differences and Mutual Influence," *Human Communication Research* 13, 3 (Spring 1987): 323–43.

[35] Audrey Nelson, "Women's Nonverbal Behavior: The Paradox of Skill and Acquiescence," *Women's Studies in Communication* 4, 2 (Fall 1981): 18–31.

[36] Janet Lee Mills, "Body Language Speaks Louder Than Words," *Horizons: University of Cincinnati Alumni Magazine* (February 1985): 8–12.

[37] J. Schneider and M. Schneider-Ducker, "A Social Relations Analysis of Nonverbal Communication Accuracy in Married Couples," *Journal of Psychology* 74 (1984): 166–69 as cited in Holley S. Hodgins and Miron Zuckerman, "The Effect of Nonverbal Sensitivity on Social Interaction," *Journal of Nonverbal Behavior* 14, 3 (Fall 1990): 155–70.

[38] Hodgins, Holley S. and Miron Zuckerman, "The Effect of Nonverbal Sensitivity on Social Interaction," *Journal of Nonverbal Behavior* 14, 3 (Fall 1990): 155–70.

Chapter 5

Intimacy

Intimate relationships are complex. Some scholars say men and women have different expectations of intimate relationships, expectations ranging from intimacy as a sexual union in a heterosexual partnership to intimacy as deep and lasting bonds that develop in a variety of interpersonal relationships. These differences in expectations, combined with individual differences in communication styles, can cause confusion in partnerships, friendships, and family connections. To address that confusion, we must find ways to understand the complexity of each unique, intimate relationship. We can begin by discovering what our social training in gender and our exposure to gender stereotype have taught us about our desires for close connections with others.

CHAPTER OVERVIEW

To better understand how intimate relationships develop and mature, we must explore differences in what we mean when we say "intimacy." In this chapter, we will investigate how differences in ways women and men define intimacy result in different communication expectations. We also discuss how intimacy is related to the feminine stereotype and to individual health conditions. The complex nature of intimate communication emerges during discussions of different kinds of relationships, including both friendships and partnerships. Finally, we will discuss one of many relationship development models and consider the effects of conflict and conflict styles on intimate relationships.

DEFINING INTIMACY

Some people explain intimacy by reporting what it is not. Determining what intimacy is not seems to present fewer difficulties than determining what it is. Intimacy is not merely sharing with another or experiencing a feeling of cohesion or togetherness.

While sharing is not the sum total of intimacy, it seems to constitute a large part of same-sex intimacy although not different-sex intimacy. Some scholars explain that women are more likely to define intimacy in terms of affection, expressiveness, openness, or self-disclosure and men are more likely to include sexual relations in their definitions, identifying intimacy with partnered relationships more than friendships. While verbal sharing is salient in women's definitions, sex is salient in men's. Physical contact and sex were key components of intimacy for males; women subsume these behaviors under the category of appreciation.[1]

Therefore, defining intimacy only in terms of verbal expressiveness may focus on ways women are intimate but may exclude ways men are intimate.[2] Other research into men's definitions of intimacy indicates that men may cognitively define intimacy in affective terms similar to those used by women; however, when men describe intimate relationships they have experienced, they use terms indicating more competitive, hierarchical relationships[3] and they emphasize sharing activities rather than self-disclosing.[4] In other words, men talk about closeness, self-disclosure and trust when they describe an intimate relationship, but they rely on activities and experiences when they have an intimate relationship. That same division is not true for women. Women's descriptions and experiences of intimacy—both of which include the affective elements such as closeness and trust—are more congruent with each other.[5] The contrast between experiences with intimacy and how the United States culture teaches us to conceptualize intimacy is greater for males than for females.

Similarities in the ways men and women define intimacy outweigh differences, but we focus on the differences because they cause misunderstandings. Boys and girls experience such different life events that they construct separate definitions of intimacy based on the reality they know. The sometimes subtle, sometimes dramatic differences in those definitions can cause confusion in cross-sex friendships and in both heterosexual and homosexual romantic relationships.

Another way to think about intimacy is to consider outcomes of an intimate relationship. Intimate relationships can be unpredictable and they take time, effort, and interpersonal work. So why would people seek out intimacy? Intimate relationships can help individuals—both men and women—achieve higher self-awareness and emotional clarity. Through the relationship, people learn more about themselves. A person's physical and psychological health can be affected by the presence or absence of an intimate relationship. Some people seek intimate relationships to find a sense of connection and for the opportunity to know detailed information about another's life and experience.

INTIMACY AND THE FEMININE

In the United States culture, intimacy has been linked with women and femininity. Family roles have cast women in the caring function, thus associating femininity with concern for others, expressiveness, and warmth. Women continue to have the responsibility in relationships for inquiring about feelings and monitoring the emotional barometer. The feminine sex role is associated with intimacy regardless of the sexes in the relationship.[6] Results of one study indicated the level of femininity in a male's gender accounts for differences between males who are high and males who are low in intimacy.[7] Age also interacts with high and low levels of intimacy. Some researchers conclude that intimacy is more salient in young women than in middle-aged women.[8] People in late adolescence often feel compelled to establish intimacy and identity.[9] We will explore the relationship between identity and intimacy later in the chapter.

Comparing the relationships of men and women in their study, Fischer and Narus conclude that women develop more fully intimate relationships than do men.[10] The intimacy women share with men is not as great as that which they share with each other. The female-female relationships scored highest in intimacy, and the male-male relationships scored lowest. Both men and women report they value love and caring,[11] but caring seems to be the principal category that differentiates one sex from the other.[12]

Historically, intimacy in the United States culture has not always been associated only with women. In the early 1800s, young men displayed fondness for their male friends in open, affectionate, physical gestures. Daniel Webster wrote that the only person to whom he divulged his most secret thoughts was his best friend. Evidence from diaries and personal correspondence suggests that many young men of the time engaged in close, personal relationships with other men without apprehension or social condemnation. Acceptable intimate behaviors for males included a wide range of what today are stereotyped as feminine behaviors.[13]

Some scholars explain that as early as adolescence, males in the twentieth-century United States culture learn that adopting feminine values to achieve intimacy will bring negative responses.[14] Boys experience social sanctions against self-disclosure.[15] While men and women and interpersonal scholars generally agree on the need for intimacy as an interpersonal development, males continue to struggle against the traditional stereotypes that cast intimacy in the feminine domain.[16]

INTIMACY AND HEALTH

Researchers have found that intimacy is not only associated with femininity but also with good health. The presence of intimacy often has been linked to good health; the absence of intimacy has been linked with problems of both mental and physical health. In research on the aging, the happiest and healthiest participants were or had been involved in close, intimate relationships. Both men and women find energy and motivation to live productive lives through one or more intimate, dyadic relationships.

The absence of intimate male relationships strongly affects male and female adults and children in deleterious ways. Negative effects of divorce, for example, seem to be more enduring on boys than on girls.[17] Clearly, divorce includes many other factors besides dissolution of a once-intimate relationship; however, adolescent girls adjust better and more quickly to divorce than adolescent boys.[18] In addition, adult male children of divorce develop hostile interpersonal styles more frequently.[19] Males develop higher anxiety than females with response to divorce and males are lower overall in psychological adjustment. These harmful effects last longer for males than for females.[20] Some research connects males' gender socialization toward sexual aggression with lower capacities to create intimate and empathic relationships.[21] Increased risk of mental illness and lower levels of physical well-being among single and divorced persons is also attributed to loss of intimacy.[22]

Positive life-long effects seem to result from the experience of a satisfying, intimate relationship. Research even makes some correlation between lack of an outlet for intimate emotional disclosure and such ailments as cancer, heart disease, and infection. Overall, intimacy and intimate relationships are dynamic life experiences that enhance satisfaction and prolong longevity.

INTIMACY IN SAME-SEX FRIENDSHIPS

Within same-sex friendships, the sexes experience intimacy very differently. Men in the United States culture often describe as best friends those males with whom they play sports, have beers after work, or talk over the back fence about their gardens, cars, or the stock market. Most women, in contrast, describe as best friends people who talk with them about their relationships, career decisions, family events, and personal hopes or frustrations. For men, then, friendships provide predictable companionship through activities and talk about those activities. For women, friendship serves to provide a human connection, with particular topics being explored as needed but not being the primary reason for contact.[23] One result of this widespread difference is that two women may remain friends for many years even when they do not work together or live in the same community, while men's friendships often die off when the men are no longer sharing jobs, hobbies, or neighborhoods.

Patterns of intimacy within same-sex friendships emerge at adolescence and continue throughout our personal development. Psychologists explain that intimacy is particularly important to us at the adolescent stage. If we are not able to achieve intimate friendships, we have heightened experiences of isolation, loneliness, and depression. Our desire for self-disclosure increases because we are learning about ourselves as individuals, separate from our families. We begin to look to our peers for confirmation and validation of our worth. At that point in our lives, our self-esteem is closely related to our intimate relationships.[24]

During adolescence, we consciously develop for the first time intimate relationships we use for personal growth. Initially, many of those relationships are same-sex friendships. Several characteristics of same-sex friendships distinguish the sexes. Generally, females are more self-disclosing in their friendships than are males. Young men express desires to be able to disclose more in their same-sex friendships; however, they disclose more and expect to disclose more only in their relationships with females.[25] Girls generally develop friendships in dyads where they favor frankness, sensitivity, trust, exclusivity, self-disclosure, emotional closeness, and loyalty. Boys develop friendships as parts of larger groups, favoring giving and sharing, taking and imposing, meeting concrete needs, having support when they get into trouble, and engaging in common activities. Boys' friendships are described as "not as deep or attached as relationships among girls."[26] Boys choose friends on the basis of being able to confide in them and have fun with them. Girls choose friends to whom they can talk freely and become confidants.[27] Girls' friendships often center around talk; boys' friendships more often center around doing an activity.

Boys seem to develop friendships in large networks, sometimes in conjunction with sports or other activities they play with one another. They learn to follow rules and get along with all kinds of people, even people they do not like well. Girls seem to develop more exclusive friendships—"best" friends with one or two others—in which they talk about feelings and learn to attend others' feelings.[28] Research in Russia, Hungary, and Israel reveals similar patterns between boys and girls, reporting that girls prefer smaller, intimate groups of friends and boys identify close friends as those who help them out if they have trouble.[29]

Many of you reading this book may have experienced your school life as a "gifted" student. Research about gifted boys and girls and intimate same-sex friendships indicates that gifted students may have higher levels of achievement orientation than other students. While their abilities to achieve are encouraged and nurtured, gifted students often receive no more instruction and education about relationship development than other students. Gifted students follow patterns more comparable to boys' patterns in general, showing more preference for intimate friendships with higher degrees of cognitive and task-oriented activities. These students seem less inclined to maintain emotionally intimate friendships; one researcher suggested that gifted children conceive of friendships from more mature perspectives than others of the same age so their expectations of intimacy may be greater than those of their friends.[30] While gifted students may act independently to reach advanced achievement goals, they need equally perceptive partners with whom they may pursue intimacy. Without a wide variety of possibilities for partners, they may not have the opportunities to investigate or achieve intimacy at the accelerated pace with which they may pursue cognitive topics. Even with gifted students, however, girls disclose more than boys and perceive their friendships to be closer and more intimate than boys'.

General patterns of intimate, same-sex friendships continue in adult relationships. Females report they are more comfortable disclosing to other women than to men.[31] Women experience higher emotional intensity in their relationships than do men. Women tend to have dyadic, exclusive, collaborative friendships; men's tend to be group-oriented, competitive, and fairly hierarchical.[32] Women's friendships are likely to be more nurturing and expressive; women have more positive attitudes toward touching behavior as signs of closeness.[33]

Males may face social censure for expressiveness in same-sex relationships. Males acknowledge that they expect to be more open mainly in other-sex relationships.[34] Some researchers found that males judge negative disclosures in the relationship as more intimate than positive ones. In other words, Peter would consider his talk about his trouble in math as more intimate than his revealing awards he received for his computer work. Negative disclosures made about a variety of emotions, various topics, and differing intensities of emotions were considered more intimate than were positive disclosures about those issues. Males rated the intimacy higher as the disclosures intensified.[35] These perceptions raise important questions about differences between presumptions made by males and females when considering the role of disclosure in intimate relationships. Since meanings for disclosures are so closely woven into relationship expectations and relationship context, differences in presumptions of those disclosures could dramatically affect a partner's desire to disclose or a partner's understanding of the meaning of the disclosure.[36]

Some researchers suggest that the element of competition in the male sex role in the United States interferes with the development of intimate relationships between men. Women who may be seen by men as companions rather than competitors do not elicit those competitive responses. To maintain their competitive edge, men may restrict some kinds of communication based on sex. For example, males more actively avoid touch with other males than females do with other females; men avoid touch less with females than females do with males.[37] Touch avoidance and restriction of emotional expressiveness with other males may be attributed to the high degree of homophobia in United States culture. Stereotypical masculine gender is defined in part by the absence of femininity. Some people with stereotpyical masculine genders may fear their status in the competitive hierarchy would be damaged by insinuations of homosexuality or femininity.

Homophobia is an irrational fear of homosexuality or of being seen by others as homosexual. Homophobic people exhibit an extreme fear of affectionate bonds between two males or two females. In the case of males, the fear or distrust of two men who show affection to each other remains strong except in certain structured settings. Football and basketball players often swat each other's behinds or hug each other after a particularly good play. Males also engage in playful blows to the shoulders. Other forms of touch allowed between men is violent behavior exhibited in times of major stress; that behavior often is called a display of "temper" or "letting off steam." In much of the United States culture, a man who lets down his guard to show warmth to another man risks being socially demeaned and misdefined, as most young men recognize.

Currently, the United States society shows more evidence of homophobia than many other countries, even though some of the legal barriers to social interaction between same-sex pairs have been relaxed. (Twenty-six states used to have laws protecting private sexual expression between pairs of adults, but in July 1986 the United States Supreme Court ruled that such laws are not protected by the U.S. Constitution.)[38] Recent initiatives in Oregon and Colorado generated significant personal and political conflict about the rights of gay citizens. In several instances, the conflicts resulted in physical violence against homosexual people; this kind of violence signals the volatile and dangerous nature of this rhetorical issue of sex and gender.

One example of how dangerous homophobia can be occurred as the result of an appearance on a television talk show. The guest had been told that he was to appear to meet (for the first time) a person who professed to have been secretly in love with the guest for some time. Unknown to the guest, the secret admirer was male. The guest showed some embarrassment at the revelation, but talked cordially with both the admirer and Jenny Jones, the host. A few days after the show aired, the guest shot and killed the young man who had professed his love on national television.

Homophobia is a learned behavior. Whether it is based in the family, religion, the community, or folklore, homophobia is not biologically generated. People with homophobic convictions often equate sex with gender; their inability to tolerate a range of genders from a single sex mirrors expectations of the culture's sex stereotypes. While only a minority has voiced openly homophobic opinions, many people in the United States experience and exhibit homophobia in certain situations.

While sources of homophobia are clearly cultural and rhetorical, questions are not resolved about the biological and/or social source(s) of homosexuality. From a power perspective, homosexual people hold a minority status in the United States culture. Recent developments with regard to HIV and the AIDS virus have profoundly affected the status of homosexuals. The Names Project (a collection of individually designed quilt pieces each of which commemorates a person who died of AIDS) calls attention both to the victims of AIDS and the general national response to those victims. The power perspective shows that homophobic behavior claims dominion over homosexual people by relying on adherence to heterosexual sex and gender stereotypes. In addition, homophobics depend on others' willingness to abandon the vantage point of knowing homosexuals as individuals in favor of the vantage point of stereotyping homosexuals as a generalized group.

In the following account, a heterosexual, male, undergraduate student described his own experience of succumbing to homophobia:

I was sitting in my dorm room with several other guys, waiting for my roommate to return from taking a phone call. When he returned—crying heavily, his shoulders shaking with the force of his sobs—I reached out to him as soon as I saw him, and I held him in a close hug for several seconds while he continued to weep. Then suddenly I pulled my arms away and stood almost three feet away from him, abruptly breaking the physical contact of the hug. I feel terrible about it now, but I know I made this sudden move away from him for one reason only: I had just remembered there were other guys in the room, and they might think the two of us were in a gay relationship.

Views about same-sex intimacy are evolving toward greater acceptance of the idea that love can occur between two people of the same sex. Yet the pressure to avoid the stereotype of being gay or lesbian keeps many heterosexual individuals from communicating as they might with people they would enjoy having as close friends.

SEX AS A COMPONENT OF INTIMACY IN OTHER-SEX FRIENDSHIPS

Friendships between men and women have generated interesting questions. Can women and men in a largely heterosexual culture establish friendships without addressing sexual issues? Do sexual relations necessarily exclude the relationship from a "friendship" status? Are these friendships trial periods, testing the possibilities for the development of romantic relationships? How do these men and women navigate through the very different expectations and experiences of friendships they have developed with their same-sex friends?

While answers to these questions are not clear, most people can distinguish between their romantic friendships and their nonromantic ones. Think of someone of the other sex who is your friend. Now think of someone of the other sex with whom you are or have been romantically involved. Do you experience differences in the feelings you have, the activities you share, and the kind and amount of disclosing you do? How is your friendship different from your romantic relationship? In the course of developing your friendship, did you address issues of sex and romance? In *When Harry Met Sally*, Harry claims that no cross-sex friendship ever can evolve without confronting the question of sex sometime along the way.

Some researchers argue that men in the United States culture are pressured by social norms to behave in highly masculine-gendered ways. To that end, men explicitly pursue sexual activity partly as a means to fulfill the social expectations of being male.[39] As a result, men may have more trouble than women dealing with the issues of sexual relations in cross-sex friendships.

The covert expectation of sexual relations between men and women in close relationships often can develop into suspicion. Generally in the United States culture, women and men in heterosexual marriages are expected to confide in their partners and be "best friends." Outside-the-marriage, cross-sex friendships frequently are discouraged and avoided. Suspicion can be raised when, for example, a husband develops a friendship with woman or a wife develops a friendship with a man.

Sexual innuendo in cross-sex friendship emerges as a culture-based characteristic. For example, age, ethnicity, educational level, class, and race can comprise cultures that influence these norms. Gender stereotypes, sexual preferences, and intercultural experiences also can affect how friends deal with implications of sexual relations. College students, for example, have the highest incidence of cross-sex friendships.[40] Increasingly, researchers are studying how cross-sex friendships develop and how cross-sex friends manage both the sexual component and intimate communication differences between them.

INTIMACY IN PARTNERED RELATIONSHIPS

When you read the title of this section, did you immediately presume the section would be about men and women in committed relationships? Most people in the United States culture presume couples to be composed of a female and a male; often the presumption is that the couple will be gendered feminine and masculine. Heterosexuality forms the basis for other presumptions about partnering as well, such as who does what role in the relationship. As a result, issues about who nurtures and who plans vacations can be inextricably tied to issues about masculinity and femininity.

These roles cannot be assessed by sex in homosexual couples. In fact, even the gender of a homosexual partner does not clearly predict behavior.[41] While socialization forces still play central roles in relationship dynamics, homosexuals face some different combinations of freedoms and pressures in negotiating intimate partnerships.[42] Sanctions against homosexual marriages create barriers for couples seeking a socially reinforced and socially recognized union.

Heterosexual marriage and intimacy often are equated in the United States culture even though not all marriages meet the definitions discussed for intimate relationships. In heterosexual marital relationships, frequent talk that is considered supportive increases both men's and women's relationship satisfaction. In a study of husbands and wives, wives found support and encouragement to be most important to their satisfaction in marriage. In addition, they reported talking as critical. They valued expressing ideas and feelings verbally. Husbands also named support, encouragement, and expressing things verbally as important elements in their relationships; in addition, they also described their desires for both partners to tolerate the "less pleasant aspects" of their mates.[43]

Some researchers find significant differences between the communication behaviors of husbands and wives. When both husbands and wives report about their own communication behavior and that of their partners, wives' reports were similar to those their husbands made about them. However, the reverse was not found to be true. The husbands' reports of their own communication behaviors were not similar to those their wives made about them. Researchers concluded that wives' communication behaviors were clearer to both husbands and wives than were husbands' communication behaviors. Perhaps that clarity of communication relates to the facility each sex has with intimate communication. The socialization that results in the pairing of intimacy and femininity may contribute to wives' abilities in intimate relationships to communicate more clearly to husbands than husbands do to wives.

Socialization may account in part for differences in intimate communication styles. In addition, Ruthellen Josselson asserts that the sexes develop identity differently. Those differences may affect how men and women communicate intimately as they develop relationships.

IDENTITY AND INTIMACY

What we believe about the relationship between identity (who you believe yourself to be as a separate self) and intimacy (your abilities to closely relate to others and become part of a "we") may affect both your expectations about yourself and your expectations of your intimate partners. Different patterns of development of identity and intimacy may complicate personal relationships between males and females. Conflict, trust, and expectations of relationship participation all may be affected by presumptions made by both males and females in regard to personal development.

Erik Erikson, a psychologist, constructed in the 1950s and 1960s a life-cycle model of psychosocial development. Erikson concluded that people meet eight critical crises in their lives—crises such as trust/mistrust, autonomy/doubt, identity/role confusion, and intimacy/isolation. As people resolve these crises, Erikson theorized, they move toward maturity. Crises of one stage must be resolved before a person could move on to the next. Erikson created the phrase, "identity crisis" because he purported that people must resolve the identity stage—usually during adolescence—before they could move on to the intimacy stage. The order of his developmental model became an influential standard for the measure of a person's progress toward maturity.

As was common at the time, Erikson used mostly males in his research; although he did not pursue research about females, he suggested that for them intimacy might precede identity. During the 1970s and 1980s, many other scholars agreed that for women, intimacy may precede or develop simultaneously with identity. In the late

1980s Ruthellen Josselson explained that adolescent females seem to grapple with the identity stage while maintaining closer ties with family members and without needing the distancing and separation apparent in adolescent males. Josselson writes that for women, "To know is to connect rather than to master."[44] As a woman resolves her "identity crisis," she does so through her connections with those close to her.

Changing Erikson's "people" to "males," we can see a contrast between these two developmental plans. According to Erikson, identity is developed throughout a lifetime; however, during adolescence males become aware that they do not have to continue being the person they have been. They can make their own choices and revise their thoughts and behaviors if they so choose. During this identity crisis, they can experiment with the ways they have traditionally acted. To conduct those experiments, they sever connections with people to whom they have been close. They isolate themselves to try out new ways to look, ways to act, ways to think. Only after they have finished with their experiments and have made decisions about how they are going to be can they turn their attention back to others where they then are ready to make intimate connections. This model, first outlined by Erikson, laid the foundation for the adage that we must first know ourselves before we can make attachments to others.

Josselson explains that the moment of the identity crisis may occur in much the same way for women with one important distinction. As with males, adolescence brings an awareness of the female's ability to shape herself in ways other than those to which she is accustomed. Like males, females examine the lifelong collection of personal traits and characteristics, experimenting with changes and revisions. Unlike the males, however, Josselson explains that females also retain their connections with people to whom they have been close as they conduct their experiments. Females use the perspective of the "other" as well as their own perspective to examine the alternatives they now see for their own development. In this model, the identity crisis and the intimacy crisis are not distinct and separate. In other words, while males may process first identity and then intimacy, females may process identity and intimacy together.

Traditional ideas about appropriate self-development follow patterns derived from research about males. Those traditional ideas assert that appropriate development moves from dependence to identity to intimacy and then to a balance of identity and intimacy. Josselson suggests that women may develop in a different pattern: dependence to a juxtaposition of identity and intimacy and then on to a balance of identity and intimacy. Josselson explains that females may be confused if they compare their own development to the standard model. They may be judged as "immature" because they engage in intimacy during their identity development; the standard model calls for them to resolve identity crises before they address intimacy needs. Josselson asserts that females' simultaneous attention to identity and intimacy crises works effectively as a developmental plan; indeed, both patterns can result in similar states. As a result, the key to understanding developing intimate heterosexual relationships between young adults is to consider the more complex interplay between these two patterns.

So how might these two developmental patterns affect a male and a female who are developing a relationship together?

Consider the differences between whether a person believes that (1) separation and distinction accomplishes identity (and identity is a recognizable goal that must be secured before moving on to intimacy) or (2) connection provides an essential source of information for developing identity (and intimacy interplays with identity throughout the life cycle). A person with the first orientation (and hypothetically we'll call this person male) may view intimacy as a threat to identity. Intimacy may blur the lines of identity, making him less clear about how he is distinct from the other. A person with the second orientation (and hypothetically we'll call this person female) may view intimacy as an exciting prospect that creates opportunities for new knowledge about herself.

In our hypothetical example, the male may see the female's actions in the intimate relationship as unrestrained and without critical regard for self. She may seem too willing to self-disclose and express feelings. Her willingness to reveal this information to him may appear problematic, and he may try to help her sort out all the details into a clearer, distinct identity package. From his vantage point and perspective, his partner may seem dependent. He does not perceive the interdependent nature of her acts. Likewise, the female may see the male's actions as distancing and unresponsive. He may seem to her to be uncooperative in this exploratory adventure and in some ways unwilling to contribute his part in this integrative effort. His unwillingness may appear problematic to her, and she may try to help him learn to open up and reveal more of himself. From her vantage point and perspective, her partner may seem separate. She does not perceive the maintenance of self in his acts.

These differences may endanger the development of this relationship because one common characteristic of partnered relationships is the expectation of longevity. Sexually intimate partnerships historically have been expected to be lifelong. But that expectation has changed. Predictions that half of all heterosexual marriages will end in divorce indicate our presumptions are changing about how relationships work and options we have when the relationship does not develop as we desire. Several scholars have created theories about general communication patterns in developing relationships. While the theories do not encompass the uniqueness of each partnership, each one provides a generic pattern you might recognize as similar in many relationships you have experienced.

A RELATIONSHIP DEVELOPMENT MODEL

The model below, originated by Julia T. Wood and later developed along with Gerald M. Phillips, may help you recognize sequences you experienced in a variety of relationships. This model provides one explanation for development of different kinds of relationships, some of which became close friendships, some of which remained acquaintances, or some of which dissipated.[45] Not all relationships move through all stages. Thinking of the model as a general explanation rather than as a specific measure of relationships helps avoid the inference that relationships at one stage are "better" than relationships at another or that all relationships fit this form exactly. What each of us experiences at the various stages and what we learn about ourselves and our partners affects our next encounter with relationship development.

The twelve stages in relationship development, each with its own characteristic communication patterns, can be outlined in the following way:

1. The individual is not involved in any particular partnership but is receptive to relationship possibilities.

2. The invitation stage involves coming into contact with various people and making initial assessments of those people we prefer (brief meetings may produce no sense of personal connection).

3. Exploration through talk occurs with one person who offers possible compatibility (either or both may end their relating here).

4. Intensity or euphoria occurs, in which the other is idealized and talk is intensely personal (a stage of total immersion).

5. Revising and reevaluating occur, and the likely chances for the relationship to succeed are assessed (termination may occur here).

6. Bonding is an act of committing selves to a future of intimacy with the other (one may be ready sooner than the other).

7. Maintenance or navigation involves finding a workable structure for the ongoing relationship and dealing with changes that occur.

8. Differentiating means increasing focus on the individual instead of on the pair.

9. Disintegrating means the falling apart of the pairing bond, whether or not the two people admit it.

10. Stagnating means operating on a nonintimate basis, but not breaking the bond officially.

11. Terminating occurs either clearly and dramatically or through a process of incremental divisions that produce specific messages to each other that the relationship is ending.

12. Partners return to individual status, changed by the experience of having been in a relationship.

Several comments can be made about the twelve stages. First, relationships do not always deteriorate or end. The deterioration process may or may not occur for a given pair of people. You may become a casual acquaintance with someone you have dated; you may become good friends who confide in each other about other people you are dating; you may continue to know this person throughout your life, communicating at holidays or seeing each other at reunions. Even if a relationship has "ended," you may find you think about experiences you had in that relationship and you may continue to use those experiences to influence your behaviors in other relationships. The connotation of a "terminated" relationship simply means that the person no longer functions in your life as a possible long-term, committed partner.

Second, the stages are not absolutes, occurring in only one direction. You might go through a particular stage more than once. For example, a woman breaks off her engagement but later decides to marry the same man; she later divorces him for many of the same reasons she had once hesitated to marry him. She may have gone through the revising stage with one set of criteria, only to change those criteria later in her life to match changes in her circumstances or her perceptions about herself, her partner, or her life. Another possibility is that a process of looping back to an earlier stage might occur. Sometimes women or men go through major reexamination of their personal values in mid-life or beyond, leading first to a differentiation stage (#8), then back to a renewed exploration of the bond with their partners

(#6). Relationships do not always end because tension or change occurs within them. Skills in communicating about the stress and frustrations of change can help people more clearly understand if they need to change their relationship or if they can live through their changes together.

Because of their socialization and their experiences with same-sex communication, women may communicate their receptivity in different ways than men. Having learned collaborative, relational expectations, women may appear more receptive to sharing a relationship than men who learned competitiveness and individuality. However, both sexes express a desire for pairing and a desire to find someone with whom to share their lives.

INITIATING RELATIONSHIPS

The initiating stage of relationship development happens continually, even when we are not aware of our actions. We assess others through all sorts of means: how they dress, how they talk, what they talk about, where we meet them, how sophisticated or unsophisticated they seem to us, and so on. Our communication "sieve" begins work immediately, using our past experiences and preferences to determine whom we consider attractive and interesting.

To make contact, we may simply follow our daily routine or we may make special choices that we believe will bring us into contact with possible relationship partners. College students often find their routine life creates myriad opportunities to make initial contact. Classes, club meetings, sporting events, concerts, organization sessions, and night life all present contexts rich with new faces, new experiences, and new opportunities to meet others. Our friends introduce us to their friends who introduce us to others. On the other hand, single people in workplaces may find that opportunities to meet others are less available; they may choose other ways to create contacts. Recreational programs, churches, public concerts, and volunteer organizations provide means by which working adult singles can meet each other. Contacts increasingly are made through the Internet or by placing descriptive ads in special newspaper columns carried nationwide.

Making the initial contact simply means we meet others who might share similar interests or who interest us for other reasons. This stage may occur through conscious effort; however, often it occurs because others who interest us are doing things we also are interested in doing. As a consequence, we meet and spend enough time together to warrant going on to the next stage of relationship development.

EXPLORATION

After discovering potential relationship partners, you move on to the explorational communication stage. Extended conversation with one individual reveals whether you want that person to receive more of your attention and time. You and the other will begin to share information to discover common interests and to test each other's receptiveness to topics you want to talk about. In addition, you will be listening for implicit relational messages that give you clues about whether your interpersonal sieve has worked properly and you have engaged a person you might like to get to know better.

In the exploration stage, self-disclosure guides the relationship development. Tentative communication by both parties stimulates the reciprocal nature of revealing information in small increments. Self-disclosure may be preceded by self-description, where each person shares general information like their names, where they live, where they work, and so on. The relationship moves deeply into the exploration stage when self-disclosure begins. Self-disclosure means intentionally sharing information about oneself that is not readily available to the other person. The conversation begins to include not only description but topics considered by the speaker to be personal and revealing, perhaps including beliefs, values, or opinions. This information need not be deep, dark secrets; what is considered disclosure is determined by the discloser.

Self-disclosure is complicated by gender because the sexes often don't think of "self" or "disclosure" in the same ways. A man may seem to a woman to be talking about the outside world when he discusses his latest sales figures or his company's plan to merge his division with another. To him, however, this kind of information may be as much "self" as anything he can think of, since he is a sales manager and this activity comprises much of his life. Conversely, he may not talk to others about this topic, if he considers this type of talk "disclosure."

On the other hand, a woman may believe she is talking about "self" when she expresses her feelings about a person she is uncomfortable with, while the man may hear this kind of comment as asking him to make a judgment or to suggest how to avoid the problem. She may consider "disclosure" as central to intimacy and disclose not only to share information but also to establish relationship dimensions. Each person may thus be sending and sharing a great deal of information the sender considers essential to intimacy but the receiver finds pointless.

Why do men and women talk past each other in this way? One answer may lie in the two-cultures explanation for different beliefs in men and women. Many of us learned early to look at certain topics as the basic stuff of conversation and other topics as necessary but uninteresting aspects of life. Girls generally disclose in dyads, searching out aspects of life regarding personal connections between feelings, responsibility, and life events. Boys generally disclose in groups, searching out aspects of life regarding activities and rules.[46] Both the kind of information exchanged and the reason for exchanging it with regard to the relationship differ. Girls learn to use personal disclosure as relational adhesive; boys learn that personal disclosure makes them vulnerable in competitive situations. How each regards and uses disclosure results from life experiences. When the two sexes come together to share a relationship, each refers to previous experiences to make meaning and thereby understand both the content and style of the communication. This difference of focus was reinforced when males went away from the home to do paid work, while women worked within the home setting. Each received and sent messages in their own environment, and each set of messages became familiar and valuable.

Studies of conversational patterns between men and women have shown that women tend to work harder at initiating and helping along exploratory conversations, although women typically have fewer chances to express themselves, are interrupted more often, and have less control over the choice of topic than do the men with whom they talk.[47]

Gaps between the sexes during this explorational stage do not always occur, and they may be less noticeable when the two people have more equivalent involvements in life events. But when women have their own stories to tell, they may take on less of the conversation-maintaining burden, leaving the responsibility of conversational maintenance to be shared by the male. If he fails to share it, the conversation may die before the pair has advanced beyond exploration to intensity.

EUPHORIA OR INTENSITY

This stage of relating is of great delight to the partners in the new relationship although rarely as delightful to others who have to listen to the euphoric individuals! Observation suggests that males and females behave somewhat similarly when suddenly excited about a new relationship, although their reasons for feeling euphoric may differ. The euphoric person often talks long-windedly about the most minute episode of interacting with the loved one: the speaker's face may become animated, the memory of mundane details of daily life may fade, and the awareness of others' concerns, worries, or schedules may decrease to the point of disappearance. In the intensity stage, people are overcome by the apparent miracle of the other's presence and interest in them. Nothing else is as interesting to talk about; in fact, it is hard for roommates or family members to manage any semblance of dialogue with the euphoric person.

Having established interest and attraction in the exploratory stage, the couple enters "limerence."[48] Self-disclosure expands to personal areas often reserved for only the discloser. Couples spend long hours together, talking about histories, discussing values, or sharing activities. During the intensity stage, couples often reduce time spent with others, sharpening the focus of their communication on their new relationship partner.

During this stage, interpretation of meaning is mediated by the euphoria of the relationship. Behaviors and messages are eagerly noted by the partners and generally are interpreted in the best light possible. She may laugh that he picks her up nearly an hour late for their dates. He may smile when she forgets to make dinner reservations. Frequently, gender stereotypes play out in behaviors, behaviors that later will be revisited and revised. During this stage, however, both men and women disregard specific characteristics in the other in favor of the euphoria of discovery.

Communication patterns during euphoria include high levels of self-disclosure, talk about intimate and personal topics, prolonged close proximity, increased touching behaviors, sexual activity, exchange of personal items, and increased talk by partners about partners to others. Some people characterize this stage as love. Some men and women have been known to move from partner to partner, developing the relationship only long enough to experience euphoria before moving to the next partner.

Sexuality is a major source of intensity or euphoria. Codes of behavior still exist about who may have sex, when sexual relations are appropriate, and what consequences accrue from violation of the codes. While the specific parameters of the codes may have changed, the division between the sexes remains. Women receive harsher criticism for random or multiple sexual interludes than do men. Men can receive criticism—especially from other men—for *not* having random or multiple sexual interludes. During this stage of relationship development, the couple negotiates—either through conversation or behavior—their sexual relationship. The Harry-Met-Sally question may be centrally responsible for the intensity of this stage.

Assuming that a given pair of individuals can work out their initial relationship regarding sexual activity, they may both be extremely happy to find a partner who seems to have the same likes, background, life goals, and music preferences that they do. As far as we can tell, the sexes are similar in their capacity for experiencing intense delight with another person; however, talking to others about their happiness may still be more acceptable for females than males.

THE REVISING STAGE

Communication at the revising stage can occur largely within the self, or it can be communicated to the partner or to a trusted outsider such as a parent or a same-sex confidant. Revising often occurs when the experience of communicating with the other conflicts with initial impressions of the other. For some people, euphoria and revising occur in close succession with every new person they meet. For others, the honeymoon of euphoria goes on for months or even years.

Revising occurs in part because initially we have a tendency to interpret others' behaviors as we would our own. Therefore, when one partner forgets an important date, the other might at first interpret that act as an understandable accident. Euphoria continues undaunted. However, when that forgetfulness becomes a pattern, revision begins. Revision means looking at another individual as a human being with flaws and foibles, not as a perfect partner in every respect. In some cases the revision diminishes the partner so completely that the relationship must end. In others, it requires that both people look at their reasons for caring about each other and decide whether they will keep working to build a relationship.

Revision work again highlights differences between the sexes and genders. As couples try to work out the meanings for behaviors and the possibilities or motivations for change, their expectations and roles interact to add connotations and implications. The partners begin negotiating such issues as personal and psychological space, individualism and partnership, dependency, conflict styles, and meaning interpretation.

One example of sex and gender differences occurs with the interpretation about relationship dependency. Research often describes women as more likely to be dependent in the relationship, seeking approval and confirmation through self-disclosure. While that dependence may be interpreted by men in the euphoric stage as flattering, during the revision stage it becomes a point of conflict. How "dependence" might be interpreted varies. From the male vantage point (which may favor individualism and competitive hierarchy), questions such as, "Should I do this?" or "Can you help me?" can be interpreted as one-down and vulnerable. The speakers' dependence reduces the speakers' value. From the female vantage point (which may favor collectivism and collaboration), questions asking "Should I do this?" or "Can you help me?" can be interpreted as one-across—creating opportunity for the other person to engage in an egalitarian way. The speakers' considerateness increases their value. During revision, the interpretation of these messages is negotiated. The couple either decides the disparity is too great and changes the nature of the relationship, or they begin to devise a standard of meaning that incorporates both sets of values and interpretations.

Revision negotiations can be simple and explicit or complicated and abstract depending on the partners' self-awareness, their dedication to the relationship, and their interests in pursuing revision. Some partners learn to use each other as mirrors, each reflecting to the other reactions and responses without directing the other's life. Some partners choose to divide expertise, implicitly assigning each sex to certain specialty areas of authority in the relationship. Still others devise unique systems between them for interpreting meaning. Not all revisions are egalitarian; not all revisions are satisfying to both partners. Couples may revisit this stage many times during the life of the relationship.

Currently social sanctions seem to support ending unsatisfying relationships. People often report they do not want to remain in damaging relationships like those their parents had. Decisions to terminate conflictual relationships may be good ones since research shows children and adults in nonconflictual single relationships fare better than those in conflictual coupled relationships. However, better communication in the revision stage might increase the number of couples who establish effective, long-term relationships in which change is part of the relationship system.

The revision stage is critical to the longevity of the relationship. The desire to bond with another person can be so great that the reevaluating process is short-circuited and the individuals make a public commitment—engagement, marriage, or sharing a living space—before they have revised the communication patterns established during the euphoria stage. If they consider that public commitment as virtually irreversible, they may establish for themselves an ongoing, debilitating communication climate.

BONDING

The relationship stage in which the partners think and talk of themselves as sharing their lives with one another is called bonding. It may be a within-the-dyad commitment without a ceremony or symbolic gesture such as exchanging rings. Race, class, and ethnicity all affect the framing of this stage, but the central act is one of commitment. The relationship itself becomes a fact as well as a goal; a pair of people bonded to each other will typically think, talk, and act more as a unit than they have done before. People will refer to them as "Ted-and-Alice," almost like the phrase is one word.

But this stage, like the earlier ones, does not always occur with equal impact for both partners; one of them may feel and act on their relationship bond as a central force in their lives, while the other may treat it as a new event but not as a major focus for continuing attention. Men and women perceive "togetherness" in different ways, having been socialized with different ideas about connectedness, individuality, and relationships. While some variation in their perceptions of bonding is tolerable for long-term partners, relationships with wide discrepancies in the feelings and actions of bonding show poor promise of lasting.

ISSUES OF MAINTAINING INTIMACY

NAVIGATING

The process of maintaining an intimate relationship is as varied in detail as the individuals who make up each intimate relationship. Some relationships begin in a great deal of conflict and appear rocky to others for many years, without ever threatening either partner's view that the relationship will last forever. Other relationships look to outsiders to be "made in heaven" but fall apart within a few months. Some begin with an unplanned pregnancy or a rebound from a former relationship. Others carry the extra complexity of combining children from former marriages into a stepfamily.

One of the most widespread situations for couples currently is one in which both partners have jobs they either need economically or want professionally—jobs they plan to continue until retirement. The term *dual-career* is often used to describe a relationship in which both partners are relatively equally committed to present and future employment outside the home. In dual-career households, handling moves or transfers is one of a number of communication issues that the partners have to work out. In *dual worker* couples, one partner generally has a position that pays less, has a job less continuously, and is more attached to the home and family as compared to the other partner (who is typically the husband). In dual-worker households, the family moves follow the primary earner's professional needs.

During the bonding stage, couples negotiate not only these issues but communication rules about *how* to negotiate these issues. Implicit communication rules will emerge about such things as who may introduce certain topics, who may complain about certain behaviors, when these topics may be addressed, and ways in which these topics may be addressed. With few role models to follow from the previous generation, couples navigate these negotiations often by trial and error.

Women and men often discover that gender stereotypes and socialization norms interfere with their negotiations and other communication. Obstacles to maintaining an intimate relationship include fear of merger, fear of exposure, fear of attack, and fear of abandonment.[49] Evident more in men than women, these fears manifest themselves in nonverbal relational messages. Fear of merger means the partner communicates a fear of being subsumed by the relationship, a fear that individuality will be sacrificed to coupleness.

Fear of exposure emanates from an aversion to vulnerability; intimate communication exposes personal imperfections usually hidden from view. Fear of attack derives from the concerns and apprehensions about being criticized by someone who has learned your weak spots. Fear of abandonment is the belief that relying on another is dangerous, since that person then has the power to arbitrarily discontinue the support and sustenance on which you have come to depend. These fears filter through relationship messages between the partners, hindering growth and threatening the bonded relationship.

Gender differences receive greater focus at this stage. The male propensity for arguments and "victory" in conversation may impede relationship development. Likewise, female tendencies for self-blame and willingness to tolerate hurt feelings also may hamper effective intimacy negotiations.[50] Women often complain that men are unwilling or unable to express their emotions. Interestingly, women and men report equally their feelings of appreciation for the other, but women express such feelings more often and feel uncomfortable with men's silence.[51] Some scholars use a cultural perspective and describe men's inexpressiveness as a learned pattern;[52] others use a power perspective and interpret it as a controlling mechanism that sustains the competitive one-up position.[53] Women do not feel that men listen to them attentively. An abundance of research indicates women want more participation from and more egalitarian interaction with their partners in intimate relationships.[54] Wives report they want less controlling behavior from husbands than husbands report themselves as exhibiting.[55] Key to navigating relationship development is metacommunication between partners (communication about communication) to establish what meanings each partner ascribes to particular behaviors. As partners learn about differing interpretations, they can work to design a shared meaning system.

NAVIGATING AN EQUAL RELATIONSHIP

An "equal relationship" is one in which two people communicate their individual opinions, feelings, and preferences in a climate of self-respect and respect for the other person. People in equal relationships can see each other as peers and can negotiate their relationship arrangements rather than having either person be "in charge" all the time. In other words, a climate of synergy exists rather than one of dominance and submission. Julia Wood has implied this kind of communication process when discussing "parallel" relationships, in which the two people may have activities and interests in common but at the same time work to protect the individuality of each other.[56]

Three principles of equal relationship—integrity, reciprocity, and flexibility—suggest the values that can guide the communicative process for an intimate pair as they navigate together. The principles do not presume that both people have to be employed for pay outside the home, but they suggest strongly that the work and inherent value of both people must receive respect. The first principle, integrity, denotes honoring the basic selfhood of each partner rather than assuming that either one exists only to serve or provide for the other. Reciprocity assumes that if, for example, geographical moves have to be made to assist the career of one person, careful choices will be made to take into account the concerns of the other. Flexibility assumes that no system of decision making is flawless, so that each partner will have to do some adapting to make the partnership function acceptably for both.[57]

The limits of equal intimacy lie both in individuals and in the systems within which we all live. Many women report that they are hesitant to go back to school or to get a job because the family needs them or because their spouses are used to the convenience of them being home. Many men who want to be open to their wives' personal development report feeling nervous about the prospect of their wives losing interest in home and family or about the prospect of their wives earning a larger paycheck. Both sexes are affected by social policies that are based on the assumption of a female in the home and a male income that is sufficient for a whole family; most families no longer can survive on only one income. In this culture, work outside the home is compensated financially and work inside the home—such as raising children, paying bills, maintaining the household—is not. Financial compensation represents the presumption that people in the business place are more valuable than people in the home. These cultural presumptions underlie critical sex, gender, and economic issues in close relationships.

Further, the economic system prefers uninterrupted and unencumbered careers, so that men or women with continuous job histories win larger salaries and quicker promotions than women who have entered the workforce after having raised children and/or left jobs to follow their spouses' career moves. Given this disparity, many couples with one partner who earns much more than the other will not see it as logically "reciprocal" to make a geographic move to accommodate the educational plans of the lower-paid partner. If they do, it will be because they reject the idea that the present earning power of one of them is automatically more important than empowering the other partner for the future. Only people with stable incomes and strong support systems can afford the choice of asserting themselves in the face of strong opposing forces.

In addition, not all classes and races support the notion that both partners work. Even in the face of economic hardship, some families choose to have an adult—usually the woman—stay at home to care for the children. Navigating the bonded relationship for these couples differs from the navigation by dual worker couples. Sex role questions and issues of power are communicated through verbal and nonverbal behaviors whose meanings were established by the social context and moral standards of that family.

NAVIGATING WITH ASSERTIVENESS

For several decades, a common type of communication training has spread the idea that assertive communication is a positive alternative to either passive or aggressive ways of dealing with others. Assertiveness is included in the chapter on intimate relationships because issues of assertiveness are particularly important when two people are trying to build or maintain a long-term intimate relationship with one another.[58]

The meaning of assert, "to affirm," is important today because many messages originating in the feminist movement have been heard as strong but negative. Women who complained about sex bias were often labeled as "angry" or "strident," while the sex bias itself went unnoticed. When assertiveness training workshops were first offered in the early 1970s, critics often called them "fight training," on the assumption that the only reason women wanted to speak up was to fight with men. Yet much writing on assertiveness confirms that the most powerful result of such training is the individual experience of finding a personal voice. Saying what you believe, often for the first time as an adult, and having other people respond to you as a unique individual can be a heady experience.

We need the concept of an assertive relationship today because films, romantic novels, television, and even cartoons offer numerous images of relationships that are not constructive for either sex. Table 5.1 compares the assertive relationship with two aggressive relationships. The table indicates the kinds of behavior and feelings likely to go with each. However, assertiveness cannot prevent all conflicts. The next section will examine various approaches to how conflicts develop and how both women and men can respond to them more productively.

Table 5.1 Ways I May Relate to You or to Another Person

1. Assertive relationship (two equals have equal sets of options):

I can talk and listen.	You can talk and listen.
I respect myself and you.	You respect yourself and me.
I am willing to negotiate.	You are willing to negotiate
I can lead and follow.	You can lead and follow.

2. Aggressive + Passive relationship (this may develop if I try but am unable to influence you to respond assertively to me):

I speak and interrupt.	You prefer to stay silent.
I control the conversation.	You are controlled.
I take the initiative.	You wait for direction.
I may attack you for passivity.	You may submit to attack.

3. Indirectly Aggressive + Ambivalent (the ambivalent one may become passive, aggressive, of indirectly aggressive if left confused and uneasy for a long time):

I play the martyr.	You feel guilty.
I act so that nonverbals contradict my words.	You worry over my meanings.
I half-praise or half-agree.	You respond uneasily.

NAVIGATING CONFLICT IN INTIMACY RELATIONSHIPS

Marriages and other relationships of commitment have high potential for conflict. One reason is that in intimate relationships people may reveal or risk more of themselves and thus experience more interdependence with a partner than is true in other types of human connection. Couples seem to have high expectations for comfort, understanding, and continued sexual sharing with one another. Disappointment in any of these areas can bring resentment, active conflict, or termination of the relationship.

For men and women today, the potential for conflict is increased as they deal with a variety of stresses related to gender. For example, men and women police officers who share a patrol car might have to face questions from their spouses. Women who win long-delayed raises on the job may wonder how their unemployed spouses will greet the news. Both sexes reflect on their inevitable aging and wonder whether the partner might no longer find them appealing as they grow older. Thus, beneath the specific topics of daily discussion lies the larger issue of personal identity in the context of an intimate relationship.

The discussion that follows is focused on conflict during the maintenance, or navigating, stage of relationships. Conflicts also occur as part of the growth or the deterioration phases of a relationship. Conflict is defined here as communication about mutually incompatible desires. Conflict can arise over competing goals, disagreement over the uses of the resources in a relationship, or personal attitudes and values that one partner does not share with the other. In intimate relationships, conflict occurs on at least two major levels: intrapersonal and dyadic. Intrapersonal conflict occurs when you are in conflict with yourself about what to do or how to think about your own or your partner's behavior. It can represent a short-term problem, as in, "Should I get up and get breakfast for Pat today or not?" or it can go on for years without being resolved.

Dyadic conflict occurs frequently and predictably between people in intimate relationships. Both content and relationship issues are involved in conflict between intimates, but the heart of the conflict is usually the relationship itself: the ways the partners define it and the changes either one wants in the relationship definition. Research into conflict and relationship maintenance confirms the idea that the sex of either partner may be less important when dealing with issues such as jealousy than are factors such as personal self-esteem and one's philosophy about the relationship as a whole. High self-esteem women, for example, show fewer feelings of jealousy than men with either high or low self-esteem.[59]

Of the four perspectives discussed in chapter 2, the three versions of the power perspectives are particularly helpful in revealing important aspects of intimates' communication about conflict. Either sex may hold a strong belief that the male should be dominant and the female submissive. In such instances, if the male fails to lead or the female fails to take his direction, either can take the opportunity to criticize the other for violating the pair's tacit relationship contract. Another version of power conflict develops when one member of the pair, often the woman, brings up an item for discussion in the expectation that once she provides her partner with needed information, the two will negotiate and come to a jointly held view of what they should do. For her, the point is not for one or the other to "win," but for her to empower him with means to engage in an open communication process ending in a mutually agreeable solution. If the male partner hears the issue as involving his authority or competence, he may move into a power struggle with his partner, perhaps announcing his position and saying crisply, "OK, take it or leave it." The woman may be left wondering why a pleasant conversation took such a turn. In a third version, the woman may bring up an idea with the expectation that her partner will join into the creative process and together they will adjust and modify that idea. The man enters the conversation expecting to share his vantage points and presumptions and expecting to hear other vantage points and presumptions from his partner. Each partner enters the conversation without strategizing the end result; each leaves the conversation with new alternatives.

Every pair develops its own priorities and its own "hot topics." In constructive relationships, conflicts are managed without undermining the pair's other bases for intimacy. From the rhetorical perspective, a pair's ability to work through its conflicts over a period of time depends on both partners believing they have adequate status in the other's eyes to be taken seriously in negotiations. Yet conflict inclines many of us to heighten our emphasis on hierarchy and personal status. We often say to ourselves, if not to our partners, "My ideas and assessments are right; other approaches aren't worth considering." Differences in the structure of the hierarchy and in the bases for personal status can occur. Each couple's needs regarding conflict management skills depend on their assessment of conflict elements, an assessment influenced not only by sex and gender but also race, class, and ethnicity.

Another feature influencing the effectiveness of intimates' responses to conflict is the accuracy with which they communicate to their partners their views of the closeness, safety, and depth they currently experience in the relationship. Nonverbal channels often carry these messages, especially when one or both partners are not skilled in metacommunication.[60] Conflicts seem to be managed more successfully when both partners can either perceive the other's metacommunication messages accurately or use language about their own perceptions of the relationship.

COMMUNICATIVE STRATEGIES IN INTIMATE CONFLICT

Recent research on communicative behavior in conflict has revealed six major strategies that men or women choose at various times. Table 5.2 illustrates some of the differences in assumptions that people make when they choose one approach rather than another. We will examine some of the links between these six strategies and the gender stereotypes affecting our views of intimates' behaviors. Each strategy is based on assumptions about the standing of the self and the other, as well as about the goal to be sought. Compelling, bargaining, and persuading are strategies that suggest power defined as dominance. The one who compels may believe that he or she has absolute authority over others (as in the military) or that the act of threatening will win power that has been sought in vain before (as in terrorism). Collaborating and active listening imply the empowerment of the other or the synergism of the pair as a whole.

Table 5.2   Strategies in Conflict

Compelling	using physical or emotional force to oblige the other to do what you want done
Persuading	using your personal credibility to attempt to change the other's feelings or ideas
Bargaining	trying for a solution that is the best you can get, assuming that your interests and the other's differ and that both can't fully win
Collaborating	working together with others to resolve difficulties based on shared information about the problem
Active listening	attending to the problem that is perceived as the other's and trying to encourage or empower the other to address the problem
Avoiding/Accommodating	agreeing to the other's views and demands, or removing yourself to avoid further conflict.

Source: Speed Leas, *Discover Your Conflict Management Style* (Washington, D.C.: Alban Institute, 1984).

Avoiding or accommodating may indicate a strategy of achieving safety or escaping emotional pain at all costs. Avoiding sometimes acts as dominance; if Carlita has asked Eric to find time for the two of them to talk and Eric simply avoids Carlita to avoid the talk, he may be acting out of a desire to control the situation. Accommodating can function as dominance or empowerment. If Allegra accommodates Allan's wishes and later demands retribution for her action, she may be trying to dominate using indirect aggression. On the other hand, Ted may accommodate Elaine's needs to allow Elaine to accomplish a personal goal; his willingness to accommodate her may empower her and increase resources she has to contribute to the relationship.

Any of these six conflict management strategies could be appropriate and effective in a given circumstance. In intimate relationships, some strategies are likely to have more of a bonding impact while others may have more of a distancing or differentiating effect on the partners. For example, the bargaining strategy assumes that the partners have different, maybe even mutually incompatible, goals. If you bring up a difficult topic, such as how to improve family finances, using words such as, "I know you think we have all the money in the world, but . . .," you are setting up a model of opposition that will be hard to escape as you and your partner talk. Or you may tend to use the compelling strategy after you have been silent for a long time about the issue that is now causing conflict. The danger of the compelling strategy is that frequent use of ultimatums or threats may tell your partner either that you cannot back up your threats or that you prefer to keep the other in suspense rather than work out your problems together. Being aware of the relationship implications for each of the six strategies is helpful before using any of them as a predominant approach to conflict.

GENDER ISSUES IN INTIMATE CONFLICT

An ongoing conflict style between partners can affect relationship satisfaction. Women may perceive their work outside the home as interfering with their family lives; most men do not respond similarly. While women who work full-time jobs spend the same number of hours at work outside the home, they spend more hours in family work than men do.[61] Evidence suggests that women have higher levels of overload from family and work demands than do men.[62] One researcher explains that since women have been shown to accrue fewer benefits from marriage than men, women may push harder for change in the relationship. They express desires for more intimacy in the relationship and more day-to-day help with household chores. As a result, women were found to demand and men withdraw. This conflict pattern seemed to put the relationship at risk over time for deterioration in partner satisfaction. Some evidence shows that couples under stress may retreat to gender stereotypes for dealing with conflict.[63] Time spent talking to each other about events of the day is considered important by both men and women and seems to relate to their relational satisfaction. Wives express more concern about whether both partners receive "listening" time; wives seem to view listening and talking as activities to be exchanged equally. Husbands do not seem to draw those fine distinctions.[64]

Among the factors affecting the results of conflict between intimates are (1) the participants' own histories with regard to conflict and its impact on relationships; (2) the individuals' skills in specifying the changes they want and the feelings they have without attacking the character and motives of the other person; and (3) the extent to which both believe that males and females have equal rights to express themselves and to strive for joint solutions when in conflict.

Life histories are particularly important today, when the conflict experiences as well as the early gender training of intimate partners may differ substantially. Some adults grow up believing that true love prevents conflict, while others have seen such destructive conflict in their original families that they are determined to avoid fighting with their partners at all costs. Some partners find satisfaction in indirectly aggressive behaviors like making the other feel guilty or strategically trapping the partner. Others believe that "a good fight" will lead to exciting sex or will release all sorts of tensions in the relationship.

In the extreme, some people who take the latter view justify males' physical violence as necessary and thus "natural." In 1995 O.J. Simpson, a former professional football player, was tried for the brutal murder of his ex-wife, Nicole Simpson, and her friend, Ronald Goldman. As the case proceeded, the public was made aware of a 911 emergency call tape recording made some months earlier of Nicole pleading for protection against a physical attack by O.J. Simpson. That recording and other details of the trial generated animated discussions about male aggression and spousal abuse. During the televised trial, public debates questioned both the notion of "natural" physical aggression for males and the public sanction of socializing males toward physical dominance and hostile behavior. The rationale that physical violence is "natural" for males echoes one version of the biological viewpoint since it emphasizes the male's nature as an aggressive being.

The cultural perspective offers a different explanation for this aggressive behavior. Traditionally males have occupied the role of "protectors" in the society and as such have been conditioned to create distance and develop competitiveness. Males were—and are still—expected to go to war and, if necessary, give their lives for their country. Although females now enter the armed services in higher numbers than in the past, males continue to comprise the largest portion of the service population and only males are required to register for the military draft. Females may choose to be cast in this role; males are expected and even required to fulfill it. Ultimately, the role of protector casts males as expendable. Loss of men in war may not be desired, but both men and women still presume that in time of war, men will sacrifice their lives if necessary to protect those at home.

From the cultural perspective, then, males may be encouraged to develop aggressive and competitive behaviors. In time of war, those who defeat the enemy in dramatic ways are awarded medals and called heroes. Whole cemeteries—such as Arlington Cemetery in Virginia—are maintained as monuments to mostly male competitors who sacrificed their lives to fulfill their social role as protectors. In time of peace, males are encouraged to develop aggressiveness through certain sports, especially those dominated by males such as football, boxing, or hockey. Physical aggression and dominance are hallmarks of these activities; becoming a world-class boxer or a football star brings not only idolatry of youngsters (mostly male) but also financial gain.

Whether or not a male fulfills this protector role does not preclude him from being measured against a standard that demands competitive excellence—especially in physical confrontations such as fights on the grade school playground or physical sports—and a philosophy of winning. Advertisers play to these standards with slogans such as "No Fear" and "Second place is the first loser."

In this way, the cultural perspective helps explain how some males might develop intimate communication strategies that include distance, silence, dominance, or aggression. If conflict is perceived as competition, some males may use unexamined responses in rote ways. Since males biologically are generally larger and physically stronger than females, the conflict situation may produce communication climates that females find menacing or even threatening. Even when females act in dominating or aggressive ways, their physical size probably will not project an implicit threat of physical supremacy.

Some females may therefore avoid direct confrontation with partners of the other sex, particularly if the females perceive the topic as sensitive to that partner or if they do not perceive their intimate communication pattern as one-across or synergistic. Instead, these females may develop intimate communication styles that approach conflict in indirect ways to protect themselves from the implied danger of being physically dominated. Some males may persist in using dominant power, even in small ways, because they do not perceive advantages to abdicating what they believe is a competitive edge.[65]

These socialized lessons generate very different intimate conflict styles of communication for each of the sexes as evidenced by researchers George Bach and Peter Wyden who discovered that women expected men to become sullen or silent during arguments and men expected women to cry. Thus, it was not surprising that both sexes were "tiptoeing around the partner's hostilities and frustrations" instead of addressing their problems so that they could become more intimate partners.[66] Today the gap between the sexes' fighting styles may be less wide, but the image persists that males are verbally and nonverbally dominant in conflict and sometimes that dominance is achieved by being uncommunicative. Men's silence can be a strategy to protect their power in an intimate male-female struggle.[67] Since many women perceive talk as a connector in a relationship—not merely a conveyor of information—they may perceive the silence as a message of disconnection or distance. The image also persists that women are nonassertive and that they avoid conflict rather than engage it. Men may perceive women's actions as "one-down" on the competitive hierarchy and continue their own dominant behaviors. In a relationship climate of safety and trust, both sexes can engage conflict in more constructive and useful ways than these images project.

RELATIONSHIP DETERIORATION

How much conflict can relationships withstand and still survive? According to the model of relationship stages discussed earlier in the chapter, several things can occur when people feel themselves more separate than unified: differentiating—increasing focus on the individual instead of on the pair; disintegrating—the falling apart of the pairing bond, whether or not the two people admit it; stagnating—operating as separate people without breaking the bond officially; terminating—either by divorce or by specific messages to the other that the relationship is ending; returning to individual status—alone, but changed by the relationship experience. As with the earlier stages, we need not assume that all of these will occur in each relationship nor that a couple would move through them in only one direction. The full set of stages may not occur, or deterioration may begin only to be reversed at a later time.

A great many intimate relationships deteriorate. Part of this process occurs when a couple's lives become more separate over time, or it may arise out of one partner's life-altering experience. When people become more differentiated, they look at their present relationship more as an option than as an inevitable or inescapable fact in their lives. Analyzing the relationship can lead to greater skepticism, or it can promote a revision of values and behaviors in both partners. Programs like Marriage Encounter and Marriage Enrichment use tools such as journal writing followed by dialogue to encourage partners to self-disclose safely, helping them to find out each other's thoughts in a freeing, respectful way. Such efforts direct people back to the growth stages of their relationship, where they may discover elements of the other's individuality that had become submerged over time.

When female-male relationships end, the males often perceive the ending as abrupt, whereas the females perceive it as protracted. Males may not recognize the problem or the seriousness of the problem until the female points it out.[68] Some scholars argue that the feminine stereotype assigns to the female the role of relationship maintenance; as a consequence, males assume females are doing the work to sustain the relationship and miss important cues about relationship trouble.[69]

Divorcing couples have used "intimacy" synonymously with "communication." However, although they agree they have experienced a communication failure, they do not agree about what the word means.[70] Communication for the wives involved touch, attentive listening, nonverbal support, and expressiveness. They valued contact. The husbands preferred less of the sharing and openness described by the wives.[71]

As men and women differentiate themselves, they place more value on their individual choices about communication styles and become less interested in continuing to pursue a joint meaning system. That differentiation leads to a disintegration of whatever system had been in place; each begins to violate the implicit communication rules of the partnership in favor of other communication strategies that support their individual goals.

Sometimes financial considerations or family demands require the couple remain together. Couples who have formed a stepfamily, for example, may be reluctant to separate because of the children's attachment to the other partner. You probably know formerly intimate partners who are postponing a termination until children graduate or until job or community obligations are completed. In such cases, stagnation usurps energy from the participating partners. But relationship stagnation occurs among college students as well; couples often reach this stage of relating when they are tired of dating each other after several years but do not have a better partner available. Having been so long in a relationship, each is hesitant to return to their social group without a partner. Sometimes stagnant relationships are maintained for the sake of others outside the relationship—"What would I tell my friends?" In many cases stagnant relationships use up a great deal of the partners' energy in attempts to avoid overt conflict, and the resulting intrapersonal and interpersonal conflict make reaching a relatively clean ending difficult.

Popular writers have cited the feminist movement as a primary reason for the increase in the rate of terminating marriages in the United States. Many comments critical of feminism have alluded to women's grabbing power from men or their unwillingness to do the compromising necessary to maintain an intimate relationship. Some people claim that women's choices to enter the workplace have destroyed not only heterosexual partnerships but the family system as well. These claims point to inevitable problems of change. Many women have gone through a period of focusing more on their own individuality than on their parts in intimate relationships. If the socialization process has generated a balance in pairing the masculine and the feminine cultures—that is, the female focused on "other" while attending the relational issues and the male focused on "self" while attending the content or work issues—then when the female begins to focus on "self" and content or work issues, imbalance will occur.

Changes in the intimate relationships between heterosexual partners occur for at least two reasons: first, financial conditions require many families to generate two incomes and, second, some women have discovered they enjoy and excel at the activities required in the workplace. Financial conditions have diminished choices for those in many two-parent families, choices for one parent to work and one to attend familial and relational necessities. More and more, both partners need to earn salaries for the family to achieve a livable income. This necessity compels women to recenter their lives; their jobs consume both time and energy the women no longer can spend on their families or partners. Since the balance of the partnership is affected by this recentering, both women and men may find themselves uncertain of their roles. Negotiation is underway about how to sustain the relational needs of the couple or the family while maintaining the necessary monetary income. The consequential experimentation to find new models of intimacy and family stability may feel uncomfortable and may result in missteps.

The experimentation also may result in new, effective ways for both the individuals and the couple or family to thrive. One result of the experimentation is that many women have discovered they enjoy the adult company and individual achievement afforded by the public workplace. As men and women learn how to better communicate with one another there (a topic to be discussed further in chapter 8), possibilities for synergistic relationships increase. Movements such as the Million Man March have begun to promote males' greater involvement in and responsibility to family matters. As more voice is given to support for family values, interest increases in promoting a model of shared intimacy (and attention to relational issues) and individuality (and attention to content and work issues) for both males and females.

TERMINATING INTIMATE RELATIONSHIPS

In some cases, intimate relationships can be terminated suddenly by one partner or the other, an event called "sudden death." In other cases, partners dissolve the relationship jointly, each recognizing their mutual incompatibility. Termination of relationships involves sometimes difficult communication about personal loss and property divisions.

Legal separation or divorce mark terminations of marriages, relationships which may or may not have been intimate. Until recent years divorces almost always pitted one marriage partner against the other, based on charges such as adultery or mental cruelty. The "no-fault divorce" movement in the 1970s and early 1980s removed some of the attacks on character from the divorce courtroom, but it also led to some unfortunate results for women and children. Previously women who had been full-time homemakers were granted alimony as well as child support. Alimony is now limited in duration and amount, often specified based on the number of years estimated for the woman to find steady work. Child support is typically awarded to the children's mother, who is more often the parent with custody. Because of both noncompliance and nonenforcement, the average single mother receives from the absent father only about $1,000 a year in child support awarded by the courts to help support the children.[72]

The significance of these facts for communication and the sexes is simple: women are objectively in worse financial condition after a divorce, whether or not they have custody of children. Men are generally in better financial circumstances after a divorce. In the year following divorce, men's incomes rise by 70 percent while women's fall by 40 percent. Over half of the African-American families in the United States are supported by a single woman, a person whose sex and race mitigates against her on the job market.

Interpersonally, however, the record is reversed. Women usually have stronger support systems—people they can talk to and spend time with—than their divorced mates. Men, in contrast, fare badly if they divorce and do not remarry in less than a year. Their tendency to withhold personal information from others makes it harder for them to make friends. If they have depended upon a spouse who facilitated their friendships with other couples, they will not easily move toward other people.

CONCLUSION

A developmental approach to intimate relationships reminds us of the dynamic, ever-changing nature of all human relationships. For women and men, the nature of intimacy has become increasingly complicated as individuals' own needs have shifted and as the contexts for their intimate communication have changed as well. People place an enormous responsibility on intimate relationships as sources of pleasure, meaning, and continuity. Yet the gender training of both women and men may produce barriers to achieving that goal of intimacy.

Recognizing some of the gender-based differences in the experiences of the two sexes may help you to prevent some of the problems described in this chapter. If you are male, that will mean examining your views about friendship, about the proper amount of self-disclosure, about verbal expressiveness and silence, and about physical aggression as a "natural" response to conflict. If you are female, it will mean considering ways in which you do or do not assert yourself, reactions to conflictual situations and arguments, and the degree to which you operate according to a dominance-submission view of intimacy. Awareness of the power of gender ideals to help or hinder your chances for intimacy can be a practical resource in your daily life.

QUESTIONS FOR DISCUSSION

1. Remember "best friends" you have had in your life. Were those friends same-sex or other-sex? What has made a particular friendship unique for you? Has its nature changed over time? What characteristics of the friendship can you see are affected by sex or gender?

2. What would you categorize as self-disclosure in an intimate relationship? What kinds of information have you disclosed before in your intimate relationships? Do you disclose different kinds or amounts of information in intimate relationships with males or females? Who disclosed first?

3. Does the concept of predictable relationship stages work for or against the possibility of a romantic relationship? Explain.

4. Which of the conflict approaches in this chapter have you used, observed in others, vowed to avoid or to apply in your own intimate relationship? What were the outcomes of the conflict style you used? How did the style protect you? How did the style evoke open communication? How did the style affect your partner?

5. Some writers assert that people are more selfish now than in the past, partly out of skepticism about the prospect of long-term intimacy. What characteristics would exist in a happy, intimate relationship? Where do you rank a happy, long-term intimate relationship among your life goals? Compare with others of both sexes.

6. Various researchers have concluded that marriage affects women's emotional health negatively and men's positively. Assuming that there is some validity to these conclusions, how would you use that knowledge in establishing or altering a real-life relationship of your own?

7. What do you consider to be negative aspects of an intimate relationship with those of the same sex? Other sex? How do you incorporate those aspects into your partnerships? What positive aspects do you perceive in intimate relationships with those of the same sex? Other sex?

Cases for Analysis

Case 5.1

1. What stereotypes with regard to femininity, masculinity, and intimacy are depicted in the cartoon on the next page? What stereotypes are rebuked? Have you found these stereotypical behaviors in your relationships? Think of examples that compare or contrast with those represented here.

Reprinted with special permission of King Features Syndicate.

2. What motivations does each of these characters have for working to understand the frame of the other? In terms of caring for each other, how might that care look to each of these characters?

3. How do the ethics of separateness and connectedness relate to this cartoon? Some people joke about men coming from one planet and women from another. Does this cartoon depict the stereotypes about who lives on the "separate planet" and who lives on the "connected one"?

4. When you are in a developing relationship, how much time do you spend thinking about it? Analyzing it? What kinds of things do you consider during those times? Do you think your partner thinks about it in the same ways?

CASE 5.2 BEING NOBODY

Aaron and Kayla lived on the same floor of a coed dormitory in a medium-sized college. They had been good friends for most of the first semester. One night they sat in the dorm lobby watching a favorite movie with a large group of friends. A discussion ensued after the movie; in small groups, the other students eventually left the lobby leaving Aaron and Kayla alone. Without planning to, Aaron and Kayla became romantically involved and spent a couple of hours alone kissing and holding one another.

The next day Kayla woke up smiling and happy. She excitedly told her friends about the budding romance, saying she didn't know where it might lead but that their talk and time together had given her new insights about Aaron. Later in the day, when Kayla went to Aaron's room to say hello, Aaron acted cool and standoffish. Kayla felt confused; later that evening, she confronted Aaron about his behavior. After several hours of talk, Kayla realized she had interpreted their interlude as an introduction to a close relationship. She perceived that Aaron interpreted it as a "natural" result of being alone in a room with someone willing to make out. Over the next few months, she watched Aaron become similarly involved with a half a dozen other women. Kayla felt duped and manipulated by Aaron's actions.

1. Have you had or known someone who had a similar experience? How did she describe it? How did he? What residual feelings did she experience? What residual feelings did he?

2. What different messages are conveyed to women by physical closeness, touching, and intimacy? To men?

3. Can mixed-sex friendships evolve without talk or experimentation about how the relationship might work as an intimate partnership? What experiences have you had with other-sex friendships? Did you address this question?

4. What communication strategies might Kayla use to avoid this situation another time? Be realistic in your solution. What communication strategies might Aaron use? Who might be most motivated to try to use these strategies? Who might be least? Why?

CASE 5.3 TO MARRY OR NOT

Two seniors in high school, Cindy and Tom, had been dating for seven months when Cindy discovered she was pregnant. Tom told her that he would marry her and quit school, but Cindy decided instead to run away from home, find a place to stay where her parents wouldn't find her, and wait for the baby's birth. After having been gone for a week, Cindy called her parents. She had not told them of the pregnancy, fearing what they might say to her. But when she called they expressed concern for her well-being, and they asked her what they could do to help now. Cindy finally agreed to come home and have the baby in her hometown hospital.

After the baby was born, Tom again asked her to marry him and gave her an engagement ring. Cindy chose not to keep it, telling Tom repeatedly that she was not sure marrying was right for either of them. Tom kept going to high school part time and working part time to save money for an apartment for the three of them. Yet he was frustrated that he could not convince Cindy that the two of them should marry and live with their infant son. Meanwhile Cindy's parents told her that they felt she was extremely lucky to have a man who would stand by her, and she should not make him wait any longer.

1. How do the reactions of Cindy and Tom fit or fail to fit the gender role expectations for each of them?

2. If you were a friend of Cindy's and had a chance to talk with her at length, what would you say to her? If you were a friend of Tom's, what would you say to him?

3. Evaluate the intimacy that appears to exist between Cindy and her parents, and between Cindy and Tom.

4. Using your knowledge of relationships, make a guess about what the future will bring to Cindy and Tom if they marry; if they do not marry.

5. Which of the four perspectives can help account for Cindy's current reactions? For Tom's?

NOTES

[1] Michael E. McGill, *The McGill Report on Male Intimacy* (New York: Holt, Rinehart and Winston, 1985); V. S. Helgeson, P. Shaver, and M. Dyer, "Prototypes of Intimacy and Distance in Same-Sex and Opposite-Sex Relationships," *Journal of Social and Personal Relationships* 4 (1987): 195–233.

[2] Pamela G. Orosan and Karen Maitland Schilling, "Gender Differences in College Students' Definitions and Perceptions of Intimacy," *Women & Therapy* 12, 1/2 (1992): 201–12.

[3] Ibid.

[4] Phame M. Camarena, Pamela A. Sarigiani, and Anne C. Petersen, "Gender-Specific Pathways to Intimacy in Early Adolescence," *Journal of Youth and Adolescence* 19, 1 (1990): 19–32.

[5] Orosan and Schilling, op cit.

[6] J. L. Fischer and L. R. Narus, Jr., "Sex Roles and Intimacy in Same Sex and Other Sex Relationships," *Psychology of Women Quarterly* 5, 3 (Spring 1981): 444–55.

[7] Don G. Schiedel and James E. Marcia, "Ego Identity, Intimacy, Sex Role Orientation, and Gender," *Developmental Psychology* 21, 1 (1985): 159.

[8] Carol D. Ryff and Susan Migdal, "Intimacy and Generativity: Self-Perceived Transitions," *Signs* (Spring 1984): 477.

[9] Nancy Cantor, Michele Acker, and Carol Cook-Flannagan, "Conflict and Preoccupation in the Intimacy Life Task," *Journal of Personality and Social Psychology* 63, 4 (1992): 644–55.

[10] Fischer and Narus, op cit., p. 454.

[11] Louise Merves-Okin, Edmund Amidon, and Frank Bernt, "Perceptions of Intimacy in Marriage: A Study of Married Couples," *The American Journal of Family Therapy* 19, 2 (1991): 110–18.

[12] Hilary Graham, "Caring: A Labour of Love," in *A Labour of Love: Women, Work and Caring*, ed. J. Finch and D. Groves (London: Routledge & Kegan Paul, 1983).

[13] E. Anthony Rotundo, "Romantic Friendship: Male Intimacy and Middle-Class Youth in the Northern United States, 1800–1900," *Journal of Social History* 23, 1 (Fall 1989): 1–25.

[14] Linda Bakken and Charles Romig, "Interpersonal Needs in Middle Adolescents: Companionship, Leadership and Intimacy," *Journal of Adolescence* 15 (1992): 301–16.

[15] Carmarena, Sarigiani, and Petersen, op cit.

[16] Bakken and Romig, op cit.

[17] Silvio Silvestri, "Marital Instability in Men, Intact and Divorced Families: Interpersonal Behavior, Cognitions and Intimacy," *Journal of Divorce & Remarriage* 18, 1/2 (1992): 79–108.

[18] Eileen Nelson, Jamie Allison, and Donna Sundre, "Relationships Between Divorce and College Students' Development of Identity and Intimacy," in *Divorce and the Next Generation* (Haworth Press, 1992), pp. 121–35.

[19] Silvestri, op cit.

[20] R. A. Kulka and H. Weingarten, "The Long-Term Effects of Parental Divorce in Childhood on Adult Adjustment," *Journal of Social Issues* 35, 4 (1979): 50–78.

[21] David Lisak, "Deficits in Intimacy and Empathy in Sexually Aggressive Men," *Journal of Interpersonal Violence* 10, 3 (September 1995): 296–308.

[22] D. H. Ingram, "Remarks on Intimacy and the Fear of Commitment," *The American Journal of Psychoanalysis* 46, 1 (1986): 76–79.

[23] See Lillian Rubin, *Just Friends* (New York: Harper and Row, 1985), pp. 59–79; and Robert R. Bell, *Worlds of Friendship* (Beverly Hills, CA: Sage, 1981), pp. 55–93.

[24] Duane Buhrmester, "Intimacy of Friendship, Interpersonal Competence, and Adjustment during Preadolescence and Adolescence," *Child Development* 61, 4 (1990): 1011–1111.

[25] John M. Reisman, "Intimacy in Same-Sex Friendships," *Sex Roles* 23, 1/2 (1990): 65–82.

[26] Orosan and Schilling, op cit, p. 202.

[27] Camarena, Sarigiani, and Petersen, op cit.

[28] Reisman, op cit.; Deborah Tannen, *You Just Don't Understand: Women and Men in Conversation* (New York: Ballantine Books, 1990).

[29] I. S. Kon, "Adolescent Friendship: Some Unanswered Questions for Future Research," in *Developing Personal Relationships*, ed. S. Duck and R. Gilmour (London: Academic Press, 1981); I. S. Kon and V. A. Losenkov, "Friendships in Adolescence: Values and Behavior," *Journal of Marriage and the Family* 40 (1978): 143–55.

[30] Ofra Mayseless, "Gifted Adolescents and Intimacy in Close Same-Sex Friendships," *Journal of Youth and Adolescence* 22, 2 (1993): 135–46.

[31] Reisman, op cit.

[32] Orosan and Schilling, op cit.

[33] Valerian J. Derlega, Robin J. Lewis, Scott Harrison, Barbara A. Winstead, and Robert Costanza, "Gender Differences in the Initiation and Attribution of Tactile Intimacy," *Journal of Nonverbal Behavior* 13, 2 (1989): 83–96.

[34] Reisman, op cit.

[35] Andrew Howell and Michael Conway, "Perceived Intimacy of Expressed Emotion," *The Journal of Social Psychology* 130, 4 (1990): 467–76.

[36] Lynn Carol Miller, "Intimacy and Liking: Mutual Influence and the Role of Unique Relationships," *Journal of Personality and Social Psychology* 59, 1 (1990): 50–60.

[37] Derlega, Lewis, Harrison, Winstead, and Costanza, op cit.

[38] See also the section on homophobia in *Gayspeak: Gay Male and Lesbian Communication*, ed. James Chesebro (New York: Pilgrim, 1981), pp. 115–61.

[39] W. K. Rawlins, "Reflecting on (Cross-Sex) Friendship: De-scripting the Drama," *Personal Relationship Issues* 2 (1994):1–3.

[40] K. Werking, "Barriers to the Formation of Close Cross-Sex Friendship," paper presented at the 1994 International Network on Personal Relationship Conference, Iowa City, IA, 1994, as cited by Lee West, Jennifer Anderson, and Steve Duck, "Crossing the Barriers to Friendships Between Men and Women," in *Gendered Relationships*, ed. Julia Wood (Mountain View, CA: Mayfield Publishing Company, 1996), pp. 111–27.

[41] P. Blumstein and P. Schwartz, *American Couples* (New York: William Morrow & Co., 1983).

[42] See Michelle Huston and Pepper Schwartz, "Gendered Dynamics in the Romantic Relationships of Lesbians and Gay Men," in *Gendered Relationships*, ed. Julia Wood (Mountain View, CA: Mayfield Publishing Co., 1996), pp. 163–76.

[43] Merves-Okin, Amidon, and Bernt, op cit., p. 116.

[44] Ruthellen Josselson, *Finding Herself: Pathways to Identity Development in Women* (San Francisco: Jossey-Bass Publishers, 1987), p. 24.

[45] Julia T. Wood, "Communication and Relational Culture: Bases for the Study of Human Relationships," *Communication Quarterly* 30, 2 (1982); and Gerald M. Phillips and Julia T. Wood, *Communication and Human Relationships: The Study of Interpersonal Communication* (New York: Macmillan, 1983).

[46] C. Gilligan, *In a Different Voice* (Cambridge, MA: Harvard University Press, 1982).

[47] Pamela Fishman, "Interaction: The Work Women Do," in *Language, Gender and Society*, ed. Barrie Thorne, Cheris Kramarae, and Nancy Henley (Rowley, MA: Newbury House, 1983), pp. 89–102.

[48] Dorothy Tennov, *Love and Limerence: The Experience of Being in Love* (New York: Stein and Day, 1979).

[49] L. B. Feldman, "Marital Conflict and Marital Intimacy: An Integrative Psychodynamic-Behavioral-Systemic Model," *Family Processes* 18 (March 1979): 69–78.

[50] Helgeson, Shaver, and Dyer, op cit.

[51] Ibid.

[52] Deborah Tannen, op cit.

[53] Jack W. Sattel, "Men, Inexpressiveness, and Power," in *Language, Gender and Society*, ed. Barrie Thorne, Cheris Kramarae, and Nancy Henley (Cambridge: Newbury House Publishers, 1983).

[54] Helgeson, Shaver, and Dyer, op cit.; J. L. Ellickson and T. Seals, "Gender and Intimacy: Cotherapy with a Premarital Couple," *Psychotherapy* 23, 2 (Summer 1986): 273–82; Paula A. Treichler and Cheris Kramarae, "Women's Talk in the Ivory Tower," *Communication Quarterly* 31, 2 (1983): 118–32; and J. L. Hawkins, C. Weisberg, and D. W. Ray, "Spouse Differences in Communication Style: Preference, Perception, and Behavior," *Journal of Marriage and the Family* 42 (1980): 585–93.

[55] Hawkins, Weisberg, and Ray, op cit.

[56] Wood 1982, op cit.

[57] Barbara Bate and James Memmott, "Three Principles for Dual Career Marriage," presentation at Northern Illinois University, March 1984.

[58] Among the books on assertive issues, three are particularly useful: Ronald Adler, *Talking Straight* (New York: Holt, Rinehart and Winston, 1977); Sharon Anthony Bower and Gordon Bower, *Asserting Yourself* (Reading, MA: Addison-Wesley, 1976); and Pamela Butler, *Self-Assertion for Women* (San Francisco: Harper & Row, 1976). See also Barbara Bate, "Assertive Speaking: An Approach for Communication Education of the Future," *Communication Education* (1976): 202.

[59] Susan Parrish Sprowl, "Cognitive, Affective, and Behavioral Correlates of Jealousy: An Analysis of Gender Differences," paper presented at the 1984 Communication, Language, and Gender Conference, Oxford, OH; see also, from the same conference, B. Christine Shea, "Gender and Relationship Maintenance Strategies."

[60] Paul Watzlawick, Janet Helmick Beavin, and Don D. Jackson, *The Pragmatics of Human Communication* (New York: Norton, 1967).

[61] Barbara A. Gutek and Sabrina Searle, "Rational Versus Gender Role Explanations for Work-Family Conflict," *Journal of Applied Psychology* 76, 4 (1991): 560–68.

[62] Linda Duxbury, Christopher Higgins, and Catherine Lee, "Work-Family Conflict," *Journal of Family Issues* 15, 3 (September 1994): 449–66.

[63] Howard J. Markman, Louise Silvern, Mari Clements, and Shelley Kraft-Hanak, "Men and Women Dealing with Conflict in Heterosexual Relationships," *Journal of Social Issues* 49, 3 (1993): 107–25.

[64] Anita L. Vangelisti and Mary A. Banski, "Couples' Debriefing Conversations: The Impact of Gender, Occupation, and Demographic Characteristics," *Family Relations* 42 (1993): 149–57.

[65] For a discussion about confrontation of high-power and low-power groups, see Judith K. Bowker, "Reporting Sexual Harassment: Reconciling Power, Knowledge, and Perspective," in *Sexual Harassment: Communication Implications*, ed. Gary L. Kreps (Cresskill, NJ: Hampton Press, Inc., 1993).

[66] George Bach and Peter Wyden, *The Intimate Enemy: How to Fight Fair in Love and Marriage* (New York: Avon Books, 1968), p. 91.

[67] Jack Sattel, op cit., pp. 118–24; and Susan Price, *The Female Ego* (New York: Rawson, 1984), p. 26.

[68] Ellickson and Seals, op cit.

[69] McGill, op cit; Ellickson and Seals, op cit.

[70] Lyman C. Wynne and Adele R. Wynne, "The Quest for Intimacy," *Journal of Marital and Family Therapy* (October 1986): 383–94.

[71] Hawkins, Weisberg, and Ray, op cit.

[72] Dan Cordtz, "Off the Dole," *Financial World* 163, 4 (Feb. 15, 1994): 24–29.

Chapter 6

Family

The family may be the most significant context in which we learn about sex and gender. While we all grow and change throughout our lifetimes, our initial presumptions about what it means to be male or female often emerge from messages we receive from our families. Family communication may be so fluid that we cannot pinpoint a specific beginning for sex and gender messages. Family communication spans international, intercultural, ethnic, and racial dimensions.[1] Intergenerational effects, experiences of parents and other family members, and community environment represent only a few of the ways families shape their expectations of boys and girls, women and men, masculine and feminine. Even before a child is born, discussions have ensued from questions like, "Are you hoping for a boy or girl?" Once a baby's sex has been announced, other messages will be sent and received that convert that first announcement of biological sex into gender-related expectations.

CHAPTER OVERVIEW

This chapter describes the family as a communication system and shows the importance of interdependence within that system.

Attention is given to the ways parents talk to parents, parents talk to children, children talk with other family members, and members of the family talk with people outside the immediate family system. The communicative importance of children's clothing, toys, and activities is also examined.

The central idea behind this chapter on the family is that *the sex of a child is treated as fact and sets the mandate for expectations of gender.* While sex is communicated explicitly and through use of nearly universal criteria, gender is communicated both explicitly and implicitly. Gender becomes the rhetorically constructed composite of those explicit and implicit messages—messages mediated by the cultural stereotypes of masculine and feminine. Whether family members concur with those stereotypes, disagree with them, or subscribe to some unique stereotype of their own, messages about gender emanate from stereotyped forms.

While the culture generates dominant stereotypes of gender, families can generate stereotypes of their own. The interplay of these stereotypes creates a complex maze of expectations that family members usually sort out in individual ways. For example, parents may express hopes and dreams about their son or daughter, projecting gender expectations with comments like, "I hope she grows up to be president" or "Maybe he'll bring world peace." These hopes project very different kinds of gender expectations from those expressed by comments like, "Maybe she'll be Miss America," or "Perhaps he'll make it big in the NFL." A female in the first example may deal with gender controversies in her family if she chooses not to enter the public workplace in favor of becoming a mother and homemaker. Likewise, a male in the second example may confront problems about gender expectations if *he* decides to stay at home to father his children and maintain his household.

Typically, we think of people generating messages about sex and gender when a baby is born into a family. Families integrate messages about sex and gender in many other scenarios also. For example, when a family member takes a partner, expectations about heterosexuality or homosexuality may emerge. Often people ask what the male does for a living or if the bride is pretty. Likewise, intergenerational conversation may include implicit negotiation of the gender expectations, negotiation that may occur between someone who was 20 years old in 1940 and someone who was 20 years old in 1995. Messages about sex and gender also inform discussions about whether an older member of the family can get along alone now that her or his partner has died. Can Grandpa cook for himself? Can Grandma keep the car in good repair? The family as a context presents numerous, varied, and complicated communication issues with regard to sex and gender.

In this chapter, we do not assume that all families are alike or that they can be represented by a single model. The importance of sex and gender and the relationship between them varies widely among families. This variance is based on a large number of influences such as geographic locale, religious belief, race, class, ethnicity, or nationality. While not all families are the same, all families deal in some way with the questions of how much and in what ways biological sex is going to be treated as the basis for messages about the *shoulds* for females and males.

THE FAMILY AS A COMMUNICATION SYSTEM

SYSTEMS THEORY

Defining what constitutes a family in the United States is more complicated now than it was in 1950. Over the last fifty years, changing roles and expectations for men and women paralleled changes in parameters of what used to be called a "traditional family": Mom-at-home, Dad-at-workplace, 2.2 children, a dog, a house, and a white picket fence. This definition not only reflected strong stereotypes for roles for women and men, it also reflected only the experiences of one segment of the United States culture—middle and upper-middle class, white people.

Many more current and more useful definitions define family in various ways as a close-knit group of interdependent people who rely on each other for financial, emotional, and physical needs.[2] Now single parent families, couples without children, and stepfamilies together comprise the majority of family experiences of people in the United States.

In keeping with this definition, we will talk about a family as a *communication system*—a theoretical construct that identifies interrelated characteristics of a family. The theory uses the term, "systems," to signify that changes to any part of that communication group will affect all other parts. To understand the concept of a system, think of a mobile. When you touch or move one part of the mobile, all the other parts bob and move. The systems theory asserts that in any communication system, these eight characteristics exist: First, *interdependence* describes the state in which the actions of one person in

the family will influence the experiences of others. Second, families are seen as *wholes* by members and observers; outsiders often think of the "Bates" or the "Bowkers" as having qualities or interests unique to them, whether or not they apply to each member. Third, each family creates a set of communication *patterns* that serve as norms for that family's interactions. Sex and gender patterns help determine what each sex may or may not say, when they may say it, and to whom they might say it. Fourth, families experience an *interactive complexity* that is punctuated to create meaning. The interactive complexity can create a circular causality that might work like this:

Judy: "Mom! Dennis hit me!"

Mom (from the other room): "Dennis! Don't hit your sister!"

Judy sneers at Dennis, mouthing: "Nah, nah, nah!"

Dennis hits Judy.

Judy: "Mom! Dennis hit me!"

Each family develops a complex means of interacting that, like this example, relies on Judy's knowledge of Mom's responses, Mom's expectation of her authority, Dennis's expectation of acceptable behavior, Judy's knowledge of Dennis's tolerance point, and so on. Each member punctuates the scene differently. Judy might say the episode started when Dennis hit her and ended when he finally quit. Mom might describe it as beginning when Judy called for help and ended when she told Dennis to stop. Dennis might say the event started when Judy pestered him and ended when he finally got her to stop. The punctuation by each family member increases the complex interaction within the family.

Fifth, families are *open* to the environment outside of the members themselves so that other events and people can influence how parents and children deal with each other. Gender messages permeate the family boundaries through sources such as neighbors, friends, the media, and the community. Sixth, different families can accomplish similar tasks and processes even though they may start at different places, use different means, and have different values. This quality is *equifinality*. In one family, males may be required to do volunteer work as a way to teach care and nurturance for others. In another family, the same value of teaching males to care and nurture others may result from certain communication rules about how members talk to one another. Differing family members, values, circumstances, and communication practices result in varying styles and processes that can produce the same goal or state.

Seventh, *adaptation* represents the family's ability to adjust to changes in the environment and within themselves. When the daughter goes to college and returns with new gender expectations, for example, the family will restructure itself to cope with the change. That restructuring could range from changing family gender norms to reinforcing more strongly norms initially established. Eighth, family systems develop *hierarchical subsystems* that inform members about who is higher or lower than themselves in a particular situation or with regard to this particular subject. Often sex and gender groups are hierarchically arranged: ask Mom if you want to spend the night; ask Dad for money; ask older sister to ask parents if you want to break curfew. These hierarchies are created on many bases, such as age, economic contribution, or capacity for confidentiality. Last, family systems use *information processing* to transmit messages. This mechanism is used to keep the parts interrelated to each other. Most families do a great deal of information processing: discussing or finding out what members are doing, when they will be available for recreational activities or household chores, and how well the family as a whole is doing in getting along with each other and with the outside world. Key types of information in the family are money, time, space, food, and feelings. Beneath these more visible topics are questions of individual identity, degrees of intimacy/comfort, and levels and types of power. Think about these issues as they were processed in your family. How did your family's communication system affect your development of gender identity or power with regard to sex or gender?

FAMILY THEMES

Each family generates themes and images that support the nature and character of that family. A theme is a simply stated directive that indicates a critical value of the family and implicitly or explicitly suggests a course of action for family members. For example, one theme a family might have at its center could be "Hard work strengthens character." Another family might have "Education comes first" as one of its centrally guiding themes. While each family might agree that both these sentiments are admirable or worthy, the family with the first theme might honor and value hard work over education. The theme might be carried out with statements like, "Mary, whether you are a physician or a gas station attendant is not really the issue. What counts is whether you are working hard and doing your best." Likewise, the theme from the second family might be carried out with statements like, "I know you like your job at the dairy, Karl, but continuing your education is much more important in the long run."

Kathleen Galvin claims that families function around central themes.[3] Take a moment to think about your own family. What are a couple of the themes you can identify very quickly? Frequently messages about sex and gender are implicit within the theme. Examine your themes for those implications. For example, in some families the education theme mentioned earlier is a theme mostly communicated to males. Females are given much less encouragement and motivation to enact the theme of pursuing formal education. Occasionally, themes and socialized gender stereotypes will clash. Imagine an adolescent male who is challenged at school about his masculinity. His family runs on the theme "We do not fight"; his peers expect him to defend himself in a "manly" way. Both are powerful influences on the choice the young man must make. Themes often represent a unifying thread evident in many parts of the family. As a result, family members receive similar messages from a variety of sources; for young children, that consistency can persuade them to develop gender roles in accordance with the family standard.

Family themes form strong foundations for communication within the family over various generations. Long before a baby enters the family these themes create webs of meaning through which family members negotiate their development. Family themes do not necessarily adhere to cultural stereotypes with regard to gender, but often the composite of family themes in a given culture constitutes the cultural norm. Assess your own family themes for messages you received about sex and gender. How are sex and gender messages in your family's themes in accord with cultural stereotypes and how are they different?

FAMILY IMAGES

Examining family images is another way to understand how the family communicates messages of sex and gender. Family members carry images of their families—metaphors derived from their vantage points on family experience. For example, some people describe their families as circuses with each family member in a separate ring acting out their best talent. These people might extend their circus metaphor by saying their families are chaotic and loud and given to crazy schemes. Another family might be described as an ocean where turbulence at the surface always is mitigated by a deep calm below. Other kinds of metaphors people use for their families include images like gardens, balance beams, war zones, or a gentle river on a Sunday afternoon.

These images are significant in both kind and variety. Think about the image that best fits your family. Assess your image for implications of sex and gender. A family image of a war zone connotes aggression, defense, and conflict. A family image of a flower garden connotes significantly different characteristics. Think of interactions of male or female family members in each of these environments. Interactions between the family members and their environments contribute to development of gender in both the members and their family images.

Having assessed your image of your family for implications of sex and gender, consider your siblings or your parents. Would they ascribe to the same family image you do? If so, how would they describe their interaction with that image? For example, do they see themselves as the circus performer or the clown? If they do not ascribe to the same family image as you, ask them about their images. In what ways does your sex affect your choices? Your gender? Understanding sex and gender in family communication through family images can reveal some of the implicit messages we receive throughout our lives, messages that guide our gender development.

COMMUNICATION OF GENDER THROUGH DEVELOPMENTAL STAGES OF FAMILY

Discussing how issues of sex and gender interact with the developmental stages of the family helps reveal the hows and whys of many messages. However, using a single model of family development is problematic. For example, families with children may expend considerable attention on the awareness levels of children and the particular circumstances that children create. Families without children develop very differently. Another variation on family development occurs because children enter some families by being born to a parent or parents; in other families children are adopted or become part of a family because parents marry or move in together. To find a model that best suits our needs, we most often will use one that includes children since one of our goals is to understand how communication in families sustains and promotes gender messages. Because we have all been children in some type of family structure, we can use our model to discuss and explain influences on gender development. The model has four stages: families with young children, families with adolescents, launching children and moving on, and families in later life.[4]

Families can be started by a single person who adopts a child or decides to have and raise a child alone. Single-parent families can also result from divorce or death. For families with one parent, the availability of a support network affects the roles and experiences of the family members. For example, research suggests that African-American mothers have less supportive networks than white mothers; their networks are smaller and dominated by family members. These mothers have fewer people to call on in times of need and have less help available to them. From a rhetorical perspective, these women have fewer options for accomplishing their family goals than do other groups of people, particularly white families.[5]

While we might predict that one-parent families might affect gender role expectations, research finds that family composition has few long-term effects. The effects that have been measured seem to indicate that family composition influences women more than men. Women whose mothers were employed seem to have less traditional attitudes than others. If parents have divorced, women seem to develop liberal attitudes toward women in politics. Sons of one-parent (female) families respond more favorably toward greater opportunities for women in politics and the public workplace.[6]

Some one-parent families become two-parent families through marriage or cohabitation. When one or both partners have children, negotiating intimacy entails not just considering the needs and desires of one another but can mean negotiating needs and desires of several others including young children, adolescents, or even adult children. Expectations about gender can complicate these broader considerations. Papernow explains how family members' initial expectations about being a stepfamily may move through a cycle from fantasy to adjustment and resolution.[7] Expectations about gender play distinct roles in stepfamily adjustment. What if Mom—who believes girls and boys should play with whatever toys suit them—chooses to partner with someone who plays roughhouse with the boys, takes the girls out for sodas, and tells jokes about dumb blondes? The tacit negotiations that ensue among all family members may affect Mom's intimate relationship as well as relationships among and between other family members.

FAMILIES WITH YOUNG CHILDREN

When Mom and her new partner—or any parent or parents—have or adopt a baby, the family moves into the first development stage. When an infant comes into a home, a family system changes in major ways. Some scholars write that parenthood emphasizes the male/female dichotomy, making mother the family's prototype for the female role and father for the male role.[8]

As the adults begin adjusting to their gender roles, communication paths must alter to make room for the new person in the household. The new family member is already the key focus of other family members' communication, particularly when it is a first child. The baby is a major source of vocal communication, loudly announcing its hunger, wetness, or desire to be held at the most inconvenient hours. Also important for our interest in the child's development in relation to gender, the infant is an active receiver of communication—from parents, older children in the household, other caregivers, relatives, and visitors who talk to the baby. The infant is also a major part of the communication environment for others in the family, affecting where and how loudly they talk and how soundly they sleep.

Not all cultures respond in the same ways to the introduction of a baby into the family. Expectations about the mothers' roles differ; as a result, how a woman might engage in her new role may in part depend on cultural expectations. For example, in a comparison of maternal role expectations of Japanese and American cultures, Nancy Shand notes that Japanese symbols are representative of the Japanese association of "woman" with passiveness, the home, and domesticity. The symbols indicate that the mother is responsible for the survival of the infant, showing the infant as dependent on its mother for physical needs and nurturance. Shand contrasts that expectation to the diverse ways that women in the United States may undertake the role of "mother." That diversity, she explains, helps account for the differences in levels of confidence that women in each culture have when they undertake the role of mother, especially the first time. While much of the focus is on the child during this stage of family development, expectations on adults in the family because of their sex also is significant.

Gender symbols and expectations emerge early in the family system, often in ways no one notices. The baby as topic of conversation receives a large amount of language and nonverbal behavior based on others' connotations for the labels "boy" and "girl." Parents have been known to bring footballs to the hospital to give to day-old sons. Friends and relatives often rush out to buy pink or blue gifts as soon as they know the sex of the baby. Observers have suggested that how fathers and mothers talk to babies depends on the sex of the child, but those differences may be smaller now that attention has been brought to the discrepancies.

Some evidence suggests that the ways fathers in particular talk about their babies may be influenced by the fathers' views of gender. The infant's behavior may be interpreted through a filter of gender beliefs and expectations. Fathers often exclaim over the baby's size when it is a boy. Fathers also have been found to comment more often on the resemblance between a girl baby and her mother, although no evidence suggests that either sex infant is more likely to look like the same-sex parent.[9]

Evidence also exists of the differences between how fathers and mothers talk *to* their children. One scholar found that fathers use imperatives ("Mow the lawn" or "Go to bed") more than mothers and use imperatives more with sons than with daughters. Fathers use more derogatory names like "ding-a-ling" and use them more with sons. Fathers use more advanced vocabulary with children, provide more complex information, and expect more information from children than do mothers. Fathers require more linguistic and cognitive sophistication from children; children display their knowledge more for fathers. Fathers interrupt children more than mothers, but both mothers and fathers interrupt daughters more than sons. Mothers are more polite in their directives. Mothers demand information less from daughters than sons.[10] When mothers talk to children, both daughters and sons, they refer less to their own feelings.[11] Throughout their childrearing years, parents influence children's notions of gender both in their conversational styles and content.

Children's pictures of gender include but go beyond biological sex. For example, even when preschool children do not know they always will be one sex, they are influenced by the social standards and stereotypes they absorb from sources other than printed words.[12] Before children can read, they learn about the culture's versions of masculine and feminine through color, activities, and games. They also learn by seeing family members with certain objects (dishes or sheets and towels versus pliers or electrical cord) or in certain rooms (the kitchen versus the garage). Babies and toddlers also learn by observing or being instructed by older siblings. In addition, the cultural gender stereotype will appear in a variety of mass media including television, children's books, print advertisements, and radio. Preverbal children will absorb gendered information long before they develop the sophisticated ability to analyze it.

CLOTHING. Clothes provide a vivid though often unnoticed example of means by which a child learns about gender. Most infant and children's clothing is differentiated by sex through color, trim, fabric, and style. Anyone who has tried to buy clothing as a gift for a not-yet-born baby knows that many clothes for newborns are made in yellow, light green, or other pastel shades, but most clothing for children over three months of age comes in pink and lavender for girls and blue and red for boys. Color crossovers seem to be allowed for girls: light or navy blue can be feminine if appropriately trimmed, and red and white clothes are available for girls at Christmas time and Valentine's Day. The reverse is by no means true; boys' clothes are almost never marketed in pink or lavender, and most parents of girls with little brothers buy new clothes for the boys (at least past infancy) rather than use the pastel clothes worn earlier by their female children.

Infants' and toddlers' clothing send additional messages to adults through the trim. Boys' clothes, if trimmed at all, show trucks, trains, airplanes, and football or baseball items—all connote action, a central theme in the masculine gender ideal. Girls' clothes usually have trims suggesting beauty and feeling, the expected province of girls: lace, hearts, butterflies, and feminine-typed merchandised characters such as Kitty-Kitty Kittens and Polly Pockets. Manufacturers are aware that children's clothing is rarely worn out by the time a given child has outgrown it. Trims make it difficult to pass clothing along to later children of the other sex and increase the likelihood of parents' purchasing many items of the same type and age range.

The styles of girls' and boys' clothing teach gender through sensory feedback to the children themselves. Boys' clothing is generally wider in both arms and legs than that made for girls. Adding to the difference, girls' pants are often gathered at the bottom so that movement is more restricted, bringing a sensation of tightness. Girls' blouses often have cuffs or gathers at the sleeve's end, restricting upward movement of the arm. Girls' skirts offer little protection against winter temperatures. Girls' shoes—especially dress shoes—often pinch toes or scrape heels. Boys' shoes generally are roomier and more sturdy. When boys dress up, their ties and shirt collars can restrict head movement and chafe necks.

As an illustration of how clothes can teach gender, imagine yourself as an infant trying to crawl while wearing a skirt. Your knee would catch on the skirt and your nose would hit the floor. The nonverbal message is clear: don't do too much of something that gets you a sore nose. This kind of event is likely to happen to girls far more than to boys because of the different clothing available to them. (Try this for yourself by putting on a long coat or a full apron and then attempting to crawl across the floor or to climb stairs.)

Another aspect of clothing that affects parents' communication to children is that boys' clothes are on the average made of heavier fabric and are of simpler styles, so they are easier to clean and less expensive to replace than frilly dresses. The fabrics remind parents (and wearers) that boys can and should be rough-and-tumble while girls should be careful with their bodies and clothes. It is easy to determine which sex is likely to hear more messages asking them to think about their appearance and their physical safety away from the home.

Some shift in the norms for young children's clothing has occurred recently, with the popularity of sweatsuits and quasi-athletic costumes for both sexes. Yet apart from sports and leisure clothing, the two sexes continue to be given distinctly different clothes along with related messages about their expected activities. As one example, many private schools still require that girls wear skirts and long socks in any kind of weather, while boys wear shirts and slacks. Even this moderate style difference reinforces the ideal of movement for boys and "femininity" despite inconvenience for girls.

TOYS AND GENDER COMMUNICATION. Another way children learn gender comes from the toys available to girls and boys and the labeling of those toys through packaging, advertising, and the uses others make of them. The most extreme gap between a "feminine" and a "masculine" toy is represented by the doll and the truck. The doll is a symbol of both beauty and nurturance, and the truck is a symbol of strength in action. Dolls and doll equipment remain major playthings for girls. Marketing experts discovered some time ago that they could make a Barbie or a Cabbage Patch or a Rainbow Brite continuously profitable by selling many forms of clothing and other equipment made particularly for those dolls, so that a young girl could concentrate on consuming ever-larger quantities of paraphernalia to fit her original doll. In 1995, a Barbie collection was added to the Air and Space Museum in Washington, DC. Barbie demonstrates how to be an astronaut in pink go-go boots. The display explains that Barbie is ready for any eventuality; in this outfit, she can be an attendant or an astronaut.

'Trek' Barbie Will Go Where No Barbie Has Gone Before

They come in peace. They mean you no harm. And toy giant Mattel hopes you'll beam them up at warp speed.

"Star Trek" Barbie—and, lest we forget that men were the original space pioneers, "Star Trek" Ken—will be available in a galaxy near you come August.

The perfectly plumed pair will be clad in first-generation Federation garb—she's dressed in red as an engineering officer, he's in gold as a commanding officer—and adorned with miniphasers, communicators and tricorders. They'll perch on the Enterprise bridge. Cost: $80 for the set of two.

Barbie fans already are buzzing about the debut.

"Lots of people are showing interest in the set, regardless of the cost," says Barbie-crazy Jennifer Warf of Indiana, who created a Barbie home page on the Internet (http://silver.ucs.indiana.edu/%7Ejward.barbie.html) and has a 300-member Barbie List of doll-savvy collectors.

"I think that combining these two collecting genres will be pretty successful for Mattel."

"The dolls are fun," says Julie Carino, historian of Windy City Barbie Club in Chicago. "I admit I'm the kind of collector that actually takes them out of the box. I most likely will make a pretend diorama of a 'Star Trek' mission with the dolls," Carino says.

But not all collectors are waiting with bated breath.

"This pair doesn't really appeal to me," says Bonnie Taylor of Killen, Ala. "I have never liked 'Star Trek,' and the outfits look really lame to me."

Regardless, sales of "Star Trek" Barbie and Ken are expected to be out of this world, meaning she'll live long and prosper.

Gannett News Service

Male children now also are being influenced to buy large amounts of equipment for their "dolls"—G.I. Joe, Z-Bots, Batman, and Megazord. Of course, these toys, made of hard plastic and not at all cuddly, are never referred to as "dolls" but "action figures" in television ads or package labels; their equipment involves vehicles and weapons instead of clothes. In 1994, sales on male action-figures rose by over 33 percent to $949 million; this category of toys was the fastest growing in the toy market. Because of this sudden rise and the popularity of the Mighty Morphin Power Rangers, toy manufacturers have begun designs of female action figures: Super Barbie, Princess Tenko (who fights evil with magic and illusion), and Sailor Moon (who protects the earth from evil Queen Beryl in a storyline based on a popular show in France, Italy, Spain, Hong Kong, and Japan).[13] In approaching children, the manufacturers appeal to each sex through gender stereotypes, intending to attract major consumers.

Dave Barry wrote a column satirizing the marketing lure of female action figures. Included was the following excerpt:

According to an Associated Press story, Sailor Moon is the blond, ponytailed heroine of a wildly popular Japanese cartoon show. Sailor Moon leads a team of female superheroes who wear miniskirts and go-go boots; according to the AP story, they "combat evil and sexism" using special powers that they get from their "magical brooches, scepters and compacts."

That's right: These heroines, striking a bold blow against sexism and outdated stereotypes of women, *get their power from jewelry and makeup.*

We can only try to imagine the plot action:

First Female Superhero: Uh-oh! It's the evil villain Lord Pustule! He's going to destroy the world!

Second Female Superhero: Not if I can help it! Toss me the eyeliner!

Chicago Tribune, April 9, 1995, Sunday Magazine, Chicagoland Final, page 28

This approach may be particularly effective on boys; some research suggests boys who understand that their sex will always be male (as opposed to children who do not yet understand sex as a constant) will play for a long time with a toy they do not find interesting if they think the toy is one other boys prefer. Manufacturers may find boys easy targets for sex-typed toy advertising.[14]

My sister and I spent hours playing with Barbie dolls. We had approximately nineteen Barbies, four Kens, the Barbie pool, Barbie house, and approximately 125 outfits in which to dress Barbie and 20 outfits for Ken. During the hours we spent playing we were always observed by my baby brother. Even at age two, he was entertained for hours watching us play with our Barbies. When he reached the age of three, we allowed him to play as well. He too spent day after day playing with the dolls, dressing them, and pretending. This all ended when it was the first day of school for my brother. In a matter of days, he despised Barbie dolls and continually threatened to do violent things to them. Eventually he requested from Mom and Dad toys such as Transformers and Atari video games. While my father was relieved, my mother recognized the influence little boys have on their peers.

While toy manufacturers still predominantly market single-sex toys, the Mighty Morphin Power Rangers are purported to be designed and marketed specifically to appeal to both sexes. Of the six Rangers, two are female. In the television version of the toy, all six Rangers take active roles. However, the central mission of the Rangers is one that holds to a masculine stereotype. The Rangers have set out to rid the world of evil Lord Zed and Rita Repulsa. While they appear to be sex neutral, they appeal largely to boys. These newer cross-sex toys seem directed primarily at increasing sales rather than providing children with new opportunities for creative play without gender stereotypes.

When I was growing up, I didn't like feminine toys. The fact that I didn't like these toys had little to do with the toy itself. I liked the Star Wars figures. I played with Luke Skywalker, Han Solo, and Darth Vader, but I didn't play with Princess Leah. Her figure could do the same things as all my other figures, but Princess Leah was for girls. Their arms and legs all moved in the same way, they all held guns, but one was a female. I didn't think it was cool to play with that one. Looking back, even the names of these characters seem funny. Darth Vader, Solo, Skywalker are all very masculine. Then there is Princess!

Toy labeling often suggests a gender requirement for certain kinds of play. Nurses' kits show only females; a toy called Mr. Work Bench gives a masculine title to a toy that used to be marketed to both sexes. Subtle differences in visuals on toys such as Lego and Duplo building blocks also differentiate between the sexes. Whereas the larger Duplo blocks made for two- to three-year-olds show girls and boys in the illustrations, the smaller and more technically complex Lego boxes for older children show almost no females in the box illustrations and include no blocks that could be labeled as feminine—flowers, house windows, and miniature figures of females. The company that produces Legos may expect girls as well as boys to play with their toys, yet the box illustrations imply boys' play by underscoring the challenges and achievements possible with the more advanced toys.

The learning cycle in the case of Legos operates in the following way. A girl who wants to build objects with Legos may find that the pictured objects are more and more like the objects her brothers play with—airplanes, trucks, tanks, and towers—and less and less like the human and household objects she may be accustomed to using. If she wishes to construct objects familiar to her, she must create them from her own imagination. Unlike her brothers, who may tell her that Legos are for boys, she may not be attracted to the toy because of its gendered connotations. These messages about distinct and separate genders operate to influence the sexes toward separate play by investing otherwise neutral objects with gender symbolism.

COMMUNICATING GENDER IDEALS. A sense of self influenced by gender ideals and expectations is no accident.[15] Dedicated parents and sometimes other family members see their responsibility to prepare the new child for a life that will be evaluated at least partly on the basis of gender in the environment outside the family system. In many families the boy's first haircut is a symbol of his ceasing to be a baby, while a girl's hair is given loving attention by one or both parents if it grows long and can be braided, curled, or tied with a colorful bow. Household duties may be divided by sex—girls set the table and boys take out the trash. Bedtime rituals can reflect gender expectations, including who kisses whom and how the recipient is to act or which sex can express aloud a fear of the dark and a desire to have a night-light left burning.

Children's expectations about themselves in accordance with their sex also extends to physical activity. Children as young as five already define football and ballet as masculine and feminine respectively. They predict their own successes at being able to do the activity also according to sex—boys rate themselves high on masculine activities, low on feminine and girls vice versa. The skills necessary for the activity are ignored; the sex type of the activity directs their predictions.[16]

Children as well as adults tend to orient children's interests toward sex-appropriate careers. Girls who wanted to be doctors may have been told, "Oh, no, you want to be a nurse." Boys who expressed interest in the visual and performing arts have been teased as "pretty boys" and challenged to show their physical prowess. Within families some effort may be made by siblings to influence each other toward gender-defined interests because the siblings themselves want to avoid the embarrassment of being associated with a family member who looks ridiculous to others.

Children frequently recount to each other the communication taboos related to gender. Taboo behaviors for males include crying, hanging close to Mother or to another caregiver, showing physical weakness (particularly in the presence of females), having a high-pitched voice, and hugging or kissing other males. In general these are restrictions against looking, sounding, and acting as girls are believed to look, sound, and act. On the other hand, taboo behaviors for girls are being loud, using profanity, looking unattractive, and beating a boy in a play or sport situation. Taboos for females work somewhat differently than those for boys. Sanctions are placed against boys for doing feminine behaviors; for girls, sanctions occur for *not* doing feminine behaviors. For a boy to compete against another boy and win is acceptable; for a girl to compete against a boy and win can produce problems for both the girl and the boy. Paradoxically, girls are encouraged to do some stereotypically masculine behaviors like excel in some sports and wear some clothes traditionally worn by men (pants, for example). Boys, however, are not similarly encouraged to do some stereotypically feminine behaviors like excel in sewing or wear clothes traditionally worn by women (skirts, for example).

Not all children act as though they are concerned about the taboos on gender communication, however. Many girls and young women describe themselves as "tomboys," defined as a female who likes the outdoors, plays sports, wears rugged clothes, and does not restrict her speech. An interesting note is that although the word, "tomboy" identifies a male universe, some perceive it has having neutral or positive connotations. Few males describe themselves as crossing over to feminine behaviors, largely because the labels for "effeminate" males carry more negative connotations than "tomboy" does for girls. Boys labeled "sissy" encounter negative nonverbal messages. The imbalance between the two stereotypes is further evidence of an unequal evaluation of the two sexes in the language.

STORIES AND FAIRY TALES. A similar effect of unequal evaluation can be found in fairy tales and stories often read to young children in families in the United States. From any perspective, the reading of fairy tales is a significant form of parent-child communication. Fairy tales often show negative relationships and extreme versions of scripts about life's troubles and ways to surmount them. Analysts of fairy tales have commented on their high proportion of violence and their ability to remain with adults as lingering dreams of romance and escape.[17] More important for the purposes of understanding parent-child or adult-child communication, traditional fairy tales often portray adults as devious or stupid. High among devious communicators are witches and stepmothers, who pervert the positive stereotype of the mother as a nurturing person. In Walt Disney's *Lion King*, the evil brother lion was depicted as a black, squinty-eyed creature slinking around in the dark. Males in that movie were admired for their fearlessness, their abilities to fight and protect their families, and their great size.

Similarly, *Pocahontas* has generated strong gender stereotypes. Promoted as a story that provided a good role model for girls, *Pocahontas* presents the male stereotype of bravery, strength, and endurance as her admirable qualities. The movie included only two major female roles, each mirroring male ideals. In addition, advertisements for the movie often hailed John Smith as the hero, inviting children to be like Smith who found "magic" in adventure. In the advertisements, Smith dominated the images; the only time Pocahontas appeared was when the narrator mentioned the "magic" Smith had found.

These movies present new versions of old messages about gender found in stories like Cinderella (where the handsome prince saves the cindergirl from a life of misery with selfish stepsisters and a wicked stepmother), Snow White (where the handsome prince saves the orphaned girl from being killed by her wicked stepmother), and Hansel and Gretel (where the wicked witch tries to eat two children left alone by a wicked stepfather and timid mother). Rather than incorporating the values of the feminine, the new stories continue the themes of conflict, violence, and rescue. The stories may assign to men or transfer to women the values of competition, violence, and mastering fate. Nevertheless, fundamental elements of the story remain similar. One argument against reducing the violent, competitive themes in modern stories is that less intense stories will not produce sufficient financial return. In this way, economic demands drive gender stereotypes. Children absorb these economically driven stereotypes through cultural stories, without the economic motivation being exposed.

HOW CHILDREN LEARN GENDER. Sandra Bem offered a Gender Schema Theory to explain how children learn gender. Since the Bem Sex Role Inventory (BSRI) is used in many research studies, we will explain its foundations; however, some findings indicate that this inventory does not predict gender as well for Hispanic-U.S. and black-U.S. groups as it does for white-U.S. groups.[18] Bem explains that children learn early (other experts estimate between 18 months and 3 years) whether they are boys or girls. The children also learn—often to their chagrin—that they cannot change that aspect of themselves. By three, they can be heard declaring that "girls don't do that" or "I don't want to because I'm a boy." They also begin to understand that if they are boys, they will never be mothers and if they are girls, they will never be fathers. While we may find their revelation amusing, the impact of this realization on the children can be profound.

Bem theorizes that the definitions discovered by the children become the framework through which they will encode and decode messages. As a consequence, even information that is not itself gendered will be decoded through this gendered lens. Because children are not critical users of communication, they do not distinguish kinds of information. In addition, they often strive to meet the expectations they perceive from their parents, siblings, and age mates.

As a result, Bem asserts, children interpret through their sex and gender lens much of the information they receive; the more they sex type information, the more likely they are to interpret future information through that same lens. As children interact with other children who also are learning the dichotomies of male and female, they help guide each other to conclusions that "girls are all mushy" or "boys are always too rough."

What are little girls made of?
Sugar and spice and everything nice.
That's what little girls are made of.

What are little boys made of?
Snips and snails and puppy dog tails.
That's what little boys are made of.

Bem outlines several ways parents can intervene in this gender schema. First, parents can teach children clear *sex* differences and talk to them about how sex and gender are different. Since children learn language literally, their interpretation of "boys don't cry" may be very different than the interpretation they will be able to make when they are older. The parent can explain to the child that crying is a choice to be made, a choice that will produce certain consequences. While a boy may or may not choose to cry, he will learn to categorize such behavior as gender—a choice he controls—rather than a mandatory requirement of his sex. His choice of behavior may differ at another time in a different situation. Children can be taught options rather than imprinted behavior.

Bem urges families to abandon stereotypical roles for male and female, adopting a person orientation rather than a role orientation. Clothes, household tasks, and activities should center around individual ability rather than sex. She also encourages parents to examine critically the children's reading material and television programs, eliminating those with strong stereotypes. In some stories, children and parents together can draw more characters on the page or change characters from male to female or vice versa to present heros and nurturers in both sexes.

Other suggestions that emerge from Bem's theory include giving children other schema upon which to base their conclusions about information. For example, a parent can say to a child, "Isn't it interesting that the person who wrote this book believed girls need help to find their way?" or "Why do you suppose Karl didn't cry when he hurt himself so badly?" These questions help children interpret information from such schema as individual differences or cultural variations. Ultimately, says Bem, parents can help children identify behaviors that deprecate others or place limits on their own and others' lives.

Bem's theory attempts to define ways a culture can change its cultural stereotypes of gender. You may see the process of creating gender as natural and necessary. Think of television or movie scenarios where characters have mistaken the sex of another character, acted on that mistaken assumption, and have been profoundly embarrassed when their mistake is revealed. Those plots are derived from the very rigid, ingrained expectations society places on its members. If you subscribe to the mandated need to be able to predict accepted behavior, you may wonder why we emphasize how gender is constructed. The point is that the traditional orientation to gender communication is not the only option, although it often appears to be. One limitation to living in a culture that dominates the world's information media is that we know far less about other cultures' patterns of raising children in relation to their sex than people in those countries know about ours. We do know that decades ago Margaret Mead discovered a society that reversed the gender communication patterns we expect in our culture.[19] In some European countries today men and boys are permitted a wider range of emotional expression (hugs, smiles, tears) than in the United States. It appears, then, that the gender communication stereotypes in the United States are one among many ways of relating biological sex and gender ideals for behavior.

The process of differentiation according to cultural stereotypes occurs in unique ways for males and females according to Nancy Chodorow. She theorizes that these unique processes can be traced to the cultural practice that women are primarily responsible for child care. Chodorow relies on Robert Stoller's work; Stoller claims that children develop a virtually unchanging core of their personalities by the age of three. Chodorow explains that until the age of three, most children have their mothers as the central figures in their lives.

Girls' development, then, is one of connection, modeling, and imitation because their sex is the same as their mothers'. To achieve gender identity, they can model behaviors and attitudes after their mothers'. Boys' development, on the other hand, is one of separation, finding the antithesis, and discovering the converse. To achieve a masculine gender identity, they must be whatever their female mother is not. As a result, Chodorow theorizes, females define their own personalities through relationship and connection to others more than do males.[20]

FAMILIES WITH ADOLESCENTS

In the United States when children reach adolescence, a key change occurs in the family. While children generally acknowledge parental authority and power, adolescents shift that power center from parents to peers. Adolescence continues—and exaggerates—the process of differentiation described by Chodorow. The trend to differentiate the sexes continues and is accompanied by sometimes extreme measures to establish identity as individuals apart from the family. Adolescents form definitive codes for behavior, dress, and talk. Adolescents' divisions between male and female become distinct and at times even rigid. Same-sex parents and their adolescents may encounter substantial conflict at this stage as the adolescent begins to reconcile norms about gender within the family culture that contrast with those of the adolescent culture.

Adolescents adopt and create cultural markers of masculine and feminine. Some girls begin to use make-up, shave their legs, wear certain clothing styles, and do "courting" behaviors. Some boys begin to publicly display behaviors to demonstrate what the culture as a whole and their adolescent culture in particular perceives as masculine—such as, develop upper-body muscles; use coarse language; repel hugs or displays of affection, especially by family members or other males; or privately take meticulous care of their physical image while publicly appearing indifferent. As we will discuss further in the chapter on education, violations of these gender codes by other adolescents can produce harsh and punitive action by peers.

My last visit to my son Josh's place was for his graduation. We arrived to find his place a mess—and dirty to boot. I resisted impulses to scrub so that he could do his own cleaning. Our biological relationships—we shared heartbeat, food, and oxygen once—binds us together in a totally unique relationship, but I am trying to move from "mother" to what? Grown-ups? Adults? So I didn't scrub.

Later, his roommate's mom came and made comments about the mess. I felt that my "mothering skills" were being judged. Why hadn't I trained my son to clean? Anyway, we—the roommate's mom, sister, me, Josh, etc.—pitched in to clean. Josh was defensive. Since my goal was to have Sam's mom see me as a "good mom," I chose a strategy of teasing and making light of the mess. Josh got huffy . . . his goal may have been to assert his maturity and deal with the uneasy situation of having his mom in his house.

That differentiation of self from family members often occurs through conflict. Adolescents and parents ascribe different meanings to the everyday, family conflicts they have with one another.[21] Both black and white females recall that as adolescents verbal messages from parents had more negative than positive and instructional value for them. Black women recall more messages from television and more nontraditional messages.[22] Adolescent boys are more likely than girls to enter conflicts with parents over issues of drugs, drinking, doing homework, or using profanity.[23] Girls may maintain a more continuous communication pattern with their mothers; initially mothers make requests by asking questions, and daughters give problem-solving suggestions or agree to their mothers' suggestions. As the girls grow older, they begin to reverse the pattern, asking questions or regulating nonverbally the conversation to confront the problem or their mothers. Mothers appear to concede to this change, encouraging autonomy.[24] Evidence suggests that adolescent girls and parents have more conflict associated with the girls' menarche; after that time, parents' (particularly mothers') and daughters' positive expressions with each other—things like laughter and enthusiasm—diminished.[25]

LAUNCHING CHILDREN AND GROWING OLDER

As children leave home, they often create families of their own, continuing the spiral of intergenerational gender patterns. As gender models, grandparents may struggle with expectations of the "loving grandmother" and "wise grandfather." Research with African-American families headed by single women finds that grandmothers expect themselves and are expected by others to be actively involved with grandchildren.[26] Grandmothers in African-American families also are presumed to help granddaughters understand better their cultural traditions—who the granddaughters are within their culture.[27]

The combination of aging and changing gender roles may generate new conditions for older family members. In the United States culture, people of older age may be less revered than in other cultures; bases for self-esteem and self-worth may change. Gender demands may be reduced, allowing androgynous behaviors to develop. As they age, black men tend to move away from the masculine gender adhered to by white males.[28] Androgyny in older adults appears to be linked to better health than in sex-typed individuals.[29]

Nevertheless, gender expectations and life circumstances related to sex and gender continue to affect peoples' lives as they age. Husbands attain their highest earning levels between 55 and 64 years of age,[30] but when they no longer are wage earners, men often struggle to reestablish their roles in the family. Women may experience retirement differently than men because they tend to retire at an earlier age and seem to derive their identities more from informal, interpersonal roles like "friend," than from formal work roles. Women incorporate their friends, hobbies, and interests in their post-retirement lives. The large majority of older people living alone are women. Often the women live on low, fixed incomes and they worry about financial problems.[31] Health problems become critical issues for both women and men. Generating activities in many different roles—such as volunteer, grandparent, student, and employee—improves health for men (especially) and women, blacks (especially) and whites.[32] Married women, more than unmarried women or married men, are more likely to receive formal health care in their lives.[33]

For some families, this stage is one of the most enjoyable. One researcher concluded that overall, older heterosexual couples reported themselves happy in their relationships.[34] Couples who spent much of their lives raising children can find time to spend with each other. Many enjoy travel or hobbies or engage in activities together they did not have time for earlier in their relationship.

CONCLUSION

This chapter has treated the family as an open communication system working through four developmental stages. Through family interaction, biological sex begins to be converted through communication into gender expectations—important to the parents as a responsibility of child rearing and to the child as a major symbol system which will affect actions throughout the life span. Clothes, toys, and fairy tales all carry gender significance, to which parents and children react in various ways. Children, like adults, influence each other's responses to gender expectations, either through stereotyping or by contributing to the process of expanding family members' opportunities as male and female individuals.

QUESTIONS FOR DISCUSSION

1. Do you recall your family as being position-centered or person-centered? What were the effects on you (or on others in the household) with regard to learning gender through that pattern?
2. What stories have been told about your birth and early childhood? To what extent do these stories focus on biological sex or on gender expectations?
3. Think of a household you know (including your own, past or present) in which the roles of female and male are the most similar; think of another household you know in which they are the most different. How have the different patterns occurred, and how well do you believe they work?
4. What was your favorite toy as a child? Who played with you? Do you now have any objects you consider to be adult "toys"?

What are they? How close are they to the traditional gender patterns for use of toys as described in this chapter?

5. Do you have siblings? Did your siblings influence your views about yourself and gender communication? How? Do you influence them now?

6. What changes do you recall occurring at the time of adolescence with regard to sex and gender? What were the codes of your friends? What did you wear? What special words did you use?

7. If you have left home, how have gender roles changed for you? For your parent or parents? What events occurred that have had an impact on the family themes and images with regard to gender and sex?

8. How might your grandparents describe their gender roles? Have you ever thought about your grandparents being intimate? What gender expectations underlie your response?

CASES FOR ANALYSIS

CASE 6.1   GO GET 'IM, TIGER

Several families were watching a championship football game together. Their small children were also present, an eight-month-old male and a pair of twins, male and female, also eight months old. The two boys were crawling on the carpet between the parents and the television when one of them started to grasp the other near the neck. The second boy looked in the direction of his mother, as if asking her, "What do I do now, Mom?" The mother was looking away at that moment, but the father, watching his son being "accosted" by the other, said, "Go get 'im, tiger!"

Within a minute after the boys' physical play with each other began, the girl twin crawled in their direction as if wanting to join the game. Just as she reached her brother, her mother got up, came to the trio, picked up the girl, and carried her back to the mother's seat.

1. Are there aspects of this scene that can be attributed to biological sex? What aspects do gender ideals explain?

2. To what degree is the football game relevant to the situation?

3. Should males be stronger and more active than females?

4. Discuss with others your reasons for agreeing or disagreeing with the mother's and the father's responses.

CASE 6.2 JUST ONE MORE GIRL

Corey is the third of four daughters in her family. She also has a younger brother, Michael, the last of the five children. Relatives and friends kid Corey's parents about their long effort to bring forth a son, and the girls have heard much of this joking. What bothers Corey more than the jokes, however, are comments such as: "Of course I love all of you dearly; you're wonderful kids. But Michael is very special to me and your dad." When Corey has asked her mother what this statement means, she has heard that now there will be someone to carry on the family name and to take over the family business. Corey feels diminished by the idea that she was one in a series of failed attempts to achieve a male child. She doesn't know how to tell her parents what she feels, and she doesn't want to hurt their feelings.

1. How do the parents' views reflect the values of the society around them?
2. What is the practical importance of "carrying on the family name"? Who can do it?
3. What can parents do to avoid giving any of their children the impression that they are second-best?
4. What communication events have you experienced or observed in the family that affected your beliefs about the value of being female or male?

CASE 6.3 HALLOWEEN

"What're you going to be?" asked ten-year-old Hilary.

"I think I'm going to be a dragon," replied eight-year-old Kyle. "What about you?"

"I'm going to be the rabbit from *Alice in Wonderland*. What about you, Colin?"

"I'm going to be an old gypsy," replied the eleven-year-old.

"You can't be a gypsy!" Hilary and Kyle exclaimed together.

"Why not?" asked Colin.

"Because you're a *boy*!" Hilary and Kyle seemed incredulous that Colin even had to ask.

"So what?" asked Colin. "In my country we dress up as anything we like. Why can't I be a gypsy?"

1. What kinds of gender expectations are communicated in this story?
2. What was your response to Colin's choice for Halloween? Where did you learn that reaction?
3. If you were Colin's parents and you understood the differences in gender expectations between the cultures, what would you advise him to do (assuming he asked)?
4. This event happened eight years ago. How likely do you think it would be for it to occur today, either in your family or in your community?

NOTES

[1] In the wake of the political upheaval in Russia, women in all classes still respond to the family positively. For more reading, see Robin Goodwin and Titiana Emelyanova, "The Perestroika of the Family? Gender and Occupational Differences in Family Values in Modern Day Russia," *Sex Roles* 32, 5/6 (1995): 337–51.

[2] Patricia Noller and Mary Anne Fitzpatrick, *Communication in Family Relationships* (Englewood Cliffs, NJ: Prentice Hall, 1993).

[3] Kathleen M. Galvin and Bernard J. Brommel, *Family Communication: Cohesion and Change*, 3rd ed. (New York: HarperCollins Publishers, 1991).

[4] Ibid., p. 205.

[5] James M. Gaudin, Jr. and Catheryn B. Davis, "Social Networks of Black and White Rural Families: A Research Report," *Journal of Marriage and the Family* (November 1985): 1015–21.

[6] K. Jill Kiecolt and Alan C. Acock, "The Long-Term Effects of Family Structure on Gender-Role Attitudes," *Journal of Marriage and the Family* 50 (August 1988): 709–17.

[7] P. Papernow, "The Stepfamily Cycle: An Experiential Model of Stepfamily Development," *Family Relations* 33 (1984): 335–63.

[8] Donal R. McCreary, "Self-Perceptions to Life-Span Gender-Role Development," *International Journal of Aging and Human Development* 31, 2 (1990): 135–46.

[9] Several related studies are summarized in Susan A. Basow, *Sex-Role Stereotypes: Traditions and Alternatives* (Monterey, CA: Brooks-Cole, 1980); see also the special issue "Perspectives on Fatherhood," *American Behavioral Scientist* 29 (September/October 1985).

[10] Jean Berko Gleason and Esther Blank Greif, "Men's Speech to Young Children," in *Language, Gender, and Society*, eds. Barrie Thorne, Cheris Kramarae, and Nancy Henley (New York: Newbury House Publishers, 1983), pp. 140–50.

[11] Judy Dunn and Penny Munn, "Development of Justification in Disputes with Mother and Sibling," *Developmental Psychology* 23, 6 (1987): 791–98.

[12] Gary D. Levy and D. Bruce Carter, "Gender Schema, Gender Constancy, and Gender-Role Knowledge: The Roles of Cognitive Factors in Preschoolers: Gender Role Stereotype Attributions," *Developmental Psychology* 25, 3 (1989): 444–49.

[13] Kenneth R. Clark, "Kid Stuff: A $19 Billion Toy Market," *Chicago Tribune* (February 17, 1995), Section 3, p. 1.

[14] Karin S. Frey and Diane N. Ruble, "Gender Constancy and the 'Cost' of Sex-Typed Behavior: A Test of the Conflict Hypothesis," *Developmental Psychology* 28, 4 (1992): 714–21.

[15] For information about messages received in childhood regarding sex roles and sexual orientation, see J. Michael Bailey and Kenneth J. Zucker, "Childhood Sex-Typed Behavior and Sexual Orientation: A Conceptual Analysis and Quantitative Review," *Developmental Psychology* 31, 1 (1995): 43–55.

[16] Charlotte Sanguinetti, Amelia M. Lee, and Jack Nelson, "Reliability Estimates and Age and Gender Comparisons of Expectations to Success in Sex-Typed Activities," *Journal of Sport Psychology* 7 (1985): 379–88.

[17] See Colette Dowling, *The Cinderella Complex: Women's Hidden Fear of Independence* (New York: Summit, 1981); and Madonna Kolbenschlag, *Kiss Sleeping Beauty Good-Bye: Breaking the Spell of Feminine Myths and Models* (Garden City, NY: Doubleday 1979).

[18] Allen C. Harris, "Ethnicity as a Determinant of Sex Role Identity: A Replication Study of Item Selection for the Bem Sex Role Inventory," *Sex Roles* 31, 3/4 (1994): 241–73.

[19] Margaret Mead, *Male and Female: A Study of the Sexes in a Changing World* (New York: William Morrow, 1949).

[20] Nancy Chodorow, "Gender as a Personal and Cultural Construction," *Signs: Journal of Women in Culture and Society* 20, 3 (Spring 1995): 516–44; also see discussion of Chodorow's theory in Carol Gilligan's *In a Different Voice: Psychological Theory and Women's Development* (Cambridge: Harvard University Press, 1982), pp. 7–10.

[21] Judith G. Smetana, "Adolescents' and Parent's Reasoning about Actual Family Conflict," *Child Development* 60 (1989): 1052–67.

[22] Monique L. Ward and Gail Elizabeth Wyatt, "The Effects of Childhood Sexual Messages on African-American and White Women's Adolescent Sexual Behavior," *Psychology of Women Quarterly* 18 (1994): 183–201.

[23] Dennis R. Papini, Steven Clark, Jawanda K. Barnett, and Catherine L. Savange, "Grade, Pubertal Status, and Gender-Related Variations in Conflictual Issues among Adolescents," *Adolescence*, 24, 96 (1989): 977–87.

[24] Julie Hakim-Larsen and Cathy J. Hobart, "Maternal Regulation and Adolescent Autonomy: Mother-Daughter Resolution of Story Conflicts," *Journal of Youth and Adolescence*, 16, 2 (1987): 153–66.

[25] Grayson N. Holmbeck and John P. Hill, "Conflictive Engagement, Positive Affect, and Menarche in Families with Seventh-Grade Girls," *Child Development* 62 (1991): 1030–48.

[26] Melvin N. Wilson, "Mothers' and Grandmothers' Perceptions of Parental Behavior in Three-Genderational Black Families," *Child Development* 55 (1984): 1333–39.

[27] Valerie Cryer McCay, "Grandmothers and Granddaughters in African-American Families: Imparting Cultural Tradition and Womanhood between Generations of Women," In H. Hamilton (Ed.) *Old Age and Language: Multidiversity Perspective*. Garland Publishing Co., New York.

[28] Ian Harris, José B. Torres, and Dale Allender, "The Responses of African American Men to Dominant Norms of Masculinity Within the United States," *Sex Roles* 31, 11/12 (1994): 703–19.

[29] McCreary, op cit.

[30] P. Glick, "The Family Cycle and Social Change," as cited in Galvin and Brommel, *Family Relations* 38 (1989): 123–29.

[31] Kaaren Hanson and Seymour Wapner, "Transition to Retirement: Gender Differences," *International Journal on Aging and Human Development* 39, 3 (1994): 189–208.

[32] Pamela K. Adelmann, "Multiple Roles and Physical Health Among Older Adults," *Research on Aging* 16, 2 (June 1994): 142–66.

[33] Jan E. Mutchler and Susan Bullers, "Gender Differences in Formal Care Use in Later Life," *Research on Aging* 16, 3 (September 1994): 235–50.

[34] Wallace Reynolds, Rory Remer, and Mitzi Johnson, "Marital Satisfaction in Later Life: An Examination of Equity, Equality, and Reward Theories," *International Journal on Aging and Human Development* 40, 2 (1995): 155–73.

Chapter 7

Education

When most of us think of education, we think of classes we take, such as history, math, and writing. However, a system of education entails much more than merely topics of courses. Each culture's system of education teaches children how that culture views the world, how individuals fit into that culture, and the means individuals may use to change or improve their situations. While attending school, children learn how to use language and how to treat others. They also learn social expectations of themselves and others. Among those expectations in the United States culture, children learn that people organize their worlds on the basis of particular distinctions, such as sex, gender, race, ethnicity, and class. One consequence of these distinctions is that educators of children—teachers, textbook writers, administrators, and even designers of school buildings—operate according to certain assumptions that expand and enforce the traditional gender symbols and expectations of the dominant social groups.

We will focus on the "gender curriculum," a term that refers to the symbols and assumptions related to gender that are embedded in the United States education system. While some curricula now include topics such as women's rights and race, students often learn about these topics through their school experience. Other communication sources—particularly other students and teachers—often are far more influential than formal course instruction. For example, preschoolers and elementary children often idolize their teachers, citing them as definitive authorities. Their teachers can convey strong messages about sex and gender through their personal styles, attitudes, language use, and directions. For adolescents, same-sex and other-sex peer groups set mandates about gender and sex. These peer groups consist of individuals known and valued to a student; they hold the power to judge actions. In addition to teachers and peers, school administrators send gender messages both in policy-setting and in personal action. Messages implying the real values guiding schools are embedded in uses of time and space, school rituals, visual displays, scheduling, kind and treatment of extracurricular activities, and sports agendas.

CHAPTER OVERVIEW

In this chapter, we will examine the workings of gender communication in the successive stages of schooling: preschool; elementary school; middle school or junior high school; secondary school; and college. These educational levels are structured in such a way that their verbal and nonverbal communication progressively resembles the home less and less and the workplace more and more. From the cultural viewpoint we discussed earlier, this means that the school and its teachers move from being an interpersonal sphere—characterized by mostly female teachers and principally feminine symbols and communication styles during the early school years—to a public sphere, inhabited by mostly male professors and principally masculine symbols and communication styles at the college level.

Our discussion covers a wide array of arrangements and assumptions about sex and gender among schools. Few schools will exhibit all the descriptions presented. However, you can predict that each school will deal in some fashion with gender communication, since parents, children, teachers, and school administrators all bring into the school environment past experiences and hopes related to one or both sexes.

DAYCARE AND PRESCHOOL

In more than half of the United States families with small children, both parents are employed full time and require child care or preschool facilities. Most single-parent families rely solely on the parent's income. Often these parents—mostly women—must find affordable, flexible child care that helps the parent both financially sustain the family and viably balance the demands of job and single parenting. Concern over children's readiness for elementary school often translates to the child spending some time in nursery school programs. The average child now begins the school experience between three and four years of age, instead of the traditional kindergarten age of five. Some preschool programs describe themselves as play groups or play centers, and many programs involve a high proportion of physical play. However, a significant number of preschools have a curriculum—a set of learning materials that children are encouraged to use—with checkpoints for the child, the parents, and the teacher to measure progress.

The discussion in chapter 6 about messages to the child from clothing, toys, and family members is relevant to gender communication at the preschool level as well. Feedback cycles continue to operate, as young girls and boys enter a new environment with few cues as to what to expect from each other and from their teachers. Clothing offers one cue, although a limited one. Girls wearing lace-trimmed blouses and hair bows may be treated as if they prefer to be passive rather than active, especially by teachers and aides whose backgrounds have led them to be careful of "nice clothes." Boys wearing brightly striped t-shirts and corduroy pants may look as if they want rugged play rather than seated activities such as coloring and puzzles. Since parents purchase most of their children's clothes and dress their children to suit their own views of gender, the clothing a child wears on a given day may not say much about the child's own interests. How much children dissociate themselves from the ways their parents dress them may depend partly on them and partly on how much the teacher can differentiate the children's personal interests from their clothing.

Parents often cite "school readiness" as the reason for having their children go to nursery school. Their goal is usually threefold: to give the children a head start in fundamental, traditional school topics such as colors, numbers, and letters; to see how the child will deal with other children in a group setting; and to receive an evaluation of the child's mental and physical abilities. The results of nearly all such evaluations are consistent. On the average, girls have better verbal skills, a lower rate of sensory problems such as dyslexia (reversing the visual images of words), and more ease interacting with others in a group setting than do boys.[1] In other words, girls begin their early school experience better prepared than boys in these areas. We will see that by early high school, girls' scores will have changed dramatically.

The preschool itself can be experienced by both child and parent as a feminine environment, that is, an interpersonal environment similar to family life at home. Unlike other cultures where young children might spend Monday through Friday living at the school, daycare centers and preschools in the United States generally operate during parents' work hours; preschoolers see their parents interact with their teachers nearly every day. Preschools often mimic the home environment and sometimes are even held in an individual's home or a building that was once a home. The separation between home and school is not as distinct as it will be during secondary school or college.

The interpersonal environment further reflects the feminine in the United States culture in the use of colors, decorations, space arrangement, and tone. Speech used by daycare workers usually closely resembles mothers' speech patterns. Even male daycare teachers' patterns are more like female daycare teachers' patterns than like fathers' speech.[2] Preschool groups are smaller than elementary school classes; a child can engage in interpersonal activities with most of the others in his or her preschool class. If a child gets hurt at preschool, she or he will usually receive a different kind of nurturance both from teachers and peers than will be expected in later school years for the same injury.

Within this environment, however, powerful messages emerge about what is male and what is female. For some children, preschool friends are their first social peer group. Through their play, children learn others' perceptions of appropriate behavior for boys and girls. Since preschoolers often are only first learning social skills, their messages can be abrupt and overt: "Boys aren't supposed to play with dolls!" or "Girls can't play football!" Sometimes the messages are more subtle: trucks and balls and dinosaurs are stored in one area while dolls and dishes and "dress-up clothes" are stored in another. The children also learn how other families assess gender: "My mom says I can't play with you because you're too rough!" Preschoolers absorb these messages about sex and gender literally with little analytical interpretation; they are not yet capable of abstract reasoning.

While preschoolers learn from their schoolmates, they place more importance on their teachers at this stage than they will later as adolescents. As a result, their teachers' attitudes—expressed nonverbally in their actions and behaviors—send messages to the children about gender. Teachers' dress, accessories, and manner model standards that children mimic. Growing up to be "a teacher, just like Miss Davis" is not an uncommon goal expressed by preschool students. The ways "Miss Davis" addresses girls and boys, the activities she chooses, the illustrations she gives, and the examples she uses all become the children's primary sources for gender information.[5]

I remember my preschool teacher, Mrs. Johnson, and remember thinking how perfect she was. She was the smartest person in the world. You had to do what she said. She was the teacher.

Because of the students' reliance on the teachers as models, the economic context for daycare workers and preschool teachers is relevant to the messages children receive from them. As with many professions dominated by women, preschool and daycare programs are economically disenfranchised; preschool teachers and daycare workers often change jobs because the pay is so low. The effects of this economic context on the communication with children is hard to assess; however, the assignment to low economic status of professions such as preschool teaching and daycare is not a norm shared by all cultures.

ELEMENTARY SCHOOL

When teachers are asked about their views on children's gender-related communication behavior, such as boys fighting or girls talking in class, they often report that they do not try to influence boys or girls toward different behaviors based on sex. Yet, research shows that even teachers with the best of intentions react to and treat the sexes differently.[3] Because sex and gender stereotypes are so intricately interwoven with cultural behavioral patterns, we may not realize how our communication patterns support those stereotypes. Myra and David Sadker suggest that teacher awareness of communication about sex and gender is a critical step toward achieving gender equity in elementary classrooms.[4]

Teachers face a difficult task with regard to teaching sex and gender equity. Most teacher-preparation programs provide little training in this area and in the overlapping areas of race and ethnicity.[5] Stu-

Doonesbury

BY GARRY TRUDEAU

dents come to school having been influenced by family members, television, friends, and personal experiences. Their communication patterns and worldviews will have been affected by both genetic and environmental influences. Children engage in classroom and playground rituals they have learned from older friends or brothers and sisters. "Friday Flip Up Day," when boys try to grab unsuspecting girls' skirts, demonstrates how messages about male-female relationships can be ritualized into informal, but acceptable, normative behavior.

Even in light of recent attention and interest in promoting women in the workplace, research in 1994 reveals that five- and six-year-old girls—from both the upper-middle class and lower-middle class—still come to school identifying themselves with traditional female careers. They express disinterest in math, explaining that "doctors should be boys" and "boys make better astronauts."[6] Studies involving sixth graders revealed similar responses. Secretary, model, social worker, and child caregiver were professions marked as feminine while professions such as pilot, sailor, farmer, and engineer were considered masculine. Boys more clearly differentiated the professions into sex-typed work than did the girls. Both sexes rated the masculine professions as more important.[7] Students coming into elementary school already hold sex and gender stereotypes that may be difficult for teachers to address. Other research indicates that not only communication about sex and gender, but issues of class and race interact together and with sex to affect children's school performances and perceptions of themselves.[8]

FEEDBACK

Differences in teachers' responses to students appear in elementary school and generally hold true throughout secondary and college experiences as well. The most significant difference is the sheer amount of attention teachers give to males as compared to females. Several research studies have shown that male students receive more critical feedback than females. White males are likely to receive the most attention, followed by minority males, white females, and minority females.[9] That means that when a male asks a question or gives a response, the teacher is more likely to interact with him, asking further questions or examining his idea in more detail.

In what has become a controversial report, Sadker and Sadker claim that boys call out in class eight times more than girls do.[10] Other research suggests that males win more praise or acclaim than do females. Teacher responses such as "Good idea" or "Yes! Good work!" are more frequently directed toward males than toward females. In some classrooms the same males may get both the criticism and the praise. Females, in contrast, receive attention for cooperative action and for quietness in getting a job done, a kind of global rather than specific, or task-based, feedback. Boys get praise and involvement from the teacher when they are actively solving a puzzle on their own, whereas girls may get help completing the puzzle and thus less feedback from doing the problem-solving task itself.[11]

America Can't Compete
Unless She Can

But in school, girls are discouraged from taking the science and math courses they'll need for America to compete in the future. Girls hear that math is too tough for them. Girls get called on less than boys in the classroom. Even tests and textbooks stereotype and ignore women and girls.

Don't let anyone tell her she can't compete.

For your free copy of "Ten Tips to Build Gender Fair Schools", call 1 800 326-AAUW.

When we shortchange girls,
we shortchange America.

AMERICAN
ASSOCIATION OF
UNIVERSITY
WOMEN

VALUES AND BEHAVIOR

Many scholars assert that the values reflected by the present system of education in the United States foster specific learning styles. As one report asserted, "[s]chools are geared more to the learning styles of white males, which tend to be individualistic and competitive. In contrast, many girls prefer cooperation over competition, acknowledging and building on others' ideas to define common meanings over individual contributions, and understanding over assessment."[12] Arguments are made that this individualistic, competitive style of education may in part account for the dramatic reduction in self-esteem for both males and females from the time they enter elementary school to the time they leave high school. That drop is greater for girls—from 67 percent to 46 percent for boys and 60 percent to 29 percent for girls. In addition, arguments are made that this drop in self-esteem for girls may affect scholastic achievement, since girls score as well in math as boys at age nine but fall significantly behind by age seventeen.[13] Although research has begun to uncover problems for girls, little research investigates how this emphasis of only one learning style limits boys' development of skills and knowledge about cooperation and understanding of others.

Life in the school shows a communication trend we will see again in later chapters: females like and seek talk more than males, and males like and seek physical activity more than females. The pattern shows up in a variety of ways:

1. In the average elementary school classroom, more boys than girls are asked repeatedly to sit down, to stop kicking, or to stand still.

2. In the average elementary school classroom, more girls than boys will be asked to stop talking with other students.

These two examples are not meant to suggest that boys don't talk or that girls are unable to move about freely, but they do suggest the value differences that begin to be apparent by the time children are in educational environments together. The girls may be glad and even proud that they are more obedient and helpful than the boys. The boys may decide, as some have reported, that the female teachers are prejudiced against them and prefer girls. Each side may feel some distance from the other, resenting either the attention they don't get or the acceptance they haven't won from the teacher.

What are the results of this major difference in types and circumstances of feedback? Girls learn that their cooperative ability is important. They receive less praise than the boys, but the praise they do receive comes from being quiet and working well with others. Boys learn that their deviant behavior attracts further attention, even special attention if they are succeeding at a challenging task after a time of making trouble. In a subtle sense, success in school for females can mean becoming invisible. Success for males can mean being noticed. Teachers and counselors work harder with "problem situations" and consider themselves successful to the degree that they solve those problems and reclaim learners who are alienated from school.

A few years ago, my sister had a problem with the teacher of a math class she was taking. She came home and told my mother that she was not doing well and that the teacher didn't help her and couldn't explain things well. At first, my mother told her that she needed to spend more time doing her homework. After a few weeks, my mom found out that the teacher had ridiculed her for asking questions.

My mother and father were so furious that they went to the principal to talk about the teacher's behavior toward my sister. One thing they found out was that the girls in the class were not doing as well as the boys.

Teacher-student communication is complex. Teachers in schools with sex-equity policies and programs may think they should act without any thought of sex differences in behavior. In trying to act toward each student as an individual, ignoring any behavioral sex differences, teachers often perpetuate their preexisting images of the sexes rather than examining them for potential change. The backgrounds of both teachers and students may lead both to depend on stereotypical personal constructs:

Girls will be talkative.	Boys will be unruly.
Girls will be neat.	Boys will be messy.
Girls will work and play quietly.	Boys will make noise.
Girls will be cooperative.	Boys will compete.
Girls do well with words.	Boys do well with numbers.
Girls are pretty.	Boys are athletic.
Girls need assistance.	Boys can figure it out.
Girls will use indirect aggression.	Boys will fight.

Both sexes look for confirmation of their preexisting beliefs or stereotypes, and both will tend to see any confirming behavior as valid and predictive of future behavior. This is called the *self-fulfilling prophecy*. Teachers have a complex task in joining theory, observation, and personal experience related to gender as they meet and try to influence both sexes in the classroom.

JUNIOR HIGH OR MIDDLE SCHOOL

Besides the students' ages, a key difference between most elementary and most middle schools is the shift from a single teacher to an array of different teachers for different subjects. This shift moves the student away from a replica of the parent-child relationship and toward a relationship with a set of teachers that may include both males and females. The variety of subjects also expands to include more abstractions (science, social science) and more physical action (industrial arts, band). The latter subjects allow more activity in the classroom, appealing to restless students.

I can remember being very academically competitive up until seventh grade. Cory Mason and I were always rivals for the number-one position in class. Then I started to get embarrassed by speaking out in class—embarrassed because I knew the answer. In addition, I felt that the boys wouldn't like me if I was smarter than them. From then on, I shifted my focus on popularity and socializing instead of studying.

My younger cousin is now entering the seventh grade. I always try to emphasize to her that women can do all the same things as men (doctor, dentist, nurse, anything) and try to get her excited about science. It is hard, though, because at that age popularity and being liked are very strong influences.

Middle school is also a time of major shifts regarding the personal importance of gender. In grades six and seven, girls rate being popular or well liked higher than academic achievement. Boys rate independence and competence as most important. Boys perceive their friends as partners for argument; talk is used to show competence. Girls are less concerned with resolution or "besting" the other and focus on understanding where others are coming from; talk is used for discovering information about the other. If girls do not excel in a subject, they tend to attribute the problem to themselves and their skills or knowledge. If boys do not excel, they describe the information as not useful to them.[14] In physical education classes, teachers observe that girls still participate in limited ways. Hutchinson writes that girls still operate under unspoken cultural guidelines such as "act like a lady," "let him win," and "be careful."[15]

At this age, girls' scores drop below boys'; the previously parallel development of boys and girls changes. Carol Gilligan describes the phenomenon as girls "going underground."[16] We don't know all the reasons for this reversal. Some contributing factors may be the gender conditioning received. Early training for males implies living up to a gender ideal of strength and competitive success; communication training for adolescent females seems to involve restricting one-self—sometimes including restricting food intake—to produce a quiet, attractive, and sociable gender ideal. While these differences are less pronounced in more academically successful students (those who often attend college), they appear striking overall.

My father has been a counselor and a teacher in elementary and junior high for twenty-five years. He tells me many things about the girls in junior high he once knew in elementary school. They used to pursue academics, he says. Now, they're dating high school boys and threatening to commit suicide when the boys break their hearts. My dad makes an extra effort toward some of the girls. He tells me that he knows how incredibly bright they are, but they don't care anymore. At this age, if they act smart, boys will label them a bitch.

In middle school, girls are frequently taller than boys, having reached puberty one and a half to two years ahead of the boys in their classes. Girls are more interested in socializing with the other sex earlier than boys are. In addition to the biological explanation for this phenomenon, a cultural explanation is that girls are encouraged to learn and develop interpersonal communication skills throughout early childhood. By adolescence, they are prepared to engage in relationship intricacies. Boys, on the other hand, are not encouraged in these ways and may not possess the sophisticated communication skills necessary for these encounters. Since boys' concerns are displaying competence and establishing their gender as separate from girls', they may avoid interpersonal encounters where they may not excel.

HIGH SCHOOL

At the high school level the directions of male and female interests continue to diverge. Particularly important at this stage are the increasing presence of male teachers and administrators, the importance of sexual attractiveness to potential partners, peer sexual harassment, college entrance exams, and the major role of interscholastic athletics in high school life.

MALE TEACHERS AND ADMINISTRATORS

Administrations in high schools in the United States are comprised largely of males. Although more than two-thirds of this nation's teachers are female, nearly 80 percent of principals are male. Likewise, even though 50 percent of the doctoral students in education are female, over 95 percent of the superintendents are male.[17] High school students are exposed to many more male models of authority and power than female models. School policies, often devised by administrators, may reflect messages and communication patterns more often associated with the masculine than the feminine.

IMPORTANCE OF SEXUAL ATTRACTIVENESS

Critical issues for students during high school accelerate the trend initiated in middle school—attractiveness and popularity. Adherence to gender scripts—often stereotyped scripts—is strong. A dominant feature of high school culture are cliques that provide validation for certain standards of behavior. Punishment for students who deviate from those standards can be harsh and punitive. People who vary in weight, agility, skin condition, or dress, for example, can elicit blunt remarks in the hall, notes in a locker, or comments made publicly in the cafeteria. Popularity often is measured by a student's adherence to or variance from the gendered norm for male or female. The greatest disdain is reserved for males who demonstrate stereotypical female characteristics and females who do not demonstrate stereotypical female characteristics. Females who demonstrate stereotypical male characteristics of athletic prowess have gained more acceptance in the high school culture recently as the image of female athletes becomes more familiar and even desired. Nevertheless, demonstration of stereotypical maleness and femaleness is a prominent feature of high school culture.

PEER SEXUAL HARASSMENT

Harassment of students by students in high school has become a nationwide problem. Studies find that 80 percent of respondents report having experienced peer harassment and one study marked peer harassment as the most common student complaint.[18] Researchers seem to agree that peer harassment is by far the most significant and most prevalent kind of harassment in the high school culture, yet policies continue to be written primarily with the teacher-student relationship in mind, giving only passing notice to harassment among students. Male students are more likely to harass female students than are male teachers.[19] Lack of attention to peer harassment may send messages to students that peer harassment is acceptable. Damage to the self-esteem of students who are harassed—mostly female—may result from lack of formal action against this behavior.

Formal action must address the perceptions of students, teachers, and administrators of both sexes. Teachers are judged more critically for harassment behavior than are students. When students are reprimanded for harassing others and the harassment is not considered severe, the student's status mitigates disciplinary actions.[20] Constructing appropriate harassment policies means dealing with the complexities of defining harassment and identifying the severity of either the harassing behaviors or the disciplinary actions responding to those behaviors. Some schools have included students' perceptions and descriptions of harassment as ways of identifying the unwelcome behaviors. High school students in one study identified four factors they considered when they determined harassment: (1) the harassing behavior; (2) how the recipient of the harassment reacted; (3) the harasser's intentions; and (4) the relationship that existed previously between the two students.[21] Writing policy that addresses such equivocal concepts as relationship history and intention confounds many administrators. Without school policy on these issues, students continue to enact peer rule with regard to harassment, often to the detriment and disadvantage of those being harassed.[22]

Sexual harassment differs from sex discrimination. Harassment means one person demeans or threatens another because of their sex. Discrimination means one person does not give another rights or privileges because of sex. Both problems exist in schools. Harassment can be identified when one student uses sex differences to taunt another or to create a hostile climate for the second student. Discrimination can be identified when a student's sex accounts for being excluded from a sport or a certain course or discussion during class.

While sex discrimination and sexual harassment are separate issues, both indicate an inequity between the sexes and an intent to subordinate one to the other. During the period 1987–1990, the Office for Civil Rights (OCR) reported a 71 percent increase in the number of sex discrimination complaints received. The impact of the Anita Hill/Clarence Thomas hearings (discussed in chapter 8) may account for the doubling in the number of cases brought before the Equal Employment Opportunity Commission (EEOC) during 1990 and 1991. In that agency's compliance review process, sexual harassment is now second only to minority special education.[23]

Not surprisingly, female high school students not only are more likely to be victims of sexual harassment, but they are targeted for more severe forms of harassment as well.[24] Since adolescent females who have been sexually harassed report feelings similar to those expressed by young women who have been raped,[25] the communication climate for disclosing those feelings is critical. In many instances disclosing the harassment does not occur because women believe they can manage the problem themselves, believe the incident was their fault, or are afraid of reprisal if they confer with others for help.[26] The high school structure is such that incidental conversations with teachers do not occur with regularity; usually a conversation with a counselor must be by appointment.

The logistics of reporting sexual harassment at school are confounding. The reporting of sexual harassment happens only in small percentages even with adults in a public or work setting. In high school, a student confronts a significant age differential. Explaining the harassing behavior to a person who, from the student's point of view, may or may not understand the vocabulary and nuances of the student's generation adds complicating factors that students may choose to avoid. Since the school (and other social institutions such as legal groups and welfare agencies) expends more attention and resources on sexual harassment of students by adult teachers, the student may well conclude that only harassment of the young by the old warrants action. If, as researchers have discovered, messages about sexual harassment may be interpreted differently by males and females,[27] one conclusion that may be drawn is that policies written by male administrators likely will not reflect experiences and interpretations of young women in high school.

Other legal developments—particularly with regard to amounts of money awarded for sexual discrimination and sexual harassment violations—have ensued from numerous cases brought against school districts across the country. The case of *Franklin v. Gwinnett County Public Schools* has expanded the means by which students can seek redress from school districts.[28] In this case, a teacher-coach made verbal advances toward a student, including pressure for sexual intercourse. A recent court ruling permits the student to seek damages against the school district and also seek damages from a band director who advised her to drop her complaint.[29]

Tension about communicating about sex and gender is amplified during high school years. Over half the students in one study reported they were sexually active.[30] Interestingly, the women reported more coerced sexual activity, and the men reported peer group pressure to engage in sexual behavior. This pattern mirrors sexual harassment patterns, where the women are harassed and the men report support from peers for harassing behavior.[31] However, the older the student, the less likely they were to support use of coercive measures in all situations, suggesting the willingness to accept sexual coercion subsides with age and experience. The problem remains that although harassing behaviors may subside with age, effects on those harassed may remain.

In their study, Feltey, Ainslie and Geib discovered that adolescents—both male and female—interpreted coercive sexual behavior to be a signal of a deeply committed relationship.[32] This disturbing finding marks sexually harassing behaviors in high schools as creating salient messages about maleness, femaleness, and attractiveness. Sexual harassment intimidates learners and negatively affects the overall academic environment, both inside and outside the classroom. Students who observe or experience sexual harassment express distrust of school policy and pessimism about education.[33]

College Entrance Exams

Many high school students aspire to attend college after they graduate. Entrance to college is in part dependent on results on nationalized tests. PSAT (Preliminary Scholastic Assessment Test), SAT (Scholastic Assessment Test) and ACT (American College Test) are used by most colleges as predictors of college success. Women's scores on SAT tests are lower than men's; males score on average 8 points higher on verbal and 45 points higher on math.[34] Three-fifths of the National Merit Scholarships, primarily awarded according to scores on the PSAT, go to males, yet women tend to receive higher college grades than men with the same SAT scores. A 1989 lawsuit charged that the SAT favored males over females. Phyllis Rosser of the Center for Women Policy Studies agrees with the ruling, citing the following example from the SAT as representative of questions that favored white males. Forty-one percent of the males answered this question correctly and 16 percent of the females answered correctly: (Fill in the blanks from the five pairs of choices below):

Although the undefeated visitors _____ triumphed over the underdog opponents, the game was hardly the _____ sportwriters had predicted.
A) fortunately.........upset
B) unexpectedly.........classic
C) finally.........rout
D) easily.........stalemate
E) utterly.........mismatch[35]

Did you answer "C," the correct answer? Supporters for SAT reform argue that the test form communicates in styles more familiar to white men than to minorities, including women. From this cultural perspective, the either/or and multiple choice questions plus the vocabulary used by the SAT as opposed to timed responses or essays all are patterns used most in the white, male world.

The college entrance exam scores generally reflect overall patterns between males and females in the United States education system. Research combining the results of six national studies indicates that boys dominate girls by a ratio of 7 to 1 at the top levels of math and science. In some science and vocational aptitude tests, only boys scored in the top 1 to 3 percent.

I was in the advanced math class all during grade school. When I entered the seventh grade, there were several girls (almost an equal number of girls and boys) in the advanced class. By the time I got to my senior year, however, there were several more boys than girls in my calculus class. Most of the girls in my classes before calculus could have probably succeeded in this class but decided not to take it because they thought it would be too difficult or because they didn't think they would need those skills. Many of them knew they would not major in math or science in college, so they stopped taking math. I think it was more a factor of not trying than not being able to do the work.

Boys also represent the largest population at the bottom of reading and writing scores. More girls than boys scored in the top 5–10 percent in reading comprehension, perceptual speech, and word association. Researchers agree that biological differences do not account for the discrepancies, but that culturally ingrained patterns have affected the learning abilities of both sexes. Evidence in this study indicates significant progress has been made with regard to improved scores for blacks and Hispanics. The sex-typed pattern found in 1994 is similar to those found thirty years ago, indicating little progress has been made in creating a test that more accurately reflects college potential of both males and females.[36]

TEAM SPORTS AND SCHOOL PRIORITIES

Interscholastic sports have major importance for both individual students and the schools for which they compete. The clearest way to identify a senior high school in most communities is by the football, soccer, or track facilities that typically surround it. In many parts of the United States, football reigns as the most important sport, and the football player is the ultimate symbol of the male gender ideal. Race, ethnicity, or socioeconomic status can be mitigated in some part by achieving athletic success. Football spawns a homecoming court, cheerleaders, marching bands, fund-raising clubs, publications, and (it is widely believed) financial support by local taxpayers for the educational program in general. In other places basketball, track, soccer, or ice hockey have equivalent importance, and the stars of these sports gain a high stature among their peers.

It is generally acceptable for girls to be competitive in sports and academics, but no boys in my school did activities that would be labeled as feminine. Even the boy involved in gymnastics was teased for being a "sissy," although he was strong and quite skilled.

Many sports programs still carry the connotation that they are male domains. Reflect for a moment about the images you conjured as you read the preceding paragraph. In this culture, when we think of marching bands, cheerleaders, and homecoming, we generally think of athletic events where the players are male. From a rhetorical perspective, the mascot names often reveal our interpretations. The men's teams are the Foxes; the women's teams are the Lady Foxes. The term, "lady," often is used in renaming teams rather than "female" or "women," juxtaposing the genteel, mild-mannered, polite referent of "lady" to the strong, athletic, active referent of the team name. To better understand the rhetorical effects of "Lady Raiders," try to imagine the parallel adjective that would be used for the male team: "Gentlemen Raiders."

Long-term effects on high school males of the overwhelming emphasis on athletic prowess are not clear. Immediate effects can include encouragement from students, parents, coaches, and teachers for males to pursue the stereotypical male gender role. For minority males, this encouragement can create complexities not experienced by white students. The interplay of maleness, race, class, or ethnicity generates complicated communication climates and intricate cultural role expectations.

High school males also experience effects of working with male superiors, their coaches. While some high school coaches teach team members personal as well as athletic development, many aspire to an extreme competitive position that only winners count. Familiar t-shirt slogans capture this sentiment: "Winning Isn't Everything, It's the Only Thing," "Second place is just another name for loser!" or "Refuse to lose." Male students use such sentiments to design their own value hierarchies; male athletes often learn to privilege winning over all else. The school and community attention male athletes receive for their efforts can function as messages about what it means to be male. Often in the political interest of fielding a winning team, coaches reduce the benefits male students can gain from high school athletics by perpetuating rigid standards for male behavior and enacting narrow models of maleness. Some coaches even pressure other teachers to pass athletes who might otherwise fail. These highly competitive behaviors often affect students of other schools as well; schools can develop fierce rivalries that result in physical fights and other violence when the schools meet for interscholastic athletic events.

In addition, male athletes learn to gain respect, self-esteem, and admiration of others from athletic prowess. How many points scored, how physical the player was in the recent game, or how well the player defended his territory become measures of his value. Males who are not athletically inclined or who are not interested in sports learn ways to deal with the discrepancy between themselves and the male stereotype. The communication climate of adolescence can allow sarcasm, put-downs, and direct verbal attacks on members of the culture who differ from the gendered stereotypes. Males who conform are rewarded; those who do not may experience discrimination, harassment, or expulsion from cliques.

Effects of the overwhelming emphasis on athletic prowess on high school females take two different forms: the first is on female athletes and the second is on females who fit a more traditional stereotype in the high school culture. Females are no longer limited to cheering from the sidelines. Educational and athletic opportunities for women have expanded with the aid of Title IX, a component of the

Education Amendments passed in the 1970s prohibiting sex discrimination in any educational institution that received federal funding. Yet, high school coaching positions—even those for women's teams—are still awarded predominantly to males, a pattern that has increased in frequency in the 1980s and 1990s. Female athletes talk to male coaches more about school matters and significant males (subjects that are peripheral to their sense to self); they talk to female coaches primarily about self-concept development and role clarification.[37] Female athletes in high school, like their professional counterparts, do not receive the same level or kind of acclaim or encouragement for their successes. This pattern is not surprising since it follows patterns for national teams. For example, many people followed with excitement the men's national soccer team as they vied for the World Cup Championship. Although the team lost their bid, team members like Alexi Lalas are still recognized by student soccer players across the country. Few people can name any woman on the national women's team or even know that team won the world championship for several years in a row. This invisibility may account for different kinds of sports participation by women than by men. Some research explains that British females, unlike males, are unlikely to continue in sports unless they have the direct support by an individual sponsor,[38] such as a coach, a teacher, or a family member. Since women's athleticism is not related to their performance of their sex role as is the case with men, many women say they are careful to display female gendered behaviors off the playing field (or court or track) to counteract their athletic ability, which can indicate maleness. One female softball player explained that she curled her hair, wore make-up, and painted her nails partly to let others know about her femininity.

For females who perceive themselves as more traditional, dating an athlete is the ultimate tribute to the woman's attractiveness and gender appeal. Whether or not the athlete is a good student typically does not matter; in fact, tutoring him may be a way for a female student to get to know him socially. What is most important is that the male athlete is admired, and his partner will be admired as well. One young woman with aspirations to achieve the feminine stereotype wanted to cross the boundary between academic success and success in the gender curriculum that centered on football. This acquaintance was a varsity cheerleader who dated a football co-captain. She giggled when people asked what her grades were and then changed the subject to the other person's concerns. Few but her parents ever knew that she earned straight As. Her voice was always soft and pitched slightly higher when she talked to men, and she appeared incapable of anger.

She had a generally friendly style with both sexes, but she was envied by many females who also wanted to succeed at demonstrating a feminine gender and achieving at academic studies at the same time. Many young women today feel duplicitous in these situations and choose images or communication styles they believe to be authentic to their individuality rather than to the stereotypical image of femininity.

COLLEGE

Earlier we noted how movement through the educational system is movement away from females and feminine symbols and toward males and the masculine gender ideal. In this view, colleges would be the most masculine of all the learning environments. Such a claim is partially true, but it needs to be qualified in two respects: (1) While male faculty still outnumber female faculty, women now comprise 51 percent of undergraduates;[39] (2) students of either sex can enroll in any course of study—from ceramics to engineering—if the requirements for admission have been met. As we look at college environments, we will consider not only the learning climate within the classroom but also how textbooks treat sex and gender and problems on campus with sexual harassment.

COLLEGE CLIMATES

One way to understand the climate on college campuses with regard to sex and gender is to compare the United States model to models from other nations and cultures. For example, at Ain Shams University in Egypt, about 25 percent of the faculty in physics are women compared to about 3 percent in the United States where only about 7 percent of physics doctorates are awarded to women. The physics department at Ain Shams is headed by a woman, Dr. Karimat El-Sayed. Similarly, at United Arab Emirates University, 70 percent of university students are women.[40] These enrollments and percentages demonstrate that women as well as men are interested in and able to study diverse topics. However, we should not conclude from these descriptions that women's educations in these cultures are given a high priority. Women dominate these positions largely because men choose not to pursue educations. Men choose not to go to college in these nations because a man's ability to amass money is not tied to his education. The climate on the campus, then, will be generated in part by expectations and messages a culture develops about which sex is allowed certain educational privileges.

Research about climates in United States' colleges suggests that experiences of men and women on campus are substantially different. Ethnic, race, and class issues interact with those of sex and gender to make experiences even more diverse; for example, black and Hispanic women face obstacles of sex and gender as well as those of ethnicity, race, and oftentimes class.[41] In 1982, Roberta Hall and Bernice Sandler described a college classroom as "a chilly climate for women" and outlined some of the subtle, even unconscious, ways that college professors and policies communicated a lower status to women. In 1986, they wrote not only about faculty, but administrators and graduate students.[42] In 1991, Sandler writes that progress has been made in policies and some attitudes, but many remain as they were in 1982:

1. Professors call on men by name more often than they do women and, when they refer to women, use nicknames more often than they do with men.

2. Comments by professors divert the discussion about a woman's work to the topic of her appearance; the same does not occur with men.

3. Faculty are more attentive to men's comments and questions than to women's questions, giving more eye contact to men and probing for more elaboration from them.

4. Examples are often worded as if no women were present, for example, "Imagine that your wife . . ."

5. Answers by males are often extended by the instructor and later referred to by the male student's name, while females' ideas often receive a quick nod or "hmm" followed by a change of focus.[43]

Observations of college classrooms reveal that college men talked longer than women and made more declarative statements even if the statements were wrong. Women responded to insufficient information by being more tentative. Sandler also asserts that professors (both men and women) "tend to call on male students more often, to make more eye contact with male students, respond more to male students' comments, [and] interrupt women more."[44]

Throughout their educations, many men and women students experience the familiar patterns described by Sandler; after twelve years in school, male students become used to speaking out more often and receiving more attention while female students become used to listening more and speaking less. Often both male and female students perceive these practices to comprise a norm that provides equal opportunity for them both. During one gender class, we engaged in a lively discussion about whether or not these patterns are prevalent and whether or not individual women received less attention in class. Most students—male and female—came to the conclusion that at our university, these discrepancies did not occur except in isolated instances and that even in this class men and women individually talked about the same amount. As we neared the end of the class period, a male student revealed to us that he had secretly kept track of our communication pattern during the discussion. He had recorded that the seven men in the twenty-five-student class had talked for 64 percent of the time and had averaged more time per talk than the women. We were all surprised by his findings and began to reexamine our presumptions!

The most current feminist movement has drawn attention to these nearly invisible presumptions with regard to their impact on women's educations. Particularly in the field of speech communication, publications about sex and gender equity in the classroom abound.[45] While some progress has been made toward making the classroom a less "chilly" place, resistance to changing the curriculum occurs in many ways: overt and covert actions, resistance based on inattention to norms, and resistance with claims that sex and gender are not relevant to teaching and learning about a particular topic.

In classes traditionally populated by males—engineering, physics, and dentistry, for example—women's experiences are even more significantly different than males'. Women in those courses frequently disclose that they learn to ignore peer comments which degrade women's abilities. One woman explained that she had learned to "be the best" in the class so others would accept her as an "equal." Responses given by women about these classroom situations differ significantly from those given by men in classes made up predominantly of women. In women's studies classes, men often remark that they are not allowed to speak out as much as they wish and feel intimidated by the instructor and/or other students. Conditioned by imbalance in the past, men may believe their talk has been unequally curtailed when the ratio is actually equal. Similarly, in communication courses in which more women are enrolled than men, women complain that men are not being allowed their share of talk when talk time is divided equally. While these kinds of problems are not yet resolved, the recent attention to them may bring change in presumptions and practices in campus climates.

Living Groups

Some living groups perpetuate subordination of women, even on the college campus. In a study of fraternities, the following account was rendered by a "little sister" of a fraternity:

I spent the afternoon at a fraternity brother's apartment with some other little sisters, drinking the shots of tequila which were waiting for us when we arrived. I took several shots, encouraged by the brothers, anticipating a need to be more relaxed for the little sister fundraiser that night. Later, as I approached the fraternity house, I saw the stage set up in the back yard with the pole in the middle of the stage. The brothers had arranged chairs and formed an audience in front of the stage. The fraternity president started the show: "Welcome to the Annual Slave Auction!" As the music started we went out on stage, two little sisters at a time, and danced for the brothers while they bid on us for one week of our "slave" services. I was really nervous and combined with the tequila I started to feel a little sick. I wanted the brothers' applause, but I did not want to embarrass myself or ruin my reputation. I danced halfheartedly and then watched from the side. The next woman went toward the pole set up in the middle of the stage. As she touched the pole, the brothers screamed and shouted, encouraging her to dance seductively: "Hump the pole, Hump the pole!" As the woman began to simulate sexual intercourse with the pole, one brother bid $60 for her. The president shouted, "Sold," and the brothers cheered. (April 1993)[46]

From a rhetorical perspective, the names of "little sister" for fraternities and "big brothers" for sororities connote superior and subordinate roles for males and females who are approximately the same ages. Connotations of "big brother" include stereotypical characteristics such as protector and provider. Connotations of "little sister" include stereotypical characteristics such as needing protection and help. From a power perspective, the structure of having a group of women who function as auxiliary support under the authority of a group of men creates inequity, imbalance, and subordination.[47] Little sister organizations frequently elicit membership from romantic partners of fraternity members. Dorothy C. Holland and Margaret A. Eisenhart write about the effects of the "culture of romance" prevalent in some colleges and universities on women's scholastic and subsequent career motivations and achievements.[48]

TEACHER EDUCATION TEXTBOOKS AND PROGRAMS

Since Title IX was implemented, overt sexism in teacher education textbooks has declined. Jordan J. Titus reports in his review that now few of the texts include any content at all about social stratification or inequality in education. Titus notes, however, that while the explicitly sexist material has been eliminated, material that addresses sex and gender inequities in the classroom have not been added.[49] Other studies find that newly graduated teachers treat males and females in classrooms similar to ways used by experienced teachers, suggesting little training in teacher education classrooms has changed teachers' practices with regard to sex, gender, and sexism.[50] Jones writes that, "Methods courses can not only provide the needed pedagogical skills for introspection but can also provide preservice teachers with the research evidence that establishes the harmful effects of biased instruction. University instructors must also model equitable teaching behaviors to ensure that teachers perceive the importance of educational equity."[51]

SEXUAL HARASSMENT AS A TWISTING OF GENDER IDEALS

Sexual harassment patterns evident in the high school environment persist at the college level. Since college students often are used as participants in scholarly research, more information is available about harassment at that level. Harassing behaviors include derogatory, inflammatory language; innuendo; and suggestive language, all of which communicate uncomfortable, and even frightening messages. Researchers find that women at universities are likely to find certain behavior harassing more than men are; men are more likely to attribute the problem of the behavior to the victim's own making.[52] College women are more likely to report harassment or discrimination, and men are more likely to fail to recognize the behaviors or to exhibit indifference.[53] Much of the research about harassment on college campuses focuses on harassment of students by faculty or of faculty by other faculty.

When a professor makes sexual contact with a student a condition for some reward—a grade, a recommendation, or even continuing goodwill—unequal power defines the arrangement. Sexual harassment is the intentional sexual exploitation of a less powerful by a more powerful individual. While this power often is defined in terms of positions—such as the professor holding a more powerful position than the student—power also can manifest itself in other ways, such as through physical size, sex, race, or class. The power difference can change based on perception. Researchers examining harassment of female professors by male students find complex power dynamics, revealing that female professors perceived the harassing behaviors more problematic than did male professors in similar situations.[54]

In light of the dominant person's power, people in the college community—professors, colleagues, students, administrators—sometimes look the other way, saying "boys will be boys" as if no "real" harm is being done. The problem spreads when members of any group in power (potentially male or female, though harassment by males overwhelmingly predominates) ignore sexual harassment because of their own presumptions about the victim, their own insecurities about sexuality, or their friendships with an offender. In any of these cases, the victim's perspective is not taken into account; she may be thought to have earned or invited the treatment, or to have no real aspirations that could be damaged.

CURRENT DEVELOPMENTS

Sexual harassment issues comprise one obstacle for women pursuing an education. Adult reentry programs at the college level have given women in particular a way to surmount other barriers to education and to find a positive educational experience that will prepare them for employment. Many women returning to college take technical or management courses rather than the liberal arts and education courses many of them began years earlier. Returning female students often focus on careers with high income potential because they are heads of households, needing to support other family members. They are often more willing than younger women to speak in class and to mention problems faced by women in various settings.

Some women find support in women's studies courses which constitute a major change in the official college curriculum. The first two courses were offered in 1969. Now courses are listed all over the United States through departments and research centers, offering majors, minors, and specialized certificates. Some schools have adopted course titles such as "Gender Studies" or "The Study of Women and Men in Society," to make clear that both sexes are affected by gender role learning. In a few universities, programs in men's studies have begun, with a focus on the particular issues males face regarding expectations for masculine behavior.

The full influence of women's studies on the gender curriculum has yet to be felt. The first efforts focused on knowledge of women's history and on filling in gaps in the traditional fields of research, an effort sometimes termed the "add women and stir" approach. Then the effort spread to deal with questions of research methodology and bias in the process of gathering knowledge. Currently a significant amount of theory building is going on, in a widening search for ways to examine and potentially alter gender-based assumptions in the academic world as well as in everyday life.[55]

The current system supports what Blythe McVicker Clinchy calls "separate knowing,"[56] with a focus on critical thinking and scientific methodologies. Clinchy and others explain in their book *Women's Ways of Knowing* that "connected knowing"[57] represents one of many other ways to think and know, ways not explored in the present education system.

CONCLUSION

In much educational literature today, schools are portrayed as places in which equal opportunity prevails. Yet in a variety of ways—teacher communication, visual and language materials, social arrangements inside and outside classrooms—schools still widen rather than narrow the gap between the communication roles and expectations of the sexes. Whereas girls perform better on the average in most school subjects until middle school, boys win more attention from teachers as well as from other boys and girls. The subtle persuasions that begin to influence children's communication during the preschool years convince many girls that they should be quiet, good, and not too noticeable. At the same time a parallel set of persuasive messages convinces many boys that they must be as aggressive and as separate from females as possible in order to succeed in the world outside the school. Some females deviate from the norm of the quiet female, and some males deviate from the norm of the aggressive male, but in both cases negative communication from public or private sources may make it hard for the girl or boy to stay self-confident in the face of the recurring message, "You do not measure up."

The disparity between the sexes' development is significant. If a female grows up in a nonsexist family and becomes a prominent attorney, she may be expanding the feminine ideal. On the other hand, if a male grows up to be an elementary school teacher and marries a prominent attorney, he may be seen as failing in the masculine ideal because he is not dominant in either arena.

To what extent do we educate women and men to conform to the system of education at hand? To what extent do we change the system at hand to integrate women's life experiences and ways of knowing? How can the system be adjusted to benefit men and allow them latitude in their gender choices? Sex and gender issues will be central to the debate about which school programs should receive tax money; decisions will hinge increasingly on the issue of what skills and values all children will need compared to the opportunities some children will want or need. Talk about schools is ultimately talk about the ways humans view themselves, their children, and the tasks those children will face in the future.

QUESTIONS FOR DISCUSSION

The following questions invite you to think about your experience of being in school. You may choose to imagine a particular time in your life or imagine a time when a vivid experience occurred. Think about any messages you received or sent to others about masculine or feminine ideals for your own or others' communication.

1. You wake up in the morning:
   Who else is home, and what do they say to you? Which clothes do you put on? Why? Who bought them or got them ready for you to wear? Who has an opinion about what you wear? What do you eat for breakfast? With whom? How was breakfast made? How do you get to school? With whom?

2. In school, who is (are) your teacher(s)?
   How do you feel about each other? What are your most and least favorite subjects? Why? How do you spend your time between classes, or waiting for class? What do you get praised or criticized for? How do you get noticed, and by whom? What do you like most and least about being in class? How can you tell who is the best student and the worst student?

3. Lunch, recess, and free periods:
   With whom do you eat? How many people? How often does this change? What do you eat? From what source? How well do you like it? What is talked about at lunchtime? What activity(ies) do you engage in during your free time? Whom do you watch or seek out? Whom do you avoid? What family rules exist about how you are to act at school or on the way back and forth between home and school?

4. General reactions:
   How do you feel about yourself today while going home from school? Do you think about the future, and if so, in what ways? What do you feel the most pressure to do or to say? What are you expected not to do or to say because of your sex? How do you know this, and how do you react to the restriction? In what circumstances do you feel the most comfortable or at ease? In the above exercise, where did it make the most and where the least difference that you are a male or a female? What experiences do you see differently now than you did at the time they occurred?

CASES FOR ANALYSIS

CASE 7.1 PLAYING GAMES

A nursery school teacher reported that she had received a visit from a pair of disgruntled parents. They announced abruptly that they were taking their three-year-old son out of the nursery school immediately. When the teacher asked in surprise what the problem was that led them to remove their son, the father answered, "He asked to play dress-up at home. He says you let him play dress-up here with Marie and Karen. We don't want a cream puff for a son. We want him to grow up to be a man."

1. What is the preschool teacher's role in this discussion? Do these values belong at home? At school? What are the implications of each?

2. Try to list all the ways messages are being sent about sex and gender among the teacher, the father and mother, the child, and other children in the room. Try to list all the messages as well.

3. Consider the fears that could lie behind the parents' words: that the boy will not be sufficiently masculine, that he will develop homosexual preferences, that he will be rejected by other boys for identifying with girls' play. Do you perceive other fears? If you were the teacher, would you address these concerns? If so, how? If not, why?

CASE 7.2 SPORTS PHOTOS

Ten-year-old Sarah came home excited about her project for class the next day. The children were to find pictures of people engaged in various sports activities. Sarah had found two pictures of male athletes, but she was having trouble finding pictures of females. Her mother tried to help by looking through a recent campus newspaper. She found a photo of a female gymnast and showed it to Sarah. The reaction was immediate: "Oh, no—the boys will laugh! They don't think gymnastics is a sport at all." Sarah's mother mentioned that there were boys as well as girls in Sarah's gymnastics class, but that didn't seem to affect Sarah's mood. The next morning she acted disgusted as she walked out the door to leave for school, apparently wanting to forget the project altogether.

Suddenly she stopped, turned around, and ran back in the house. She came out again in less than a minute, carrying a photo of a female basketball player making a jump shot. Sarah grinned. Holding all four photos, she marched out triumphantly. Though Sarah didn't explain her delight directly, her parents guessed that she was pleased she had thought of having a photo of a female athlete in a male-oriented sport. That was the one way she could do the project and avoid the boys' ridicule.

1. What does this true story tell you about a ten-year-old's ability to recognize a sex stereotype? What kind of thoughts would you expect a child like Sarah to have concerning the accuracy of such stereotypes?

2. What influence did the communication of Sarah's parents seem to have on her view of the project, compared to the stated opinions of the boys in her class?

3. What kinds of school assignments have you been given that stated or implied equal valuing of both sexes? Have any stated or implied the opposite?

4. To what extent are athletic activities still a male domain?

CASE 7.3 WHAT'S SO FUNNY?

The following joke appeared in a popular magazine: A parent hears a friend proudly stating that his son got a bachelor's degree in three years. The parent answers, "That's nothing; my daughter got a Ph.D. in two years." "Really? How?" "Easy—she married him."

1. Did you laugh? Why or why not?

2. Compare your response to the joke with that of others.

3. Humor is time-bound and personal. When might this joke have been funnier, and to whom?

4. Which viewpoint(s) from chapter 2 might help you account for the various reactions to this joke?

CASE 7.4 LAISSEZ-FAIRE AT WHOSE EXPENSE?

When I was in junior high, one of the "in things" to do was to "shift" or "pants" the girls. For the girls it was one of the most humiliating things that could happen to them. I know because it happened to me. The class clown came up and asked me a question while another boy, his sidekick, pulled my stretch pants to my feet. It was during lunch and I felt like just about everyone saw this happen. I was very upset and my friends knew it. They let our English teacher next period know. The teacher just took the "boys will be boys" attitude and said he would talk to them. I think he found it humorous as opposed to being injurious.

1. Do you consider the "pantsing" of girls to be sexual harassment? Why or why not?

2. What role did the English teacher play? How would you have handled this situation?

3. What course of action *should* this writer have taken? What course of action *could* this writer have taken?

4. Did students at your school have similar practices? How do those practices function with regard to gender ideals?

NOTES

[1] See Daniel O'Leary, *Mommy, I Can't Sit Still: Coping with the Hyperactive and Hyperaggressive Child* (New York: New Horizon Press, 1984). Observation as well as anecdotal reports from preschool teachers confirm this perception.

[2] Jean Berko Gleason and Esther Blank Greif, "Men's Speech to Young Children," in *Language, Gender, and Society*, eds. Barrie Thorne, Cheris Kramarae, and Nancy Henley (New York: Newbury House Publishers, 1983), pp. 140–50.

[3] A. L. Bryant, "Stalled Agenda: Gender Equity and the Training of Educators," *American Association of University Women* 2, 2–7 (1991).

[4] M. Sadker, D. Sadker and L. Stulberg, "Fair and Square? Creating a Nonsexist Classroom," *Instructor* 102, 7 (March 1993): 45–68.

[5] M. Sadker, D. Sadker, and S. Klein, "The Issue of Gender in Elementary and Secondary Education," in *Review of Research in Education*, ed. G. Grant (Washington, DC: American Educational Research Association, 1991), pp. 269–315; Patricia G. Avery and Constance Walker, "Prospective Teachers'

Perceptions of Ethnic and Gender Differences in Academic Achievement," *Journal of Teacher Education* 44, 1 (January 1993): 27–37.

[6] Susan Kochenberger Stroeher, "Sixteen Kindergartners' Gender-Related Views of Careers," *The Elementary School Journal* 95, 1 (September 1994): 95–103.

[7] Shmuel Shamai, "Possibilities and Limitations of a Gender Stereotypes Intervention Program," *Adolescence* 29 (Fall 1994): 665–80.

[8] Kevin Majoribanks, "Relationship of Children's Ethnicity, Gender, and Social Status to Their Family Environments and School-Related Outcomes," *The Journal of Social Psychology* 131 (February 1991): 83–91.

[9] Myra Sadker and David Sadker, *Failing at Fairness: How America's Schools Cheat Girls* (New York: C. Scribner's Sons, 1994), pp. 48–50.

[10] Ibid.

[11] Myra Sadker and David Sadker, "The Report Card on Sex Bias," report published by the MidAtlantic Center for Sex Equity, Washington, DC, 1984.

[12] Mid-Atlantic Equity Consortium Inc. and The Network, "Beyond Title IX: Gender Equity Issues in Schools," September 1993, p. 16 as cited in Charles Clark, "Education and Gender," *CQ Researcher* 4 (June 3, 1994): 481–500.

[13] American Association of University Women, *How Schools Shortchange Girls*, commissioned by the AAUW Educational Foundation and researched by the Wellesley College Center for Research on Women, a joint publication of the AAUW Educational Foundation and National Education Association, 1992.

[14] Ibid.

[15] Gayle E. Hutchinson, "Gender-Fair Teaching in Physical Education," *Journal of Physical Education, Recreation, and Dance* 66, 9 (1995): 41–47.

[16] Gilligan as cited by Charles S. Clark, "Education and Gender," *CQ Researcher* 4 (June 3, 1994): 481–500.

[17] Mary Moran, "Up Against the Glass Ceiling," *American School Board Journal* 179, 2 (February 1992): 38-4.

[18] Dan H. Wishnietsky, "Reported and Unreported Teacher-Student Sexual Harassment," *Journal of Educational Research* 84, 3 (January-February 1991): 164–69; Carren Loredo, Ann Reid, and Kay Deaux, "Judgments and Definitions of Sexual Harassment by High Schoool Students," *Sex Roles* 32, 1/2 (1995): 29–45; Perry A. Zirkel, "Student-to-Student Sexual Harassment," *Phi Delta Kappan* 76, 8 (April 1995): 648–50; and Kate Myers, "Unwelcome Touches of Student Life," *Times Educational Supplement* 4032 (October 8, 1993): SS6A.

[19] Karen Bogart and Nan Stein, "Breaking the Silence: Sexual Harassment in Education," *Peabody Journal of Education* 64, 4 (Summer 1987): 146–63.

[20] Ibid.

[21] Loredo, Reid, and Deaux, op. cit.

[22] Bogart and Stein, op cit.

[23] Moran, op cit.

[24] Bogart and Stein, op cit.

[25] Susan Strauss, "Sexual Harassment in the School: Legal Implications for Principals," *NASSP Bulletin* 72, 506 (March 1988): 93–97.

[26] Bogart and Stein, op cit.

[27] Ibid.

[28] Mark Walsh, "Students Claiming Sex Harassment Win Right to Sue," *Education Week* XI, 24 (March 4, 1992): 1, 24.

[29] Paul M. Barrett, "Students May Seek Cash in Sex-Bias Cases," *The Wall Street Journal* (February 27, 1992): B6.

[30] Kathryn M. Feltey, Julie J. Ainslie, and Aleta Geib, "Sexual Coercion Attitudes among High School Students," *Youth and Society* 23, 2 (December 1991): 229–50.

[31] Ibid.

[32] Ibid.

[33] Bogart and Stein, op cit.

[34] Karen Bogart and Nan Stein, "Do College-Bound Girls Face a Disadvantage When They Sit Down to Take the SAT Test?" *CQ Researcher* 4 (June 3): 488–89.

[35] Ibid.

[36] Larry Hedges, "Sex Differences in Mental Test Scores, Variability, and Numbers of High-Scoring Individuals," *Science* 269, 5220 (July 1995): 41–45.

[37] Sara A. Officer and Lawrence B. Rosenfeld, "Self-Disclosure to Male and Female Coaches by Female High School Athletes," *Journal of Sport Psychology* 7 (1985): 360–70.

[38] Jay Coakley and Anita White, "Making Decisions: Gender and Sport Participation Among British Adolescents," *Sociology of Sport Journal* 9 (1992): 20–35.

[39] Joan N. Burstyn, "'Has Nothing Changed in a Hundred Years?': The Salience of Gender to the Undergraduate Experience," *American Journal of Education* 101 (February 1993): 196–202.

[40] Wendy Koch, "Power Eludes U.S. Women," *Statesman Journal* (May 31, 1995): 8A.

[41] Y. T. Moses, *Black Women in Academe: Issues and Strategies* (1989) and S. Nieves-Squires, *Hispanic Women: Making Their Presence on Campus Less Tenuous* (1991); Washington, DC: Project on the Status and Education of Women, Association of American Colleges as cited in B. R. Sandler, "Women Faculty at Work in the Classroom, or, Why It Still Hurts to be a Woman in Labor," *Communication Education* 40 (January 1991): 6–15.

[42] B. R. Sandler and R. M. Hall, *The Campus Climate Revisited: Chilly for Women Faculty, Administrators, and Graduate Students* (Washington, DC: Project on the Status and Education of Women, Association of American Colleges, 1986).

[43] Roberta Hall and Bernice Sandler, "The Classroom: A Chilly Climate for Women," report of the Project on the Status and Education of Women, Association of American Colleges, 1982. A second report, "Beyond the Classroom," is also available. Ironically, in social terms the college climate is felt to be chillier by men than by women. See Norman Schultz, Jr. and DeWayne Moore, "The Loneliness Experience of College Students: Sex Differences," *Personal and Social Psychology Bulletin* 12, 1 (March 1986): 111–19.

[44] Sandler 1991, op cit.

[45] S. H. Aiken, K. Anderson, M. Dinnerstein, J. Lensink, and P. MacCorquodale, "Trying Transformations: Curriculum Integration and the Problem of Resistance," *Signs* 12 (1987): 255–75; Lynn Weber Cannon, "Fostering Positive Race, Class, and Gender Dynamics in the Classroom," *Women's Studies Quarterly*, 18, 1/2 (Spring 1990): 126–34; Julia T. Wood and Lisa Firing Lenze, "Strategies to Enhance Gender Sensitivity in Communication Education," *Communication Education* 40 (January 1991): 16–21; Carole Spitzack and Kathryn Cater, "Women in Communication Studies: A Typology for Revision,"

Quarterly Journal of Speech 73 (November 1987): 401–23; Karlyn Kohrs Campbell, "Hearing Women's Voices," *Communication Education* 40 (January 1991): 33–47; Eric E. Peterson, "Moving Toward a Gender Balanced Curriculum in Basic Speech Communication Courses," *Communication Education* 40 (1991): 60–73; Carole A. Beere, Lynda A. King, and Daniel W. King, "Gender-Related Instruments as Instructional Devices in the Communication Classroom," *Communication Education* 40 (1991): 73–93; Kristin S. Vonnegut, "Listening for Women's Voices: Revisioning Courses in American Public Address," *Communication Education* 41 (January 1992): 26–39; Jamie C. Capuzza, "Curriculum Inclusion and the Small Group Communication Course," *Communication Education* 42 (April 1993): 172–78; Leah R. Vande Berg, "Using Television to Teach Courses in Gender and Communication," *Communication Education* 40 (January 1991): 105–11; and Judy C. Pearson and Richard West, "An Initial Investigation of the Effects of Gender on Student Questions in the Classroom: Developing a Descriptive Base," *Communication Education* 40 (January 1991): 22–32.

[46] Mindy Stombler and Patricia Yancey Martin, "Bringing Women In, Keeping Women Down," *Journal of Contemporary Ethnography* 23, 2 (July 1994): 150–84, quoted from pp. 150–51.

[47] Ibid.

[48] Dorothy C. Holland and Margaret A. Eisenhart, *Educated in Romance: Women, Achievement, and College Culture* (Chicago, University of Chicago Press, 1990).

[49] Jordan J. Titus, "Gender Messages in Education Foundations Textbooks," *Journal of Teacher Education* 44 (January 1993): 38–44.

[50] M. Gail Jones, "Gender Issues in Teacher Education," *Journal of Teacher Education* 40 (January 1989): 33–38.

[51] Ibid., p. 38.

[52] Linda J. Rubin and Sherry B. Borgers, "Sexual Harassment in Universities During the 1980's," *Sex Roles* 23 (1990): 397–411.

[53] Ann R. Fischer and Glenn E. Good, "Gender, Self, and Others: Perceptions of the Campus Environment," *Journal of Counseling Psychology* 41, 3 (1994): 343–55.

[54] Kathleen McKinney, "Contrapower Sexual Harassment: The Effects of Student Sex and Type of Behavior on Faculty Perceptions," *Sex Roles* 27 (1992): 627–43.

[55] Journals such as *Signs, Women's Studies, Feminist Studies, Sex Roles, The Psychology of Women Quarterly*, and several international journals of women's studies have made available current research reports and theory-building essays about women, sex, and gender. Of interest to communication students and faculty is the *Journal of Women's Studies in Communication.*

[56] Blythe McVicker Clinchy, "The Development of Thoughtfulness in College Women: Integrating Reason and Care," *American Behavioral Scientist* 32 (July/August 1989): 647–57.

[57] Ibid., p. 650.

Chapter 8

Organizations and Employment

The various ways you define work are important to communication and the sexes, because your definitions reflect and affect your images of men and women. Although work or labor is involved in both paid employment outside the home and the activities of managing a household and family, many people equate "work" with "jobs" and evaluate the worth of jobs according to their monetary return. When work is defined as what one does for pay, it fails to include what is done in the home by a family member. The people who do "home work" are not treated, evaluated, or rewarded as they would be if their efforts occurred in the larger economic and political system. The biases in our language about work will be addressed in this chapter.

CHAPTER OVERVIEW

Most places of employment are assumed to be the natural sphere of men, based on all four perspectives described in chapter 2. The assumption has been that men are the primary workers, with women defined largely as extra, supportive, and temporary workers. Thus, women's communication in the workplace has generally been treated as marginal, no matter what the individual woman's abilities and contributions might be. Recently this arrangement of primary and secondary workers has broken down, and women are entering the professions, skilled trades, and business management areas in unprecedented numbers. Because of these developments, this chapter presents more information about women's communication in the workplace than about men's. Questions about how both sexes are coping and will cope with their new relationships on the job are the focus of this chapter.

The view advanced here is that gender communication ideals and expectations touch nearly every aspect of men's and women's talk on the job. We can expect that every level of communication pertaining to work will show the impact of gender-related meanings and values. First, we examine some ways the two sexes have been treated as distinctive communicators on the job. Second, we will learn about the influence of both verbal and nonverbal symbols on the ways women, men, tasks, and achievements are perceived. Third, the four approaches to communication and the sexes introduced in chapter 2 will be applied to various situations and issues in the workplace. The chapter ends with an analysis of current messages to both sexes about "success" and how it is to be achieved.

DOES A JOB HAVE A SEX?

The images we have of which sex is appropriate for which job often are unexamined. As we explained in chapter 7, kindergartners already have clear ideas about which jobs belong to females and which belong to males. In most cases, the image we have of a secretary or a manager is no accident: it has been built up by many instances of dealing with, reading about, or observing female or male individuals in those jobs. As an example, when Barbara first became a full-time assistant professor in a university, she shared an office with a male professor whose desk was farther from the door than hers. Approximately once a week she was interrupted by a student standing in the doorway asking where he was. When she said she didn't know, most of the visitors would respond indignantly, "Well, aren't you his secretary?" When room assignments changed two years later, Barbara moved her desk to the far side of the office so that she would be less likely to be mistaken for the secretary of her professional colleague.

Now that she shares an office with a female colleague, the problem almost never occurs. Judy notices the same phenomenon even now if she walks down to the secretaries' office to check a student's file. Often she is assumed to be one of the clerical staff simply because she is female. On the other hand, a male secretary in another academic department has reported that he has had trouble convincing students that he is in fact the departmental secretary. Likewise, when Judy's husband was ill, Judy called the Nurse Hotline for medical information. When she got off the phone, her husband asked, "What did she say?" The nurse who had answered the call was male. Our presumptions about whether jobs are for males or females are pervasive and sometimes hard for us to discover. Those presumptions can be communicated in implicit ways—like the students who presumed Barbara or Judy to be secretaries—and can affect others who are trying to do their jobs.

Sometimes those presumptions are based on expectations about who should be supervisors or managers and who should be subordinates. Sixty percent of all management and administrative positions in the United States are held by males.[1] Since a majority of the managers in most organizations have been male, promotions to supervisory positions are more likely to be decided by males than females. The United States culture's stereotypical attitude about sexuality is a major obstacle to women being promoted. Considering a woman as a sexual being may mean failing to consider her contributions in a nonsexual context. Affirmative action programs at the national and local levels have led to attempts to change the language of job titles to address this problem, but the problem has not been eliminated. Ironically, however, movements are in process to eliminate affirmative action programs.

The issues of sexuality seem to pervade attitudes about hiring, working with, and forming trusting relationships with females. For example, research about males' attitudes toward females reveals that male superintendents studied favored hiring an attractive female for a position of elementary school principal but few would consider her for a position of assistant superintendent. They worried that either they would be attracted to their co-worker—in which case the superintendents might lose support of school board members or experience marital problems—or she might be attracted to them—in which case working together would be complicated if the feelings were not mutual.[2] Similarly, female administrators express caution when they receive attention from male subordinates because the women are not sure about the intent of the messages.[3] Problems with sexuality on the job interfere with job performance and promotion.

Another problem of the sexes working with each other stems from their differences in definitions. Both females and males in educational administration report they value trust in their relationships with co-workers. However, their definitions of trust differed. Males defined trust as being comfortable enough with someone to say what you felt when you wanted to without worrying that the other person might violate the confidence. Females defined trust as dependability and as knowing the other person was reliable.[4] The discrepancy in definitions could contribute to the practice of male supervisors holding back criticism of female subordinates. Male supervisors may not believe they could not disclose feelings they had about their female counterpart without risking having the information revealed. Likewise females may not perceive males as reliable if females are unsure of the intent of males' messages.

These differences in trust definitions and expectations may result in different responses by each sex to similar situations. One research study depicted one such scenario. Male administrators were likely to give direct critical feedback to male subordinates, but they were not likely to do so with females. The females were not notified of their errors and the problems were corrected without their knowledge.[5] One conclusion could be the administrators felt more certain of another male's response to and action about criticism. They may not have felt females' reactions would be as predictable; they may have concluded that the criticism might not remain confidential. The problems generated by this behavior are evident: he feels uncomfortable or unskilled at directing criticism at her, and she feels distrusted or devalued because she is not afforded the same opportunities to correct mistakes and learn from them. From a rhetorical perspective, this kind of communication pattern can be changed. Where the patterns exist, they disadvantage females, as we noted in chapter 7.

LEADERSHIP AND MANAGEMENT

Female managers, like other female professionals, often face the problem of contradictory expectations. For example, while females and males associate attractiveness in a man with qualities that make them effective leaders, the same is not true for women.[6] Research finds that women who succeed as leaders may be identified as unattractive.[7] Therefore, an attractive female who aspires to be a leader faces contradictory demands. The contradictions increase because male leaders are seen as effective, competent, knowledgeable, and satisfying as leaders to subordinates if they behave in ways stereotypically congruent with their sex. Women are seen as satisfying and sincere, but not effective if they use feminine styles.[8] Both male and female subordinates perceive female leaders as less effective if the leaders demonstrate feminine gender characteristics.[9] If a woman wishes to be perceived as competent, she faces two double binds. In the first bind, she must adhere to stereotyped feminine styles—styles evaluated in ways that do not lead her to her public, social leadership goals. Simultaneously, she must abandon those feminine styles— styles of leadership with which she is familiar and has effectively managed her life—because social interpretations of these styles are not congruent with social interpretations of leadership. In the second bind, she must decide whether her socially sanctioned leadership role warrants abandonment of her way of knowing the world if she does not perceive leadership in these public, social ways. Enacting leadership can be a complex process for her.

I've known a woman who works as successfully and effectively as men. She is a director of a company. She works really hard and she takes the man's role. I think her work is better than most men's. I wonder why almost all male workers don't like her. They think she acts like a "bitch." Men already devalue women who have ability to do things better than them. This is a problem in the organization that is caused by gender expectations.

If a woman chooses to abandon her feminine style for a more stereotypically masculine one, she still may not achieve leadership effectiveness. Males devalued leaders who use leadership behaviors perceived as incongruent with the sex of the leader.[10] If women adopt more stereotypically masculine leadership styles—in particular autocratic or directive styles—they are evaluated negatively, especially by men.[11] Authoritative women are evaluated more negatively than authoritative men; authoritative men are perceived to be more intelligent.[12] Women also are devalued as leaders if they try to occupy a leadership position that has been male-dominated.[13] These barriers to achieving leadership cause women to endure very different leadership preparation (on a personal level) and execution than men.

I attended a business meeting which several European women attended along with several men and women from the domestic headquarters in Oregon. The European women had a completely different style of conducting business than the American women. They were aggressive, straightforward, to the point, and extremely blunt when expressing their feelings. After the meeting was finished, I expressed to a colleague of mine how interesting it was to experience different cultures in the business setting. The response was, "Yes, the European women are quite masculine, aren't they?"

Some researchers explain that expectations about the leadership role or the formal authority bestowed on the leader may be more influential than sex in determining a leader's effectiveness.[14] Whether leadership expectations or perceptions of authority can be distinguished from gender stereotyping is a critical question. Are leadership expectations or authority expectations embedded in presumptions about gender stereotypes? Perhaps one way to examine this question is to investigate leadership experienced by women in women's groups. Are leadership and authority in this situation the same phenomena as those in mixed-sex or all-male groups or organizations? Several scholars suggest that: women distinguish mixed-sex group and organizational experiences as different from those in single-sex environments;[15] women evaluate their single-sex leadership experiences positively;[16] women respond best in management training when the trainer is female;[17] and relationships among women at all levels in organizations improve when women are significantly represented at the upper levels of management.[18]

I work at a restaurant and one night I was hostessing with two other managers. One is a female and the other is a male. They are both about the same age. All three of us were standing at the front desk at the same time when a man came up to the desk. I asked him what I could do for him. He said, "May I speak to your manager, please?" I turned and said, "Here are the managers," pointing at both of them. He was actually standing in front of the female manager, but instead of talking to her concerning his problem, he walked past her and started talking to the male manager. She gave him kind of a funny look and he just kept on talking.

Until recently, the kinds of skills believed necessary for managers were identified with a masculine pattern of communication: giving directions, controlling emotion, and dominating interpersonal situations. Today a trend continues toward training managers to be consultative rather than directive, open rather than controlled, and egalitarian rather than dominant in their interpersonal relationships with workers. While we still seem to perceive consideration behaviors to be feminine and structuring behaviors to be masculine,[19] males and females seem to prefer and find more satisfying a leadership style that uses both masculine and feminine styles.[20] When leaders include all group or organizational members in a participatory style, differences in evaluating leaders by sex dissipate.[21] Women do not seem to have an advantage in expressing interpersonal sensitivity as leaders,[22] and both male and female leaders seem able to develop more sensitive attitudes towards their subordinates. One recent study of union members discovered they preferred the mixed style for both male and female supervisors. They rated themselves more satisfied and their mixed-style manager more effective regardless of their sex.[23] However, the more common image of a manager continues to be one of authority rather than inclusivity.[24]

Understanding that what we say we prefer may differ from what we choose may also be part of realizing the difficult position for female leaders. Participants in one study overwhelmingly selected non-sex-typed qualities like reliability, efficiency, and truthfulness as those they said they preferred in their leader. Yet when these same participants were asked if they preferred a male or female supervisor, 82 percent chose male.[25] Women may receive these kinds of double-sided messages and feel isolated from leadership possibilities. One study of a training session for *Fortune 500* managers found the ratio of trainees to be 218 men to 35 women; such isolated experiences by women create vulnerable membership roles in groups[26] and more precarious leadership opportunities.

People of minority groups, such as African Americans, Hispanics, Latinos, Asians, Native Americans, older workers, and physically disabled workers all face the problem of appearing highly different or deviant from the expected image of the individual in a particular job. Even if colleagues do not say in words, "What are you doing here?" their facial expressions may betray surprise. Receiving that message, the person who differs from the norm may struggle with feelings ranging from low self-confidence to anger at the unfairness of others' presumptions. Improvements can be made in these areas. Some black women in public relations report they have begun to perceive themselves as professionals with some ability to interact with management.[27] To continue these gains, organizations must take steps toward changing harmful climates. One step is to increase the awareness of people in the dominant group (largely white males) that they may be under the influence of powerful stereotypes, stereotypes that may be communicated entirely without words.

NONTRADITIONAL WORK

Some people defy stereotypes and take on jobs that are not traditionally linked with their own sex. Comparing men doing "women's work" and women doing "men's work" reveals evaluative differences between the qualifications and pay for work. Like the United States, Nordic countries of Europe sex-type occupations. Also like the United States, when men and women cross over the imaginary sex requirements for the job, women are more likely to profit than men. Motivations for women to do men's jobs is high; women in men's jobs gain autonomy, more challenging work, and increased salaries. Men, on the other hand, earn lower salaries for doing the same sort of work as women.[28] One interesting twist to this issue occurs in Czechoslovakia, where a woman's work at home *and* her work at the paid workplace regulate her retirement. Women may retire if they have been employed for 25 years and have reared five or more children. Women's work conditions there, however, mirror other cultures in that women do less desirable work under less favorable conditions and receive less pay than men.[29]

While salary differences mark the most striking sex-type job imbalance, qualifications for jobs may function similarly in some positions. In the United States, female correctional officers in men's prisons are, according to one study, more highly educated and come from more professional families than do male correctional officers. The researchers suggested the educational level may result from the problem that United States labor markets do not offer a wide range of possibilities for educated women. Female corrections officers also differ significantly from male officers in their reasons for seeking the job: males looked for security, salary, and possibilities to advance; females expressed interest in rehabilitating prisoners and performing service work.[30] These familiar gender themes continue to emerge, marking not only nontraditional jobs of today, but earmarking jobs of the future.

Computer jobs seem to be emerging as pointedly "male jobs." Regardless of the possibilities computers provide—such as working out of the home—women are not drawn to computers in the same way or with the same intensity as men. Beginning in elementary school, boys express more interest in computer science and spend more of their free time experimenting and playing games. When all students are required to take computer classes, girls do equally well as boys; however, boys perceive computers as being instruments of finance and games; girls perceived them as means to run a home.[31] Since computers change work from labor intensive to mind intensive, they create numerous opportunities for changes in traditional job assignments.[32] Muscular differences between males and females no longer would cast many job positions as more favorable to one sex than the other; however, the traditional expectations and messages we send to one another about sex and gender appear to be powerful enough to be holding the masculine and feminine stereotype in place.

ORGANIZATIONS AS SYMBOL SYSTEMS

The first level of consideration pointed to distinctions of communication practices between males and females. In this section, we will examine verbal and nonverbal systems at the workplace.

Most tasks done for pay are done in the context of an organization. When we think of organizations or businesses, we are likely to imagine AT&T or Chrysler Corporation. As we discuss issues of sex and gender in organizations and employment, keep in mind that many more people in the United States work in smaller places, such as the service station in town or the local hair salon. In our society an employer may be a small business with fewer than ten employees or a multinational corporation with a million people who depend on its success for their continued employment. Every kind of organization exists through verbal and nonverbal symbols, functioning at a variety of communication levels. Symbols that make up the organization's internal and external communication system include these:

- Slogans, such as "Just Do It!" or "No Fear"
- Visual symbols, such as the golden arches of McDonald's or the lion symbolizing Metro-Goldwyn-Mayer Studios
- Acronyms, capitalized letters that are abbreviations of organization names, such as AT&T, IBM, or BMW
- Formal and informal uniforms, such as baseball players' blue-and-white stripes, a janitor's medium-blue shirt, or a banker's navy blue suit
- Structural and environmental features, such as open offices with modular partitions for clerical or sales staff; corner offices with doors and exterior views for executives

As you read the next two sections on language symbols and nonverbal symbols in work environments, think about the symbols that convey significant, often subtle messages about the school you attend, the grocery store you prefer, the business you manage, or the club you enjoy.

LANGUAGE SYMBOLS

Every kind of organization has verbal symbols that identify it as a unique entity. What follows is a description of several kinds of language that tend to separate the sexes and to make many workplaces more comfortable communication environments for one sex than for the other.

Three kinds of language are characteristic of life in large organizations and tend to work against shared meaning and effective cooperation between the sexes, as illustrated in table 8.1. Military language focuses on hierarchy and on images of conflict with an enemy; athletic language mixes the connotations of war with those of teamwork and camaraderie among participants; and sexual language serves a variety of functions, such as reinforcing the notion that dominance equals sexual control and providing tension release through jokes among male colleagues. A great many women coming into work relationships with men are ill-equipped to interpret these military, athletic, and sexual languages in ways that will not leave them isolated as females or compromised as workers.

Table 8.1   Languages That Divide Us in Organizations

Military	Athletic	Sexual
Example: "war stories"	"ballpark figure"	"more bang for the buck"
soldiering is masculine symbol	skill and winning fit the gender ideal	conquests of women show masculinity
ultimate form of competitive action	major form of small talk throughout the year	brings comaraderie and competition at the same time
women are invisible	women are less skilled	women are target of conquest

Source: Material in this table is based on categories described by Betty Lehan Harragan in *Games Mother Never Taught You* (New York: Rawson, 1977).

My previous employer was a former colonel in the United States Air Force—a fighter pilot. He would refer to our goal as "our mission." When obstacles would cross our paths, he would say, "We need to eliminate the enemy." Or when someone would have a great idea, he would say, "We need to drop that bomb."

I guess this was his way of visualizing things. He had no previous business experience because he had been in the service his whole life. I don't think he realized that even though these ways of explaining things worked for him, they weren't very effective ways of communicating to the rest of us. When he would say something like this, most of us would just look at each other as if to say, "Has this guy lost his mind!?"

Through most of this century, organizations have been set up along military lines. Ideas such as the "span of control"—the number of people an officer could effectively command—have been transferred into peacetime organizations. Terms borrowed from combat have become part of the everyday vocabulary of organization members: clients are "targeted" by the sales "force," powerful people are referred to as "big guns," and workers are put on the "front lines" or "in the trenches" to see how they react "under fire." Most men as well as women have no actual experience in wartime combat, but any worker may be in an environment in which the language of war suggests that a parallel kind of activity occurs in organizational life. Those who dislike the images of combat or who do not respond to it may be treated as unequal to the competition and thus unfit for leadership in the workplace.

The language of athletics is probably even more widespread than combat language in modern organizations. Sports talk operates on at least two levels: current sports events are a major form of small talk used to create comfort and demonstrate general expertise in conversations between colleagues or negotiating parties; and sports terms portray the world of work as a continual game or contest in which "our" team is trying to beat "their" team. Some of the sports language is so familiar that origins are rarely contemplated: "ballpark figures" are prepared more often than "estimates"; new workers are evaluated in terms of being "team players."

According to one writer about language and bias, women are at a major disadvantage in workplace talk because many have not dedicated themselves to team sports as children or adolescents and thus do not share the feelings many men have about teamwork and winning together. Many women do not follow college or professional sports or follow only a single team. In addition, women who do play sports cannot aspire to high-paying professional sports teams, so their experiences with the sport differ from those of aspiring to be professional baseball, basketball, or football players. As we discussed in chapter 7, the world of sports dominates some aspects of high schools and colleges; football and basketball are treated as central school events. Because of its importance, the issue is more than understanding the language of sports. Young women are less likely than their male colleagues to be surrounded by and to absorb sports talk, sports history, and statistics-quoting enthusiasts. When the world of work is infused with this language, "non-native" speakers are at a distinct disadvantage.

Sexual language about women in the workplace ranges from individual words or phrases to full-scale reports by one person to others of sexual conquests within the organization. While some men make a point of apologizing to a female who happens to be present when they use obscene language, it is generally irrelevant whether females are present when males use sexual language and anecdotes. In many cases, women present respond to the language or laugh at the anecdotes; sometimes their laughter is genuine and sometimes it results from nervousness or embarrassment. In either case, their roles in the ritual are different from men's roles. Workplace talk about sex, like sexual language in other settings, exists primarily to increase a male's status with other males. One way for a male to show dominance, particularly if he has not been a soldier or an athletic star, is to boast of sexual prowess with attractive women. The character of Sam Malone on the television show, *Cheers*, demonstrated this practice. Words, phrases, and jokes can demonstrate that a man is sexually knowledgeable rather than naive. For some men, stories about sexual conquests—especially of attractive women co-workers—raise the communication status of the storyteller. "Lemme tell you about the new girl in Accounts Receivable . . .!" Once she is a topic of sexual talk, the woman's personal status will diminish, and attempting to deny the man's stories about her will put her, more often than him, on the defensive. The appearance of sexual activity on the job still carries a double standard of evaluation between the sexes.

One troubling feature of sexual language and anecdotes on the job is that it often places nonparticipant audience members in difficult situations.[33] A woman who hears a demeaning joke or anecdote about another woman or about women in general has no easy exit from the situation. If she is silent, she will be seen as judging her male co-workers or as lacking a sense of humor. If she laughs, she may lead some of her male co-workers to think of her as "one of us" or as "an honorary male" for the moment, but she may leave the situation disappointed at her own cooperation or collusion with a damaging stereotype. Judy recalls an episode when she was the only female at a table of colleagues sitting around the university pub on a Friday afternoon. As a group, they were recounting the miseries of finals week, laughing, and sharing the events of the closing semester. After several beers, one man began to describe his wife, using personal details to compare her to a barracuda. Before long, everyone at the table was laughing and adding to the image of the barracuda wife. Judy felt uncomfortable as she knew and liked the woman in question. She left the group and found her actions changed her relationship with each man at the table in varying degrees, both in the ways the men acted toward her and how she felt toward them. The situation for men not inclined toward using sexual language is somewhat similar. If they don't express enjoyment of or participation in sexual talk, they may be stereotyped as "wimps" or "mama's boys." Such men may find themselves at a distance from the informal power structure in the organization, and thus separated from chances for achievement that are reserved for consistent "team players."

Not every organization depends on military, athletic, and sexual language for its daily communication. However, these three kinds of verbal material are present to some extent in many settings. In some cases, it is even difficult to ascertain which level is operating. As an example, the phrase "more bang for the buck" is interpreted by some listeners as a World War II phrase related to the dropping of the first atomic bomb, while for others it refers to a monetary arrangement made with a prostitute. Whether you adopt the military or the sexual meaning of the phrase, the connotation of aggression underlies both versions. This connotation of aggression, the central theme behind many specific actions, may separate the sexes and make them uncomfortable with each other. For men aggression can represent success and affirmation of masculinity. For women aggression can mean danger, both on and off the job.

In settings where only females are employed, there is often a kind of "lingo" that may bind the women together and to some degree may exclude men from the community. Terms related to child care and the home often serve the function of building cohesion among women and suggesting dimensions to their lives that go beyond the present task. The use of this jargon by women is often mistaken by men as lack of dedication to their jobs. Its use is restricted when women want to be considered for advancement and for participation in policy discussions. Two single mothers who work together may begin their conversation to solve an organizational problem. In the course of their problem-solving, however, they may exchange experiences about raising adolescent boys alone.

NONVERBAL SYMBOLS

Nonverbal systems mark organizations just as verbal ones do. As suggested earlier, organizations and professional groups identify themselves by color, style of clothing, gestures, and other symbols. The symbols can shift to suit changes in the environment. The golden arches of the first McDonald's restaurants, for example, were true arches that stood taller than the restaurants themselves. When zoning laws and architectural styles both changed, the golden arches turned into a curved letter M and a small symbol on signs, food containers, and employee uniforms.

Like corporate visual symbols, some of the clothing symbols that show employee status have shifted somewhat over the years. Most accountants employed by large accounting firms used to have wardrobes of navy blue suits, white long-sleeved shirts, dark ties, and wing-tip shoes. One firm had an official policy in the 1950s that a felt hat would be worn until a specified day in the spring, when a lighter-weight hat would replace it until a specified date in the fall. No particular provision was made for hats worn by females, since few women were employed at the professional level at that time. Nowadays those dress codes are usually obsolete. During the past several years, yellow, pink, and bright red have become popular colors for men's neckties; pink as a shirt color for men is accepted in some offices; and the most popular current shoe style for men is the tasseled loafer. For women in female-identified jobs, a wide range of clothing types can be seen: dresses, skirts and jackets, and sportswear, including pants. For women in corporate or professional work settings, the clothing norms in the past decade have been similar to those for men: tailored skirt suits in muted colors, with neckline decoration on the woman's blouse as a softer parallel to the man's necktie. In a trend for even more relaxed dress codes, many offices practice "casual Friday" when jeans, casual shirts, and tennis shoes often function as a unisex uniform for everyone.

Nonetheless, the more formal uniform for both female and male professionals tends to be expensive. For women it is also complex to achieve. The woman is urged to convey the image of authority that men can gain from wearing suits, while remembering at all times that her value in any communication setting lies partly in her attractiveness to those of the other sex. A working woman who dresses for function rather than for interpersonal appeal is at risk of being labeled "unfeminine" or "antisocial." She may be subtly or explicitly left out of the informal communication networks of her organization.

Four Perspectives on Gender and On-the-Job Talk

All four perspectives about communication and the sexes—biology, culture, power, and rhetoric—inform the analysis of gender issues on the job. Because job situations so often fall into a hierarchical pattern—who does the best job, gets promoted, or earns the most money—the power perspective becomes most salient. Nevertheless, by applying all four perspectives to communication and the sexes in the job setting, you can discover a rationale for actions by someone with whom you must work—yet you find troublesome. People rarely make specific plans to destroy the effectiveness of others. More often they seek ways to confirm or to justify their own views of the world in the face of change and conflict. Anyone you work with will have a view of you, of the job, and of himself or herself. Finding out more about that person's perspective may make communication more productive. If dialogue remains difficult or impossible, you still have the satisfaction of understanding more about the situation than you did before.

BIOLOGICAL PERSPECTIVE

Believers in the biological view of communication and the sexes see the physical attributes of both sexes as natural and sufficient causes for job placement, task performance, and evaluation of various kinds of human labor. The greater muscle mass in most males is treated as a clear sign that physically demanding work is intended for men. The female's ability to bear and nurse children is treated as a clear sign that females should perform child care, nursing, and other human service jobs. This point of view is not new, but it has become more controversial as technology has freed an increasing number of jobs from the necessity of frequent physical exertion.

Males may then be cast in job positions where substantial physical strength is required. In construction work, for example, females may direct traffic with road signs while males dig the ditches or carry materials. Some females do not have the physical strength to accomplish these males' tasks; those females who are strong enough may face unspoken skepticism from other workers. Physically strong women may have to "prove" themselves before their position as a co-worker is established.

In jobs where a worker's life may depend on other workers' physical strength—jobs such as firefighter, police officer, or some military jobs—tension may generate from doubt about a woman's physical abilities. Arguments may arise about whether or not these jobs are appropriate for females. Some hold a strict biological view about the fit between a worker's sex and job demands. Those people believe women should not fill jobs with harsh personal or environmental conditions, that require great physical demands, or that keep women away from the home. People with biological perspectives also would find men suspect if they elected to work as child-care professionals, clean houses, work as nurses, or stay at home with children. From this perspective, males' physical strength and ability to endure hardship may be critical parameters for job selection.

Some jobs have a more subtle or indirect connection with physical strength than those of firefighter, construction worker, or military soldier. Truck drivers are often depicted as burly, no-nonsense individuals who can control a large rig as easily as a child might control a bicycle. In an age of power steering, power brakes, and largely machine-run loading and unloading of materials, the truck driver may not need to be a tall, muscular male; in fact, female truck drivers are becoming more familiar. Yet a day spent at any major truck stop will demonstrate how the image of the driver as a physically dominant male helps support the image of the driver's job as one of physical challenge. (One midwestern trucking company receives many comments and questions about its name: each of its trucks bears the words "Jim Johnson and Daughters.")

The biological perspective asserts that people decide on task allocation based on the sexes' physical capacities to serve family needs. Infants have always been dependent on adults for food, shelter, and nurturing during their first few years. If the mother nursed the child during its first year or years of life, other productive work by the mother might need to be limited to the area immediately around the home, so that she could attend to a child while doing the other tasks. In this interpretation of work arrangements, the important thing is the mother's ability to do two essential tasks at a time: nurse children and prepare food for the family and community. Men hunted and provided shelter. From these historical roots, the biological perspective interprets what are "natural" jobs for males and females. The relative importance of each of these jobs affects judgments people make both about the job to be done and the group doing it. If hunting is the center of interest, men's tasks get more attention; if home and family are the center of interest, women's work will be valued.

In the late twentieth century we see some parallels to this interpretation of early humans' working and living arrangements. Employed mothers are still expected to be physically and emotionally closer to the home than are employed fathers. Employers often assume that mothers will treat their away-from-home work as secondary to their responsibilities as parents, particularly if their children are very young or ill. Employers also consider how pregnancy might affect a woman's work schedule. As women began to enter the public workplace with more frequency, issues about how to consider pregnancy (Is it a temporary disability? Is it a special circumstance that calls for special work conditions?) became more widely debated. While other countries have long had maternity leave and child-care provisions in their workplace community, the United States lags far behind. In 1982, when Lillian Garland tried to return to work after her maternity leave, she was refused a job at the Los Angeles branch of the California Savings and Loan Association. Since then, companies all over the United States have entered into policy debates about how these family issues fit into the workplace community.[34] So women in female-identified jobs often get wages, benefits, and job incentives that are structured with the expectation of high rates of absenteeism and turnover. While many people talk about changing times with regard to these ideas, mothers still are largely responsible for family affairs and must juggle these along with job demands.

The biological basis for this kind of thinking is not always expressed, but the implied message is that mothering is natural for women and thus should take a more central role in the life and work of a female parent than in the life and work of a male parent. Businesses that refuse paternity leave to new fathers (and the vast majority do) treat the father's presence with a newborn child as a convenience for the father or mother, not as a biological necessity. It is the mother's "nature" and thus her responsibility to be with her child. The father's "nature" and responsibility from the biological perspective is to be a strong leader of the family, the provider of its food, clothing, shelter, and security.

Following the Persian Gulf War, public debate ensued when the biological perspective was presented during testimony before the Senate Armed Services Committee, Subcommittee on Manpower [sic] and Personnel in June of 1991. Becky Constantino, former chair of the Defense Advisory Committee on Women in the Services argued that women should be allowed to serve in the military in any capacity for which they are physically fit and trained. She agreed that physical sex differences "which could negatively impact combat readiness would be valid reasons for closing positions for women." Arguing against women in the military, General Robert H. Barrow contended that

Combat is finding and closing with and killing or capturing the enemy. It is killing, that is what it is. . . . It is uncivilized, and women cannot do it. Nor should they be even thought of as doing it. The requirements for strength and endurance renders them unable to do it. And I may be old-fashioned, but I think the very nature of women disqualifies them for doing it. Women give life, sustain life, nurture life, they do not take it.[35]

Military issues generate animated debates because these issues emerge from cultural values directly tied to the connections between the biology of sex and the performance of gender. How can military culture incorporate women? Results of the Tailhook scandal indicate that women may be viewed as sexual beings rather than soldiers even when they serve as officers. The Tailhook scandal occurred when in 1991 the Tailhook Association, a society of Navy and Marine Corps carrier pilots, met for a convention at the Las Vegas Hilton. Female officers reported that during the convention, they were subjected to a series of humiliating incidents including being forced to walk through a gauntlet of males who subjected the women to unwanted physical contact. Eighty-three women reported being assaulted during the course of the convention. Navy officer Paula Coughlin became the focus of the ensuing investigation of Tailhook. She eventually resigned from the Navy, explaining she continued to experience ongoing harassment. Admiral Frank B. Kelso, II, head of the United States Navy at the time, was supported by government officials who encouraged that he be allowed to retire with all his stars; several female senators and members of Congress objected. At its conclusion, no one was fired as a result of Tailhook and the charges were dropped. Nevertheless, most observers agree that Coughlin's actions opened opportunities for women in the Navy.

Should women in the United States be drafted? Should women resist the draft and work toward constructing a political climate that honors compassion more than aggression?[36] What is the connection between the cultural function of femininity and the military or war? During wartime, ironic gender developments affect both males and females. Men who have served in wartime, particularly World War II, Korea, Vietnam, and the Persian Gulf, attest to dramatic changes in their pre- and post-war selves. Frequently, these men become more alienated from old stereotypes of masculinity and develop different perspectives, particularly with regard to aggression and violence. The willingness and eagerness they once felt for combat and aggression is replaced by compassion and regard for human life.

Women who have not served in the military, on the other hand, frequently have the experience during war of performing roles otherwise reserved for men, not only in the workplace but also in terms of roles in the family. As Sandra Gilbert writes, wartime affects the individual's and the culture's demonstration of gender, thereby giving each sex new experiences with being male or female.[37] Positions regarding the inclusion or exclusion of women in the military often revolve around the biological perspective.

CULTURAL PERSPECTIVE

Chapter 2 described the cultural perspective about communication and the sexes as presenting men and women from two distinct spheres, having different belief systems and approaches to experience. Women are in the private sphere of home and family; men occupy the public (and financially rewarded) world of business and civic affairs. As noted earlier, some writers take this division of the world into two spheres as natural and fortunate. Others treat it as negative for both sexes, preventing all of us from understanding each other and preventing each from treating the other's ideas as important to humans in general.

In this chapter on employment, the word, "culture," has a meaning in addition to those just mentioned—one that is compatible with earlier uses of the word that denote sets of beliefs and practices characterizing a group of people who are geographically and socially linked with each other. Analysts of organizational life have coined the phrase "organizational culture" to refer to the clusters of symbols that give meaning and identity to the individuals who are part of a particular organization.[38] The organization's culture, much like geographically based cultures around the world, involves the verbal and nonverbal cues, the uses of time and space, and the expressions of belief, attitude, and value that make up the official or unofficial story or saga of that particular group or organization.

A company may have a tradition that some of its heroes are honored and cited in order to inspire heroic actions on the part of other employees. Certain stories of past and present organizational characters or events may be told widely to bolster participants' sense of solidarity with the whole and to provide comic relief through laughing at "the time when Crocker got caught with his hand in the till!" Generally the shared symbols of an organization's culture develop the members of that group into a community, whether of five or of fifty thousand members.

In terms of women and men, the existence of organizational cultures has both positive and negative effects on their attempts to work together. On the positive side, a large number of current management theories advise executives to emphasize strong working relationships with employees and to foster and reward initiative from any member of the organization. This kind of direction suggests a democratic climate, one in which the newest mailroom assistant and the oldest member of the typing pool have some chance to be treated as worthwhile members of the community. On the negative side, the military symbols prominent in most large organizations and the preference of many men to conduct business in exclusively male communication settings produce a subtle kind of separation which many women are unwilling or unable to fight. Sexual jokes and casual talk about sports tend to reinforce male-to-male friendships and to leave the lone woman in a group without a comfortable way to join the conversation or the choice to abandon her own sense of self to "fit in" to a different culture. While organizational theories suggest a more open and humane climate for workers and bosses alike, the language and nonverbal components of organizational culture can communicate to the individual of the other sex, "The company rules may *say* we operate that way, but our rules are different. If you want to get along, you better follow our rules."

The idea of men and women operating out of different spheres can be extended to mean that the away-from-home workplace belongs to men who share it with women as a matter of generosity or convenience—or even grudgingly if complying only because of legislation. In this culture, men are defined as "the workers" because their world is by definition "the world of work." Work done at home or in the private sphere is thus not "work." "Career man" has reference only to extended military service and is an unnecessary phrase to use about employed civilian males. "Career woman" in contrast is a necessary phrase to indicate that a given woman expects her involvement in vocational activities to be central and continuous. Often when people ask a woman, "Do you work?" they are asking if she is employed outside her home. The question eclipses work such as organizing family affairs, scheduling, cleaning, doing laundry, attending sick family members, managing finances, buying family supplies, buying or making clothing, preparing food, attending kinship needs, and volunteering for community tasks. The "Do-you-work?" question reflects the culture's hierarchical order where public work is visible and financially rewarded and private work becomes invisible and presumed. That order is further supported by business policies that exclude daycare considerations, omit time off for family events, and incorporate only meager (or no) vacation leave. Other cultures structure this hierarchy differently. In France, for example, every worker receives four weeks vacation each year; French people often respond with amazement at vacation time practices in the United States. They ask how the family finds the necessary time together for recreation and leisure. The differences in national policies reflect differences in values.

If women's primary sphere of influence is taken to be the home and the family, then women's work in the paid work force is logically (1) secondary to the women themselves; (2) of secondary importance to the organization itself and (3) of secondary value in determining the family's total income and worth. These points may seem obvious and correct to you, or they may seem biased and outdated. However you see them, you are moving toward the heart of a bitter debate about the fairness of wages paid to women compared with those paid to men. Research studies explain that pay inequity has less to do with equal pay for equal work and more to do with subtle mechanisms in the workplace that usher women into certain positions that are not paid as highly as positions held by men. People who want wage rates changed to reflect the levels of skill and responsibility in jobs such as librarian, nurse, and executive secretary argue that the pay rates for these "women's jobs" have stayed unnaturally low because women have held the jobs, while less-skilled jobs such as groundskeeper, janitor, or truck driver have become better paid simply because historically men have held these jobs. People opposed to changing these pay rates say that the marketplace is a reliable determinant of wages and that it makes no sense to ignore the marketplace in favor of an abstract concept of wage justice.

The comparable worth, or pay equity, debate is ultimately an argument about whether women should be considered as a separate and secondary category of workers because they are actual or potential wives and mothers. If a woman is a family member first, and a worker only under certain household circumstances, a two-culture perspective supports the view that she is not a worker in the same sense as a man: not a provider, not a continuous jobholder, and not a career-oriented individual. Thus paying her differently, on a lower wage scale even for highly skilled jobs, is seen as fair. The basis of the arrangement is that one type of worker, the male, is symbolized as being in the public world; the other, the female, is seen as a member of the private world, even when she enters the public world to earn money.

At one time this situation reflected rather accurately the experience of many women in the United States. Women's lives now show patterns of employment that are increasingly like those of men, including the requirement that they be providers for dependent children. Most women are now paid workers for a longer portion of their adult lives than they work at mothering. Because of a high divorce rate, most work at mothering longer than they are wives. The paid worker status, in other words, is a constant or near-constant element in most women's lives. Portraying women as living in stable homes, employed for pay only when it is convenient or interesting, is a stark aberration of reality.

Almost 70 percent of all adult women are now in the paid work force, and half of those have children under six years of age. Despite the image of being "extras" in the paid work force, women make up nearly half of all employed people in the United States. Only about 10 percent of American households are like the "Dick and Jane" family of the 1950s, in which a single male wage earner provided for children and a spouse living at home. Of the women currently employed, many are in two-worker families whose incomes would fall below the poverty level without the wife's contribution. Among the 30 percent of families who have only one parent, over half live below the poverty level.

Evidence suggests that many women would not be working full-time outside the home if they had satisfactory alternatives. The earnings gap between males and females affects both women's need to work full-time and their frequently high level of dissatisfaction with that arrangement. Throughout the 1980s and into the 1990s women employed full-time have earned approximately 60–70 percent of the salaries of the average full-time employed male. A major economic reason for this difference is that 80 percent of employed women are clustered in occupations with historically low pay rates: secretary, nurse, bookkeeper, sales clerk, and waitress.

Salaries alone do not account for the feelings people have about their jobs. Indeed, some women find great enjoyment in being the skilled, supportive assistant whose competence helps a boss do better work; others in similar settings believe that their skills are as significant a contribution to the whole effort as are those with incomes five or six times greater than their own. In such cases, the salary discrepancy may cause less dissatisfaction to the woman than does the continual experience of being invisible in the eyes of visitors, colleagues, and clients while her boss receives honors for work she has done.

One of the ways these women cope with being invisible or unrecognized in an organization is to form a distinct subculture of their own, by keeping their language and nonverbal patterns and their expressed attitudes and values separate and at times secret from the dominant members of the organization. Subculture members thus find ways to affirm themselves without violating the accepted practices of the dominant group. Women working closely with each other in a large office sometimes develop a code for talking about people they find difficult or unpleasant. For example, Barbara knows of three secretaries who had worked together for several years. They would signal each other when "#3"

cathy®   by Cathy Guisewite

was on the phone, so that one of them could rescue the other from #3's long-windedness by a trumped-up long-distance call. We have begun to learn more about how women and other muted or silenced groups find ways to express their own forms of organizational culture, even when they lack power within the formal organization.

The emphasis placed on work and the greater value ascribed to work than home does not affect only females. Since the beginnings of the latest feminist movement in the 1960s attention has been focused—mostly by women—on the problems generated for women who try to enter the culture of the paid workplace. Little attention has yet to be given to the effects of that culture on males or on males' training or education to enter the home culture. Just as the workplace culture presumes women will honor home and family first, job or career second, it also presumes men will do the opposite. As work hours lengthen and job travel increases, men are expected to conform to company demands; few organizations recognize as legitimate a man's argument that he prefers to expend his energies toward his family rather than meet all the demands of his job. While women have openly and in large numbers expressed their discontent with being excluded from the culture of the workplace, men have not made similar objections to being taken away from home. While some might say that males are the leaders of these companies and can make decisions as they wish, most men who work are not the decision makers of their organizations. Some men without corporate power may operate as subordinates to dominant forces; their social education based on principals of competition and hierarchy may function to perpetuate their positions.

Recent movements by men's groups such as Promise Keepers and those organizing the Million Man March have drawn attention to the devaluing of a father's role in the family. Controversy abounds over the way to frame the problem: some believe men should be reinstated as patriarchal heads of the family; some believe men should be allowed the same latitude of work and home as women are allowed; some believe men should redesign their family roles to limit the work culture and increase skills to nurture and care. As is often the case with movements promoting social change, the message from these groups and intent for change are not clear.

The change for men to enter the homeplace differs from the one for women to enter the workplace. One central difference entails education. When women decide they want to develop a career or take a job, they can enter job training programs or go back to school. In fact, returning students (people who have been away from school for a long period and now are returning to earn or complete degrees) largely are comprised of women. These women can train themselves or gain education that qualifies them for specific jobs or careers.

If a man decides he wants to reenter the homeplace, create a different balance between home and work, change his communication style, and redesign his family roles, he has fewer resources for education. A woman may incur loans for her education because she anticipates earning money later to repay them. A man will not be likely to accrue financial improvement for his decision; in fact, he may decide to give up extra benefits from the office to devote more time to home. He also will not be as likely to discover a community of other men who are making decisions like his. The impetus for males to review and redesign their roles is not pervasive across the various cultures of men.

The "men's movement" may grow in size and power. Its growth may be slowed by the lack of a tangible gain for change. Whereas women point to income—a tangible, measurable mark—men may not find such a concrete icon. Men—particularly white, middle- and upper-class men—may learn about gains through conversations with other men and with women about the rewards of living in a culture where self-disclosure, collaboration, and interdependence balance or sometimes replace competition, hierarchy, and product.[39] Key to the success of the men's movement will be means to motivate such conversations.

POWER PERSPECTIVES

Often we think of power in terms of authority, control, energy, or force. When we think of authoritarian power, empowerment, and synergistic power with regard to jobs and organizations, we find that power has both positive and negative connotations. By using power, people can propel the business or organization toward goals both with regard to people and product; they also can manifest organizational climates of subordination, inequality, and sexual harassment.

The older, more familiar authoritarian style links power with position in a hierarchy. People with powerful positions—chief executive officers (CEOs), directors, or vice-presidents—can communicate more freely with their employees than the employees can with them. One instance of this power discrepancy is the varying use of first and last names to mark status differences among workers. First names are used mutually by people at the same level of responsibility and by people who are friends with each other. Use of first names by two people suggests that, whatever their titles may be, they see themselves as interdependent members of the organization who need and value each other's contributions. With different job levels, the person of lower status can be called by a first name but is often expected to use Mr. or Ms. when talking or referring to the person of higher status. This custom becomes awkward when a fifty-year-old secretary addresses a twenty-year-old manager, yet the name distinction is particularly important in this instance to counter the tendency for people to believe older people hold more prestigious jobs than younger ones.

Several effects come from this first-name-last-name ritual. One is that the person whose first name is used will have a familiar, casual identity, more likely to be paired with "Carla, can you do this for me?" Using a first name could protect the employee from having unwanted clients call or visit outside office hours, but it also can deprive the person of a way to identify the self in formal, sometimes more adult ways. Another by-product of the name difference is that people who are called by first names are subject to an uninvited intimacy. Strangers walking into an office might feel more free to touch a shoulder or make a casual observation to "Sarah" than to "Mrs. Trapp." Females are more likely to be addressed by their first names than are males. This practice may influence the implicit permission some superiors feel that they may initiate sexual encounters unwanted by the other. The subordinate is defined by the connotations of language that the superior has more behavioral latitude.

Name rituals vary a good deal depending on the size and type of organization and on the product or service it offers. In some places of employment everyone is on a first-name basis, and status distinctions are minimized in everyday communication. In others, no manager ever dials or answers the telephone, and clerical staff screen every caller and visitor. How names, titles, and communication channels such as these are used will tell you a great deal about the ways dominance or empowerment are communicated in a particular place of employment.

For men as well as for women power is a complicated subject to talk about. When women enter the paid workplace, do they usurp men's power? One argument is that women and minorities take positions away from white men. Research finds that males lose no autonomy or decision-making authority in their jobs as more females enter the paid workplace because women are segregated into positions that do not intersect with those activities. Men enjoy their positions by virtue of years on the job. Women achieve them only by having years of education on their resumés.[40] Do men believe they should retain power in paid work? Most men agree when asked in opinion surveys that women should have equal power and opportunity in their work. On the other hand, recent legislation limiting or abolishing affirmative action attests to discontent with special programs that help women and ethnic minorities attain positions and promotions. The appearance of women, African Americans, Asians, Native Americans, Latinos and Hispanics in advertisements and in visible organizational roles suggests to many that no one today is disadvantaged and that special access programs are now unnecessary. Some white males express uneasiness that the competitive edge now goes to women and minorities, giving these groups an unfair advantage in getting jobs.

Women and minority workers describe their experiences as disadvantageous. Researchers find that people of minority status often work in contexts where they occupy "solo status," meaning they are the only member or one of a small number of their race or sex in the job. Being isolated in this way affects their job effectiveness because they have no familiar support networks. Some black women report they feel they must outperform those in the majority in order to receive recognition and status. They describe their work experience as one of isolation, and they feel doubly disadvantaged because they are both female and black. They believe black women experience greater discrimination than white women. Their observations are that men advance more quickly, are promoted more quickly, and hold negative stereotypes about roles women play in the paid workplace. These black women feel pressure from the majority group to conform to norms and standards of that culture. Their positions require them to deal with their frustrations by themselves, adding an even greater burden to their already increased work expectation. Since they have few or no mentors, they have to learn the job and the organizational culture on their own.[41]

These black women are not alone in their assessments of male power. Many women draw conclusions that men in general have plenty of power and have cooperated with each other to prevent women from attaining power in the workplace. Presuming that men in general have power and that every man has power on the job are not the same idea. A great many men as well as women feel that they are not powerful in their work. Feeling unable to negotiate power, sources of power, and uses of power can generate frustration and resignation in workers, detracting from their productiveness. Men who feel powerless may respond with bitterness or disgust to being criticized for using power unfairly.

Mentoring and networking are two means for increasing power on the job; these strategies have gained attention for their use by women, although both have been present for a long time as options for men. Mentoring involves a junior-level person being advised and assisted by someone more senior, who often is not in a direct line of supervision but is knowledgeable about the kind of career options open to the junior person. Having a mentor is not the only way to succeed professionally, but it can be one useful way to discover the informal ways to advance and to meet influential people who can aid one's career. Women in the past have rarely had mentors, but the publicity given to this concept has increased the number of women who actively seek out a person to advise them. The evidence suggests that women often find more than one person to help them at various times, while men who report they have had mentoring say that one individual has advised them over a period of years. Not everyone needs or desires mentors; but one study of mentoring in a utility company showed that women with assertive styles can be protected somewhat from strategic errors or criticism by having a highly placed mentor as an adviser and advocate.[42]

More recent research has shown that Hispanic women who mentor young Latinas can have a profound influence.[43] Mentoring processes for women pursuing their doctorate degrees also have produced more positive results.[44] One organization in New York City makes a business out of mentoring; WOMEN Unlimited matches women in midlevel positions with higher-ranking women or men and has met with considerable success.[45]

Both women and men tend to expect more power, more excitement, and more control over their time than they actually get on their first jobs. Added to this disappointment are the complications of gender roles, which encourage both women and men to express only limited aspects of themselves to strangers and co-workers of the other sex. Because these features of the employment situation complicate life for both sexes, much of the communication about power within and across the sexes expresses a mixture of attraction and hostility.

On the job, the masculine gender ideal promotes invulnerability and a love of competition; the feminine gender ideal promotes cooperation and the avoidance of conflict. Whether persons of either gender accomplish these ideals is less important here than the existence of the stereotypes. Anyone trying to live up to one of these ideals is likely to feel scornful, envious, or confused in dealing with someone who is working hard to achieve the other gender ideal. If you are a woman who has been trained to believe that skill and effort will be noticed and rewarded naturally, you may resent the male co-worker who is intent on having the first and last word in every conference and on making sure his projects are noticed by superiors at every turn. If you are a male who has been trained to think that you must make yourself noticed or face a deadly anonymity, you may become angry when you learn that the "quiet girl" next to you has been producing ideas that might be seen as superior to yours. In both cases, competition itself produces some tensions, but the tensions are made worse by the gender-based beliefs that the game of succeeding on the job is not being played fairly by the other person.

SEXUAL HARASSMENT. Power plays sometimes take the form of sexual harassment. As we mentioned earlier, sexual harassment differs from sexual discrimination. In the latter, people are treated differently because of their sex: they may be passed over for promotion, not given a particular job, or moved to a certain part of the office because of their sex. Discrimination on the basis of sex is illegal. Sexual harassment also is illegal. It is defined in two ways: quid pro quo and hostile environment. Quid pro quo harassment means someone has requested or demanded something in return for something else. In other words, quid pro quo harassment occurs if a male boss asks a female secretary for a date intimating that she will receive a raise if she complies. Another example would be if a female who makes the office schedules indicates she would give her male colleague better hours if he does not break off his relationship with her.

Hostile environment harassment is broader. This type of sexual harassment creates an uncomfortable environment for a worker based on sex. Repeated requests for dates, sexual jokes, teasing, references to seductive dress or attire, or displays of cartoons or pictures that convey sexual messages all are examples of communication in a workplace that can create a hostile environment. Whether or not these messages constitute a hostile environment is perceived from the vantage point of the receiver of the messages rather than the creator of them. Women have been found to interpret behaviors as more definitively sexual harassment and more damaging to their job performance than men do.[46] Differences in the way the sexes make meaning from nonverbal and verbal behavior play significant roles in understanding and interpreting sexually harassing acts.

Often, hostile environment sexual harassment occurs at a low, continuous level that makes its confrontation difficult. Phrases woven into conversations, consistently pointed nonverbal messages, or subtle reminders of sexual implications may pervade the organizational culture. If a male relates a sexual joke and then says, "Oh, sorry Belinda. I didn't mean for you to hear," while smiling at his cohorts, the duplicity of the message may encourage Belinda to deal with her own frustration over the episode and not confront the group. Hostile environment sexual harassment can subordinate one sex to the other.

Confronting sexually harassing behavior can be problematic. Often the harassment emanates from someone in a higher status, so the person being harassed is faced with the dual problem of losing a position (and perhaps income) and confronting a superior. Women often do not confront sexual harassment because they fear losing their jobs and because they have accepted the behavior as inherent in the workplace. Although affirmative action offices report that only one percent of complaints turn out to be falsely filed, people who are sexually harassed sometimes refrain from reporting the behavior because they do not want to be accused of being too sensitive or being vindictive.

In nontraditional job situations where women are physically more equal to men—such as female firefighters who describe themselves as bodybuilders—black women report they respond to sexual harassment with explicit, confrontational strategies that are effective in stopping the harassment. However, these women also report that the harassment they encounter is not physical in nature, as is the harassment often reported by college students and white-collar women.[47] These findings are similar to those about female autoworkers, thus implying that the nature of the harassment may be related to the kind of work women do.[48]

Sexual harassment has connotations for women that may not be true for men. Louise F. Fitzgerald explains that one of every two women will be harassed at some time during their educational or working experiences.[49] Sexual harassment has embedded within it the threat of use of power. When women are the receivers of the harassment, this threat implicitly can include the use of physical power. When women are the harassers, often their power bases are economic ones or bases derived from hierarchical status. When men are the harassers, their power bases can include both economic and status as well as the implicit physical advantage of being male.

Men often believe that women are powerful in their ability to use their sexuality to influence others. Women often believe that their sexuality is both a positive attribute and a danger, because it is so often seen by men as a woman's primary characteristic. When a man feels distracted by the presence of a female co-worker, he may conclude that she has sent intentional sexual messages to him. He may respond to her on the basis of these assumptions and then be surprised or even offended that she does not continue the process of intimate communication that she had supposedly begun. Out of this process emerge comments such as, "She's a real tease" and agreements among male colleagues that, "Someone oughta tame that one."

In 1991, a landmark event brought sexual harassment to the forefront of debate. Clarence Thomas was nominated to the Supreme Court by then-President George Bush. In the course of any Supreme Court nomination, the Senate conducts an investigation of the nominee. Typically, a nominee will appear before a Senate subcommittee to answer questions about qualifications. In this case, Thomas was in the final days of his questioning before the Senate Judiciary Committee, which was composed of fourteen white males. National Public Radio announced a story that Anita Hill, a professor in Oklahoma, had previously given evidence through the Federal Bureau of Investigation (FBI) to the Judiciary Committee that during her tenure with Thomas at the Equal Employment Opportunity Commission ten years earlier, Thomas had sexually harassed her.

Hill was summoned to the hearings for an unprecedented, televised, two-day presentation of testimony. Hill and Thomas both read statements to the committee after which two days of questioning and testimony by co-workers and friends ensued. Hill alleged several episodes when Thomas spoke to her in sexual terms, indicated his desire to date her, recounted pornographic films, and described sexual acts. Thomas denied all the allegations and asserted he had supported Hill and mentored her throughout her career.

This single event dramatically spotlighted the issue of sexual harassment in the paid workplace. Immediately following the hearings, more than half of respondents to national polls expressed disbelief in Hill's story. For the next few months, complaints of sexual harassment soared; media coverage included television talk shows, newspaper features, radio call-in programs, and films about sexual harassment. People reported increased discussion of personal stories about sexual harassment in their workplaces. In academia, some journals devoted whole issues to the topic. At the end of six months, national polls revealed a reversal in public sentiment: most people now believed Hill's story and recognized her experience as similar to those they had experienced or had begun to hear.

By that time, another interesting development had occurred with respect to this case. The black community responded vociferously to the hearings, asserting that the white community had brazenly presumed it could interpret the events meaningfully. The black community contended that white individuals could not know the intricacies of being black in a white-dominated culture and how that dynamic affected the relationships between black men and women. Many black scholars responded angrily that race had been virtually ignored as the nation debated the experience of an alleged harassment by a black man of a black woman.[50] Furthermore, black scholars explained that historical precedent must be understood to fully comprehend the role of a black female in United States society.[51]

On many levels, then, the Hill/Thomas sexual harassment case embroiled issues of sex, race, and class.[52] Attitudes, ways of knowing, and opinions about sexual harassment swirled in the public debate. Some scholars suggest that creating the symbol (the word, "sexual harassment," was only introduced in the mid-1970s) gave people a way to recognize and address the issue. They explain further that when the Hill/Thomas hearings sparked narratives of sexual harassment, those stories revealed life experiences that had previously been invisible or ignored.[53] Once those narratives received public attention, they prompted policy changes in organizations and businesses to attempt to address the difficult circumstances of sexual harassment in the paid workplace. Efforts to understand, recognize, and eliminate sexual harassment continue.

RHETORICAL PERSPECTIVE

The previous three perspectives have dealt with ways women and men differ in their life experiences and in the values they attach to communication. The biological perspective stresses the physical strength and risk taking of men and the childbearing capacity of women as having disparate implications for their talk and their appropriate tasks. The cultural perspective focuses on the idea of two spheres of activity and two separate types of belief systems, with women as home and relationship-centered and men as work and leadership-centered. The power perspective emphasizes differences in the ways men and women respond to hierarchical or lateral relationships with others inside organizations.

The rhetorical perspective helps us understand alternative systems within which women—and other minorities—may construct messages. Rather than imposing norms of the dominant communication system on these messages, the rhetorical perspective allows us to understand meaning generated and derived from within minority culture.

The rhetorical or strategic approach, presumes that all men and women construct and use ways to make meaning, negotiate that meaning with others, and influence their worlds. Examining communication between men and women from a rhetorical perspective means discovering and explicating those different strategies and meanings. From this perspective, each of us can be considered to be taking "rational action" even when our communication strategies backfire badly or appear senseless to another person.[54] What is and is not rational no longer is defined from a prevailing viewpoint but from the point of view of the person who designs and uses the communication. A stereotype of women as irrational and illogical beings cannot be sustained when a particular woman's pattern of reasoning is examined in strategic terms.

For example, many women tend to take into account several areas of their lives at once, such as job tasks, relationship concerns, and home and child-care management. A question put to them about one of these areas in isolation may be considered—often aloud—in terms of how it affects the other areas before an answer is given to the original question. For a given woman that process may be helpful; for a supervisor who does not conduct life as a situation of multiple commitments, such a response may sound like gibberish.

Another difference in communication styles stems from the ways men and women go about seeking solutions to problems. Many men have been trained to think and talk in terms of problem-solution sequences and final results. They may seek the "bottom line" in conversations or negotiations. In a competitive workplace with little time to reflect on alternatives, the skill of "getting to the point" is highly valued. When men and women work together and a woman begins to reflect on the various elements of a situation, a man may interpret her comments as presenting a problem for him to solve. He might quickly offer a solution to the problem (as he hears it), as a final step or closure to her concern. If she hears that proposal as cutting off her thinking, she may choose not to raise future concerns in this person's presence. On the other hand, if she fails to adopt his idea, he may consider her unable to work effectively on a team.

Differences in rhetorical strategies can also be seen in negotiating practices of women and men. Some researchers have concluded that sex has little bearing on the negotiation of salaries by men and women; however, the same studies also explain that males set higher salaries than females as goals for their negotiations and that while women and men bargain with the same frequency, men receive higher offers for their efforts.[55] The rhetorical perspective causes us to see this discrepancy as embedded in the meaning and strategies expected and presumed by each sex. Men's salary expectations are higher so men pursue a different goal than women. In pursuit of that goal, men use more interruptions, talk more, use a lower voice pitch, take longer, and ask more questions than women.[56] These differences in senders' rhetorical strategies are matched by differences in receivers' interpretations. One study showed that if people are watched by a male during their negotiations, both men and women are more contentious, using strategies like putting down the other party.[57] Negotiating salaries with a male superior, then, might create a more competitive climate than negotiating with a female superior. These differences may change the communication climate in which men and women negotiate and also may change the outcomes of those negotiations for each sex.

Perhaps the largest contribution the rhetorical perspective can make to understanding job-related communication is to reveal that the communication of people of both sexes is constrained by gender stereotypes. If you think you must prove you are strong and adventurous in order to be promoted, you are not going to spend your time on low-profile or invisible projects that improve interpersonal relationships but do not show your individual skills. If you think you must get along with everyone in your office, you will have a hard time responding forcefully to efforts by a co-worker to establish a sexual relationship in which you have no interest. Issues related to sexuality, to power differences, to beliefs about jobs and life-style are not simple matters of right and wrong or of skillful and unskillful communication. They are bound up with the views you and others hold about yourself, gender, and work.

CONCLUSION

Changes occur so rapidly in the paid workplace that some statements in this chapter may become obsolete within a few years. Both sexes seem to experience a connection between their competence on the job and their self-esteem.[58] Yet gender stereotypes and the constraints they put on both sexes may interfere with both self-esteem and job performance. Some evidence indicates a trend toward greater cooperation and more peer relationships between men and women on the job, as well public expressions of the wider value of these more collegial arrangements between the sexes. For this effort to be successful, we will need to address some of the gender-based difficulties considered in this chapter. Until the disparity in the numbers of women and men in decision-making positions in organizations changes we can expect differing perceptions to create misunderstandings in the workplace.

The chapter as a whole has focused somewhat more on women's communicative experience on the job than on men's for two reasons. First, despite the risk of appearing to compare females to a male standard of talk, it has been important to reconsider some of the long-standing stereotypes and myths about women's communication, placing them in the contexts of the four perspectives so that the rationales for individuals' choices might become more clear. Second, when men believe that a dominant or aggressive communication style is the only way to lead others successfully, they will not examine the impact of that style on women or on nondominant males. When more than one model of interpersonal influence becomes visible, and when the negative effects of imposing one communication system on other systems are observed and analyzed, both sexes benefit from enhanced understanding.

QUESTIONS FOR DISCUSSION

1. A popular idea for having workers participate in decisions about their jobs is the idea of quality circles, in which groups of workers meet often to discuss what they are doing. What implications for such small group discussions can you draw from this chapter?

2. Sexual harassment as perceived by a woman is often thought by a man to be typical, friendly behavior. How do you distinguish between "typical, friendly behavior" and unwanted language or touch or fondling on the job? How would you communicate your interpretation to the other person? What other responses might others make? How would you respond if you were that other person?

3. What do you think about women serving in the military? With which of the four perspectives presented in this book would you identify your view? What messages are sent to men and women with regard to the Tailhook scandal and to men and women serving together in the Persian Gulf War?

4. Do you agree or disagree that "the battle of the sexes is alive and well and living in the workplace"? Why? How are the metaphors in this statement conforming to or repudiating sex stereotypes?

5. How would you go about constructing an organization (social service or manufacturing, for example) that was sex-bias proof?

CASES FOR ANALYSIS

CASE 8.1   TASKS VERSUS TITLES

Louise has worked for a semi-public organization for the past fourteen years. She did mainly typing and filing when she began working for IMEX. Two years later she was asked to do some testing of materials as well. When her boss learned that she was a good writer, he asked her to write drafts for reports he had to submit to regulatory agencies. She would write the drafts; he would make one or two changes; then he would have her type the final copies with his name on the cover. Louise was not very happy with this arrangement, but she had an ailing husband and two children at home, so she did not complain about her job for fear of losing it.

Last year, after thirteen years at IMEX, Louise was told she could sign her own name to a report for the first time. She was also given the largest raise—10 percent—that she had ever received. She decided to go to the boss and ask him to give her the title of Assistant to the Director, since she was doing the work of a professional and was the only person reporting solely to him. He reacted impatiently: "Well, Louise, you want a lot! You mean that big raise and your new status aren't enough to satisfy you?"

1. What would you encourage Louise to say next to the boss?
2. How do you believe the boss would respond to assertive behavior on her part? Would her chances for success be increased?
3. What explanations can account for Louise's long willingness to work in the shadow of her boss?
4. How important is a job title to you, compared to money or job task? Explain your answer.

CASE 8.2 CORPORATE TRACK SHOES

In a large midwestern city, female riders on commuter trains began wearing track shoes and socks for their commute to the office. The contrast between stylish, tailored suits and briefcases and the track shoes and socks earned the notice of observers and led one of them to concoct a pun: "Is this the ultimate symbol for those of you on the 'fast track'?"

One firm took its employees' mixture of styles without humor. A memo came from top management to all staff members in the downtown office, requesting that female employees change into their business attire—meaning dress shoes—before entering the elevators that went up to the corporate offices. Management's reasoning was that running shoes would not be perceived as appropriate professional attire by any potential clients who might happen to see the individual enter the corporate office.

Some women employed by the firm took exception to the memo, citing it as a case of regulating personal choice. Other women agreed that it was important to be seen as a competent professional at all times during the workday.

1. What is your reaction to the idea of women wearing track or other walking shoes during travel to and from a workplace?

2. In what other situations has personal appearance been a job requirement?

3. What do you think about rules against female employees wearing pants on the job?

4. Do you see the track-shoe question as an issue of gender, power, or another factor not mentioned here?

CASE 8.3 DOUBLE MEANINGS

Laura is a woman in her mid-twenties who is professionally employed in a graphic design firm. She recently telephoned a radio talk-show psychologist to say that she was scared to go back to her office because of what she called an episode of sexual harassment. When asked what had happened, she described it as follows.

She had received some design help from Ed, a male colleague in his late twenties employed by the same firm. When she told him she had won an award for the project, he had said, "Hey, you owe me a drink for that." She said that she had replied in a happy, energetic tone of voice, "Oh, I owe you much more than that!" Ed immediately began to act as if he expected her to go to his apartment that evening. Laura left the office at the end of the day, unnoticed by Ed, but was afraid to return to the office and see Ed again.

Laura told the psychologist that she felt afraid of being "harassed" again, but she was uncertain what she could do to avoid the problem.

1. What levels of meaning do you find in her statement to her colleague? In his statement to her? How likely do you think it is that both people had the same denotations and connotations to their messages?

2. Assuming that Laura is confused about her communication experience with Ed, how could you help her to clarify her situation?

3. Has this sort of double-meaning situation ever happened to you? If so, what did you conclude about yourself, your words, and the other person?

4. Discuss this story with two other people, one male and one female. See what conclusions each makes about the woman, the co-worker, and the words each uses.

5. Under what circumstances would you call this event "sexual harassment"?

NOTES

[1] Virginia Schein, "Her Say: Stereotyping Still Barrier to Top," *Chicago Tribune* (May 5, 1996), Section 13, p. 9.

[2] C. Shakeshaft, "The Gender Gap in Research in Educational Administration," *Educational Administration Quarterly* 25 (1989): 324–37.

[3] C. Shakeshaft, *Women in Educational Administration* (Newbury Park, CA: Sage, 1987).

[4] E. Garfinkel, "Ways Men and Women in School Administration Conceptualize the Administrative Team," unpublished doctoral dissertation, Hofstra University, Hempstead, NY, 1988.

[5] Shakeshaft 1987, op cit.

[6] Joyce Hickson, "Differences in Influence of Physical Attractiveness on Evaluations of Leadership Behavior for Men and Women in Higher Education," *Journal for Higher Education Management* 9, 1 (Summer/Fall 1993).

[7] L. Gale, "Gender and Leadership: The Implications of Small Group Research," *Initiatives* 10 (1988): 19–32, as cited in Hickson, op cit.

[8] Michael Z. Hackman, Marylyn J. Hills, Tracey J. Paterson, and Alison H. Furniss, "Leaders' Gender-Role as a Correlate of Subordinates' Perceptions to Effectiveness and Satisfaction," *Perceptual and Motor Skills* 77 (1993): 671–74.

[9] Betsy Q. Griffin, "Perceptions of Managers: Effects of Leadership Style and Gender," paper presented at the Annual Meeting of the Southeastern Psychological Association (38th, Knoxville, TN, March 1992).

[10] Krystyna Rojahn and Tineke M. Willemsen, "The Evaluation of Effectiveness and Likability of Gender-Role Congruent and Gender-Role Incongruent Leaders," *Sex Roles* 30, 1/2 (1994): 109–19.

[11] Alice H. Eagly, Mona G. Makhijani, and Bruce G. Klonsky, "Gender and the Evaluation of Leaders: A Meta-Analysis," *Psychological Bulletin* 111, 1 (1992): 3–22.

[12] Griffin, op cit.

[13] Eagly, Makhijani, and Klonsky, op cit.

[14] Rojahn and Willemsen, op cit.; Cathryn Johnson, "Gender, Legitimate Authority, and Leader-Subordinate Conversations," *American Sociological Review* 59 (February 1994): 122–35.

[15] Ernest B. Gurman and Keith Long, "Gender Orientation and Emergent Leader Behavior," *Sex Roles* 27, 7/8 (1992): 391–400.

[16] D. Butler and F. L. Geis, "Nonverbal Affect Responses to Male and Female Leaders: Implications for Leadership Evaluations," *Journal of Personality and Social Psychology* 58 (1990): 18–59; L. Smith-Lovin and C. Brody, "Interruptions in Group Discussions: The Effects of Gender and Group Composition," *American Sociological Review* 54 (1989): 424–35; both as cited in Gurman and Long, op cit.

[17] Edward B. Klein, Ellen Ernst Kossek, and Joseph H. Astrachan, "Affective Reactions to Leadership Education: An Exploration of the Same-Gender Effect," *Journal of Applied Behavioral Science* 28, 1 (March 1992): 102–17.

[18] R. Ely, *An Intergroup Perspective on Relationships Among Professional Women*, unpublished doctoral dissertation, Yale University (1989), as cited in Klein et al., op cit.

[19] Arnie Cann and William D. Siegfried, "Gender Stereotypes and Dimensions of Effective Leader Behavior," *Sex Roles* 23 7/8 (1990): 413–19.

[20] Hackman et al., op cit.

[21] Griffin, op cit.; and Alice H. Eagly, Steven J. Karau, and Blair T. Johnson, "Gender and Leadership Style Among School Principals: A Meta-Analysis," *Educational Administration Quarterly* 28, 1 (February 1992): 76–102.

[22] Sara E. Snodgrass, "Further Effects of Role Versus Gender on Interpersonal Sensitivity," *Journal of Personality and Social Psychology* 62, 1 (1992): 154–58.

[23] Doreen Geddes, "Sex Roles in Management: The Impact of Varying Power of Speech Style on Union Members' Perception of Satisfaction and Effectiveness," *The Journal of Psychology* 126, 6 (1992): 589–607.

[24] Patricia Hayes Andrews, "Sex and Gender Differences in Group Communication: Impact on the Facilitation Process," *Small Group Research* 23, 1 (February 1992): 74–94.

[25] A. Cann and W. D. Siegfried, "Sex Stereotypes and the Leadership Role," *Sex Roles* 17 (1987): 401–8.

[26] J. H. Astrachan, *Mergers, Acquisitions, and Employee Anxiety: A Study of Separation Anxiety in a Corporate Context* (New York: Praeger, 1990).

[27] Marilyn Kern-Foxworth, Oscar Gandy, Barbara Hines, and Debra A. Miller, "Assessing the Managerial Roles of Black Female Public Relations Practitioners Using Individual and Organizational Discriminants," *Journal of Black Studies* 24, 4 (June 1994): 416–34.

[28] Kaisa Kauppinen, Elina Haavio-Mannila, and Irja Kandolin, "Who Benefits from Working in Non-Traditional Workroles: Interaction Patterns and Quality of Worklife," *Acta Sociologica* 32, 4 (1989): 389–403.

[29] Zdenek Salzmann, "Portrayal of Gender Relations in Contemporary Czech Mass Media," *East European Quarterly*, 23, 4 (January 1990): 399–407.

[30] Nancy C. Jurik and Gregory J. Halemba, "Gender, Working Conditions and the Job Satisfaction of Women in a Non-Traditional Occupation: Female Correctional Officers in Men's Prisons," *The Sociological Quarterly* 25 (Autumn 1984): 551–66.

[31] G. Kolata, "Equal Time for Women," *Discover* (January 1984): 24–27.

[32] For a discussion about women and technology, see Mary Cianni and Anna D. Weitz, "The Technological Society: Implications for Women in the Workplace," *Journal of Counseling Development* 64, 8 (April 1986): 501–3.

[33] See Julia Wood and Charles Conrad, "Paradox in the Experiences of Professional Women," *Western Journal of Speech Communication* 47 (Fall 1983): 305–22. We have heard women say that they feel either "invisible" or like "honorary men" in many conversations with men on the job.

[34] For a discussion of recent debate on this issue, see Lise Vogel, "Debating Difference: Feminism, Pregnancy, and the Workplace," *Feminist Studies* 16, 1 (Spring 1990): 9–32.

[35] Becky Constantino, "At Issue: Should Women Be Allowed in Combat?" *Congressional Quarterly, Inc.* 2, 36 (1992): 849.

[36] For a discussion of this debate, see Clyde Wilcox, "Race, Gender and Support of Women in the Military," *Social Science Quarterly* 73, 2 (June 1992): 310–23.

[37] Sandra Gilbert, as cited in Allison Berg, "The Great War and the War at Home: Gender Battles in *Flags in the Dust* and *The Unvanquished*," *Women's Studies* 22 (1993): 441–53.

[38] Michael Pacanowsky and Linda L. Putnam, eds., "Special Issue: Interpretative Approaches to the Study of Organizational Communication," *Western Journal of Speech Communication* 46, 2 (Spring 1982).

[39] For a discussion about motivation for a high-power group to engage a low-power group on noncompetitive terms, see Judith K. Bowker, "Reporting Sexual Harassment: Reconciling Power, Knowledge, and Perspective," in *Sexual Harassment: Communication Implications*, ed. Gary Kreps (Cresskill, NJ: Hampton Press, Inc., 1993), pp. 195–205.

[40] David Jaffee, "Gender Inequality in Workplace Autonomy and Authority," *Social Science Quarterly* 70, 2 (1989): 375–90.

[41] Deborah C. Fontaine and Shelia P. Greenlee, "Black Women: Double Solos in the Workplace," *Western Journal of Black Studies* 17 (1993): 121–25.

[42] Charlotte Kinder Shelton, "The Relationship of Mentoring and Behavioral Style to Selected Job Success Variables," Ph.D. diss., Northern Illinois University, 1982.

[43] Christina Diane Fernandez, "Career Comadres," *Hispanic* 8, 8 (September 1995): 46–48.

[44] Kathleen T. Heinrich, "Doctoral Advisement Relationships between Women: On Friendship and Betrayal," *Journal of Higher Education* 66, 4 (July 1995): 447–69.

[45] Hagar Scher, "New Mentor Matchup Programs," *Working Woman* (January 1996): 17.

[46] Paula M. Popovich, DeeAnn N. Gehlauf, Jeffrey A. Jolton, Jill M. Somers, and Rhonda M. Godinho, "Perceptions of Sexual Harassment as a Function of Sex of Rater and Incident Form and Consequence," *Sex Roles* 27, 11/12 (1992): 609–25.

[47] Janice D. Yoder and Patrica Aniakudo, "The Responses of African American Women Firefighters to Gender Harassment at Work," *Sex Roles* 32, 3/4 (1995): 125–37.

[48] J. E. Gruber and L. Bjorn, "Women's Responses to Sexual Harassment: An Analysis of Sociocultural, Organizational, and Person Resource Models," *Social Science Quarterly* 67 (1986): 814–26, as cited in Yoder and Aniakudo, op cit.

[49] For a review of prevalence and consequences of sexual harassment, see Louise Fitzgerald, "Sexual Harassment: Violence Against Women in the Workplace," *American Psychologist* 48, 10 (October 1993): 1070–76.

[50] Robert Chrisman and Robert L. Allen, eds., *Court of Appeal: The Black Community Speaks Out on the Racial and Sexual Politics of Clarence Thomas vs. Anita Hill* (New York: Ballantine Books, 1992); and Morrison, Toni, ed., *Race-ing Justice, En-Gendering Power: Essays on Anita Hill, Clarence Thomas, and the Construction of Social Reality* (New York: Pantheon Books, 1992).

[51] Norma J. Burgess, "Gender Roles Revisited: The Development of the 'Woman's Place' among African American Women in the United States." *Journal of Black Studies* 24, 4 (June 1994): 391–401.

[52] Dan Thomas, Craig McCoy, and Allan McBride, "Deconstructing the Political Spectacle: Sex, Race, and Subjectivity in Public Response to the Clarence Thomas/Anita Hill 'Sexual Harassment' Hearings," *American Journal of Political Science* 37 (August 1993): 699–720.

[53] For discussions about Hill/Thomas hearings, see Judith K. Bowker, "Believability: Narratives and Relational Messages in the Strategies of Anita Hill and Clarence Thomas," in *The Lynching of Language: Gender, Politics, and Power in the Hill-Thomas Hearings,* ed. Sandra Ragan, Christina Beck, Lynda Lee Kaid, and Dianne Bystrom (University of Illinois Press); Judith K. Bowker, "The Hill/Thomas Hearings: Voice and Visibility," in *He Said, She Said, We Listened: A Communication Perspective on the Hill/Thomas Hearings,* ed. Paul Siegel (Hampton Press, in press); Judith K. Bowker, "Reporting Sexual Harassment: Reconciling Power, Knowledge, and Perspective," in Gary Kreps, ed., *Sexual Harassment: Communication Implications* (Cresskill, NJ: Hampton Press, Inc., 1993), pp. 195–205.

[54] Bette Stern, ed., *Women in Management,* 2d ed. (Englewood Cliffs, NJ: Prentice-Hall, 1985).

[55] Cynthia Kay Stevens, Anna G. Bavetta, and Marilyn E. Gist, "Gender Differences in the Acquisition of Salary Negotiation Skills: The Role of Goals, Self-Efficacy, and Perceived Control," *Journal of Applied Psychology* 78, 5 (1993): 723–35; Barry Gerhart and Sara Rynes, "Determinants and Consequences of Salary Negotiations by Male and Female MBA Graduates," *Journal of Applied Psychology* 76, 2 (1991): 256–62.

[56] Joyce Neu, John L. Graham, and Mary C. Gilly, "The Influence of Gender on Behaviors and Outcomes in a Retail Buyer-Seller Negotiation Simulation," *Journal of Retailing* 64, 4 (Winter 1988): 427–47.

[57] Dean G. Pruitt, Peter J. D. Carnevale, Blythe Forcey, and Michael Van Slyck, "Gender Effects in Negotiation: Constituent Surveillance and Contentious Behavior," *Journal of Experimental Social Psychology* 22 (1986): 264–75.

[58] Donald C. Beitzes, Elizabeth J. Mutran, and Maria E. Fernandez, "Middle-Aged Working Men and Women: Similar and Different Paths to Self-Esteem," *Research on Aging* 16, 4 (December 1994): 355–74.

NOWADAYS, ADS DONT JUST SELL A PRODUCT. THEY SELL AN ATTITUDE! LOOK AT THIS ONE!

HERE'S A COOL GUY SAYING NOBODY TELLS HIM WHAT TO DO. HE DOES WHATEVER HE WANTS AND HE BUYS THIS PRODUCT AS A REFLECTION OF THAT INDEPENDENCE.

SO BASICALLY, THIS MAVERICK IS URGING EVERYONE TO EXPRESS HIS INDIVIDUALITY THROUGH CONFORMITY IN BRAND-NAME SELECTION?

WELL, IT SOUNDED MORE DEFIANT THE WAY *HE* SAID IT.

MM.

Chapter 9

Mass Media and Mediated Communication

Responses to the growth and popularity of mass media range from delight to scorn to alarm. Delight is expressed that new forms of mediated communication are almost constantly being introduced and marketed with success. Scorn is often directed at "mindless" and violent computer games and "antisocial" rock music lyrics. Alarm often centers on the apparently endless power of mass media to promote the buying of products, the presentation of simplistic solutions to complex human problems, and the substitution of mediated communication for interpersonal communication.

CHAPTER OVERVIEW

This chapter focuses on two powerful influences on sex and gender stereotypes in the United States culture: mass media and mediated communication. Mass media includes public forms of message sending that do not occur face to face, such as film, television, radio, newspapers, and magazines. Mediated communication encompasses any communication that is mediated by technology and that can be controlled by an individual, such as the fast-growing computer industry and its products like the Internet, the World Wide Web, word processing programs, computer games, and electronic mail (often called e-mail). The key difference between what is deemed mass media and what is deemed mediated is the communicator's private and individual control of the message.

In this chapter, we will investigate how both mass media and mediated communication portray and influence both sexes. We will try to connect theoretical knowledge about media and mediated communication with the daily experience of consuming media materials and using computer-related means as they affect gender. Mass media and mediated communication help create and recreate gender stereotypes because they are present in nearly all settings and are able to reflect and reinforce certain communication patterns. Current treatments of the sexes in print, broadcast, and film media reflect some social changes such as the increase in two-career marriages, single parenting, and active women in retirement age. Mediated communication also has become the means by which these messages are traded, not only within this culture but with cultures around the world. Two serious problems regarding sex and gender persist: (1) the problem of a skewed reality in which women are underrepresented, misrepresented, or marginalized and devalued in a variety of media and mediated forms and (2) the problem of reinforcing stereotypic and destructive patterns of relating for both sexes. The male gender stereotype of physical strength, the ability to accommodate pain and to control emotions, and successful aggression remains a central image in films, television, magazines, and computer games. Female physical beauty is emphasized by the same media—even in story lines ranging from women as mythical to self-improvement programs urging goals such as career fulfillment.

MASS MEDIA

BACKGROUND: THE GROWTH OF MASS MEDIA

In the 1880s, most people in the United States were likely to get their information about the world from a few sources: by word of mouth from acquaintances, from a newspaper or newssheet based on material conveyed by telegraph, and in a very few cases from a telephone. Fifty years later the radio and newspaper were the two kinds of mass communication people depended on for news reports. Some teenagers had access to movie theaters and phonograph records by the 1930s, but many did not.

Today the array of mass communication forms is staggering. Most homes have a minimum of two televisions and multiple radios plus at least two of the following:

stereophonic or quadraphonic recording equipment

videocassette recorder (VCR)

films on videotape

audiocassette tape recorder

compact disks

video disks

video recorder

citizen's band radio

T-shirt, jacket, or jeans advertising a saying, place, or product

satellite dish

Your household probably receives one or more local, national, or professional newspapers, a news magazine, and one or more special interest magazines dealing with gardening, home decorating, fishing, parenting, or beauty. Moreover, you are likely to get multiple mailings from companies promising sweepstakes prizes, investment counseling, or store specials. Some of these items may not seem to be mass media communication, but each qualifies because it uses technology for the production and distribution of its messages to audiences that are not face to face with the message sources.

The term "media smorgasbord" underscores the fact that, like a dinner table covered with more items than any one person can consume, the number and variety of mass media available today are more than any of us can use all at once. Even with the advent of on-line newspapers, at least 1,700 different daily papers are being printed in the United States, in addition to weekly newspapers and local advertising papers. Ninety-nine percent of American homes and 95 percent of our automobiles contain radios; portable radios and cassette players allow users to be "tuned in" constantly if they choose. Fewer book publishers now produce hardbound books than was true decades ago, but a great many more paperback books are now published, and bookstores are typically included in large shopping malls; these stores sell not only books but a wide range of newspapers and magazines. As a result of this media smorgasbord, you can choose how to receive certain kinds of information and how much of it to receive.[1] You can hear news on CNN and some radio stations all day and all night. Some cities have morning and evening newspapers, plus two national dailies (*The Wall Street Journal* and *USA Today*). You can be a "news junkie," searching for news in all possible sources, or you can get your news from only one source and try to avoid other sources of information. With all these options available for finding out about the world, you have some degree of individual choice about the sources and amounts of mass media information you will absorb.

One feature of the media smorgasbord is that the effort to reach a particular audience with an appealing message has become highly expensive. Producers of media material target their articles, programs, and advertising to a specific segment of the general population. Marketing representatives refer to various "publics" that are to be reached with a particular commercial or a specific series of articles. Media organizations do this tailoring to specific audiences because profits depend on sales, sales depend on size of audience receiving the message, and audience size depends on the success of fitting messages to their existing interests. One way to emphasize the importance of economics in mass media is to say that a media organization exists to deliver audiences to its sponsors or advertisers. Commercial time during the 1996 Super Bowl cost $2.2 million per minute. That charge was acceptable to sponsors in light of the fact that the game might be watched by more people than any other televised event during the 1996 viewing season.

With the exception of public broadcasting in radio and television, media organizations exist to make profit. Even the public stations now devote days of air time to requesting donations to offset the loss of federal government grants. Market research is central in the planning of programs. A local TV station may begin a 6 A.M. exercise show after finding out that most early risers will not watch either a cooking show or a soap opera at that hour, although many would like to do aerobics at the start of their day. The resulting show will have appropriate commercials about fitness equipment and low-fat yogurt. Generally, you can assume that product marketing determines most of what you read, hear, and view in the mass media.

The current growth of video recorders, rental movies, special cable television channels, and specialized magazines illustrates another aspect of mass communication. It is mass in the sense of involving millions of people, yet demassified in the sense that people can view widely differing films and read about highly diverse areas of interest. In most locations more cable than noncable channels are available. One can subscribe to premium movie channels, a children's channel, a sports channel, a religious channel, a music video channel, and an arts and entertainment series, just to name a few. Substantial overlap occurs within this potential diversity. Subscribers to premium movie channels will find that approximately half of the same movies show up on all the channels, since the same film distributors are used by most of the cable organizations. Thus the selections made by one media source will limit the choices of films that can be made by millions of viewers.

News Media and Gender Stereotypes

The fact that media messages are more alike than we expect them to be is particularly relevant to the gender messages, nonverbal and verbal, you receive from multiple media. In terms of news events, both broadcast and print news sources depend largely on national wire services and the three or four broadcast networks to learn of stories outside their own localities. What appears on a wire service report or in a prior newspaper account will usually be taken as fact by a radio, television, or newspaper staff unless a reporter is on the scene to be consulted. As a consumer of news, you will likely hear, see, and read many similar accounts of the same news events if you consult several news sources during a given period of time.

These features of media affect our knowledge of the sexes, and particularly our knowledge of the actions and opinions of women, in four ways: (1) by separating or omitting information about women or of interest mainly to women; (2) by portraying stereotypical masculine behavior of males (although some research suggests this trend may be slowing[2]); (3) by focusing on the deviant, the dramatic, or the violent behavior of either sex; and (4) by treating the sexuality of women as a primary theme that overrides other content of news stories about them. We will discuss each of these points separately, although they are interrelated in practice.

First, let us consider the way news is defined. Hard news is defined by newscasters as national and international politics, crime, disasters, and threats to public safety. Men are represented more often than women in these arenas of activity. The expected arenas of action for women are the home, relationships, and community services. These arenas are viewed by most editors and news directors as soft news, appropriate for the "life-style" or "community" section of the newspaper and the last few minutes of a televised news broadcast, but rarely fitting into radio news. Information related to women may not appear on wire services at all, or if it does it may not be used by local news reporters.

Within those stories deemed as hard news, stereotypical masculine images and behaviors are reported: government leaders making decisions, rescue workers saving victims, judges handing out sentences, and financiers conquering the stock market. Even when the central figure in the story is female, the masculine stereotype honoring leadership, strength, protection, and decision making is featured. When we read those lists of news stories and characteristics, we may say, "Of course those are the reported items. Those are news!" We may not recognize the circular pattern of our thinking: we determine what will and will not be called news and then identify events around us as news depending on whether or not those events fit our criteria. In the presentation of the news, insofar as females are integrated, the masculine experience of events continues to be projected.

What makes the public action of an individual or group "newsworthy" is its difference or deviance from expected practice and its dramatic quality as a "story." Thus a rapist is more interesting than a couple enjoying a successful interpersonal relationship, and a labor union strike is more newsworthy than a successfully negotiated contract.

The sexuality of women, and particularly that of young women (the media often refer to them as "girls") who are long-haired, long-legged, and large-breasted, is perceived to be of interest to many or most males in a reading or viewing audience. Thus photographers of televised sports events and parades frequently hold the camera on buxom females, while writers about rape cases often give details of the rapist's attack that do not increase the likelihood of capture but do provide sexual or violent images for some readers or listeners to savor.

Women's contributions to public life are not entirely absent from the print and visual media, but they are more difficult to learn about than the pursuits and achievements of men. Further, focusing on women's sexuality gives male audiences a pleasurable "media massage." The problem is not due to a planned conspiracy on the part of wire services, news directors, or photographers; instead it grows out of a long-established gender bias that affects decisions about what is news and what will most interest the desired audiences. The problem is difficult to address because individual instances often appear to the sources as accurate and effective, not biased.

The treatment of the sexes in the news is in some ways quite different from the treatment of the sexes in narrative films or cartoons or romance novels. A common element does run through all the forms of media: the search for an interesting, memorable story. The search for a story or drama makes news reporters compete not only with each other for the most up-to-date and detailed report of the same event, but also with the narrative forms of entertainment that people might choose instead of the news. The sensational, especially in a visual image, can hold audiences. This preference was the foundation for the interest in the O.J. Simpson trial. Each day, reporters found the most tantalizing detail to pique receivers' interests. In this way, viewers and listeners were motivated to return day after day, month after month to observe trial testimony. Not all cultures treat these kinds of events this way. In England, for example, media are prohibited from coverage of the crime once police arrest a suspect.

Message sources within any of the media must deal with limitations of time and space. Because not every piece of available information can be presented, selectivity is required. Choices are often made on the basis of drama, sensation, the memorable, or the unusual. However, to message receivers, who do not know the whole array of possible messages, the selection process is invisible and the resulting story or report appears to be not only the truth but the whole truth.

In the 1960s, when a group of feminists demonstrated publicly against the exploitation and restriction of women's bodies, a wire service reporter coined the phrase "bra burning." The phrase has continued to be used in popular literature and in conversation as a shorthand term for feminist protest. Media exposure can bring almost immediate fame to an individual, but it can also produce nearly insurmountable difficulties when people try to present an issue or situation that is more complex than a visual or verbal cliché. The topic of gender role changes is frequently reduced to misleading or simplistic generalizations. How mass media are implicated in this process has been a question of interest to observers and theorists during the past several decades.

GENDER AND THEORIES ABOUT MASS MEDIA

As the media organizations themselves have expanded over the years, theories about the operation and impact of the mass media have expanded as well. Among the various viewpoints, some are optimistic, others neutral, and still others critical about the operations and impact of the mass media. Optimistic views focus on the unique services media can deliver to readers, viewers, and listeners. Neutral views analyze the ways information is processed and the developing forms of technology which change the means by which receivers take in that information. What are referred to here as critical theories focus on the problems media produce for audiences and participants, especially through the influence of a market economy on mass communication. Among the theories discussed during the past few years, many have dealt with television in particular, since it reaches almost everyone in the United States and large numbers of people in other countries as well. An outline of prominent ideas from the three vantage points will show you some of the different concerns that are expressed about the same media organizations and events.

OPTIMISTIC VIEWS OF MEDIA

One of the optimistic views of mass media, that of Marshall McLuhan, is based on a historical look at human communication over many centuries. Before the printing press was invented in the sixteenth century, most people depended entirely on oral communication for education, history, and amusement. As a result, people relied on their sense of hearing more than any other sense; remembering what you heard was an essential skill. Today we may have a hard time imagining the memorization of a poem of many thousands of lines. In ancient Greece individuals recited *The Iliad* or *The Odyssey* from memory and taught these epic poems to others orally. McLuhan claimed that since the invention of the printing press, humans have depended on sight more than hearing as a way to take in new information. Reading and writing became ways to distinguish the educated from the uneducated. At the turn of the twentieth century, the radio and phonograph renewed the emphasis on the auditory element in media. Then film and television combined the visual and the oral so that people could experience a multisensory message. Whether or not they are literate, people in countries all over the world now receive similar visual messages and thus know more about each other than was ever before possible. This worldwide spread of mass communication is seen as creating a global village with the help of the mass media. In this global village people are enabled by their new knowledge about the world to develop a more caring attitude about others—a positive result of mass communication.

One of McLuhan's most famous statements is, "The medium is the massage." He also said that "the medium is the message"—suggesting that radio, television, newspaper, and film each has a distinct communicative impact derived from its own form of technology. The first statement in this paragraph is even more important for our purposes in this chapter. A mass medium itself can convey subtle yet powerful gratification, apart from the information it contains.[3] When a mass medium acts as a "massage" for a receiver, the information conveyed within the channel of communication becomes less important than the soothing experience of being in the presence of the channel itself.

None of us may be conscious of what we are learning about ourselves or gender ideals when we choose a medium such as television, radio, or a magazine simply for relaxation. Advertising messages are planned to elicit exactly that sort of uncritical attention; in fact, the many subtle appeals in advertising to sexual needs, fear of death, and loneliness have been called subliminal seduction.[4] Despite the ethical question raised by these persuasive appeals, theorists with a positive view of the mass media claim that, in general, mass media render us better off by extending our knowledge and connecting us with the rest of the world.

NEUTRAL VIEWS OF MEDIA

Students of television and other visual media have tried to understand the popularity and apparent influence of these communication forms. One area of study has been of the way people process pictures as compared to words. Humans learn visual materials more easily than they learn purely verbal or conceptual materials. Psychologists have found that visual images stay in the mind longer and can be retrieved more easily than other forms of information. Visual imagery, such as photographs, has powerful socializing effects that can shape cultural consensus with regard to gender.[5] Language that can be pictured—whether single words, sentences, or paragraphs—will be more memorable.[6] This means that producers of television shows and commercials have an advantage in influencing viewers, since they can show pictures and use words that paint pictures at the same time. Add to these features a jingle with an easily recalled melody and the prospect for persuasion rises significantly.

Another analysis of mass media asserts that messages are experienced not in isolation but in layers or waves across a number of media at the same time. Certain images, ideas, events, and controversies appear in several media settings at the same time, making them seem more central or important by this multiple presence. In other cases, a character or idea may be seen or heard in few media settings but become familiar and even expected over a period of time. Because of this layering or accumulation of communication events, questioning whether a single media message has influence by itself does not make sense. If you have experienced a mixture of many forms of an image or event, your prior learning and your expectations for the future may make you more or less receptive to the message to come.[7]

A third notion about the way visual media in particular can affect their receivers is by providing genderisms, or visual repetitions of various expected relationships between males and females. Relative size can be used to photograph males so that they will appear taller than their female companions. Mock assault rituals suggest simultaneously that the sexes are enjoying playful combat and that the male could hurt the female if he chose to fight in earnest. These ritual relationships in advertisements serve as a kind of visual shorthand that allows receivers to identify with gender ideals without examining their validity.[8] Ongoing research with regard to these criteria has produced some conflicting findings.[9] We still are unclear whether the new research reflects changing stereotypes, changing roles for men and women, or differences in researcher methods.

All three of these means used by the media—using pictures and words, using layers of media, and providing genderisms—are based on the belief that mass media can in some way influence human thinking. Denis McQuail widens the discussion by presenting six possible changes media might produce in audiences:

cause intended change (conversion)

cause unintended change

cause minor change (in form or intensity)

facilitate change (intended or not)

reinforce what exists (no change)

prevent change[10]

We have no conclusive proof about which kinds of change related to gender and communication are either caused or prevented by the various mass media, but the above set of options allows us to consider how messages from the mass media are likely to operate in human consciousness. Their influence may be positive or negative, either educating the sexes toward greater mutual understanding or deepening stereotypes and preventing a clear analysis of complex social problems.

CRITICAL VIEWS OF MEDIA

Critics of mass media, and particularly of television, claim that the technology as well as the content of televised mass communication renders receivers less critical than they should be about the ways their ideas and values are being altered by the media messages. Part of the problem is in the physiology of television viewers, especially children. The visual and auditory signals from television can produce more alpha waves in children than do other kinds of experiences such as reading or active play. The result, according to critic Jerry Mander, is that children become mentally relaxed, in a state somewhere between waking and sleeping, taking in images without questioning their truthfulness. For adults as well as children, one result of this process of being uncritical in front of a television screen is becoming convinced they should adopt life-styles, purchase products, and defend political or social values that they have seen in televised images but have not examined for themselves.[11]

Complex issues or experiences do not fit the time and space limitations of television. Intentionally simple messages are presented that show problems being solved through magic, violence, or by simple denial that a problem exists. Problems are dealt with in convenient time segments, usually of one-half hour or one hour interrupted periodically for commercials. Because television, and to some extent film, as a visual medium implies that it is conveying reality to its audiences, many receivers of televised messages experience the characters and stories of television as equally real as the individuals in their neighborhoods, families, and workplaces. Audiences for commercials as well as programs are encouraged to develop would-be interpersonal relationships with televised characters, often to the degree that viewers talk about characters as personal friends or enemies rather than as actors who play their parts according to scripts. Several magazines and newspapers exist to help soap-opera viewers maintain those would-be interpersonal relationships by summarizing the plotlines for each week's programs. (This could be called "bound gossip.") Other magazines and tabloids report sensational stories on the behavior or problems of the celebrities of television and film. If you are inclined to dismiss these relationships and interests as trivial or limited to a few people, observe the number of people in supermarkets and drugstores who look at the celebrity magazines. Consider also that thousands of college students plan their class schedules to avoid missing a favorite soap opera.

THE COLONIZED VIEWER. Besides claiming that receivers are kept from analyzing what they see and are encouraged to form unreal relationships with products and characters, Mander claims that television viewers in particular are colonized toward an affluent life-style by the images they see continually on the screen. In colonization, the behaviors and customs of the ruled nation or group will imitate those of the ruler nation or group. In Mander's theory, colonized television viewers have become members of a consumer-colony dominated by materialism and a narrow definition of attractiveness and success.[12]

Lifestyles of the Rich and Famous embodied the fantasy and wish fulfillment implied by the colonized viewer concept. It offered microscopic personal details about celebrities who were already headline material for tabloids and *People* magazine. The celebrities were treated as newsworthy even when doing the most mundane or boring activity. The *Lifestyles* program exemplified the working assumption in much current advertising: being rich is a universal desire, so anything you can learn about rich people will improve your life. In fact, the reverse of that claim is likely to be true: people who continually hear and see the glamorous details of the lives of celebrities may become more negative about their own state of relative deprivation. By focusing on the material circumstances of the famous—their four homes on as many continents, or the number of servants stationed in each of the homes—the producers of these messages teach receivers to emphasize the visible features of life rather than other issues, such as the celebrities' political or religious perspectives, which would not translate easily into visual images. Emphasis on the physical appearance of females, and to a lesser degree that of males, can thus be understood as rooted in the features and constraints of a visual medium as well as in the producers' biases.

GENDER MESSAGES ACROSS THE MEDIA

The mass media theories have been presented above to provide a context for the discussion of gender-related media messages that follows. However, they are only part of the story. An array of careful research studies have demonstrated that, as compared to men, women are less visible, more stereotyped, and less accurately portrayed in most print and broadcast media. The problems revealed by this research include both the lack of factual accuracy in the ways women's lives are depicted and the strong evidence that children identify with male characters and demean female characters. In terms of aggression and the masculine gender stereotype, a series of national studies concluded that "television violence is as strongly correlated with aggressive behavior as any other behavioral variable that has been measured."[13] This research supported certain claims about communication and gender: (1) girls and women fail to see themselves realistically represented in the mass media; (2) girls develop a preference for male characters when there are few or no female models in the media; and (3) an aggressive gender stereotype for boys and men is reinforced by violent media programming. One regulatory effort may increase the visibility of women. The FCC has embraced a policy to grant licenses to minority and female-owned media facilities.[14]

Although the visibility of women has increased significantly in some of the mass media during the past decade, the problems cited above have not disappeared. Treatment of women's careers and of varied family forms is somewhat more accurate now; but the gender stereotypes of control and aggression for men and of beauty and passivity for women still predominate. The examples that follow from various print and visual media show the subtle and often paradoxical ways these gender ideals emerge and persist in the mass media.

NEWS

In trying to discover how the media affect attitudes of men and women about the economic environment, researchers found that newspapers have greater affect than television on both sexes. Researchers explained that television provides summary stories and quick reviews. Newspapers, on the other hand, can present the complex and slowly evolving political issues in their editorials and feature articles. Men in this study tended to answer questions about economic concerns and base their attitudes on their knowledge of the issues; women were twice as likely as men to say they did not know answers to the questions. Although men answered the questions, they were more likely to guess at the answers and get them wrong. One explanation is that the gender stereotype for males is that they should know about public issues; for example, men may feel pressure to be knowledgeable about economics. At a competitive level, men may feel embarrassed to appear uninformed. The stereotype for women, on the other hand, does not require them to be competent in public matters so they may be more relaxed about answering that they were not familiar with issues questioners mentioned.[15]

The news also seems to affect viewers' perceptions of political candidates with regard to sex. The patterns of coverage used by news producers and reporters can change viewers' interpretations about male and female candidates. For example, Pat Schroeder was sharply criticized in 1987 when the media publicized her teary decision not to run for president. One columnist wrote that Schroeder's face "looked like a Cabbage Patch doll."[16] Viewers' ongoing sex stereotypes interact with the news media treatment to affect viewers' judgments about gubernatorial and senatorial candidates.[17]

CHILDREN'S PROGRAMMING

Children's television programs, according to a 1995–1996 program schedule, are a mixture of education and entertainment. Public television airs several programs that entertain and inform at the same time: *Barney and Friends*, *Mister Rogers*, *Reading Rainbow*, *Lamb Chop's Playalong*, *Shining Time Station*, and *Sesame Street* are cheery, energetic shows that include music and the arts, science, and relationships, as well as words and numbers. The pace of these programs is fast and backed with rock-style music, except for *Mister Rogers*, which is much slower paced than the others and depends on talking directly to viewers rather than on technology and visual effects.

The biggest block of time devoted to children's programming is Saturday morning, beginning at 7:00 A.M. on NBC, ABC, and CBS and lasting for two to four hours. Programming for children's cartoons has changed substantially in the last fifteen years. Mornings previously devoted to superheros and magic have changed to a variety of venues, although the superheros and magic remain a significant part. Most of the morning's choices still feature males as the main characters. For example, ABC offers *Fudge*, *Free Willy*, *The New Adventures of Captain Planet*, and *The Bugs Bunny and Tweety Show*. NBC starts the morning at 6:30 A.M. with *Bill Nye the Science Guy* followed by *Saved by the Bell: The New Class*, and two hours of news. CBS provides the most stereotyped programming, including *Little Mermaid*, *Aladdin*, *Teenage Mutant Ninja Turtles*, and *Skeleton Warriors*. While it does not air on Saturday mornings, *Mighty Morphin Power Rangers* represents one of the most popular children's programs.

I remember all of the programs we used to watch when I was a child. One day I was sitting around with my three-year-old female cousin when we got to talking about cartoons and I asked what her favorite cartoon was. She replied, "Smurfs." So next I asked, knowing all the Smurf trivia possible from growing up with them, who was her favorite Smurf. She answered, "Smurfette, because she gets to hang around with all those boys and just play with them." My cousin is a tomboy. I thought that was the funniest answer. She was smart enough to realize there is only one female and all those male Smurfs. I wonder if ever there were any little-girl issues to deal with in the Smurf village. I guess not.

Characters on children's television generally follow gender stereotypes. Males use aggression more effectively and females show affection twice as much as males do. Only one in five Saturday morning characters is female. Girls surveyed said they would create very different characters for girls if they were creating the programs.[18]

Plot details vary across programs, and characters range from animals to superheros. Whatever the stated plot, one of the essential elements of the programs' messages remains the same: implicit messages to children about sex and gender imbedded in the stories and characters.

1. Some problems are beyond the realm of human action; magic solves these difficult problems.
2. Individual action, even physical violence, is simple and dramatic, but without long impact.
3. Strong male leaders often lead both "good" and "bad" sides in a struggle.
4. Females are often victims, gentle characters to be protected, witches, or sometimes sisters or assistants to the main character.

Some programs provide exceptions to these four points, but by and large these ideas pervade not only narrative cartoons and other children's programs but also their commercials, which come in bunches of four to six messages at least five times during a half-hour program. The cartoon programs and commercials show basically the same problem-solution sequence of action, but the commercials add the specifics about a product that a child can obtain. Commercials for children, as for adults, are typically stories with happy endings: we experience a lack, we find the product to fill that lack, and we enjoy the benefits of having that product. What adds to the power of commercials laced through Saturday morning cartoons is that the cartoons themselves do a major part of the persuasion. In several cases the characters in the cartoons represent products currently for sale. Willy the Whale, Little Mermaid characters, Aladdin characters, and Ninja Turtles are all on sale as dolls and emblazoned on children's clothing, lunchboxes, and bookbags. So a story, and the mood of adventure attached to a story, can make a product-character appealing enough for a child to recall its visual image or name when shopping for other items.

The product-character connection looks rather obvious under the kind of analysis done here, but consider the more subtle aspects of persuasion through visual and structural message elements in programs. The first in the list of four messages to children is that magic solves difficult problems. If you find yourself in trouble, you can hop on your carpet and fly away. Decades ago child psychologist Jean Piaget wrote about a magic phase in child development in which children don't know how cause-effect relationships work but believe in magic connections between one event and another.[19] This kind of fantasy presents for children the unrealistic thinking that personal and relational issues not resolved through action and negotiation can be dealt with magically. When they encounter confrontative situations, young boys can be seen mimicking the Ninja Turtles or the Mighty Morphin Power Rangers (who magically move through space). While their actions may look like play to adults, children may not clearly understand the line between fantasy and reality.

In most of the children's programming—and much adult programming as well—the characters' actions are simple, dramatic, sometimes violent, and without much long-term consequence. Bugs Bunny and Sylvester beat other characters with large mallets or drop large objects on other characters who are flattened by the force. Sylvester, a large character, stalks Tweety, a small character, who always is saved or manages to foil Sylvester's plan. These actions provide little consequence in the programs; children may not be able to interpret what they see at such an abstract level. One of our neighbors, a four-year-old boy, stood out in the middle of the road in front of his house one day, his arm extended and his hand flattened. He refused his parents' imperatives that he come back in his yard and cried loudly when his parents carried him out of the traffic lane. He said he wanted to stop traffic and that he had seen his favorite cartoon character do it earlier that morning. The propensity for children, particularly boys, to emulate models they view on television demonstrates the power of such modeling.[20] Characters often engage in dramatic action—sometimes violent action—and yet "win" in the end. Some stories, like *The Lion King*, show children scenes of violent physical conflict. The conflict is almost always resolved by the "good" character's triumph over the "bad" character.

Like *The Lion King*, many children's programs feature males for both the central protagonist and antagonist. Saturday morning television for children shows stereotypes especially aimed at boys and consumed by both boys and girls; the leader figure in many shows continues to be male. *Free Willy* features a boy who befriends a whale who is pursued by bad men; *Aladdin* features a boy who protects a beautiful girl from bad men. Ninja Turtles are male characters triumphing over mostly male antagonists. The Mighty Morphin Power Rangers (a group which includes two females) dress and behave in stereotypically masculine ways except for the two females, who dress in pink and yellow, Barbie's signature combination. The Rangers exhibit dominant male traits of physical action such as karate chops, flips, and great speed, all to destroy Lord Zed (male) and Rita Repulsa (his female sidekick). The Power Rangers are described as "modern-day heroes"; their ominous uniforms feature dark, slanted eye covers that omit the possibility of eye contact. Typical of their talk is this line from their comic book: "Power Rangers—ATTACK! We have to stop this Tyrannosaurus Rex or we'll never get back to save the earth **in time!**"[21] Only *The Little Mermaid* has a female as lead; neither the title of the program nor the stories generally cast the mermaid as an action hero.

This tendency to stereotype the sexes—more strongly toward males—occurs in other cultures as well. Japanese children's programming also overrepresents males and reinforces them for acting in sex-appropriate ways. Females are presented as weak, younger, and less mature; males are presented as powerful, older, more likable, and more mature.[22]

The stereotype of females as victims or as people in need of protection is carried through children's commercial television in somewhat more subtle ways than occurred ten years ago. In the Power Rangers' story, the males design and direct the plans used by the rangers against foes. Males rarely smile. The following exchange between the Yellow Ranger (a black female) and the White Ranger (a white male) demonstrates both verbally and nonverbally the guidance of female by male:

> *Billy:* (White male) Well, when we activate each zord's power, the feedback should generate a "time hole" at the center. The hole should be easy enough for **us** to leap through, but there's **no way** for the thunderzords to accompany us! **We'll** be back in our own time, but the zords will be **lost here for all time!**
>
> *Yellow Ranger:* (Black female) The zords? Lost? Power Rangers with **no zords!?** Lord Zedd will stomp us for **sure!**
>
> *White Ranger:* (White male. His serious face turned toward Yellow Ranger, his hand on her shoulder) Don't **worry**, Aisha . . .You're the **yellow ranger** . . . even without your **zord** . . . even without your **weapon** . . .You're a **power ranger**—one of the **team!**
>
> *Yellow Ranger:* (Smiling towards white ranger) You . . .You're **right**, White Ranger. I'm sorry I panicked. Let's **do** it! **Let's go home!**[23]

When females are not characterized as victims or in need of protection, they often are given male characteristics as a means of achieving equity. Plots, character descriptions, and action scenes of the Power Rangers include females in these ways more than we saw a decade ago in children's programs. For example, Aisha, the Yellow Ranger, is described as "a devoted martial artist, observant and quite intelligent. . . . Aisha becomes a razor sharp tiger with lightning reflexes once her training takes over."[24] However, nowhere in children's programming is there visible a positive female character who is not related to or following after a male leader. And nowhere do we find male leaders whose principal strength derives from gentleness or nurturing qualities. Producers and marketers appear to believe that girls are so accustomed to thinking of boys as leaders that they would not watch a female star who was not linked with admired males. More significantly, boys are expected not to watch a female star unless she is identified with powerful males, and boys are expected not to see themselves as temperate or moderate.

Music Television

Music videos have gained attention from viewers and researchers in the past decade. Central themes in the videos consistently appear: romance, sexual attraction, and sexually suggestive behavior. Strong adherence to stereotypes occur both in the videos themselves and in MTV commercials. Females are most often depicted outside the paid workplace, often in the home or fashion showroom and rarely in nontraditional professions. They are portrayed as more affectionate than males and are shown behaving in implicitly sexual and subservient ways. Women pursue and are pursued in explicit and implicit sexual ways; they are the objects of someone's gaze more than males, and they exhibit fear more often than males. Familiar MTV images show fearful women in dark places or women exhibiting anxious expressions when they are left alone or lost. Nonwhite females show more sadness, nurturance, and dependence than nonwhite males. Nonwhite females are seldom shown in white-collar jobs.

Males appear in MTV commercials and in videos more often than females; in both commercials and videos, men display more dominance and violence. They are four times more likely than females to display aggression. Men are seen stalking women, fighting with women or other men, and chasing victims. They are also more frequently the target of violence than females.

When only one sex is targeted for a commercial, that sex more often is male; more than twice as many single-sexed commercials involve only males than only females. Commercials for females most often are for personal products such as beauty products like lipstick or mascara; commercials for males most often tout entertainment products such as stereo equipment or computer games.[25] MTV promotes boldly stereotyped images of both men and women, extending the images to commercials as well. These stereotypes promote and perpetuate traditional expectations and descriptions of men and women.

ADULT TELEVISION PROGRAMMING

Programming for adults on major networks has been affected by the ready availability of cable channels, satellite television, and pay-per-view options. Profit rather than social good drives the commercial television networks, not only in the United States but in other countries as well.[26] United States commercial networks strive to attract viewers in number and in amount of viewing. In a visual metaphor of the results of that pursuit, twice as many blondes appear on television than exist in real life.[27]

Programming for afternoon television has undergone major revisions in the last decade. Soap operas, watched by both men and women, have been re-examined in light of women's "different" or "feminine" voice.[28] However, differences in viewers' perceptions occur less on the basis of sex than on the basis of viewers' status as "fans" or "nonfans." The allure of the soap opera may emerge from the vantage point taken by fans. Fans (who are largely women) focus on the possibilities among characters and events in the story. Nonfans (who are often men) focus on the repetitiveness of events and the lack of conclusions or end points.[29] These vantage points on stories may reflect women's theoretical center on connection; skills in detecting links and connections through verbal and nonverbal messages between people may be tapped during soap opera stories where the complexities of possibilities at any given communication point in the story are emphasized. Likewise, men's theoretical distinction and separation orientation might support beginnings and endings, distinctness and parsimony. Rather than expect the soap opera to represent "real life," fans may be attracted to soap operas for reasons similar to those that attract people to crossword puzzles. The complexity of the interplay of words in the puzzle compares to fans' perceptions of the complexity of interplay among interpersonal relationships in the story.

Sonia Livingstone explains that reactions to talk shows, which compose a significant portion of afternoon network television, may follow similar patterns. Livingstone explains that talk show audiences, largely female, value the confrontation of "elite experts and ordinary people," enjoy the diversity of attitudes and opinions offered, and may construe the shows as providing critical social cohesion in the form of lay debate over personal and everyday issues.[30] Other researchers view talk shows not from this vantage point of process but as a social force that creates a stereotyped, gendered product. Because of the network commitment to high ratings, they believe, the "real" debate that ensues on these shows is contrived to reinforce social convention and therefore attract viewers.[31] Oprah Winfrey, the highest paid talk show host on afternoon television, attempted to defy the imperative to encourage such contrivances. She determined to engage "normal" topics discussed by everyday people. Popularity ratings for her show immediately dropped. This kind of public preference for overdramatization may be related to the frequent media portrayal of sex stereotypes as polar opposites.

Although stories, characters, and events displayed on television may be contrived, adults who watch a lot of television tend to apply the perceptions they have seen on television to their real lives.[32] They often do not distinguish between televised characters and people they know; they may even talk about televised characters as though they were real. Characters on television become acquaintances. Images— even images of violence—become familiar and unalarming. These viewers identify with characters who hold views like their own. Adults who hold ideas about the sexes that coincide with cultural gender stereotypes tend to forget or distort information they see on television that contradicts those ideas. Androgynous people or people whose gender schema differ from the cultural stereotype remember and more accurately describe things they saw on television that did not support the cultural stereotype.[33]

People who adhere to traditional gender stereotypes and watch a lot of television, then, may find their stereotypes reaffirmed by programming like sports programs, news programs, *Wheel of Fortune*, *Matlock*, *McKenna*, *Coach*, and *Walker, Texas Ranger*. Viewing an image that affirms a stereotype may produce a relaxing, consonant mood for the viewer. One study showed that men viewed television to escape negative moods; it also reported that watching wrestling—a sport that definitively portrays a masculine stereotype—was favored for this purpose.[34]

Even many shows that attempt to present the sexes more equitably include a greater number of central male roles than female roles. *Seinfeld* revolves around four friends, three men and one woman. *Wings* includes two male lead roles as pilots, and three supporting male roles as an airline owner, a mechanic, and a taxi driver. The female lead runs a lunch counter and eventually marries one of the pilots. The female supporting role is a former flight attendant whose current job is announcing flights to customers. Two attempts have been made to add another female to the cast, a female pilot (who was dropped from the show) and a sister of the woman who runs the lunch counter. Nevertheless, some of the males and females on both *Seinfeld* and *Wings* are presented with more varied dimensions than characters in sitcoms that aired thirty or forty years ago.[35]

Interpersonal strategies depicted on United States soap operas and situation comedies rely on fewer stereotyped behaviors than many critics allege, especially when compared to a generation ago. However, characters often are still treated in stereotypical ways.[36] Some shows intentionally attempt to oppose the traditional gender stereotypes, particularly in the presentation of females. These attempts produce characters of mixed, but sometimes stereotypic behaviors. Few individuals engage indiscriminately in behaviors traditionally ascribed to one sex or the other. More frequently, equity seems to be conceived as females engaging in masculine behavior or males engaging in masculine behavior gently. Murphy Brown dominates her news station as a hard-nosed reporter; her behaviors often are strongly masculine in nature. In some ways, the gender message is that using masculine behavior accrues success. Brown also parents a small child; the child was originally cared for by Brown's male, ever-present, handy-man-artist who often displays very stereotypical feminine attitudes.

One popular show that presents an equal number of males and females is *Friends*. Dialogue addressing issues of sex, gender, and the relationship among them often frames individual episodes. As is true for music videos, the themes of romance and attraction underlie interactions among the three male and three female leads. Tension throughout one season was sustained by Ross's undeclared affection for Rachel. In one scene, Chandler advises Ross not to go on his laundry date with Rachel carrying Snuggles, his fabric softener. Ross exchanges his container of Snuggles for a product with a harsh-sounding German name. In the laundromat, Ross teaches Rachel how to do laundry, reversing typical sex roles. However, in the more dominant plot, Rachel and Ross adopt stereotypical roles when Ross teaches Rachel how to be aggressive toward an older woman (stereotypically grouchy) who tries to claim one of Rachel's washing machines. Over the course of the show, Ross is presented as a professional paleontologist with a high-paying job. Rachel is presented as a shopping addict forced to take a job as a waitress after she broke off her engagement to a man with a career.

Abandoning the old, inequitable stereotypes presented in the media seems commendable, but directions are unclear about how to do so, what to replace them with, and whether such a move is economically rewarding. Answering viewer expectations still outweighs pro-social goals in the United States. In many ways, gender equity in the United States is defined as integrating the masculine stereotype into the feminine stereotype. Reconfiguring gender into a palate of behavior choices for men and women is much more complicated.

MAGAZINES FOR TEENAGERS

In 1981 researcher Cheris Kramarae published an account of the differences in teen magazines written for one sex or the other. Many of the differences she found are still in evidence. Males' magazines, like *Popular Mechanics*, *Hot Rod*, and computer game guides give how-to information on building vehicles and electronic equipment. They contain no information or advice about interpersonal communication. For example, the July 1995 *GamePro* offers in its table of contents an array of computer game instructions with descriptors like "On location with new PlayStation developer 47-Tek, plus 92 PlayStation games and counting!" or "This new GamePro series explains how games are made and takes you behind the scenes to meet the people who make them" under the article titled: "The GameMakers: Meet the Talent Behind the Titles."[37] The magazine uses black pages and dark colors; on the cover is Judge Dredd, dressed in a shiny black space suit with gold epaulets, and poised with a space gun to shoot a shadowy enemy superimposed behind him. The red-lettered caption reads: "HE IS THE LAW!" These same black, sinister images appear in *Batman Forever*, a comic book adaptation of the Batman film. Male images throughout the magazine depict physically strong, magical male figures battling disfigured, villainous male creatures. Females are presented with long, flowing hair and cleavage; they often are scantily dressed. The magazine is printed on black pages, emphasizing the violent scenes of males injecting females with syringes, blasting each other with torches, threatening women with knives, attacking each other with chains, and pursuing women who have frightened looks on their faces.[38]

The magazines written for teenage females, such as *Teen* and *Seventeen*, concentrate on appearance and relationships, with how-to articles on applying makeup and winning attractive males as dates. Kramarae's observations and descriptions of the foci of these magazines remain valid. In the August 1995 *Teen*, girls were instructed in a thirteen-page article about "100 Best Back-to-School Trends" that included "Coed classics that'll take you to the head of the class," "Measure up in the cutest skirts around," and "Pick a study partner . . . the subject is style!"[39] The magazine not only teaches girls that clothes, grooming, and style are the measure of excellence, but the themes indicate that females should "study" these topics to achieve personal success and status. Both *Teen* and *Seventeen* lead their tables of contents with the fashion and beauty segment. The August 1995 *Seventeen* included articles that dealt with issues like "help for nail-biters, [and] making lip gloss last," "seven straight-from-the-runway ideas" for hair, and "classroom cool: preppy, punky, sporty, or mod? Mix 'em up for maximum results."[40]

Cosmopolitan, one of the top-selling magazines, represents the myriad women's publications that blatantly embrace sex stereotypes. While it appears to be a magazine for women, it is read largely by teenage females. Familiar covers feature models with flawless skin, usually prominently displaying cleavage in the middle or upper half of the cover. Examples of articles include "Acts of Courage for Mousy Girls Can Make *WONDERFUL* Things Happen," "Why *POWERFUL MEN* Are Superstars in the Bedroom," and "10 Ways to Win Him—Without Losing Yourself." Kramarae made the point that females are being taught by their own magazines that femininity means beauty and skill in heterosexual intimacy, while males are being taught by their magazines that skills working with tools, machines, and technology represent masculinity.[41] Thus, two separate communication cultures are reinforced, and the gap between the sexes' views of the world and of themselves widens as they read their separate magazines.

ADULT MAGAZINES

Over the last thirty years, women's magazines have decreased the presentations of women as mothers, wives, and homemakers and increased articles dealing with social and political issues.[42] Nevertheless, photographs of women's faces, both on magazine covers and in advertisements within the magazine, conform to sex-role stereotypes.[43] Smiling women wearing appropriate makeup and current hair styles dominate both advertisements and feature pictures. Even fitness magazines entreat women not to overdevelop their hips or exercise in ways that reduce their busts. Themes in mainstream magazines still endorse the traditional stereotypes about women. *Ladies Home Journal, Redbook, McCalls,* and *Good Housekeeping* (which boasts 28 million readers monthly) frequently include articles such as "Lose 10 Years in 5 Minutes," "The Fashion That Led to Passion," "Flatten Your Tummy: 5 Superfast Exercises," "Look Younger at 30,

40, 50," "The Most Important 4 Minutes in Your Marriage," and "The Best of Summer: 27 Fast, Fresh Recipes—From Salads to Shortcake." The magazines display advertisements for food, cleaning products, feminine hygiene products, collectables, and beauty products.

Men's magazines, like those for male teens, are designed around cars, guns, hunting, sports, and woodworking. Magazines such as *Gentlemen's Quarterly (GQ)*, *Esquire*, and *Playboy* represent those aimed at more general audiences. These magazines feature longer, more dense feature articles and often include several works of fiction. Unlike the women's magazines that lead their tables of contents with personal grooming, recent issues of these magazines led with feature stories about the Los Angeles County high-crime area, the presidential bid of Lamar Alexander, features about Mickey Rourke and Andy Garcia, and several specials about militia groups in the United States.

In the fashion department, the target of the dress message differs from that of the women's magazines. In women's magazines, females are encouraged to dress for "their men." *GQ* asks if the reader is worried about how the boss will react to fashion choices and whether the change of seasons affects comfort.[44] *Esquire* explains that "Designer Miuccia Prada goes beyond her women's accessories to create simple yet luxurious men's wear with an industrial edge."[45] The only other fashion article leads this way: "Physical Attraction. Forget the baggy shorts and stretched-out T-shirt. Why not look as good on the Nautilus as you do at the office? Chic workout wear with a 1930s twist that lets you sweat in style."[46] Other topics treated in men's magazines include money, travel, sports, politics, and music. Advertisements, which are fewer and less intrusive on the articles, feature liquor, automobiles and trucks, cigarettes, clothes, and shoes.

BEAUTY CONTESTS AND PIN-UP CALENDARS

Beauty contests and calendars with scantily dressed females have long been popular with many men and sources of complaints by many women. Each year, *Sports Illustrated* publishes a special issue in January that has come to be known as the "swimsuit" issue because it features women in scant swimsuits in provocative poses. *SI* uses the issue in appeals for new readers. From the standpoint of the male viewers, the beautiful female body is to be admired. To the women offended by such calendars, focus on the female body alone implies that women exist primarily for their sexual value to men. In addition, women object to the dangerous standards projected in these images, where air brushing and touch-up techniques create flawless texture and artificial color. Debates about photographed bodies have become more bitter as more nudity and more overt and violent sexual behavior have been depicted in "adult" films and magazines.

The same debates about the use and abuse of presentations of the female body has generated controversy over beauty contests for girls and women. As an example, the Miss America Organization announced that viewers of the 1995 pageant would decide by call-in vote whether or not contestants would compete in swimsuits. One newspaper headline announcing the story made clear the contest was a sporting event: "Will Miss America Suit Up?" While the plan appeared to be a response to complaints about having women compete to see who had the best body, it also increased viewer interest in the pageant which had in recent years lost the attention it once enjoyed. Viewers voted during the pageant; many people watched the event both to vote and to see the outcome of the vote (the swimsuits "won"). In addition, organizers profited from the calls, which cost callers 50 cents a minute.[47]

Messages about men's appearance are increasingly visible in the national media market as well. All-male calendars usually feature men who look between 20 and 30 years of age. The men may be fully clothed (in open-collared sport shirts), or in various stages of undress. Usually the models have attractive features, a clear-eyed gaze toward the camera, and smooth, though not slick, hairstyles. Nowhere on the calendars are the men identified as individuals. The calendars treat the men in much the same ways as makeup commercials do women: models who are visually appealing, implicitly sexual, but in no way individual. Again a reversal in presentation of the sexes has occurred, not because a calendar company has decided to make a statement about sex equity, but simply to reach the market of female buyers of wall calendars.

ADVERTISEMENTS AND COMMERCIALS: GENDER TEACHING

Advertisers attempt to respond to audiences' current interests and attitudes so that audiences will be attentive to the sales pitch for a product or service. We may try to avoid commercial messages as much as possible, but a typical receiver sees or hears millions of commercials during a lifetime. Apart from the incidental learning of new information we may experience from watching commercials over a period of time—for example, what is NutraSweet?—commercial messages are subtle indicators of the interpersonal communication norms of the time. Humorous commercials often carry to extremes the typical messages of daily life. More serious commercials use slight twists on common patterns of talk so that they will be remembered long enough to affect buying attitudes.

Some of the most telling commercials in the media are those written by individuals for "Personals" columns. A popular feature in newspapers across the country, men and women write descriptions of themselves and descriptions of their preferred mate; couples meet and sometimes develop extended relationships from these columns. However, a study that examined mostly Caucasian, heterosexual men and women in the United States discovered that writers described their physical selves in ways more typical of sexual stereotypes than in keeping with characteristics representative of the general population. In addition, advertisement writers described stereotypes in their partner preferences. Men looked for women five years younger, fit, petite, or tall. Women looked for men three years older, tall, fit, and athletic.[48]

Descriptions written in these columns coincide with general depictions of men and women in television commercials, where sex-role stereotyping occurs pervasively but more often during daytime programming.[49] Some researchers indicate that advertisements during the daytime target the female audience while advertisements during prime time target male audiences. The portrayal of gender differs for the time of day and the sex of the target audience.[50] Male voice-overs dominate television commercials during prime time. Although the commercial might show a woman mopping her kitchen floor, the voice-over announcer describing the product most often is male. Men are portrayed in three times as many occupations as women; women are not seen outside the home as often as men.[51] Even in children's commercials, more boys than girls are featured and boys are shown outside the home more often.[52] Male characters appear more often in advertisements during sporting events and males more often speak in those advertisements. In what some might consider a positive finding, the appearance of scantily-dressed women in advertising during Sunday football was no more frequent than during advertising on regular, prime time weekdays.[53]

This use of bodies teaches viewers how to view, what to view, and how to value people's bodies. Like print or advertisements, television commercials show women's bodies more than men's and men's faces more than their bodies.[54] Body images—particularly women's bodies—are used to promote sales; the display of sexual symbolism sells products. One researcher discovered that the use of sexual symbolism in liquor advertisements increased the likelihood viewers would buy the product.[55] Women's perceptions of their own bodies can be affected even with short episodes of viewing female bodies in these ways.[56] When women see female bodies repeatedly used to sell liquor or attract attention to an automobile, they may learn to develop negative images of themselves and their own bodies.

The media teach gender stereotypes that emerge in personal columns and depictions of physical bodies; media advertising also presents (and therefore teaches) clear sex roles that are firmly fixed in viewers' minds. Even viewers with considerably different ideologies (conservatives and nonconservatives alike) seem to interpret in similar ways the sex roles depicted by television advertising. Viewers know clearly what roles the media teaches each sex to fulfill.[57] Media adherence to stereotpyical roles appears to be established not only in the United States, but in England, Australia, and even more firmly entrenched in Italy.[58]

Advertisements also teach associations between gender and status. One group of researchers examined viewers' reactions to both men and women in high-status positions on television. Viewers interpreted both male and female television characters in high-status roles as rational, independent, dominant, ambitious, and possessing leadership qualities. Characters in low-status roles were assessed as followers who were emotional, dependent, submissive, content.[59] The researchers drew the conclusion that sex inequity had emerged from the consistent assignment of females to subordinate or low-status positions. Whether we derived those characteristics from gender roles or derived gender assessments from those characteristics is not clear.

Feminists may be more sensitive than the general population to the sex typing of females in advertisements. As advertisers have responded to feminist criticism, the response often has been concerned with business and profit rather than sex equity; advertisers are warned to study carefully the demographics of female audiences to determine how to represent gender within the commercial. The message reads, "Advertise to the tastes and interests of your audience."[60] An unfortunate finding of one research team is that young females seem more aware than young males of publicly portrayed images, and these young women seem more responsive to advertising.[61]

WOMEN AND MEN IN FILMS

Movies produced for theatres, television, and home viewing share an emphasis on gender stereotypes as a major theme. In earlier decades of this century, strong women were at times major characters in film, but by the 1970s movie plots focused on male-male camaraderie and female characters were marginal or absent.[62] In the 1980s a renewed interest developed in women characters in films.

One film that has been noted for portraying both individual grit and love among women was an Academy Award nominee in 1986 for Best Picture of the Year. *The Color Purple*, based on the novel by Alice Walker, depicted two black sisters who had been subjected to incest, beatings, and verbal abuse as children and teenagers. One of the two, Celie, is able to survive a long separation from her sister through the loving support of other women. Almost as interesting as the film itself is the criticism heaped on it by several black male columnists, who charged that the film was racist both for portraying black males as villains and for suggesting that racism was not a major problem for blacks in the South. The critiques ignored the fact that Sophia, one of four central women in the film, was beaten and separated from her family for years simply because she had said to a white woman, "Hell, no!" when asked if she'd like to work as a servant. The black male critics never referred to that scene, nor to the poverty in which most of the blacks were shown. Most notably, these critics failed to mention that the film was not really about men but about four black women— women seen as interesting and strong human beings. Each of the four distinct women in *The Color Purple* face major problems, and each helps the other women to survive their struggles. The spirit of community among the four black women is so vivid that it suggests that the human spirit can rise even in the middle of a racist, sexist environment.

The tone in that film was similar to several others which have followed in the last decade: *Thelma and Louise*, *Steel Magnolias*, *Working Girl*, *Waiting to Exhale*, and *Fried Green Tomatoes*. Based on a novel by Amy Tan, *The Joy Luck Club* told the generational story of four women, their mothers, and their mothers' mothers as they experienced life in China and the United States. Even the role of the main character in *Silence of the Lambs* represented a change in perspective about how females appear on film.

When Harry Met Sally and *Singles* provided a look at heterosexual relationship development in Caucasian couples. Discussion about the impact of sex on cross-sex friendship, the gender expectations of each sex during and after sexual intercourse, and the nature of love provided an explicit dialogue that often occurs implicitly in real-life experiences. Like *Annie Hall* of years earlier, these movies attempted to uncover some of the unspoken cultural presumptions about males and females together both in friendships and partnered relationships.[63] They differed significantly from other courtship hits, like

While You Were Sleeping, Bed of Roses, or *A Walk in the Clouds,* all of which depict the more stereotpyical romance scenario.

A few films have presented a changed or at least less rigid perspective about male roles. *Forrest Gump* offered a positive male character who was slow-witted, emotional, and deeply appreciative of relationships. In *Dead Poet's Society,* Robin Williams plays a professor who tries to teach poetry and art to young boys in the midst of a highly structured, rule-bound private school setting. *Dances With Wolves* presented the story of a soldier who deserted his regiment to pursue peace. *Philadelphia* told the poignant story of a man suffering from AIDS in the midst of a male-dominated corporation. Sometimes, the male leads donned female roles; *Mrs. Doubtfire* featured realistic makeup and costuming to transform Robin Williams into a matronly housekeeper. One film, *Junior,* even promoted a story about a male (Arnold Schwartzenegger) pregnancy.

However, sex stereotypes remain the more common way for males and females to be presented. The successful Disney film, *The Lion King,* produced not only stereotypical sex role models, but generated myriad products to continually remind children about the film: lunch boxes, posters, pencils, toys, animal figures, and collector tins. The graphic, physical combat featured in that animated film paled in comparison to the level of violence produced in many movies in which the stereotypical male character dominates. Perhaps in response to the blurring of sex roles by other films, males' violence in films continues to be explicit, pervasive, and habitual. As special effects improve, the level and explicitness of the violence increases. *Under Siege, Under Siege II,* and *Universal Soldier* represent the viciousness and ruthlessness of the male persona. Other films like the *Die Hard* and *Lethal Weapon* series promote images of males as superhero types: afraid of nothing, resourceful, witty, physically able to endure any pain, ruthless, and violent. Sylvestor Stallone's *Judge Dredd,* (hailed by critics as a movie to dread), played to a consistently large adult audience that continues to support male violence at an increasingly higher level. *Judge Dredd* gives us a look at the future, one with no hope and inconsequential female characters. Dredd is characterized as a law officer, jury, and prosecutor, rolled into one, who displays no emotion and is feared by all. Diane Lane, cast as a peer judge but without the mega-persona of Dredd, engages in the stereotypical task of trying to pry emotions out of Stallone. Violence in the media—and particularly violence linked to males—is one of the significant problems regarding sex and gender and communication— an issue discussed further in the concluding chapter.

The danger in abbreviated presentations of explicit violence and complex problems is that receivers will come away with misinformation or with the wrong impression that social, psychological, or medical problems can be solved within 100 minutes and that overcoming these problems requires a high level of violence. Many of the violent film images are designed to appeal to young boys and young men.[64] According to the catalyst theory of media effects on receivers, the great majority of watchers would not take the explicit violent action as a model to imitate; however, a person who is already unstable or troubled may look at a media model and decide to do the same thing.[65] The advisability of creating violence in films, even films like *Pulp Fiction*, for example, is unclear. Was the violent rape scene in *The Accused* informative and educational or exemplary? No firm consensus has been reached about how to predict when a media image, particularly a violent image, will lead a person to act out that violence directly. As we noted earlier, however, the existing research shows a strong correlation between the repeated viewing of televised violence and acts of violence by young viewers.[66]

THE MEDIATED SELF AS AN OBJECT

One disturbing result of the breadth and availability of gender messages in the visual media is a widespread tendency among heavy media consumers to act as if women (and sometimes men) are objects to be marketed or judged by others rather than as individual human beings. People have always measured themselves against ideals and felt happy or sad based on their own evaluations. However, it is now almost impossible to avoid images of media celebrities—people with apparently perfect (airbrushed) bodies and exciting lives—presented to us on magazine covers, in television commercials, in movie posters, or on record album covers.

What happens to men and women surrounded by human symbols of perfection? For one thing, they are less able to rationalize that visual ideals are possible only in artists' and poets' fantasies. They are faced with what appear to be straightforward photographs of people who are without blemish, apparently happy, and in situations that imply pleasure and intimacy. For men, images of young women always are available on the covers of *Playboy, Penthouse,* or *Hustler* as well as most women's magazines such as *Cosmopolitan* and *Self.* For women, television heroes abound, particularly on shows like *Beverly*

Hills 90210, Melrose Place, ER, or even *Friends.* The visual images in these cases are usually young, usually white, and nearly always sexual. Such images can addict a teenage girl to thinness and a male to bodybuilding. Kenneth Burke's phrase "rotten with perfection" becomes ironically fitting when applied to a young woman who obsesses over gaining weight. Visual images of human perfection, for both women and men, are difficult to escape and exhausting to emulate.

The driving force of the media to present these images is clear: the images generate money. Although we may feel comfortable pointing a finger at media moguls condemning their programming and filming choices, we also must recognize our individual contributions to these sex stereotypes. The media gain wealth by making images of these ideals; what do each of us gain from reproducing them? Why do we *want* to look like these ideals? Why do we acquiesce to social norms of "beauty" and "strength," often even refining and fortifying those norms? Why are we not satisfied with our own individuality and sense of self? In what ways does our communication with one another reinforce sex and gender stereotypes that ultimately restrict, contain, and sometimes control us? Answers to these questions need to inform our choices with regard to interpersonal communication and its effects. Time and energy can be spent rethinking our own reasons for maintaining old patterns. That kind of critical thinking can lead us to redesign our individual communication priorities to eradicate negative effects of sex and gender stereotyping.

MEDIA CHANGES IN PROGRESS

A number of interesting changes have been occurring in the treatment of gender roles and in the visibility of the sexes in the mass media. Books, newspapers, magazines, and television all have increased their coverage of gender issues. Given this increase of information, the level of public awareness about gender ideals and restrictions for both sexes may rise higher than ever before. At the same time, the sexual tease in magazines, billboards, television advertising, and popular music lyrics is more explicit and more confrontational toward receivers than ever before. Advertisers and music video producers invite viewers to interpret their messages as a mixture of eroticism and aggression.[67] Necklines and leglines on female models' swimsuits begin to approach each other, and a male model in a glossy advertising

STYLISH. RESPONSIVE. FUN.
IF IT WERE A MAN YOU'D MARRY IT.

Let's face it, there are a lot of similarities when it comes to choosing a car and a mate.

While this may seem surprising to some, even more surprising is that in today's society

the chances for a lasting relationship just may be greater with a car.

Especially if that car is the new Paseo. Toyota's legendary reputation for reliability,

the safety of dual air bags, responsive handling and eye-catching style make Paseo fun

to be with whether you're on a date or just going to the store.

Drive the new Paseo. Fall in love. Your future awaits — down the road.

TOYOTA PASEO
I love what you do for me

brochure for a major department store is shown with a forefinger pulling down his American Express-printed beach towel, as if promising that he might disrobe completely at any moment with the right partner. These and other media messages imply, especially with their nonverbal cues, that sex not only sells, it addicts the receiver, so that advertisers need simply feed the addiction with visual messages in order to arouse the audience's instinct to buy.

Several recent media events add interesting postscripts to the discussion of media in this chapter. For example, the Soviet government named two new parks for the two American women who were on the *Challenger* flight that ended in a tragic explosion on January 28, 1986. The decision to name the parks for Christa McAuliffe and Judith Resnick was reported in a brief story in American daily newspapers. No public response to this Soviet action was made by American officials.

The former "women's pages" in newspapers are now called by names like Lifestyle, Tempo, and Living, all sexually neutral terms, and the fashion sections of these pages sometimes carry prominent articles about clothing for men. Attractiveness to the other sex is now treated as worthy of men's interest as well as of women's, though women are still the primary audience for clothing advertisements.

Magazine and television advertisements often show prepared foods or cleaning products without a human figure in the picture. This exclusion allows both male and female receivers to imagine themselves as users of the products rather than specifying that the product is within one sex's "job." Although the reason for this focus may be economic (to increase the buying public for a product), the result is a slightly smaller number of advertising messages that portray women as tied to the house, as silly creatures needing Mr. Clean to rescue them, or as "natural experts" informing men that women alone know how to remove "ugly toilet bowl scum."

Although sports are still considered more a male than a female interest, advertisers are now buying commercial time for sports events based on their projections of female as well as male audiences. This practice generates less revenue from football and basketball games (other than the national championships) because both beer and automobile commercial sponsors also attempt to reach female audiences by buying time on other types of programming competing with the most expensive sporting events. Interestingly, the 1996 summer Olympics reflected the increasing attempts to make sporting events appealing to women. NBC broadcasts focused on gymnastics, swimming, diving, track and field. In addition, the network wove personal anecdotes and histories into an entertaining story surrounding the athletic event to hold viewer interest.

MEDIATED COMMUNICATION

Mediated communication is distinguished from mass media. Whereas mass media refers to those messages produced usually by a corporation or organization for a mass audience, mediated communication entails public messages produced and controlled by individuals. The message is mediated by technology. Using personal computers to send e-mail or communicate across the Internet, leaving a message on an answering machine, or sending a fax are all examples of mediated communication. Ways to mediate communication have increased dramatically in the past decade. Consider your use of the following:

> cordless telephone
> answering machine
> facsimile machine
> personal computer
> laser printer
> portable computers
> cellular telephone
> beeper

These technological developments produce a new means of communication that can function at public—and sometimes anonymous—levels; when we use their capacities to generate and respond to messages, we enact new ways to create and recreate gender. As we invent more technologies that travel with us—such as the cellular phone, the beeper, and the hand-held micro-computer—we will accrue the consequences of continuous and ever-present mediated communication.

Some people predict that mediated communication will reroute our public and perhaps even our private talk back to orality (remember our discussion earlier about dramatic shifts in cultural patterns with the introduction of the printing press). Predictions are that mediated communication might generate a new shift away from formalized, written words in structured formats, to a more spontaneous, less guarded message pattern. Long, involved conversations over electronic bulletin boards may be the precursors to forms of public debate similar in some ways to the Greek forums. With the fast-changing face of technology, the future may bring small, portable communication devices capable of instant access to worldwide locations. These devices may become as familiar and widespread as telephones, televisions, or automobiles.

WOMEN AND MEN IN CYBERSPACE

Male themes and practices dominate the computer field.[68] Some experts argue that the greatest deterrent to females entering the computer industry are the organizational cultures that espouse masculine ideals. These ideals may be represented by organizational metaphors of battle and maleness.[69] Taking a cultural perspective, basic language use presents analogies and images more conducive to male cultures than female ones. Some might argue that the feminine culture would not have selected "abort" as a principal command used to end a session. Other terms like "Gameboy" also fit better in the masculine culture. While some companies are attempting to design a "Gamegirl," their misreading of basic sex and gender issues is evident both in the obvious target of males with the first wave of computer games and the apparent attempt to co-opt masculine interests into feminine ones as a way to attract girls. Confusion regarding the Gameboy and Gamegirl reflects issues of differences between males and females with regard to mediated communication. Sex-related differences about learning and using computers occur at all educational levels, although why they occur and what consequences may accrue are not clear.[70] Men seem to use computers to get ahead; women use them to catch up and survive in the workplace.[71] Some researchers suggest women will transform computers just as they did the telephone. Initially identified as a technology for the workplace, women reinvented the telephone as a necessity in every home.[72] At present, however, women are less involved with computers than men are.

Ironically, women and women's issues are intricately connected with computers.[73] Early pioneers in the development of computers were women, including Ada Byron Lovelace and Grace Murray Hopper. Lovelace, credited with being the world's first computer programmer, developed programming basics as early as 1846.[74] Now, computers are routinely used in ways that benefit women. For example, they predict and record information about women's health issues, such as breast cancer.[75]

Aside from the question of organizational structure, reasons women are not as attracted to computers as men is not yet clear. This is not to say no women use computers with the same enthusiasm exhibited in general by men. In some cases, women seem to adopt or access computers more readily than men do.[76] But those cases do not represent the norm; more often, girls and women do not engage in computer activities.

Recent discussions over the Internet have engaged the debate about women and men together in cyberspace. Men far outnumber women on the Internet; estimated ratios vary from 3:1 to 9:1. Women complain that if they allow their sex to be known (for example, by giving themselves female names), they are harassed, cybernetically stalked, or treated poorly.

The anonymous nature of communication in cyberspace provides great latitude in interpersonal encounters. Whereas face-to-face communication provides nonverbal cues and an amount of culpability owing to the personal identification through sight, cyberspace communication occurs largely through keyboard entries. Participants in the MUD (Multi-User Dimension) activity, for example, assign themselves odd and bizarre names as they enter "rooms" where they have "conversations" with real people they have never met from places unknown. Possibilities abound for communication that does not conform to usual cultural mores, expectations, and "rules." Some males log on to these kinds of activities using female names in efforts to search out females online.

This anonymity lends itself to the overtly pornographic communications that plague cyberspace. Unlike mass media forms that can be recognized by form and controlled in some ways, pornography over the Internet can be accessed by any computer user. In addition, individuals responding to requests on electronic bulletin boards or even sending individual electronic mail messages can spontaneously create pornographic or violent messages. The quality of anonymity in mediated communication has emerged as a central feature to be addressed. Just as people abuse answering machines to leave rude or obscene messages, so does the Internet provide latitude for new kinds of communication problems.

These concerns have led to attempted legislative actions to limit and confine Internet access and content. To date, those attempts have been unsuccessful. Arguments against such censure cite free speech rights. Children's ability to access the Internet create new considerations not included during historical debates about censorship of literature and art. The advent of mediated communication and its use by children presents challenging policy issues regarding sex, gender, and communication.

Problems caused by anonymity are not the only characteristics that seem unappealing to females. The association of computers with science and math also form bases many females find unattractive.[77] In addition, girls report being bored with computer games that strongly attract boys. While boys may respond generally in more lively ways than girls—as boys do to video media, popular music, and television[78]—the plots of the games may be what attract boys and bore girls. Many of the computer games have as their central plot lines the "man rescues woman" theme. Super Mario Brothers, one of the original Nintendo and Super Nintendo games with later Gameboy and computer versions, required the player to survive multiple layers of challenges—often violent challenges presented by monsters throwing large objects at the player or bomb-like objects that explode on the player—before rescuing the princess at the end of the game. Most computer games (Nintendo, Super Nintendo, and the Sega series) feature violent weaponry and require the player to shoot other players or other creatures to accomplish the goal. Some games use realistic pictures and sound to enhance the violence. These brutal, active games may be consumed by males who can be as young as three or four although the users are predominantly preadolescents and adolescents.

Although little effort has been made to curb the violence and male stereotyping in computer games, education experts and programming designers have made significant efforts to address females' disinterest in and even rejection of computer games, personal computers, and computer activities.[79] The paid work force is rapidly moving away from physically demanding services that historically have excluded women because of their lack of physical size and strength; it is moving toward services based on intellect and computer skill where the possibility for sex equity in jobs could be more plausible. Yet boys outnumber girls in computer science classes. When girls are required to enroll, they fare as well as boys. However, girls do not frequent the computer labs after school and during free time the way boys do. Nor are they as likely to own or use a home computer.[80] Female participation in cyberspace does not appear to be growing at the pace of male participation.

CONCLUSION

The influence of mass media and mediated communication on stereotypes and images of sex and gender in the United States culture is dramatic. With the television and computer able to reach inside families—and indeed, inside the minds of children—the responsibility is critical to assess sex and gender messages sent by these means. Children often are more attuned than adults to the rapid evolution of technology. The dazzling variety of products and capabilities may deflect our attention from the consequential perceptions of sex and gender being promoted. On the other hand, the advent of these technologies also offers unexplored possibilities for generating equitable and psychologically healthy ideals for both women and men.

QUESTIONS FOR DISCUSSION

1. Gender, race, class, and age have all been treated selectively by mass media. Consider your current images of Hispanic, Asian, or African-American women over 50, and think about where these images originated. Consider East European or Asian men over 70 or Hispanic men and women in their teens. Identify specific sources in the media for these images.

2. Interpret the phrase "action movie." What does the phrase imply about dramas that would be excluded from such a category?

3. Survey your friends about their uses of computers or the Internet. Find out how people got started using their computer and for what reason. Ask them how much time they spend computing or sending e-mail and what they enjoy/don't like most about it.

4. Subliminal seduction theorists say that you are influenced to buy through indirect appeals to your sexual needs. When and how do you believe that your buying decisions, including clothing, have been influenced by sexuality?

CASES FOR ANALYSIS

CASE 9.1   RADIO TAGS

An early morning radio host for a music show has a calm, resonant speaking voice which is easy to listen to. He likes to talk to the people in his radio audience as if they were present and able to converse with him. One of his frequent techniques is to ask a question by making a statement first and following it with a brief tag. He often goes on to make a response to his own words. For example, one morning he played a male chorus from Victor Herbert's "Vagabond King," and at the end of the chorus said, "Well, that really celebrates virility, doesn't it?" Later in the same broadcast he read the rainy weather report and followed it with the words, "This would have been a great day to stay in bed, wouldn't it?"

1. The language pattern shown here has been called a "tag question" by linguist Robin Lakoff, who calls it an example of powerless feminine speech. Do you see it as powerless? As feminine? Why or why not?

2. How do you react to questions being asked by a person you cannot respond to face to face? Does it help or hurt your enjoyment of a media message?

3. What if a woman were using the same lines quoted above?

4. Are there features that to you characterize "masculine," "feminine," or "androgynous" vocal styles in radio or television personalities?

5. Discuss the style of a radio talk-show host. What masculine features do you notice? Feminine ones?

CASE 9.2 SEXIST LANGUAGE

Recently, an undergraduate in a gender class previewed four episodes of *The John Larroquette Show*. She reported to the class that she observed no instances of sexist language. Several students in the class agreed and asserted that the media presents some sexist images, but little sexist language is used because of the PC (Politically Correct) movement.

1. Do you agree that the media presents little sexist language? What would you define as sexist language?

2. How does the PC mandate affect gender stereotypes or people's gendered behaviors?

3. Think about a show you watch on a regular basis. Are you aware of the specific language used there? Can you assess the language as sexist or nonsexist?

4. Think of a show you believe to be particularly nonsexist. What about the show indicates its nonbiased presentation? Is this show different from others you can name? If so, how?

5. When you watch a show, are you aware of the level of sexist or nonsexist messages presented during the commercial breaks? Do

you talk about these issues when you watch the commercials? How do you and others respond?

CASE 9.3   COMPUTER DATING

A caller to a radio talk show gave this account of his experiences with computer dating. "I have moved three times in the last few years," he explained, "so I have used the Internet and e-mail to meet new people wherever I moved. In all three cases, I met someone in cyberspace with whom I arranged a blind date. In all three cases, the women turned out to be ugly and definitely not my type. I'm never going to try dating by computer again."

1. What advantages for interpersonal relationships can you see as emerging from communication through e-mail or the Internet? Have you met people this way? What do you learn about them through computing?

2. Why do you think this person had such similar experiences each time he arranged his blind dates? What expectations about sex do you think were operating in this story? What significance do you see to the fact that he was telling his story on a radio talk show?

3. What are the implications of anonymity on the Internet? What advantages might it present? Disadvantages? Do you think it advantages or disadvantages one sex or the other? How could disadvantages be avoided?

4. How might interpersonal conversations of this kind affect international or global relations among people? Since the Internet is worldwide and growing constantly, what might you predict for future interpersonal relationships between people of different cultures?

NOTES

[1] Parts of this summary are derived from Teri and Michael Gamble, *Introducing Mass Communication* (New York: McGraw-Hill, 1986).

[2] Penny Belknap and Wilbert M. Leonard, II, "A Conceptual Replication and Extension of Erving Goffman's Study of Gender Advertisements." *Sex Roles* 25, 3/4 (1991): 103–18.

[3] Marshall McLuhan, *The Medium Is The Message* (New York: Random House, 1968), and *Understanding Media* (New York: Signet Books, 1964).

[4] Bryan Key Wilson, *Subliminal Seduction* (Englewood Cliffs, NJ: Prentice-Hall, 1973).

[5] Belknap and Leonard, op cit.

[6] Allan Paivio, "On Exploring Visual Knowledge," in *Visual Learning, Thinking, and Communication*, ed. B. S. Randhawa and W. E. Coffman (New York: Academic Press, 1978), pp. 113–31.

[7] Samuel Becker, "Visual Stimuli and the Construction of Meaning," in *Visual Learning, Thinking, and Communication*, ed. Randhawa and Coffman (New York: Academic Press, 1978).

[8] Erving Goffman, *Gender Advertisements* (New York: Harper Colophon Books, 1979).

[9] Belknap and Leonard, op cit.; Amy G. Halberstadt and Martha B. Saitta, "Gender, Nonverbal Behavior, and Perceived Dominance: A Test of the Theory," *Journal of Personality and Social Psychology* 53, 2 (1987): 257–72.

[10] Denis McQuail, *Mass Communication Theory: An Introduction* (London: Sage Publications, 1983).

[11] Jerry Mander, *Four Arguments for the Elimination of Television* (New York: Morrow, 1978), esp. argument three.

[12] Ibid.

[13] National Institute of Mental Health Report, *Television and Behavior; Volume 1*, Summary Report (Washington, D.C.: Department of Health and Human Services, 1982), p. 6.

[14] Donna Allen, "FCC Needs Proof of the Obvious: Women Add Diversity to Programming," *Media Report to Women* 23, 1 (Winter 1995): 12, 11.

[15] J. David Kennamer, "Gender Differences in Attitude Strength, Role of News Media and Cognitions," *Journalism Quarterly* 63 (1986): 782–88, 833.

[16] Bonnie Miller Rubin, "Fears for Tears," *Chicago Tribune* (January 28, 1996), Section 13, pp. 1, 5.

[17] Kim Fridkin Kahn, "Does Gender Make a Difference? An Experimental Examination of Sex Stereotypes and Press Patterns in Statewide Campaigns," *American Journal of Political Science* 38, 1 (February 1994): 162–95; Kim Fridkin Kahn, "Does Being Male Help? An Investigation of the Effects of Candidate Gender and Campaign Coverage on Evaluations of the U.S. Senate Candidates," *Journal of Politics* 54, 2 (May 1992): 497–517.

[18] Jennifer Mangan, "Fine Tuning: Diversity and Realistic Roles Sought for Girls on Television," *Chicago Tribune* (May 26, 1996): section 13, p. 1.

[19] This fits the magic phase that is said to occur early in a child's development. See a summary of Jean Piaget's concept of the magic phase in Ruth Beard, *Piaget's Development Psychology* (New York: Mentor Books, 1969).

[20] The powerful, white male model is even emulated by black boys. See Carolyn A. Stroman, "Television Viewing and Self-Concept among Black Children," *Journal of Broadcasting & Electronic Media* 30, 1 (Winter 1986): 87–93.

[21] From Hamilton Comics, "Sabens' Mighty Morphin Power Rangers" No. 2 (of a four-issue series) July 1995, published monthly by The Bruce Hamilton Company, Prescott, AZ under the Gladstone imprint, and Saban Entertainment, Inc. & Saban International N.V.

[22] David R. Rolandelli, "Gender Role Portrayal Analysis of Children's Television Programming in Japan," *Human Relations* 44, 12 (1991): 1273–98.

[23] "Sabens' Mighty Morphin Power Rangers," op cit.

[24] Ibid.

[25] Information drawn from Rita Sommers-Flanagan, John Sommers-Flanagan, and Britta Davis, "What's Happening on Music Television? A Gender Role Content Analysis," *Sex Roles* 28, 11/12 (1993): 745–53; A. Huston, E. Donnerstein, H. Fairchild, N. Feshback, P. Katz, J. Murray, E. Rivenstein, B. Wilcox, and D. Zuckerman, *Big World, Small Screen* (Lincoln: University of Nebraska Press, 1992); Steven A. Seidman, "An Investigation of Sex-Role Stereotyping in Music Videos," *Journal of Broadcasting & Electronic Media* (Spring 1992): 209–16; Nancy Signorielli, Douglas McLeod, and Elaine Healy, "Gender Stereotypes in MTV Commercials: The Beat Goes On," *Journal of Broadcasting & Electronic Media* (Winter 1994): 91–101.

[26] Zdenek Salzmann, "Portrayal of Gender Relations in Contemporary Czech Mass Media," *East European Quarterly* 23, 4 (January 1990): 399–407; Everett M. Rogers, Ankila S. Chandran, Jeffrey D. Robinson, and Thomas M. Hirata, "Television Promotion of Gender Equality in Society," paper presented at the Western States Communication Association, Albuquerque, New Mexico, February 1993.

[27] Gretchen Metzger, "Is a Blonde, Blonde?" *American Demographics* (November 1992): 51.

[28] Carol Gilligan, "Preface" to *In a Different Voice: Psychological Theory and Women's Development*, 2nd ed (Cambridge, MA: Harvard University Press, 1993).

[29] Sonia Livingstone, "Watching Talk: Gender and Engagement in the Viewing of Audience Discussion Programmes," *Media, Culture, & Society* 16 (1994): 429–47.

[30] Ibid.

[31] E. D. (Adie) Nelson and B. W. Robinson, "'Reality Talk' or 'Telling Tales'? The Social Construction of Sexual and Gender Deviance on a Television Talk Show," *Journal of Contemporary Ethnography* 23, 1 (April 1994): 51–78.

[32] Tamar Zemach and Akiba A. Cohen, "Perception of Gender Equality on Television and in Social Reality," *Journal of Broadcasting & Electronic Media* 30, 4 (Fall 1986): 527–444.

[33] Jennifer A. Renn and Sandra L. Calvert, "The Relation Between Gender Schemas and Adults' Recall of Stereotyped and Counterstereotyped Televised Information," *Sex Roles* 28, 7/8 (1993): 449–59.

[34] Azra S. Bhatia and Roger J. Desmond, "Emotion, Romantic Involvement, and Loneliness: Gender Differences Among Inner States and Choice of Entertainment," *Sex Roles* 28, 11/12 (1993): 655–65.

[35] For an historical review, see Mary Beth Haralovich, "Sitcoms and Suburbs: Positioning the 1950's Homemaker," *Quarterly Review of Film & Video* 11 (1989): 61–83.

[36] Rogers, Chandran, Robinson and Hirata, op cit.

[37] "The GameMakers: Meet the Talent Behind the Titles," *GamePro* (Infotainment World, July 1995): 6.

[38] Dennis O'Neil, Michal Dutkiewicz, and Scott Hanna with Adrienne Roy, *Batman Forever*, The Official Comic Adaptation of the Warner Bros. Motion Picture New York: DC Comics, 1995).

[39] *'Teen* (August 1995).

[40] Contents, *Seventeen* (August 1995).

[41] Cheris Kramarae, "Dreams for Teens," in *Women and Men Speaking* (Rowley, MA: Newbury House, 1981), pp. 82–89.

[42] Jack Demarest and Jeanette Garner, "The Representation of Women's Roles in Women's Magazines Over the Past 30 Years," *The Journal of Psychology* 126, 4, (1992): 357–69.

[43] David K. Dodd, Veronica Harcar, Barbara J. Foerch, and Heather T. Anderson, "Face-ism and Facial Expressions of Women in Magazine Photos," *The Psychological Record* 39 (1989): 325–31.

[44] *GQ* (August 1995).

[45] "On Fashion," *Esquire*, 124, 1 (August 1995): 107.

[46] Ibid.

[47] Associated Press, "Will Miss America Suit Up? You Decide," *Statesman Journal* (July 13, 1995): 1D.

[48] Arnold E. Andersen, Paul J. Woodward, Adela Spalder, and Marlene Koss, "Body Size and Shape Characteristics of Person ("In Search of") Ads," *International Journal of Eating Disorders* 14, 1 (1993): 111–16.

[49] Diana S. Rak and Linda M. McMullen, "Sex-Role Stereotyping in Television Commercials: A Verbal Response Mode and Content Analysis," *Canadian Journal of Behavioral Science* 19 (January 1987): 25–39.

[50] R. Stephen Craig, "The Effect of Television Day Part on Gender Portrayals in Television Commercials: A Content Analysis," *Sex Roles* 26, 5/6 (1992): 197–211.

[51] Lynn T. Lovdal, "Sex Role Messages in Television Commercials: An Update," *Sex Roles* 21, 11/12 (1989): 715–24.

[52] Lois J. Smith, "A Content Analysis of Gender Differences in Children's Advertising," *Journal of Broadcasting & Electronic Media* 38 (Summer 1994): 323–27.

[53] Daniel Riffe, Patricia C. Place, and Charles M. Mayo, "Game Time, Soap Time and Prime Time TV Ads: Treatment of Women in Sunday Football and Rest-of-Week Advertising," *Journalism Quarterly* 70, 2 (Summer 1993): 437–46.

[54] Christine C. Ijima Hall and Matthew J. Crum, "Women and 'Body-isms' in Television Beer Commercials," *Sex Roles* 31, 5/6 (1994): 329–37.

[55] Philip N. Myers, Jr., "The Elastic Body Image: The Effect of Television Advertising and Programming on Body Image Distortions in Young Women," *Journal of Communication* 42, 3 (Summer 1992): 108–33.

[56] William J. Ruth, "Effects of Freudian Sexual Symbolism in Advertising on Self-Reported Purchasing Tendencies: A Preliminary Intrabrand Analysis," *Psychological Reports* 67 (1990): 1207–10.

[57] Dennis J. A. Melville and Ian M. Cornish, "Conservatism and Gender in the Perception of Sex Roles in Television Advertisements," *Perceptual and Motor Skills* 77 (1993): 642.

[58] Carmela Mazzella, Kevin Durkin, Emma Cerini, and Paul Buralli, "Sex Role Stereotyping in Australian Television Advertisements," *Sex Roles* 26, 7/8 (1992:) 243–59.

[59] Florence L. Geis, Virginia Brown, Joyce Jennings, and Denise Corrado-Taylor, "Sex vs. Status in Sex-Associated Stereotypes," *Sex Roles* 11, 9/10 (1984): 771–85.

[60] John B. Ford and Michael S. LaTour, "Differing Reactions to Female Role Portrayals in Advertising," *Journal of Advertising Research* 33, 5 (September 1993): 43–52.

[61] Stephen J. Gould, "Gender Differences in Advertising Response and Self-Consciousness Variables," *Sex Roles* 16, 5/6 (1987): 215–25.

[62] For an historical look at ways women have been represented in film, see Michael Renov, "Advertising/Photojournalism/Cinema: the Shifting Rhetoric of Forties Female Representation," *Quarterly Review of Film & Video* 11 (1989) 1–21. For a review of gender and emotions in film, see Stanford M. Lyman, "Anhedonia: Gender and the Decline of Emotions in American Film, 1930–1988," *Sociological Inquiry* 60, 1 (February 1990): 1–19.

[63] For information about films, friendship, romance and the sexes, see Janet Sigal, Margaret Gibbs, Bonnie Adams, and Richard Derfler, "The Effect of Romantic and Nonromantic Films on Perception of Female Friendly and Seductive Behavior," *Sex Roles* 19, 9/10 (1988): 545–54.

[64] For an ethnographic study about adolescent males and film, see Melissa A. Milkie, "Social World Approach to Cultural Studies: Mass Media and Gender in the Adolescent Peer Group," *Journal of Contemporary Ethnography* 23, 3 (October 1994): 354–80.

[65] The theory has been developed by Norman Felsenthal in *Orientations to Mass Communication* (Chicago: Science Research Associates, 1976), and cited in Phillip Tompkins, *Communication as Action* (Belmont, CA: Wadsworth, 1982), chap. 9.

[66] National Institute of Mental Health Report, op cit.

[67] Barry Sherman and Joseph Dominick, "Violence and Sex in Music Videos: TV and Rock 'n Roll," *Journal of Communication* 36, 1 (Winter 1986): 79–93. The authors note that violence frequently is done by women in the videos they studied. Perhaps such violence serves as a fantasy outlet for fear and an imagined justification for aggression.

[68] Paul N. Edwards, "The Army and the Microworld: Computers and the Politics of Gender Identity," *Signs: Journal of Women in Culture and Society* 16, 1 (Autumn 1990): 102–27.

[69] Fiona Wilson, "Language, Technology, Gender, and Power," *Human Relations* 45, 9 (1992): 883–904.

[70] Pamela E. Kramer, "Mismeasuring Women: A Critique of Research on Computer Ability and Avoidance," *Signs: Journal of Women in Culture & Society* 16, 1 (Autumn 1990): 158–72.

[71] Jean Brunet, "Formal Versus Grass-Roots Training: Women, Work, and Computers," *Journal of Communication* 39, 3 (Summer 1989): 77–84.

[72] Sue Curry Jansen, "Gender and the Information Society: A Socially Structured Silence," *Journal of Communication* (Summer 1989) 196–214.

[73] Ruth Perry, "Women and Computers: An Introduction," *Signs: Journal of Women in Culture & Society* 16, 1 (Autumn 1990): 74–101.

[74] Chuck Beardsley, "The Lovelace Letter," *Mechanical Engineering* 113, 1 (January 1991): 4; Denis W. Gurer, "Pioneering Women in Computer Science," *Communications of the ACM* 38, 1 (Jan 1995): 45–54.

[75] Paul McCarthy, "Breakthroughs: A Crystal Ball for Cancer," *Health* 20, 6 (June 1988): 28.

[76] Lori A. Collins-Jarvis, "Gender Representation in an Electronic City Hall: Female Adoption of Santa Monica's PEN System," *Journal of Broadcasting & Electronic Media* 37, 1 (Winter 1993): 49–65; Susan Vernon-Gerstenfeld, "Serendipity? Are There Gender Differences in the Adoption of Computers? A Case Study," *Sex Roles: A Journal of Research* 21, 3/4 (August 1989): 161–73.

[77] For interesting reading about women and science and technology, see Cheris Kramarae, "Got to Go Myrtle, Technology's at the Door," In *Technology and Women's Voices: Keeping in Touch*, ed. Cheris Kramarae (New York: Routledge & Kegan Paul, 1988); Evelyn Fox Keller, *Reflections on Gender and Science*, (New Haven, CT: Yale University Press, 1985).

[78] Robert Kubey and Reed Larson. "The Use and Experience of the New Video Media Among Children and Young Adolescents," *Communication Research* 17, 1 (February 1990): 107–30.

[79] Yvonne Gebhardt, "Computer Materials: Breaking the Barriers," *Arithmetic Teacher* 38, 7 (March 1991): 56; Isabelle Bruder, "Equity for Girls Supported by Women's Action Alliance," *Electronic Learning* 8, 3 (November 1988): 18; Beatriz Chu Clewell, "The Prevalence and Nature of Mathematics, Science, and Computer Science Intervention Programs Serving Minority and Female Students in Grades Four Through Eight," *Equity & Excellence* 25, 2/4 (Winter 1992): 209–15; Ellen F. Mappen, "Guest Comment: Creating a Support System for Women in Science—Combining Co-curricular Programming and Student Life at Douglass College," *American Journal of Physics* 59, 12 (December 1991): 1065.

[80] Kubey and Larson, op cit.

Chapter 10

Contemporary Issues about Sex, Gender, and Communication

Alice B. Toklas recalls a conversation in which Gertrude Stein spoke her last words: "What is the answer?" Stein asked. Toklas was silent. "In that case," Stein continued, "what is the question?"[1] Whenever we confront difficult or complicated problems, we search for definitive, conclusive answers. You may realize by now that in issues of sex, gender, and communication, we do not find definitive, conclusive answers. Information in this book can inform readers, but it cannot provide "right" answers about what to do in certain situations; it cannot dispense step-by-step instructions about how to develop the "right" communication style. As is frequently the case with complex issues, becoming informed about sex and gender means learning to search out important questions more than it means finding absolute and unequivocal answers. Now that you have examined the research, considered different perspectives, and contemplated various communication practices, you may find the questions posed in the next section important ones to investigate.

CHAPTER OVERVIEW

In this chapter, we will consider three related sets of questions about sex, gender, and communication:

- What are the women's and men's movements? What prompted their emergence? What ideologies do each represent and how do they reflect or influence conversations between women and men?
- How is sexual violence—such as rape, incest, spousal abuse, child molestation, and aggressive pornography—related to interpersonal communication? Is this violence related to the rhetorical construction of gender? If so, in what ways?
- In each new generation, people make new presumptions about communication between men and women, presumptions based largely on the gender ideals touted by their cohort group. These presumptions create new and different challenges. What challenges persist in the United States as we navigate into a new century? How might some of those challenges be met?

At first glance, these questions may seem unrelated. As we engage them, however, we will find they are woven together in a tapestry of human identity and purpose. We will explore the questions, considering not only how to create a conscious focus on gender in human interaction but also how to generate conversation about these questions both at the personal and public levels. In addition, we will consider carefully the ethical implications for individuals, communities, and societies.

THE WOMEN'S MOVEMENT AND THE MEN'S MOVEMENT

THE WOMEN

The women's movement and the men's movement have very different origins, histories, and ideologies. The most recent women's movement—often referred to as the feminist movement—has been a major source of discourse for nearly 40 years. Its influence may be in part responsible for the advent of the most recent men's movement.

Although feminism and the feminist movement do not generate questions for all communicators, the feminist social movement begins this chapter because of its impact on the communication of both sexes.

A mistake people often make is assuming that feminism represents a single ideology. In addition, they often presume that all feminists hold the same beliefs and that feminism is an attitude. Feminism is not an attitude or a behavior by itself. Actions described as feminist emerge from ways of thinking about and knowing the world, but conclusions and pursuits differ widely. Referring to the collection of ideologies as "feminisms" would be more accurate. Moreover, in the context of its history, feminism has many different meanings. Nevertheless, we believe most feminisms include in some measure these three principles: (1) women, like men, are complete and important human beings whose ways of knowing and modes of thinking have derived from unique experiences as women; (2) some practices within human social systems—particularly those perpetuating unexamined stereotypes and attempting to direct human development in monolithic modes—bar women's realities, sending both implicit and explicit messages that women are not valued as persons; and (3) all living beings have immanent value.[2]

Many people believe all feminists hate men. Contemporary feminism in the United States takes a number of diverse positions, some of which advocate the exclusion of men. More common positions focus on oppressive behavior men do. Still other positions focus on women only, promoting women in ways not stereotypically familiar. Some feminists focus on both men and women, looking to discover principles that apply across sex and gender. Recently feminists in the United States have begun to realize that, in general, the movement centered on white, middle-class people. Feminist ideology had prompted the voices of other female minorities, who began to assert that they had not been integrally braided into the fabric of feminism. Feminists began to recognize that their exclusion of women of various classes, races, ethnicities, physical abilities and ages ironically enacted on those groups the fate feminists had objected to for themselves. In the last decade, efforts have been made by most feminist groups to make visible these minority women, incorporating images and voices of many diverse individuals, recognizing the immanent value of each.

These efforts have met with varying degrees of success. Some feminists who have tried to live by the third principle—that all living beings have immanent value—have experienced frustration and even disillusionment. They may struggle to find ways to live a philosophy that inherently contradicts the hierarchical and competitive goals that exist in much of public life, particularly in the business world.

Ecofeminists, for example, promote lateral relationships not only among people, but between people and their environments. Many kinds of feminists continue to search for successful ways of incorporating their ideologies into their ways of life and their communities.

Efforts to make visible and valuable different ways of knowing and different ways of thinking challenge traditional stereotypes. Feminist theories often propose not *additional* rhetorical theories or theories of interpersonal communication, but *different* ones. If we see gender in its complex form, we can understand the kinds of changes many feminists seek. When a female, for example, conceptualizes her own gender, she may do so on many levels. The gender she believes herself to be when she is alone exists in one arena. The gender she believes is most appropriate in any given public situation may be different for a number of reasons. She also may have a gender she enacts with her partner and one she expects or hopes for from her partner. In addition, she may conceptualize feminine gender differently if she applies it to a male than if she applies it to a female. Many of the enactments of these genders may be mitigated by the cultural stereotype for male and female. In short, purporting a single gender or even a single gender stereotype becomes problematic.

Now if we return to the question of "additional" or "different," we find a difficult problem. Who is to determine the cultural stereotype for males? For females? If females are coerced to enact the feminine gender as it is conceptualized by males, is that the same gender females might conceptualize for themselves? And is androgyny for women accomplished by the integration of the male version of feminine gender (for women) and the male version of masculine gender (also for women)? Some feminists even ask if androgyny is a desired goal. They question whether the homogeneity implicit in the ideal of androgyny would effectively represent the communicative diversity among people since more interpersonal communication differences exist within each sex than between sexes. Most feminists work to make visible not the cultural or stereotyped version of feminine gender, but the variety of versions of feminine gender that emerges from activities of people who are feminine—largely women. Feminists' insistence on their own language—or at least some words of their own—reflects their desire to manifest within the culture a feminism that functions in a viable, dynamic, and visible way similar to that of the masculism that is more dominant in the United States society.

Throughout this book, we have made the claim that gender stereotypes are taught and learned by individual males and females. These communication stereotypes are not "natural" or unavoidable. Human beings have expanded the biological distinctions between the sexes because of long-held and often subconscious beliefs about human beings according to their sex. For example, changing a married woman's name to her husband's name without changing his name to include hers is not a universal custom around the world. Yet in this society it continues to be the predominant practice, paralleling the idea that the husband will be the head of the household and his name will be perpetuated by any children borne by the couple. When feminists expose this and other cultural practices in pursuit of their principles, they may encounter strong opposition accompanied by confusion, misunderstanding, and suspicion.

THE WINGS AND BRANCHES OF CONTEMPORARY FEMINISM

The latest women's movement in the United States has never been a single movement. In the past twenty-five years in particular, several differences of approach and philosophy have emerged, resulting in diverse types of public communication and diverse public images of feminists themselves. Distinctions among the various branches or approaches of the feminist movement are difficult to outline without being unfair to any of them. Adding to this communication problem in writing about feminism is the fact that previous writers do not agree among themselves about how to characterize the wings or branches of contemporary feminism. In light of this, we will describe the movement in terms of: (1) the rhetorical situations out of which feminist groups arose; (2) the current communication arenas in which feminists function, whether as groups or as individuals; and (3) the expressed goals of various feminists.

Consider first the rhetorical situations that helped give birth to feminist activity in the latter half of the twentieth century.[3] As described in chapter 2, a rhetorical situation comprises those features that promote, allow, or hinder one from initiating communication. The constraints of a situation may make life so frustrating that you will decide to speak up about it. Alternatively, someone may encourage you to talk about your career plans with a teacher or counselor, whereas without that brief encouragement you might have said nothing at all. In the case of women and feminism, the actual circumstances of life, as well as the availability of others to talk with, have led a great many women to see feminism as a communication opportunity for themselves. The following are two major examples of that fact.

BETTY FRIEDAN AND THE NATIONAL ORGANIZATION FOR WOMEN.
One set of women, most of them white, middle class, and politically liberal, became aware during the 1960s—many by reading Betty Friedan's *The Feminine Mystique*[4]—that they suffered from a lack of meaning and purpose in their lives. Often isolated in suburban homes with large families, the women found to their surprise that "the problem that has no name" (Friedan's term) was shared by many other women. Friedan and others urged women to look at their need for identity and participation in the larger world outside the home. In 1966, they started the National Organization for Women (NOW) to bring women and supportive men together so that women would gain social, political, and economic equality of opportunity. Their goal was to reform existing institutions into fair, open environments.

Many women in NOW were married; some were divorced, widowed, or single. Some had the leisure to reflect on their possible futures, while others had to support themselves and other family members on limited incomes. Many NOW members hoped to pursue higher education or to enter professions such as law, medicine, and the clergy (all three were still largely closed to women in the 1960s despite the civil rights laws of that decade). Their goals had some similarities to those of black civil rights leader Dr. Martin Luther King, Jr.: integration into the institutions of society and the use of public persuasion to address human rights and human opportunities rather than the separateness of the races or the sexes.

NEW LEFT POLITICS AND THE "RADICAL FEMINISTS". The second major situation that led women to commit themselves to feminist activities resulted from experiences in protest groups working against the Vietnam War, racial injustices, and wrongs by American government and business. Women participants, most of them young and single, frequently found that their male co-workers treated them as sources of sexual recreation rather than as thinking adults and equals. Black leader Stokely Carmichael was widely quoted as saying that the place of women in protest groups was "prone." As they came to see that many male civil rights and peace activists were selective in their view of equality, some of the women developed the theory that socioeconomic class differences, central to Marxist thought, were not the ultimate form of human inequality; sexual inequality was even more basic. If sexual inequality is the foundation of all human institutions, then all institutions are flawed and should be rejected. That was a revolutionary statement, and along with scattered acts of violence it convinced some audiences that feminists as well as other protesters threatened an armed revolution.

Feminists in the New Left did not unite behind a single strategy. Some became separatist, in that they avoided dealing with capitalism and with the nuclear family as much as possible. Others developed lesbian relationships or started women-only communes, farms, or artist collectives. Others published newspapers and journals of women's writings or opened feminist bookstores to sell the works of feminist writers such as Germaine Greer, Shulamith Firestone, Kate Millett, and Simone de Beauvoir. Activities on a small scale were more typical of New Left-originated feminists than of the women in the National Organization for Women, which sought and won tens of thousands of members during its first decade.

By definition the New Left, or radical wing, of contemporary feminism is difficult to summarize, as these feminists wanted to avoid large institutions and single, enforced answers on how to affirm being a woman in a repressive society. Yet, the term "liberationist" suggests one common feature of their background and concern, for they sought separation or liberation from male domination as a central objective. Table 10.1 lists some tentative distinctions between the liberation and equal rights wings of contemporary feminism. The descriptive phrases in the table suggest different directions but not absolute differences, for many people have been involved with actions led by both branches. Also, any language describing a large and varied social movement is necessarily limiting.

Table 10.1 Two Directions in Contemporary Feminism

Equal rights wing	Liberation wing
Problem is defined as women's isolation and lack of identity	Problem is defined as sex bias against women in all groups and movements
Older on average	Younger on average
e.g., National Organization for Women (1966)	e.g., Radical Feminists (1967–1968)
Institutions need reforming	Institutions are unworkable
Goal of equal opportunities	Goal of destroying patriarchy

Source: This framework is suggested by the analysis done by Jo Freeman, "The Women's Liberation Movement: Its Origins, Organizations, Activities, and Ideas," in *Women: A Feminist Perspective*, 2d ed. (Palo Alto, CA: Mayfield, 1979), pp. 557–74.

CONSCIOUSNESS RAISING. Rap sessions and consciousness raising have been common elements in the development of both branches of contemporary feminism. Small groups meet, typically on a regular basis, to allow women to tell their stories about personal experiences, including frustrations and aspirations. Members respond with empathy, support, and sometimes ideas about how similar problems have been addressed. Most important, the individuals in the group are encouraged to examine the connection between their negative personal communication experiences (often thought by the speakers to be their "fault") and the politics of being a woman in a culture where women are considered "the other." A shorthand phrase for the desired result of consciousness raising became a theme of feminist education in general: the personal is political. With the help of the group setting and interpersonal support, a woman could recognize that a past experience was not her fault but was linked to structural biases in the world around her.

THE ISSUE OF NEGATIVITY. Feminists have been criticized for a negative approach to many areas of everyday life. While there are certainly individual reasons a person sounds negative or brings up negative personal issues, a wider reason for this phenomenon exists in the case of feminism. Whenever a tradition exists for a long period of time, it becomes the assumed reality. Questioning it is a negative act: "Why should we do this any longer? It is unfair." Many feminists said "no" to public practices or private customs that had not been examined before; they objected to customs that appeared on the surface to be neutral or positive. Consequently, the negative label was attached to their refusals. This response to change is not new. The response may be particularly strong against feminists because the traditional stereotype requires women to cooperate and create connection rather than resist and assume assertive or aggressive positions.

The negativity associated with the most radical feminists often is cast over all groups claiming the label. Learning to differentiate ideologies among groups who espouse feminism—through exploratory conversations aimed at discovery rather than attack—can help clarify similarities and differences among feminists that might otherwise be stereotyped with a generality.

THE IMPACT OF THE FEMINIST MOVEMENT

While many individuals have not thought through their feelings about gender ideals or feminism, others have concluded that feminism is now a past event. Expanding job opportunities for women and the visibility of women in news broadcasting and other professions lead some to conclude that feminism has done its job and is now obsolete. Other observers disagree, pointing to the increasing numbers of women with incomes below the poverty line; the poor record of this country in sex education, infant mortality and child abuse; and the low wages paid to women who teach young children and work in female-identified professions. The difference of opinion on this issue is profound. Focusing only on individual employment rights for white middle-class females in the United States, the success has been quick although shallow. Women are being hired but not promoted along with their male peers. Focusing on poverty-related matters, the failure of society to address the "human issues" involving women parenting families alone as well as women in paid employment is shocking.

In the last 35 years, the number of families headed by a single parent raising children under age 18 has tripled. That number is estimated to increase by 4 percent a year. Approximately nine of ten single parents are female. Over half of all single mothers live at an income below the poverty level; only one-fifth of dual-parent families share that economic status.[5] Mothers head 90 percent of the 5 million families on welfare; only one in twenty absent fathers provide even $200 a month in child support.[6]

For feminists, women like those who comprise these statistics continue to struggle to build lives within systems that work against them. These feminists often agree that some large, very visible changes have occurred, such as women wearing pants in public and business settings. They disagree that the need for feminist action has passed; they see a continuing mandate to identify, make visible, and replace the more subtle, more subjugating structures of present systems, both interpersonal and political.

THE MEN

The men's movement is younger, smaller, and more scattered than the women's movement. Some people assert the men's movement emerged as a "backlash" to the feminist movement; others claim it exists in its own right. The intents of the various groups in the men's movement vary from reasserting family roles to developing new ideologies as males. The movement experiences wide controversy about its purposes, its methods, and its leaders. Two groups in the movement are particularly visible; we will examine the texts and events of each to gain a better understanding of this emerging social force.

Poet Robert Bly is at the heart of one group in the men's movement. This group sometimes is described as mythopoetic because Bly's approach uses myth, narratives, and dramatic enactment as part of the search for identity.[7] In workshops held across the United States,

Bly encourages men to rediscover their primal male spirit. He explains that males feel a disconnection to their own male characters. Males, he says, feel isolated in their world, unsure about their own roles and identities. In their attempts to become more sensitive, Bly suggests men have not become happier[8]; they do not feel a sense of self-fulfillment. Bly uses his experiences with his alcoholic father to shape the intense investigation into men's instinctive selves.

Bly uses a poetic style to shape a new—not a revised—idea of maleness. Using a kind of mythology of maleness and what one writer calls a mass therapy[9], Bly incites men to actively seek mentors in other males. He explains in *Iron John*[10] that "[i]t is in the old myths that we hear, for example, of Zeus energy, that positive leadership energy in men, which popular culture constantly declares does not exist; from King Arthur we learn the value of the male mentor in the lives of young men. . . ."[11] Bly notes that the 1990s mark an "important and fruitful moment now, for it is clear to men that the images of adult manhood given by the popular culture are worn out; a man can no longer depend on them."[12] Bly's mythology points to a new maleness that awakens the wild man in every man. Other leaders who sometimes are compared or grouped with Bly include James Hillman, Michael Meade, and Robert Moore.

Criticism of Bly's movement ranges widely. Some have called it a backlash against the feminist movement.[13] Some feminists believe Bly's views exclude women, marking those ideas as anti-women. Other critics reject Bly for exactly the opposite reasons. One of these critics calls followers "Blysters" and sees Bly's position as one that misinforms men and panders to women.[14] These opposing assessments of the mythopoetic branch of the men's movement are typical of the sometimes fractious character of the fledgling men's movement. Supporters of Bly's ideology report that this leadership helps them escape the formulated social expectations of their sex, leaving them able to discover new ways to experience being male.

A second group in the men's movement focuses on men's roles as fathers. This group is represented by several national organizations like the National Fatherhood Initiative, the National Center for Fathering and Promise Keepers. The goal of Promise Keepers is not only to reaffirm men's roles as fathers but also to encompass men of all ages and races. Begun in 1990 by former Colorado University football coach Bill McCartney, the group brings men together usually in football stadiums across the country for what have been described alternately as evangelical, fundamentalist religious messages and messages about men's spirituality and relationships. Attendance is limited to males only.

The most dominant criticism of Promise Keepers is that the group not only excludes women but promotes a traditional, patriarchal hierarchy in relationships between mothers and fathers. Some critics claim the group advocates the principle that females should be subordinate to males. Other critics laud the group for working to promote solidarity among men of all backgrounds and for its message of racial reconciliation.

One significant project supported by Promise Keepers was the Million Man March on October 16, 1995. Organizer Rev. Benjamin Chavis hoped to attract one million men to the event in Washington D.C. His stated goal was to create a community of men who could then take that spirit of kinship back to their individual communities across the nation. He and other organizers of the march declared they hoped to rekindle a sense of place and responsibility for men in their neighborhoods and their families.

Controversy swirled around the march in large part because of the significant leadership role played by Louis Farrakhan and the Nation of Islam. The NAACP (The National Association for the Advancement of Colored People) refused to endorse the march. Accusations of racism and sexism were leveled against the march and its organizers. Nevertheless, an estimated 400,000 men (an estimation reached through a process Farrakhan later charged as racist) spent the day listening to presentations by Farrakhan and others, such as Jesse Jackson, Maya Angelou, Rosa Parks, and Stevie Wonder. Assessment were mixed about the effectiveness and value of the Million Man March.

ISSUES OF NEGATIVITY

Like people who label themselves "feminist," men who label themselves as members of the men's movement may receive negative feedback. Male behavior that does not conform to the male gender ideal stereotype can be met with derision. In addition, the strong religious ties present with some men's groups can heighten perceptions of difference. Since the men's movement has fewer members than the feminist movement, males who venture into new behavior and communication practices may not readily find a community of men with whom to talk and share ideas. Confusion in the movement remains about whether to search for new gender parameters or to revise old ones; negativity can emerge from that confusion.

IMPACT OF THE MEN'S MOVEMENT

The impact of the men's movement is smaller and more diffuse than the impact of feminism. The men's movement is younger and less widely shared. Hundreds of small workshops for men are held throughout the country each year, each with a slightly different agenda and slant than the next. Without a unifying theme—such as economics played in the early years of feminism—some suggest the movement may remain segmented.

SEX, GENDER, AND VIOLENCE

While many individuals are trying to find more humane ways to talk to each other, a growing number of messages created publicly exploit sexuality and link sexuality with violence toward women. Their existence, and their increase in the past few years, can be understood better if one looks first at the assumptions behind this book as a whole:

1. Biological sex categories are treated by a great many people as central symbols for individuals' identities from the day of birth.
2. Sex is quickly and importantly elaborated into separate gender communication ideals for the two sexes, on the assumption that one must achieve success in life as a female or male rather than simply being a person who happens to have one or the other set of sex-linked body parts.
3. The stereotypical behavioral components of gender for males include power—defined as the ability to control others; for females, relatedness is a pertinent issue—defined as the ability to attract and maintain a relationship with another person, particularly with a male.
4. Once these differences of focus and value have been learned, most of us accept them as general truths. The gender filter developed in both sexes prevents each from seeing how the others' minds work and what the words of the other sex mean in context.

Biology does not require that the sexes develop these differences in focus. Culture, especially in the United States, emphasizes action in male children and beauty in female children. The result is significant differences in the knowledge we obtain about the worlds outside and inside ourselves and in the communicative means we use to obtain and reinforce that knowledge.

ACTS OF SEXUAL VIOLENCE

Biology does, however, generally bestow greatest physical power on males. Therefore, if a male chooses to act on the stereotyped gender requisite that he be powerful and aggressive, he may choose to do so. Overwhelmingly, most males choose not to dominate others physically, but the incidence of male violence against females continues to rise not only in the United States but worldwide. The United Nations appoints a Special Rapporteur on Violence Against Women[15]; the ARCC (Economic Commission for Africa and the Africa Regional Coordinating Committee for the Integration of Women in Development) continues to shape legislation to define violence against women and make punishments more severe.[16] Problems of violence in the home and other violence against women such as genital mutilation were topics of concern at the United Nations' 4th International Women's Conference in 1995. Rape and violence against women in Bosnia-Herzegovina, Croatia, and Serbia during the most recent war were cited as reasons for United States military intervention. The rape of a twelve-year-old school girl in Okinawa by three United States servicemen in 1995 also demonstrates the international dimensions of violence against women.

Within the United States, one in eight women will be raped in their lifetimes.[17] As you look around your classroom or think of the females in your family, you may realize you probably know or will know someone who will contribute to these statistics. A 1995 rally in Washington, D.C., called for an end to domestic abuse. Domestic violence is the leading cause of injury for women between ages 15 and 44 in the United States.[18] Some people have objected to the term "domestic violence" or "domestic abuse" because they believe "domestic" reduces in some people's minds the magnitude of the violence. In fact, one study discovered that arrests for "domestic" assault were inversely related to the level of intimacy of those involved. In other words, a stranger who abuses another stranger would more likely be arrested for that behavior than an intimate who abuses another intimate.[19] These perceptions about intimate relationships may contribute to national data showing women more likely than men to experience nonvoluntary intercourse during childhood and adolescence.[20] They also generate from the fact that one-third of cases of sex-

FOR BETTER OR FOR WORSE copyright (1996) Lynn Johnston Prod., Inc. Dist. by
UNIVERSAL PRESS SYNDICATE. All rights reserved.

ual assault occur in the victims' homes. Rape is the fastest-growing crime in the United States, where a woman is raped every six minutes.

Violent behavior against women encompasses women of all ages. One author explains that rape of women over 50 goes virtually unnoticed; that most evidence of these crimes is based on anecdotal information.[21] Sexual violence on United States campuses is increasing dramatically; the incidents now total about 6,000 each year.[22] Many women believe college disciplinary boards are not equipped to deal with rape and that women's security is therefore jeopardized.[23]

Sexual assaults of acquaintances ("date rapes") are now reported on college campuses. Evidence suggests that many more date rapes occur than female college students are willing to report. In family settings, father-daughter and stepfather-stepdaughter incest cases also appear to be increasing. In many instances, the situation is complicated by the child's financial dependence on the male parent and by the male parent's success in convincing the child that she promoted the sexual relationship and therefore must protect herself by keeping it secret.[24] According to some estimates, physical abuse will occur in one in four or one in five marriages, predominantly by the husband toward the wife.

Actions with regard to these alarming statistics include rhetorical sanctions against sexually aggressive behavior as well as punitive legal ones, but problems remain. In 1993, a United States Senate Judiciary Committee concluded that the justice system did not protect victims by effectively prosecuting rapists or violent sex offenders. As a result, the committee approved the Violence Against Women Act which, among other provisos, allowed women who were abused or raped to sue their assailants in federal court. Some critics argued the act was overreaction. Ironically, these legal trappings may deter some women from reporting rape, especially women who do not realize they can file a report without pressing charges.

The communication climate between men and women functions in the foreground of this ongoing tension. Clearly, most adult males maintain positive, loving relationships with their partners and avoid the extremes of violent communication outlined here. Nevertheless, many women operate with a low level of awareness of the implicit difference in physical power between men and women. If they are asked to work late at the office, women may have to take different precautions than men, especially if the women must work alone at night and leave by walking out to a car in an unlighted parking lot. A woman who walks down a street at night alone often is haunted by images of lurking danger inspired by the statistics discussed above. The sound of footsteps behind her may cause very different sensations from those a man would experience in the same situation. Some women develop a keen sense of sensitivity toward their partners with regard to anger. These women often can identify the parameters of what they feel safe to discuss and how they may discuss those issues. Especially in times of intense conflict or risk, women may take a significantly different vantage point than men.

MESSAGES OF SEXUAL VIOLENCE

Although many women will not experience rape during their lifetimes, they are reminded repeatedly by social custom and the media that at any time they could be victims of sexual violence. Many women spoke out against the "hero's welcome" awaiting Mike Tyson after his release from imprisonment for rape. Tyson returned to professional boxing with much celebration and financial gain. Music performer Snoop Doggy Dog successfully markets CDs with lyrics and pictures that depict demeaning and sometimes violent images.

Images of sexual violence are not uncommon in a variety of consumer products and are particularly exploited in pornographic material. Pornography refers to verbal and visual material intended to arouse sexual desire. Many people distinguish it from erotica, the artistic depiction of sexual feeling and experience, because pornography exploits sexual experience for a profit and typically portrays male dominance and female subordination. Pornography is therefore an act of power and control. The assumption behind pornographic films, writing, and photography is that the female in particular is controllable and is appropriately under the control of a dominant male. Both within the story or photograph while it is being experienced and in producing the tale or photograph, the point of view is that of an individual who uses another person to produce a sensuous image. The woman may act as if she is "out of control" in her dramatized lust, but the important thing is that she is portrayed as having been made to feel that way by the person behind the camera: a powerful, skillful sex partner and/or film director who is able to "free" her "natural sensuality." The main character, then, is not the woman in front of the camera but a man (or in rare instances another woman) who has the power and skill to produce these visual images of desire.

Problems of pornography on the Internet have sparked a heated debate about censorship and the freedom of speech. Undergraduate Marty Rimm of Carnegie-Mellon University produced a controversial (drawing criticisms about methodology and ethics in data collection) study entitled, "Marketing Pornography on the Information Superhighway: A Study of 917,410 Images, Descriptions, Short Stories and

Animations Downloaded 8.5 Million Times by Consumers in Over 2000 Cities in 40 Countries, Provinces and Territories." Rimm testified before Congress where the Communications Decency Act was being debated.[25] One critical issue in dealing with pornographic material is the definition of pornography and its distinction from erotica. In this case, "indecency" was defined as "any comment, request, suggestion, proposal, image, or other communication that, in context, depicts or describes, in terms patently offensive as measured by contemporary community standards, sexual or excretory activities or organs."[26] As you read that definition, you can understand the ambiguities (in such words, for example, as "patently offensive," "contemporary," or "community standards") that make difficult the translation of value into symbolization. What constitutes censorship rests in the interpretations of those symbols.

Educators feared the effects of the telecommunications bill on the education system because of interpretation differences. They worried they might be held liable if students accessed the pornography via school computer systems. Because young children had access to the pornographic sites on the Internet, various school officials tried software products like SurfWatch designed to block sexually explicit sites. The effectiveness of the action was hampered by questions about the company's right to block sites and by problems with the software. Universities worried that the language in the legislation would restrict students' access to research sites in certain subjects. Some universities eliminated sex-related bulletin boards or flashed notices to students that if they accessed certain Internet sites their status at the university would be jeopardized.[27]

Varying degrees of punitive measures have been used in attempts to curb pornographic material on the Internet. Fines as high as $100,000 and prison sentences of up to two years were outlined in the telecommunications bill for offenders who knowingly exposed minors to on-line pornography. In addition, federal agents raided homes and offices, arresting cyberspace child pornographers.[28] The fears, debates, and actions taken with regard to sexual violence have directed relationships to the culture's construction of gender and communication about sex.

Effects of Acts and Messages of Sexual Violence

We do not yet know conclusively what causal links exist among mediated messages, individual histories, biological factors, and acts of sexual violence. Some researchers claim connections exist between exposure to sexually violent media and the development of thought patterns that support violence against women.[29] Others find in their studies that heavy metal rock music seems to increase males' gender stereotyping and increase negative attitudes toward women.[30] Exposure to sexually explicit material seems to produce acceptance of rape myths and less concern for rape victims.[31] Clearly, the fabric of some mediated communication experiences provides a strong theme of aggressive sexuality and other forms of violence. Aggressive pornography, which depicts acts of graphic physical damage to women's bodies, is the most blatant example of connecting sexual images with violent acts toward women.[32]

Media messages indicate both men and women are sexual objects. One example of males as objects is a recent Coca Cola commercial in which several women wait at their office window for a muscular young man to take a break from his hard physical labor, during which he takes off his shirt to drink a Coke. More messages appear using females as objects, and most sexually violent messages target females. In a study of college women, researchers found that exposure to media that featured aggression against women increased the women's feelings of being restrained and losing personal power. Repeated messages of sexual violence may affect both women and men in destructive and negative ways.

COUNTERMEASURES

The first step toward changing the environment of sexual violence is awareness of its intensity, pervasiveness, and negative effects on general communication between men and women. Exposing the undercurrent of threat through which many women navigate during their communication helps explain the more intense response they may have to sexually harassing situations, for example. The point here is not that every woman believes every negative comment made to her carries an implicit threat of violence. The effect is much more subtle. The point is that women often must use a subtle detecting system to warn them of potential danger in the communication situation. Many males better understand females' messages when they consider sexual violence as part of the larger sexual context in which many females exist in the United States culture.

Some people favor censorship as a way to change that sexually violent environment. In one study, more than two-thirds of respondents were in favor of censoring sexually violent media[33] that sent messages like these or those directed at males. Some experts believe that ultimately, censorship will not curb the production of sexually violent messages. They are researching intervention via education.[34] Through reading this book, you have learned about various perspectives you might take to better understand the messages of both sexes. Using these skills and helping others use them seems to be the strongest agent against the negative and debilitating practices of sexually violent individuals and sexually violent media.

While none of the four communication perspectives discussed in chapter 2 precludes violence between men and women, recognizing one or more of the four assumptions as operating in particular situations can help participants or observers produce clearer communication about the issues and their roots. Violence in children often erupts when things are not making sense. Violence in adults today, in thought as well as in action, often erupts because the gender communication ideals of early life have failed to bring what they promised. We often blame each other for our discomfort, ignoring the wider circumstances that hinder our satisfaction. Women and men can examine these wider circumstances and the gender-based divisions between individuals that may be open to change. Ultimately the specific techniques of producing aggressive pornography or violent sexual messages are less of a danger to humanity than are the more general attitudes that permit some people to manipulate the bodies and minds of others for profit.

CHANGING PERSONAL COMMUNICATION STYLES

For many people social movements are a distant part of the landscape. Much closer to home are the needs to improve oneself and to deal successfully with other people. Self-help books and workshops by the thousands offer to help people reduce the fat on their thighs, increase the return on their investments, or extend their life through better eating habits. In the past two decades, communication books and short courses have offered numerous guidelines for improving human relationships at work and in intimate situations.

Goals to improve relationships have inspired two major incentives toward changing individual communication styles: recent business publications emphasizing human development and the altering or ending of marriage relationships. We discussed in chapter 8 the fact that communication arrangements in many marriages have been affected by the time constraints of dual-career and dual-worker house-

ANNE GIBBONS copyright (1996). Reprinted with permission of Hot Pink Productions. All rights reserved.

holds. Women as well as men bring home job-related work to complete; women now have "war stories" from the job to share with their partners; and relationships face additional stress because of commuting or long hours at work. In such households, men and women have largely the same communicative concerns, and both sexes may have the responsibilities for children, the buying or making of meals, and the various household tasks.

While the evidence is spotty and contradictory, it appears that in many families the day-to-day communicative activities of men and women are becoming similar. This means that men have more of the tasks of relationship maintenance than their fathers had. Men who do not shift their communicative activities at least somewhat toward more involvement as listeners to spouses, caregivers to children, and planners of household logistics appear more likely to experience separation or divorce than those who adapt to multiple communication

roles in a household. A few who leave or lose those family ties seek counseling or join men's groups to examine their communication values and practices, in the hope of doing better the next time. In contrast, many men renew their search for the "real woman" who will treat them as they deserve and not expect so much adapting to the female world of home and parenting.

ALTERNATIVES FOR GENDER COMMUNICATION

As indicated in these summaries of changing situations, both sexes have been encouraged to make personal changes in light of the women's movement, altered household arrangements, and a competitive market economy. Table 10.2 presents some options for change in women's and men's communication styles. None of the four options in the table has become dominant thus far. Some of them receive more active encouragement and modeling than others from various communication arenas—television advertising, business and professional schools, counseling groups, or families, for example. In individual cases, the boundaries between styles may blur as people adapt their messages within an interaction. The patterns do give some indication of the range of efforts people may make to communicate effectively in the context of shifting gender ideals.

Table 10.2   Alternative Models for Communication by the Sexes

Heightened gender identification	The man or the woman exhibits and defends intensely his or her sex-typed verbal and nonverbal patterns.
Gender reversal	The person moves forcefully in the direction of emulating the other gender communication ideal.
Gender neutrality	The communication behavior is intended to be free of any identifiable links with either sex-typed style.
Inclusive or androgynous style	Strengths of both sexes' traditional styles are respected, and wide variations are allowed in fitting behavior to circumstances.

I'm really funny about issues such as housework, laundry and grocery shopping—even cooking. I know it's because my whole life I saw my mom doing all of these things while my dad sat in front of the television. She would even wait on him—and, of course, he'd have my sister and me do the same. We did it, against our will, because he was our dad after all and we didn't want to rock the boat. To this day, my parents' situation remains the same.

I am not like this. I made it clear that I will never be like this. When my husband and I got married, I was both going to school and working. I wanted to appear to be "the perfect little wife" so I did a majority of the things until I got tired, opened up my eyes and saw a reflection of my mother. Enough was enough! My husband and I argued about this for a long time. He thought that mowing the lawn, maintaining our vehicles, etc., was equal to all the things I was doing.

He finally realized it wasn't—especially once when I brought up what we would do once children entered the picture. I certainly wasn't superwoman.

HEIGHTENED GENDER IDENTIFICATION. The style of heightened gender identification often appears in situations where stereotypes are intended to amuse an audience. A beer commercial with a dozen men and one woman may present the woman as high-voiced, large-busted, and asking silly questions. In life outside television, some men report informally that on hunting trips, for example, they enjoy "letting loose" with language, jokes, and fantasies they believe women would not allow them to express. Middle-class women in same-sex communication settings, such as a YWCA locker room, may talk about their fitness programs or their partnered relationship. If they are mothers, they may recount a child's funny comments or share advice about the details of child care. In all of these cases the talk connects with a gender communication role: the "macho" male ideally should emphasize his physical prowess and sense of adventure, while the "moderate" female should attend to child care and personal appearance.

These conversations are presented in more extreme form than you may have experienced them, but most people have a sense of the ritual communication topics that fit particular settings. The positive side of this pattern is that a pleasant camaraderie can develop within these same-sex groups. The limit is that the rituals imply boundaries as well as permission: a man on a hunting trip may feel constrained not to talk about his loss of a promotion at work; a mother dressing her child in a locker room may feel that it is inappropriate to talk with other mothers in the room about completing a project on the job.

GENDER REVERSAL. Gender reversal sometimes results from an individual's effort to neutralize the negative effects of gender communication ideals. Janet Lee Mills says about nonverbal communication that women tend to move between extremes of nonverbal behavior when they are trying to adapt their actions to the contradictory commands, "Be powerful" and "Be feminine."[35] Men often move from one extreme to the other as well, particularly when it involves adapting to demands for language change or being asked to express emotions. In attempts to express "his feminine side," a man may act in ways that appear inappropriate or insincere. Observers may accuse him of trying to be a "nineties kind of guy."

Pendulum swings of behavior do not always occur by choice, however. Men who are experiencing a power shift outside their control may also move from one extreme to the other, without being aware of doing so. The man who jokes loudly about "that nutty woman I'm married to" may become passive and less boisterous in conversation after hearing that his 20-year job or 25-year marriage is in jeopardy.

GENDER NEUTRALITY. The style of gender neutrality is advantageous to use when you are in situations where one or the other sex-typed style has been misunderstood or devalued. Women eager to attain the best possible jobs have been told in numerous magazine articles, books, and personal advice columns that they need to beware of feminine communication patterns that could make them appear flighty, confused, or unable to lead others. Thus hedges ("I'm not sure, but . . ."), qualifiers ("It is sometimes true that . . ."), and tag questions ("We need to do that today, don't you think?") are treated as dangerous language forms for women to use if they want to be taken as seriously as their male colleagues. As a counterpart, men in many work environments alter language patterns such as swearing or sexual jokes to show respect for the women working around them. A key difference in the two examples, however, is that men often mention to each other that they had to change their language practices for the women. The comments may be accompanied by a roll of the eyes or a knowing smile.

This third communication option has unequal implications for the two sexes in another respect. Males can still be respected and liked when using qualifiers and other supposedly feminine-style language forms, as long as they are otherwise seen as intelligent communicators. Many young women in professional settings go to great lengths to limit their topic choices to items related to work. They are careful about mentioning families, friends, intimate partners, or personal interests outside work, hoping to neutralize any element of communication that would suggest that they are not dedicated to their work. In this respect, the neutralizing of an interest in relationships that has been identified with women makes the supposedly neutral style more masculine than feminine, and thereby more of a source of communication stress for women in the workplace than for men.

THE INCLUSIVE STYLE. Idealized in some of the writing about women and about changing gender roles, the inclusive style allows an individual to adapt to varying communication situations so that the communication strengths needed—regardless of their stereotypical assignments—can be used. Inclusive people can be supportive to an injured child as well as independent in expressing an opinion different from that of a work colleague. They can lead others effectively while also being able to enjoy sensory pleasures like playing with a cat or dog.

Organizations have a major role in leading people to develop communication skills that are desirable in the contemporary workplace. Men who are in management, for example, are now hearing in many of the *Fortune* 500 companies that leadership and supervision require sensitivity, active listening, encouragement and praise to subordinates, and opening oneself to team problem solving rather than acting as the sole leader. Women who enter professional fields such as medicine, the ministry, and trial law are advised to develop their nonverbal and verbal authority so that they will not be questioned about their professional qualifications because of nonassertive gestures, voice, or phrasing.

Many writings about gender and communication suggest that women have made more progress toward an inclusive style than have men. Perhaps the necessity that most women work has demanded in a more tangible way that women find ways to achieve a successful communication style in a male-dominated environment. Assertiveness training and support groups attended by many women have offered examples of confident expression of opinions, without advising women to give up gentle and caring communication patterns. Less reinforcement is available for men, especially on the job, to include the other sex's traditional patterns of talk. While the management literature encourages an inclusive style of talk to colleagues and subordinates, it does not encourage the integration of relationships and responsibilities into the corporation. Ultimately, the most valued goal of most corporations is money; thus, only when strategies result in higher productivity or more efficient (and thus less costly) operation will they become valued behaviors in the industry. In private terms, anecdotes suggest that male workers now sometimes talk to female co-workers about home, children, and personal concerns, but they appear to talk very rarely to other men about such concerns. The reward system in most kinds of employment—and in many households as well—makes it more dangerous for a man to move toward feminine-identified patterns of communication than for a woman to move toward masculine-identified patterns.

The focus of the inclusive model is on determining what communication patterns fit the self, the others involved, and the situation. It overlaps with the idea of assertiveness discussed in chapter 8, for it suggests that self-respect and regard for the other are the primary bases for choosing what to say in a given case. From a rhetorical perspective, you cannot adopt a single script that will be used with every person. Each situation brings different constraints and possibilities to its specific actors. One often has to make a conscious choice to overlook the current gender-based expectations and to look instead at the actual components of the situation, the intended goals, and the concrete personal relationships involved.

COMPLEXITIES IN CHANGING COMMUNICATION PATTERNS

Now that you have examined four models for changing one's communication style, consider some of the complexities that are involved in actually making such a change. When you or another person takes a major step in redefining self, job, or requirements for intimacy, your own world as it relates to that person will become unpredictable. Unpredictability and our reactions to it cause a great many communication problems within and between the sexes. Physical and emotional stress levels rise when you are unable to predict whether you will be praised or criticized for a report you have prepared, or you are left guessing whether the one you love will be receptive, antagonistic, or preoccupied when you next encounter him or her.

A predictability drop can occur when a man or a woman changes status and consequently changes activities. For example, when a woman who has been supporting her spouse while he is in law school quits her job in a medical office and starts night school to become a physician, her communication behavior may change in a variety of ways—depending on how her view of herself and her world changes. She might start to act more self-reliant and less concerned with her spouse's opinions of her actions. She may develop a picture of herself as a woman who is becoming a professional person in her own right. On the other hand, if she had a high level of responsibility or respect in her job she may be impatient with the student role, suddenly dependent on instructors for work assignments and evaluations. In this case she may try to get back her sense of personal power by acting more demanding and critical in her communication at home. Whatever the new events, they will influence the view of the self and the expectations of the relationship. Often the other member of the relationship has not seen these changes coming and is shocked by the size of the ripples affecting them both.

One particular direction of change in an intimate relationship occurs when each partner moves to identify more strongly with the other gender stereotype. Though this change may seem unlikely, it can occur in intimate pairs where some pressure for change has been brought to bear either from inside or outside the pair. If one or both has been heavily identified with their same-sex gender stereotype, a crisis or a major change in goals may lead to a gender reversal pattern. If a conflict has occurred between the partners or within one or both individuals about their own communication effectiveness, the two may not stay closely in touch with each other about how and why they are changing. Ironically, each may be trying to adapt to meet the other's desires while unaware that those desires have changed.

This crossover pattern also can occur when the two partners have been reared according to polar gender expectations. Often the main thing that attracted one to the other was that each seemed to supply missing qualities, elements of style or awareness that the first person felt lacking in himself or herself. (Recall the proverbial statement "Opposites attract.") Once the two join together, the attractiveness of the previous gender stereotyped qualities—her soft speech, perhaps, or his certainty in stating his views—disappears. The balance provided by difference is lost and the similarity may be perceived as irritating. They may find themselves tending to act more as competitors than as partners, each wondering where their once-ideal "opposite number" has gone.

Not all couples go through such a process, but many of us find ourselves redefining what we want our partners to be because we are developing new skills or patterns that make us act more like the romantic partner we once sought in order to complete ourselves. In a relationship system, as we change, those around us will change, and we cannot predict the exact form of their adjustment. This redefinition suggests a different basis for seeking intimate partners. Rather than trying to complete an otherwise incomplete or inadequate self, you might try searching for people who are enough like you to be understanding yet different enough to lead you to grow in the process of knowing them.

IMAGES AND REALITIES ABOUT COMMUNICATION STYLES

Significant gaps exist between the mass media images of everyone's communicative options and the realities of the demands most adults face. Women encounter many advertised images of the Superwoman/Superwife/Supermom, a person who can make fresh sandwiches for her kids, get everyone to school or work on time, be well dressed, calm, and brilliant at her fascinating job, look wonderful when she and her spouse go out on the town, and in some extreme versions study Spanish in her "spare time." Personal damage from this image can be substantial. Women ask each other and themselves how they can "work smarter" in some way so that they will have time for Spanish or spouse. Personal isolation while in pursuit of the

Superwoman myth may be worse now because employed women today have less time for same-sex friendships that are not job contacts.

For women, the struggle can be between the new communication situations she encounters and the personal goals she continues to pursue. Her job might be saying to her, "Create and maintain your credibility, establish a presence, and assert your ideas. Be creative in your attempts to generate excellence on the job, but always remember some people want to see you as a female." The internal dialogue she may hear, especially when she is with her partner, may be quite different. "Okay, so you've found ways to communicate in a man's world. Now where's the counterpart? Where's the part where you have a deep conversation at home about your life and your goals and your feelings? Why is he not more intuitive? How can you have the kinds of conversations where you each discover yourselves and the world? Why can't he talk to you in the ways you need, like you can talk to him?" She may feel cheated, as though she has taken on an extra effort only to discover that her partner and the society now expect her to "do it all." She may ask herself, "Is this an improvement? Am I now expected to live in both worlds while he only has to navigate one?" For many women, the communication world is more complex than ever, demanding different styles of talk several times in a day and allowing almost no time to renew the self for the day to come.

For men, the internal feeling of pressure toward perfection in appearance and behavior may be somewhat less strong because men have long secured social permission to "let off steam" through participating in or watching athletics and relaxing with the constantly advertised beer. However, in a world where jobs may be hard to find, living with a stereotype that you must always be the best and always make the most money can be taxing. In addition, uncertainty about how or when to try to meet the newer gender requirement of being sensitive and insightful can generate anxiety and frustration. A gap remains between the public and the private images; the cost of that gap may be greatest in the intimate relationships men have or hope to have.

Two equally strong sources of influence can act on men. The popular culture seems to be saying, "We know you're out there, guys, being batted around in the Monday-to-Friday rat race and trying to appear as if you are in charge of it all. Now sit down here and relax with the boys in your well-earned time out. When we get together, in the bar, on the golf course, or in front of a good game on TV, we men really understand each other."

The voice competing with this males-only voice is quite different. It may come from an internal dialogue within an individual man, or as the echo of the words of a tired and exasperated spouse. This voice typically says, "Well, of course you have worked hard, but so has she, and you did promise long ago that you would do half the cooking and baby watching and laundry along with those masculine tasks of garbage and lawn. So what kind of person are you, anyway?" This second voice promotes guilt, where the first one had promised relief, enticing the man to recall long-ago days of "real freedom" when he could watch the game or head for the fishing stream with no questions asked. He may ask himself, "Is this an improvement? Have I gained a 'family business partnership' but lost a place I can come to relax?"

The scenarios and discussion presented here are meant to illustrate some of the complexities, both within and between individuals, of trying to alter one's communication patterns. None of this is meant to suggest that making change is bad in itself or that efforts such as assertiveness training or counseling lack value. What is meant is that changes in one person affect other people as well and change that brings gratifying results can take time, effort, and perseverance. Lacking that realization, we can all do as much to damage our relationships as to improve them by planned efforts at self-help in communication.

Complications exist at the public levels of communication as well. Changing the self is not sufficient to change larger systems. People are sometimes misled into thinking that becoming assertive will win them promotions or will change sexist policies in large organizations. While people may become better persuaders when they are more confident and better prepared, individual messages do not by themselves produce change in systems. Organizational systems have been built essentially on one gender stereotype, so they will not easily change to deal with other people and assumptions. However, since organizations and institutions are comprised of individuals, perseverance by educated members of those organizations can present united efforts to address problems. Public discourse can bring behaviors into the foreground—make them available for discussion—that have been unconsciously accepted in the past. Calling attention to a different perspective on previously accepted behavior can cultivate identification with the new views and values. Of course, effective discussion depends on the skills of the communicators. Framing an issue by selecting new areas of emphasis which differ from previous patterns of interpretation opens the possibility of negotiation. Humans, as symbol users, routinely organize the information they receive. If new patterns of organization are presented as new opportunities and participation is invited and encouraged, all parties can negotiate a new, more accommodating reality which can result in more "liveable" gender expectations for both sexes.

CONCLUSION

This chapter has described three gender issues that are receiving current attention and deserve careful examination. The first has to do with the women's and men's movements and their impacts on communication. The two main branches of the women's feminist movement were described in order to show how the mediated view and general perception of the movement is distinct from the experiences many women (and men) have had through consciousness raising and the growth of their personal confidence. Developments in the newly forming men's movement indicate the uncertainty of today's male roles. Perhaps we will see new directions for both movements as we head into the next century.

The second issue deals with the increase of sexually linked violence and the possible connections of that violence to pornography, explicitly sexual media, and personal communication styles. While no final proof has yet been provided, the connections between the tendency toward a detached view of women's bodies, men's distance from their own bodily and emotional experience, and the widespread visual images of women's bodies as a sexual tease appear to be more than coincidental.

The third issue deals with the degree to which women and men should change their own communication patterns to make themselves more effective with other communicators. While the mass media as well as interpersonal advice sources provide support for changing styles, the complexities of making changes from within existing relationships and institutions are substantial. Options for change show the range of possibilities and consequences that accrue with a shift away from earlier behavior patterns. Finding ways for the sexes to communicate more humanely requires that both have opportunities to imagine the experienced world of the other sex, and that both develop the skills and concern to work at understanding both their differences and their similarities as human beings.

QUESTIONS FOR DISCUSSION

1. Choose one of the three issues discussed in this chapter and develop a brief position statement of your own that you could present to a family member, a friend, or a work colleague.

2. Carol Gilligan argues that men develop their moral positions based on abstract principles and women develop theirs based on concrete human relationships. Apply this distinction to the pair of arguments below about the appropriate public response to pornography.

   Side 1. Pornographers violate human and civil rights by placing women in harmful physical and psychological situations while making pornographic films.

   Side 2. Restricting the production of pornography violates the First Amendment's free speech clause.

3. Do you believe that either sex can, in fact, change not only their surface communication patterns but also their basic beliefs about communication and gender? Why, or why not?

4. Interpret the sentence, "I'm not a feminist, but I believe in equal rights for everyone and equal pay for equal work."

CASES FOR ANALYSIS

CASE 10.1 FEMINISM (STUDENT CONTRIBUTION)

White males are having a tough time these days. The feminist movement is one group of women with whom I am having problems. Our school newspaper is a breeding ground for anti-white-male issues. One of these issues is rape. Last term I was walking back from lunch and thought it would be a perfect day to walk to the quad. I could hear a female's voice on a loud speaker. I saw Mark Thompson just before I reached the quad. He warned me that my kind shouldn't go through the quad today. The female on the loud speaker was talking about men and rape, punctuated with a periodic loud bang on a huge gong to emphasize that "every [?] minutes a women is raped by a man." It seriously ruined my mood of happiness because I am a man.

1. Have you had an experience like this one? If so, identify the gender presumptions you and the speaker at the rally do not share.

2. Why do you think these kinds of feelings—on both sides—are raised?

3. How are gender ideals or expectations related to happiness? How does the author connect unhappiness to his sex? How does the speaker at the rally connect unhappiness to hers?

CASE 10.2 SEX CRIMES

After reading the following essay from *Sports Illustrated*, discuss the contents.

Sending the Wrong Message

In shamelessly recruiting a sex offender, coaches were too quick to forgive and forget

by Johnette Howard

When the news surfaced late last week that Utah was among four or five college basketball programs interested in New York City schoolboy star Richie Parker despite his felony conviction for sexual abuse, Ute coach Rick Majerus told the *New York Post* he saw nothing wrong with the recruiting of Parker because "everyone I've spoken to in New York says he's a great kid." Utah assistant coach Donny Daniels proved even more callous by suggesting that too much sympathy was being showered on Parker's victim when Parker himself had endured "an emotional trauma."

It's not as if the facts of the crime are in doubt: On Jan. 4, 1994, Parker and a classmate lured a freshman girl into a basement stairwell at Manhattan Center High and forced her to perform oral sex on them. The 6' 5" Parker, now 18, pled guilty to first-degree sexual abuse a year later and was sentenced to five years' probation. The classmate pled guilty to attempted sodomy.

Yet 10 days passed between Parker's guilty plea and Seton Hall's decision to rescind its November scholarship offer to him. Seton Hall's laggard withdrawal—which came only after heavy criticism of the Catholic university—allowed a school like Utah to pursue Parker, a guard who averaged 25 points as a senior. Asked how a convicted sex felon might be received in Salt Lake City, site of the Utah campus and headquarters of the Mormon church, Majerus said, "Isn't the essence of religion about forgiveness?" And Daniels, 40, the father of two girls and a boy, said Parker was an overlooked "victim."

"Will he ever be able to forget it?" Daniels asked. "She probably will get a doctorate and marry a successful guy and live over in the Hamptons. . . . This girl could have damaged Parker for life. Five years from now this will haunt him. They both made a mistake, they shouldn't have been there. . . . But everyone's worried about the girl. What about him?

"There are much worse crimes," Daniels added. "If he was a child molester, we wouldn't take him."

What a comfort.

It's unfair to seize on a few coaches and suggest that their lamebrained remarks prove college sports is a cesspool. (Utah president Arthur Smith denounced Daniels's comments, though sterner disciplinary action against the coach seems warranted, and Utah will no longer recruit Parker.) But this is also true and deserves to be shouted from the mountaintops: When it comes to attitudes about sexual assault, the tolerance shown for the athlete and the contempt for the victim are nothing new. Nor are they rare.

Though the people and particulars change, there are identifiable patterns that persist across cases and time. Indiana basketball coach Bob Knight's infamous 1988 reprise of the old line that "if rape is inevitable, why not relax and enjoy it?" wasn't all that different from Daniels's comment, "Who's to say [Parker's victim] did something she didn't want to do?"

And the support that Parker has received even after his guilty plea is not all that different from the warm embrace that convicted rapist Mike Tyson has received from a flock of ministers and holy men—one of whom was accused of offering Desiree Washington up to $1 million to drop her charges against Tyson.

And when Tyson was recently released from prison, crowds lined the highway and cheered him—a spectacle that was hauntingly similar to the one that accompanied O.J. Simpson's excursion in his Ford Bronco. The crimes are different, but Simpson's supporters said precisely what Majerus said about Parker: He's a nice guy. Could everybody be wrong?

Yes, people can be pleasant company and murderers both. A few years ago a woman writer I know was propositioned and harassed for months by a baseball star. When he finally tired of her unwavering rejections, he asked her, "Let's get this settled up front. If I raped you, how much would it take to keep you quiet?"

Women are not making up these stories. Yet the men accused or convicted of these sexual improprieties often chug along with their careers intact. And female victims who speak up risk being stigmatized. Women are often judged by a moral standard that blames them even when they are not at fault: *You shouldn't have gone down that stairwell, shouldn't have worn that dress, shouldn't have gone into that hotel room.* But that's akin to saying that there are some conditions that justify uninvited sexual aggression by men. And that's an idea that deserves to be ground beneath the heels of our shoes.

Apologists for athletes are right about one thing: The sickening tolerance of sexually inappropriate behavior doesn't exist only in sports. But awarding an athletic scholarship to a convicted sex felon gives the impression that sexual assault is not a serious offense. It suggests women are expendable. If coaches really want to be kind to kids, they should realize this: Social justice extends to women *and* men. It's an intellectual swindle to say sports is the only thing that can save kids like Richie Parker. Sometimes it's the opposite. Sometimes it's the problem.

1. What is your reaction to some sports figures' abilities to gain financially regardless of their sexually violent behavior?
2. What could an individual do to really affect a change if they desired one?
3. What effect does sports status have on sanctions against sexual violence?

CASE 10.3 GETTING HER DRUNK

A group of males attend a large party together, and after a time they look around for something interesting to do. They notice a quiet female who stands on the sidelines and seems not to have any dancing partners.

"I've got an idea. Let's give our little friend here her first drink of real alcohol and see how she handles it."

One of the males goes over to the young woman and asks her if she'd like some refreshments. He brings her a glass of vodka-spiked punch and sits talking with her until she finishes the glass. Then one of his friends comes up and asks her to dance, followed by another round of the punch. By the time the second glass has been emptied, she is looking flushed and is laughing loudly.

The first member of the group now turns to the third, and says, "You get the best part. You get to take her upstairs to a quiet place to talk, and we'll follow you after about twenty minutes to get our share."

1. Imagine yourself as either the third male in this group or as a female watching the progression of events. What would you do?
2. While many men would not engage in this kind of behavior, others find it stimulating and entertaining. What kinds of large, social actions could affect these attitudes and behaviors? Should institutions—such as schools and churches—be involved? What kind of plan could be implemented? By whom? With what possible effects?
3. What are the current situations in which you believe that a male should be "more experienced" than a female? Discuss your views with others.

NOTES

[1] Last words of Gertrude Stein, paraphrased from *What Is Remembered* by Alice B. Toklas (New York: Rinehart and Winston, 1963).

[2] The last principle is proposed and explained in Sonja K. Foss and Cindy L. Griffin, "Beyond Persuasion: A Proposal for an Invitational Rhetoric," *Communication Monographs* 62 (March 1995): 2–18.

[3] For background on feminist rhetoric, see Karlyn Kohrs Campbell, "The Rhetoric of Women's Liberation: An Oxymoron," *Quarterly Journal of Speech* 59 (February 1973): 74–86; Judith Hole and Ellen Levine, *Rebirth of Feminism* (New York: Quadrangle Books, 1971); Gayle Graham Yates, *What Women Want: The Ideologies of the Movement* (Cambridge, MA: Harvard, 1975); and Barbara Deckard, *The Women's Movement* (New York: Harper & Row, 1975).

[4] Betty Friedan, *The Feminine Mystique* (New York: Norton, 1963).

[5] Peter L. Benson, "Family Patterns Today," *Education Digest* 60, 6 (February 1995): 47–49.

[6] Dan Cordtz, "Off the Dole," *Financial World* 163, 4 (February 15, 1994): 24–29.

[7] Elizabeth Walker Mechling, "The Jung and the Restless: The Mythopoetic Men's Movement," *Southern Communication Journal* 59, 2 (Winter 1994): 97–111.

[8] Steve Chapple, "Wild Man," *Men's Health* 4, 4 (Winter 1989): 80–83.

[9] Lance Morrow, "The Child Is Father of the Man," *Time* 138, 7 (August 19, 1991): 52–54.

[10] Robert Bly, *Iron John: A Book about Men* (New York: First Vintage Books, 1992).

[11] Ibid., p. ix.

[12] Ibid., p. ix.

[13] "Robert Bly," *Current Biography* 54, 3 (March 1993): 7–11; Asa Baber, "Call of the Wild," *Playboy* 38, 4 (April 1991): 98–100.

[14] Asa Baber, "Men: Calling All Blysters," *Playboy* 39, 3 (March 1992): 32.

[15] "Women and the United Nations: Special Rapporteur on Violence against Women Appointed," *WIN News* (Women's International Network) 20, 4 (Autumn 1994): 11.

[16] "Women and Violence: Violence Against Women in Africa," *WIN News* (Women's International Network) 20, 4 (Autumn 1994): 34.

[17] Julie Gannon Shoop, "One in Eight U.S. Women Raped, Survey Says: Most Victims are Young," *Trial* 28, 7 (July 1992): 110–11.

[18] *Uniform Crime Reports*, Federal Bureau of Investigation, 1991.

[19] Eve Buzawa, "Responding to Crimes of Violence Against Women: Gender Differences versus Organization Imperatives," *Crime and Delinquency* 41, 4 (October 1995): 443–66.

[20] Kristin Anderson Moore, "Nonvoluntary Sexual Activity Among Adolescents," *Family Planning Perspectives* 21, 3 (May 1989): 110–14.

[21] Ronnie Polaneczky, "The Sex Scandal America Overlooks," *New Choices for Retirement Living* 35, 6 (July 1995): 42–46.

[22] Ric Dolphin, "Rape on Campus," *Macleans* 101, 45 (October 31, 1988): 56.

23 Michele N-K. Collison, "Increase in Reports of Sexual Assaults Strains Campus Disciplinary Systems," *Chronicle of Higher Education* 37, 35 (May 15, 1991): A29–A30.

24 Janet K. Larsen, "Private Discourse of Batterers: The Rhetoric That Controls," paper presented to the Speech Communication Association, Denver, CO, November 1985.

25 Thomas J. Deloughry, "Researcher Who Studied on-line Pornography Gets Invitation from Congress, Criticism from Scholars," *Chronicle of Higher Education* 41, 45 (July 21, 1995): A19.

26 Thomas J. DeLoughry, "Upset with Internet Law," *Chronicle of Higher Education* 42, 23 (February 16, 1996): A21, A26.

27 Amy Wahl, "University Creates 'Cyberporn' Warning for Students," *Chronicle of Higher Education* 42, 8 (October 20, 1995): A23.

28 ". . .And a crackdown on child porn," *US News & World Report* 119, 12 (September 25, 1995): 24.

29 Neil M. Malamuth and John Briere, "Sexual Violence in the Media: Indirect Effects on Aggression Against Women," *Journal of Social Issues* 42, 3 (1986): 75–92; Charles R. Mullin, "Desensitization and Resensitization to Violence Against Women: Effects of Exposure to Sexually Violent Films on Judgments of Domestic Violence Victims," *Journal of Personality & Social Psychology* 69, 3 (September 1995): 449–59.

30 Janet St. Lawrence and Doris J. Joyner, "The Effects of Sexually Violent Rock Music on Males' Acceptance of Violence Against Women," *Psychology of Women Quarterly* 15 (1991): 49–63.

31 D. Linz, "Exposure to Sexually Explicit Materials and Attitudes Toward Rape: A Comparison of Study Results," *The Journal of Sex Research* 26 (1989): 50–84.

32 The strongest research in making these links is that done by Edward Donnerstein and his colleagues. See, for example, Edward Donnerstein and Daniel Linz, "Mass Media Sexual Violence and Male Viewers: Current Theory and Research," *American Behavioral Scientist* 29 (May-June 1986): 601–18; Bernard Malamuth and Edward Donnerstein, *Pornography and Sexual Aggression* (Orlando, FL: Harcourt Brace Jovanovitch, 1984). The U.S. Attorney General's Commission on Pornography also asserted in July 1986 that pornography and sexual violence are connected; their report continues the debate on these points because it omits significant qualifiers that Donnerstein added to his own research claims.

33 Randy D. Fisher, Ida J. Cook, and Edwin C. Shirkey, "Correlates of Support for Censorship of Sexual, Sexually Violent, and Violent Media," *The Journal of Sex Research* 31, 3 (1994): 229–40.

34 Daniel Linz, Barbara J. Wilson, and Edward Donnerstein, "Sexual Violence in the Mass Media: Legal Solutions, Warnings, and Mitigation Through Education," *Journal of Social Issues* 48, 1 (1992): 145–71.

35 Janet Lee Mills, "Body Language Speaks Louder than Words," *Horizons: University of Cincinnati Alumni Magazine* (February 1985): 8–12.

Index

AEE-5219